# The British Shotgun
## Volume Two 1871–1890

by

I. M. Crudgington and D. J. Baker

ASHFORD
Southampton
1989

Published by Ashford
        1 Church Road
        Shedfield
        Hampshire SO3 2HW

© I. M. Crudgington and D. J. Baker 1989

British Library Cataloguing in Publication Data

Crudgington, I.M.
  The British shotgun.
  1. British shotguns, 1871–90
  I. Title   II. Baker, D.J.
  683.4'26'0941

    ISBN 1–85253–133–9

Printed in Great Britain

# Contents

# Foreword

Most of the British sporting shotguns in use today are over fifty years old, and many are closer to a hundred, which says much for the quality of the materials and workmanship employed in their manufacture. Less obvious, perhaps, is the durability of the designs to which these guns were built. Both in Britain and abroad, guns are still being made that incorporate inventions dating from the last century, and the period 1871–90 was probably the richest for innovation in the history of the sporting gun. Volume Two of *The British Shotgun*, therefore, deals in history that has, in many respects, direct relevance to the present day. This increases its appeal and I hope that sportsmen, as well as collectors, will find enjoyment in tracing the design origins of their guns.

Proprietorial pride and ease of manufacture are sometimes relevant to the life of an invention, but the designs that have survived the longest are, in the main, those that have proved to be the most practical and reliable in service. As a result, a representative sample of working guns would reveal only a small proportion of the inventions identified in this work.

Fortunately, the authors' appetite for hard information, gathered from examples, patents and other sources, is matched by their patient identification and elucidation of individual designs. Anyone who has ever sought to comprehend a mechanism from its patent specification will appreciate the scale and difficulty of the authors' achievement and Ian Crudgington has generously volunteered that the major credit belongs to David Baker. Also impressive is the order given to all this material by the identification of groups and sub-groups of related mechanisms. This structure is a valuable aid to comprehension, as the incidental biographical vignettes are refreshing interludes in the flow of technicalities.

Volumes One and Two of this work stand independently, but form part of an unfinished whole. By 1890, the shotgun had come of age, but had not yet reached full maturity. Stylistically, the guns of 1890 tend to appear archaic to modern eyes and there were still important mechanical developments to come (particularly in relation to single-trigger systems and over-and-under actions). Therefore, at least one more volume is required to complete the story and I look forward to the next with keen anticipation.

Christopher Brunker
Christie's, South Kensington
London

1989

iv

# Preface

With this second volume of *The British Shotgun*, we take up again the story of the sporting shotgun in Britain. In order to make sense of the mass of material contained within our two decades, we have adopted a policy of considering features on a like with like basis. An unfortunate, but unavoidable, result of this policy has been that where a gun has a range of novel features the resulting description will be found scattered in several chapters.

It has been our intention to illustrate every mechanism, either with a photograph of an actual gun or with a drawing. In the main, the drawings we use are one of the several that appear on a typical full patent specification. It should be borne in mind that most provisional patent specifications are unillustrated and so, where our sole knowledge of a mechanism derives from this source, we are unable to produce an illustration. Unless otherwise stated, the actual guns illustrated are 12-bore.

Another aspect of our researches has been the locating of a photograph and some personal details of inventors whose contributions were of real significance to the development of the shotgun. These individuals were often involved in the development of a number of different patents. However, a decision has been made to include biographical detail in the context of what we consider to be an inventor's most important design. For the rest, the personal details noted with each invention also largely derive from the patent specification and this approach can give rise to confusion as men with common surnames change their addresses and their own descriptions of their gunmaking specialities over the years. In general, we have not attempted to confirm relationships or check on the pernicious practice (from a researcher's point of view) of naming sons identically to their fathers. Indeed we seriously doubt whether, after this lapse of time, this would be possible.

It is our hope that, armed with the information in this book, an enthusiast will be able to identify any shotgun mechanism that was invented in Britain during the period 1871 to 1890. However, we accept that a work such as this cannot be truly definitive and would welcome correspondence from readers on the guns or their makers in the hope that a future edition can be more complete.

I. M. Crudgington
D. J. Baker
1989

# Acknowledgements

To produce a volume such as this requires the help and co-operation of many people and it gives us great pleasure to be able to record our sincere thanks to all concerned.

We are especially grateful to Her Majesty the Queen for graciously granting us permission to consult the Royal Photographic Archives at Windsor, to examine and photograph the Royal sporting guns at Sandringham and to reproduce the photographs.

We should also like to mention the following, for their various contributions: Avon County Library; Lynne Baker (for typing, advice and support); Dick Banks; Roger Barlow; Mike Barnes; Alfred Bedford (Proof Master, London Proof House); Freda and Eve Beesley; John Bogg; James Booth (Sotheby's, Ltd) John Booth; Geoffrey Boothroyd; Reg Bretnor; Nigel Brown; Christopher Brunker (Messrs Christie, Manson & Woods Ltd); Cambridge City Library; Cambridge University Library; John Clarke (Arthur Turner, Sheffield, Ltd); Mike Delanoy; Frances Dimond (Curator, Photograph Collection, Royal Archives, Windsor Castle); The late Mark Dineley; Tony Eminson; David Fairbrother; Derek Fearn; Richard Fosbery; Maureen Gooding (Local History Library, London Borough of Ealing); Graham Greener; The Guardians of the Birmingham Proof House; David Harding; Holland & Holland, Ltd; Interarm Co. Ltd; H. Lee Munson; Rob Knowles; Roger Lees (Late Proof Master, Birmingham Proof House); Adrian Lemmon (Cambridge Gun Repairs); George Lewis (Messrs G. E. Lewis & Son, Birmingham); The Master, Wardens and Court of Assistants of the Worshipful Company of Gunmakers of the City of London; Peter McGowan; Monks of Chester; The Naval Historical Library; The late Harry Needham; The British Library Newspaper Library, Colindale; Olive Parsons (Taunton Dean Borough Council); The Patent Office (especially the Staff of the Printing and Sale Branch, St Mary Cray); David Powell (Messrs Wm. Powell & Sons, Ltd, Birmingham); Richard Rattenbury (Curator, Winchester Museum, Buffalo Bill Historical Center, Cody, Wyoming); Emil Rosner; Ted Shoebridge; *Shooting Times & Country Magazine*, Alistair Sinclair (late of Messrs John Dickson & Son, Ltd, Edinburgh); Jackie Szpera (Edinburgh Reference Library); Pat Watley; Robert Wilson; Dave Winks; Denis Wood; Keith Woodvine; John Wilkins and the York Castle Museum.

# CHAPTER ONE

# The Lever-cocked Hammerless Gun

In telling a story as tangled and interwoven as that of the evolution of the British shotgun, where or where not to end a particular period is largely arbitrary. However, one reason which led us to conclude Volume One at the end of 1870 was that the following year, 1871, saw the appearance of a gun which thereafter altered the development of shotgun design. This turning point was the introduction of the hammerless shotgun, patented by Theophilus Murcott, who was then in business as a gunmaker at 68, The Haymarket, London. Murcott's patent, No. 1003, was registered at the Patent Office on 15 April 1871 and it is from information such as this, and, more importantly, clues from other sources, especially editorial coverage in *The Field*, that we can piece together if not the full story of the Murcott, then at least a proportion. And this, then, would seem to be a good place to start Volume Two.

Murcott advertised in *The Field*, and also in its rival *Land and Water*, not with a page-spread as we might feel befits the herald of a new era, but with an inch of text amid scores of others of like size. However, we now recognise its importance and reproduce his advertisement complete:

THE LAST GUN OUT – **Theophilus Murcott, Gunmaker, 68 Haymarket, invites the attention of the nobility, gentry and the sporting world generally to the new GUN he has recently patented. The advantages offered by it are rapidity of action, perfect security, nonliability to accident, extreme simplicity of construction. The first is attained by the lever, which opens the barrels to receive the cartridge, also cocking the gun, the second is insured by the bolt on the top indicating whether or not the gun is ready for discharge, the third is exhibited in the entire absence of all external projections, while the fourth is shown at a glance at its mechanical principles. Its shooting powers are guaranteed to be second to none. An inspection of the gun is respectfully solicited by Theophilus Murcott, Patentee & Maker, 68 Haymarket.**

*Murcott's 'Mousetrap' gun;*
*built by T. Murcott on his patent No. 1003 of 1871*

The subject of Murcott's fine advertisement is, essentially, a very simple gun. Its design incorporated a lever which pivoted just ahead of, and followed the sweep of the bow of, the trigger guard. This lever continued inside the gun so its upper part moved backward as the underlever was thrust forward. This backward movement withdrew the barrel-bolting catches and also, via an inward projecting stud on the top of each tumbler, cocked the locks if they had been fired.

The barrel-bolting is either a simple, single bolt engaging with the rear lump or a Purdey double-bite (the locking-bolt has a slot through which the internal lever slips). The single bolt can also be used in combination with a round bolt that slides from the top of the head of the action into the top rib. This round bolt is also slotted onto the internal lever. (Incidentally, this latter feature is very like that of William Wellington Greener's patent, No. 2231 of 1863, which, in view of the subsequent history of Murcott's, may be significant.)

So much for the gun as actually seen. (The patent specification in addition shows several variations on the basic theme. We will defer considering these until later when mechanisms that share the features are described.) Toward the end of 1872 the Murcott advertisement changed, providing more information regarding technical detail and manufacture.

By modern standards, conditioned as we are to mass-production, 100 guns sounds a meagre total. However, we are considering a gun that was largely handmade and, by the fashion of the day, novel. Since this gun can be claimed to represent the beginning of the popularity of the hammerless shotgun, we should understand how it became accepted.

Firstly, we must not underestimate the value of the publicity that the Murcott received from editorials in *The Field*. Second, certainly to the shooting man not deeply interested in the mechanical intricacies of his gun, the Murcott with its push-forward underlever hammerless action bears more than a passing resemblance to the hammerless Martini-actioned rifle that the British Army had officially adopted in 1871. Thirdly, aside from the concealed striking mechanism, it was not really a very strange gun. The bar-action sidelocks even then were a design that was some 200 years old. The push-forward underlever was far from original. Finally, the safety catch was completely simple and easily comprehended. So we can well envisage the salesman in Murcott's front shop removing a lock, or perhaps having a stripped gun on show, to demonstrate to a wavering customer that this 'new' gun was after all reassuringly familiar. The customer would, too, be encouraged to feel himself in the front of fashion without committing himself to some untried and bizarre mechanism such as the double bolt-action Bacon gun (see Volume One).

*Theophilus Murcott advertisement of 1873*

*Detached lock from T. Murcott hammerless gun*

The acceptance of the Murcott was demonstrated by a feature in *The Field*, published on 6 July 1872. This was illustrated with a wood block engraving of the gun and its lockwork. The engraving was used by both Greener and Dr Walsh in their standard textbooks and has been even more widely copied in modern times.

William Wellington Greener and Dr J. H. Walsh will appear frequently in this book. Greener was a gunmaker and entrepreneur and author of *The Gun and its Development*, published in 1892. Dr Walsh was a leading commentator on guns and gunmaking and he, too, was an influential author. He wrote the standard textbook, *The Modern Sportsman's Gun and Rifle*, published in 1882, and was editor of *The Field*.

The feature in *The Field* was to provoke a small correspondence as to who had first used the Murcott. In this we have the claim by H. Cholmondeley-Pennell that he was 'one of the first to use the gun in the field in pursuit of wild game and the first to use one at the Live Pigeon Traps'. So we have a picture, admittedly fragmentary, but nevertheless contemporary, of the early growth in popularity of the Murcott gun. It even earned for itself the nickname of 'Murcott's Mousetrap'. As is so often the case with such sobriquets there seems to be no definite information as to who so christened the gun or indeed why. A modern author, Macdonald Hastings, in his *English Sporting Guns and Accessories* (1969) refers to the Murcott as 'strange box-like'. The present author (DJB) has shot from time to time with a Murcott hammerless. Its boxiness is no more pronounced than many another gun and the noise, caused by the underlever slapping against the trigger guard, is no different to other guns of a similar layout. We feel that the most likely explanation of the name is that it is an amusing alliteration coined by a rival gunmaker who did not have a hammerless gun of his own.

It is regrettable that there appears to be little published biographical detail on Theophilus Murcott. Like George Daw, he made a crucial contribution to the development of the British shotgun, but, apart from street directories, the records of the Patent Office and a few advertisements, he has left no other record that we can now discover. His hammerless gun is, as far as the Patent Office records are concerned, his only invention and other guns bearing his name are thought to be completely conventional.

The Murcott business closed sometime in mid-1878. In *Land and Water*, dated 1 June of that year, there is a notice that the stock was for sale by auction by Ellis Gun Sales whose auction rooms were at 21, Old Bond Street. This sale, the advertisement stated, was 'at the direction of W. W. Greener' who had bought the business. Interestingly, among the items listed in this advertisement are several Greener guns which leads us to wonder if there was some prior connection between the two businesses or if Greener was taking advantage of the opportunity to sell off some dead stock. The premises at 68, The Haymarket, were to become Greener's London showrooms for the next 42 years and were, at that period, known as 'Greener House'. An echo of the Greener takeover of Murcott's appeared in the next year in the shape of Greener's patent, No. 769 of 1879, which covered a modification of the Murcott gun in which the tumblers and the cocking lever had a common pivot axis for greater ease of cocking.

A crucial factor in assessing the acceptance of the hammerless gun is the appearance of a competitive hammerless gun. A study of the patent records reveals a lull of just under two years in between the Murcott and the next hammerless patent. However, with the benefit of hindsight, we now know this to be a vital period. In these months, early work led to designs which were to last for the next decade and a half. In this hiatus, the hammerless gun was doubtless the subject of much discussion and speculation in interested circles.

The design which broke the lull after the Murcott was the Gibbs and Pitt. It was to become perhaps the most successful of all the British lever-cocked hammerless guns. It is a gun that an enthusiast is most likely to encounter and its design is such that many subsequent guns relate to it. The essential feature of the Gibbs and Pitt patent, No. 284 of 1873, is the use of a rearward projection from the barrel-locking bolt which goes into, and cocks, the lockwork. The patent describes several variants on this basic theme, depending on whether a push-forward underlever, a turning underlever or a turning top lever is used to work the barrel-locking bolts. However, our story is complicated by the fact that while it was the push-forward underlever design that was first exploited, by the end of our present period it was the top lever model that had become popular. Having noted this, we propose to describe the push-forward underlever version, since this has the greatest resemblance to the Murcott; we shall return later in this chapter to the other variants and couple them with the designs which share their mode of external manipulation.

The Gibbs and Pitt push-forward underlever action first produced was perhaps most usual and distinctive in that the lockwork, which is of the trigger plate type, extended downwards into the trigger guard in a slim box-like projection. The trigger guard has no forward bow: instead it slopes backwards in a slight curve to which the underlever is closely fitted. The snap spring for the underlever, and indeed for the whole action, forms the bottom of the centre of the action bar. The final, immediately noticeable, feature is a very wide top strap which, at its forward end, is formed round the head of, and

strengthens, the stock, which is much cut away to make room for the large tumblers to work in. A point that should be made about this action is the close resemblance of the lockwork to the Farquharson single-shot rifle action that was patented the previous year and was being built by Gibbs and Pitt.

Patent drawings often show, in addition to the essential mechanical details of a design, other points of style or quirks of construction which are peculiar to the maker or firm who obtained the patent. Therefore, it is all the more remarkable that we have a drawing of a gun, patented as No. 3424 of 1874, by the famous gunmaker William Middleditch Scott of the Birmingham firm, W. & C. Scott and Son. This so exactly copies all the points of style and construction described above for the Gibbs and Pitt gun that, prior to the discovery of this patent, if shown an unmarked gun or drawing we would unhesitatingly have called it a Gibbs and Pitt. The mechanism is, in fact, subtly different; with the Scott gun it is the head of the underlever that pushes backwards a lever in the head of the stock which in turn pushes back the tumblers. The reason for the close similarity of

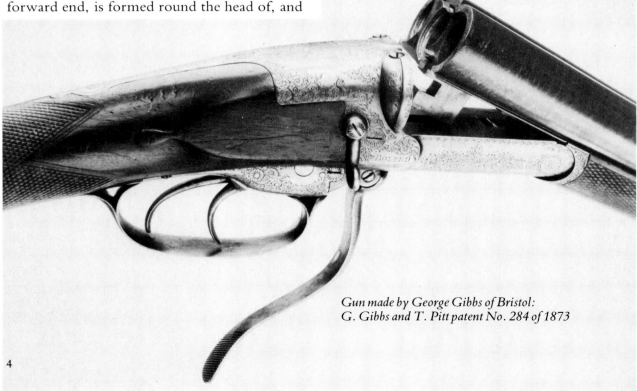

*Gun made by George Gibbs of Bristol:*
*G. Gibbs and T. Pitt patent No. 284 of 1873*

these two guns both in style and mechanism we can now only guess at, but it represents a subtle snare for the present-day enthusiast who may not be able to strip a particular gun to check on its internal parts and authenticity.

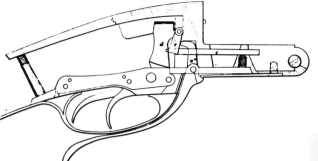

*William Middleditch Scott patent No. 3424 of 1874*

The essential difference between the Gibbs and Pitt and the Murcott is that in the former it is the locking-bolt that indirectly cocks the locks; in the Murcott it is an extension of the underlever that does this directly. Following the success of, and the publicity generated by, these two guns there was something of a vogue for push-forward underlever hammerless guns and it will aid our description of these if we group together those that resemble one or other of these two pioneer guns. For the sake of continuity we will first describe the Gibbs and Pitt type, those that use the barrel-locking bolt as the basis of the cocking mechanism.

*Sidelock gun made by George Gibbs of Bristol: G. Gibbs and T. Pitt patent No. 284 of 1873*

However, of the true Gibbs and Pitt guns, some examples were produced with conventional bar-action sidelocks – as far as we can now tell, more or less concurrently with the trigger plate form. Gibbs and Pitt were one of the many firms who had more than one serial number series. Those with no prefix to their serial were best-grade guns actually made by Gibbs. Those with a B were made in the trade but finished and regulated by Gibbs. The C series were the second-quality guns and the E series were the third; these last two series were entirely made in the trade.

In the drawing for the patent, No. 1145 of 1878, obtained by Edwin Charles Hodges, an action-filer outworker to the London gun trade, we find an upward projection on the rear of the locking-bolt. The bolt is, in fact, drawn in the form that Hodges had patented some seven years before as No. 251 of 1871, but this is not vital to the working of the action. The projection from the bolt is in plan a T-shape with the head of the T, when seen in elevation, relatively broad. The purpose of this is both to force back the tumblers, for which purpose two hardened steel rollers are carried on the cross-piece of the

T, and to withdraw the firing pins. The latter have small downward projections from their heads to engage with the cocking piece. The drawing shows trigger plate lockwork that uses the lower limb of the mainspring as a sear spring.

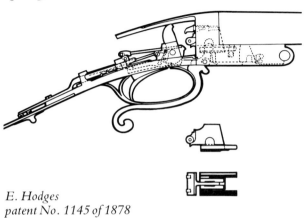

*E. Hodges*
*patent No. 1145 of 1878*

James and Thomas Adsett took out their patent, No. 574, in 1879. They styled themselves 'Gun Manufacturers of Canterbury, Kent' and from street directories it would seem they were in business for the better part of the last quarter of the nineteenth century, the last listing occurring in 1894. The central feature of their design is a lever that is V-shaped and hung with its point uppermost at the rear of the standing-breech. The limbs of this V are not quite equal in length and the forward one is just a little shorter than the rear one and hangs vertically down when the barrel-bolt is for-

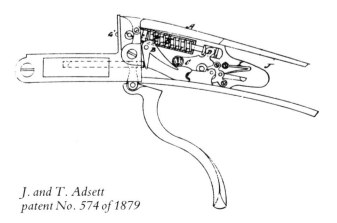

*J. and T. Adsett*
*patent No. 574 of 1879*

wards. As the push-forward underlever forces the bolt back, so it in turn bears on the short limb of the V and thus the long limb moves back and up to raise and cock the tumbler. Like so many of these early hammerless guns, a novel form of lockwork is shown, in this case using spiral mainsprings which are round the rod-like striker. To enable the motion of the V lever to compress the mainsprings, the tumbler has a head that slots into the rear of the striker.

Henry Walker, who, like so many others, simply tells us he is a 'Gun Manufacturer of Birmingham', was another to propose many variations on a theme in his patent, No. 4294 of 1878. Two of these variations are push-forward underlever-cocked hammerless guns which we will consider here. The central idea of all these variants is to have a lever pivoted high up in the head of the stock where the top strap joins the standing-breech. The length of this lever is such that its bottom is pushed back by the locking-bolt as this is withdrawn from the bites. It is this lever, swinging back, that lifts the tumblers to full cock. On the push-forward underlever version the locks are shown as various forms of sidelocks.

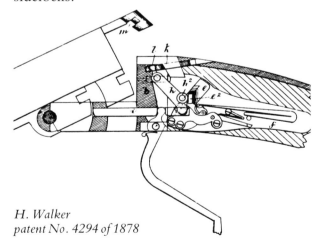

*H. Walker*
*patent No. 4294 of 1878*

The second push-forward underlever version of this gun uses the same motion to cock the locks, but this time the swinging lever is, in side view, triangular and is hung at its apex. The bottom front corner is the actual locking-bolt which swings over a rearward projection from the rear lump. To compound the variations on this theme, this patent also describes how, via an incline on the rear of the front lump, these actions could be cocked by the fall of the barrels. This idea of using the locking-bolt forced back in this way was one which appeared many times and which we will return to when we come to consider those many actions cocked by the motion of the barrels.

A recurring feature throughout the history of the British shotgun is that we encounter ideas which have later enjoyed considerable vogue. For instance: the idea of a spiral spring fitted round the striker that reappears in the Francis Robertson and John Joyce provisional patent, No. 3466 of 1881. Now one hundred odd years later, due to the ease with which it fits into machine manufacture, it is a much-used idea. We mention this mechanism at this point because these spiral spring-loaded strikers were to be cocked by projections from the sliding barrel-bolt beneath them, the bolt in turn being forced to the rear by a push-forward underlever.

There remain within our grouping three un-illustrated provisional patent specifications: No. 2328 of 1873, in the name of John Henry Apted, 'gunmaker' of Knights Hill, Lower Norwood, London; No. 2163 of 1878, taken out by Isaac and Reuben Bullock; and No. 4902 of 1879, granted to Lionel Gye. Little is known about these patents, but all appear to describe variants of the push-forward underlever Gibbs and Pitt theme.

We now can return to those hammerless actions that resemble the Murcott action and, in so doing, consider a design that can be regarded as intermediate between the two basic ideas.

This is, to a degree, questionable as the fine illustration which accompanied the patent specification would appear to show a small calibre rifle but we have decided to include it because it forms so useful a link. The patent, No. 3002 of 1884, was granted to two famous men from the Birmingham gun trade, Charles Pryse and Edwin James Cashmore. Their idea was to have a small horizontal cocking lever pivoted at its centre and hung fore-and-aft in the lockwork. On the forward end of this a rearward projection from the underlever bears, so that, as the underlever is thrust forwards and down, the rear of the cocking lever would lift the tumbler up to the full-cock position.

Before we go further we need to take a backward glance at the Green hammerless gun of 1868. While the shape of the internal parts is different, the basic principle of its action is exactly the same as that of the Murcott. What influence, if any, this design had on the latter we can only surmise, but the Green hammerless must be borne in mind to maintain a true perspective. The essential feature of the Murcott, as we have seen, is a projection of the underlever into the lockwork that cocks the action. It is evident that this idea was highly thought of in the late-1870s and we can point to a sub-group of successful designs during this period.

If, within this sub-group, we work in a chronological sequence, we are immediately reminded of the utter impossibility of forming neat discreet groups out of our tangled material, for we are faced with none other than a lever-cocked version of the William Anson and John Deeley patent, No. 1756 of 1875 (considered in

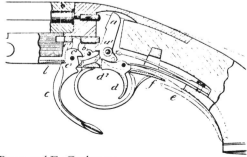

*C. Pryse and E. Cashmore*
*patent No. 3002 of 1884*

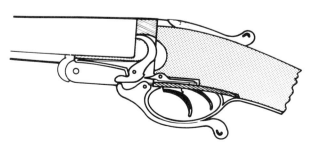

*W. Anson and J. Deeley*
*patent No. 1756 of 1875*

far greater detail in Chapter Four), which we can only regard as very much a make-weight for no other reason than that the push-forward underlever merely cocks the locks while a conventional top lever is also drawn, presumably to open the gun. This two-lever operation was a very definite retrograde step and it is doubtful if a gun of this type was ever made. However, the mechanism proposed is exceedingly simple. The tumbler and striker are combined as a single component and are shaped like a backwards capital letter C, set vertically in the action and pivoted on a transverse axis about one-third of the way up the curve. The push-forward underlever has a forward projection which, as the lever is thrust forwards, bears on the bottom of the tumbler and rotates it backwards to cock.

The next design in our sub-group is that of James Adsett, whom we have already met. However, since his two designs are so dissimilar, there is no real chance that they can be confused. Adsett's patent, No. 1981 of 1877, is an ingenious mechanism which could be loosely said to have half the lockwork made upside down so that, while the tumblers are in their expected place, the bent for the sear is cut in the top of the tumbler and the long sear lies along the top of the lock. The exact details of construction are not stated so we cannot be sure if this mechanism is a trigger plate type or is hung from a web down from the top strap. Even a sidelock configuration is possible if a rather box-like shape to the top of the head of the stock is acceptable. The combined tumbler and striker is basically shaped like a capital letter C, if the gun is viewed from the right-hand side. The pivot is through the bottom end of the letter and formed on the back is an upward projection on which, via a swivel, the mainspring pulls upwards. Bearing in a wide slot above this projection is one side of the head of a T-shaped cocking piece, the bottom of which is fixed to the underlever behind the latter's pivot so that as the underlever is thrust forwards and down the tumbler is pulled back to cock. We are not shown how the barrels are bolted, but presume the mechanism is worked by the underlever as no other is shown.

We are indebted to Greener's *The Gun and its Development* from which we frequently quote. In the case of our next gun it would seem that he had first-hand knowledge for he describes it as 'one of the cheapest guns on the hammerless system that has yet been constructed and one requiring great force to cock'. Bearing these remarks carefully in mind we will look at the gun, which was patented by Thomas Danby Cross, James Wheeler Cross and William Wheeler Cross. On the patent, No. 126 of 1879, they are described as gun action-filers of Birmingham; as to their relationship there is no clue. The novelty of this gun lies in its lockwork with a coil mainspring set forwards in the action bar which pushes back the bottoms of the tumblers and hence the heads forwards since the pivot is above the spring. The sear has no bent in the normal sense of that term: instead, as the tail of the sear is raised, its nose slips below a shoulder on the bottom of the tumbler.

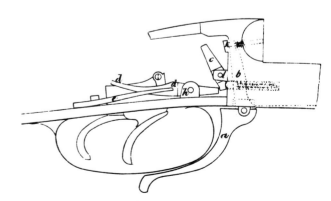

*J. Adsett patent No. 1981 of 1877*                    *T. J. and W. Cross patent No. 126 of 1879*

With all the interest in the hammerless gun, of which the activity recorded in the Patent Office is evidence, it is easy to be led to believe, as some writers have been, that the hammerless gun was coming into general use as the 1870s drew to their close. This is a fallacy; a look at a gunmaker's records tell a very different story. For instance: the very first hammerless gun listed by Thomas Horsley of York is one made in 1879 and it is not until 1885 that hammerless guns account for even half those listed. These, it must be remembered, are new guns being sold. The composition of the guns in a shooting party would be different again and would, to a degree, vary with the affluence of the men present. However, it is likely that in a shooting party made up of knights and peers, a hammerless gun would have been a rarity in 1879.

Obviously, there was growing interest in the hammerless gun and one important milestone was the patenting by several top London gunmakers of their own designs. This top echelon produced, fairly close together, patents for their own hammerless guns. These form a neat group in that mechanically they are so very similar that the patentees were probably very wise to adopt, as they apparently did, a policy of live and let live rather than engage in wasteful legal wrangles. The group bore the prestigious names Woodward, Lang and Rigby and the patents are respectively: Thomas Southgate and James Woodward, junior, No. 600 of 1876; James Lang, No. 545 of 1878; and John Rigby and Thomas Bissell's, No. 1411 of 1879.

Of these three, the guns of Woodward and Lang are, in the authors' experience at least, the most commonly encountered. The Woodward, called variously the 'Automaton' and the 'Automatic' – the latter more usually on the actual gun – appears from time-to-time with other makers' names, both metropolitan and provincial,

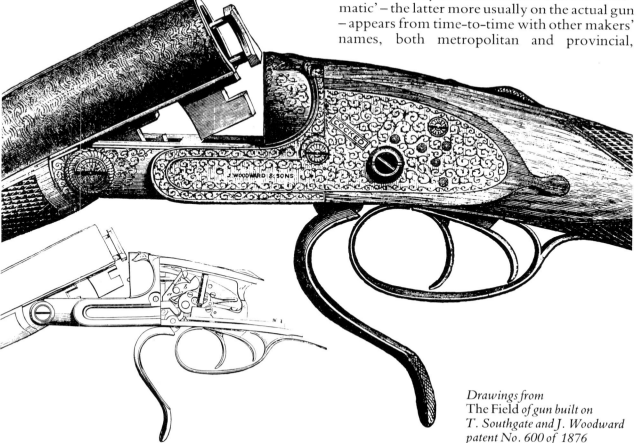

*Drawings from*
*The Field of gun built on*
*T. Southgate and J. Woodward*
*patent No. 600 of 1876*

which suggests some sort of licensing arrangement. By contrast, with but one exception, all the guns of the Lang design we have seen were so named. One of them, in shootable condition, used to belong to the author (DJB). Because it carried a fair degree of choke it was reserved for late in the duck season when the quarry was well educated. But perhaps the most remarkable feature of the barrels was that the chambers were bored with sharp shoulders rather than the normal cones. Probably the original owner had a predilection for brass cases that were then coming into limited use. Tucked away on the beautifully made trigger plate action was the stamp 'J. Stanton' and from this we get a glimpse of the organisation of the trade and the buying-in of parts, which was normal practice. In use this was a remarkably easy gun to operate. Even when both barrels had been fired, the lockwork cocked with scarcely noticeable effort and the thrust of the underlever would cause the gun to spring open as if it were some sort of self-opener. The trigger plate action was surprisingly compact and the head of the stock on this Lang was not as big as that of some hammer guns. In addition to all this, the position of the lockwork is well to the rear and the action bar slim, so that the centre of gravity of the gun is also well back. This made for a responsive gun that was, in all ways, a delight to use.

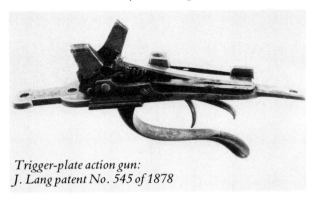

*Trigger-plate action gun:*
*J. Lang patent No. 545 of 1878*

We feel it is appropriate at this point to digress and say something of the several men, prominent in the British guntrade at this time, who had the surname of Woodward. We are not aware of any blood relationship between them, but feel it necessary to write of them as a group

if only to counter some of the confusion that already exists. The most potent cause of this confusion is the fact that there were two Thomas Woodwards; one was a Birmingham gunmaker with premises at 10, Steelhouse Lane, from 1868 to 1886, and then at 7, Bath Street until 1888. In the main his products seem to have been the sound, honest but unpretentious guns, pistols and rifles that made Birmingham's reputation in the last century.

The other Thomas Woodward, also a prolific patentee, was the man who established in London Messrs Holland & Holland's first factory at 527, Harrow Road, London, and managed it until forced by ill health to retire in 1914. He was thus responsible for the transition that Hollands made in their style of business from being retailers of guns made for them by outworkers and firms specialising in working for the trade, into the true manufacturers of the majority of guns and rifles that bore their name.

The final, famous Woodwards who add another possibility for confusion were James and his sons, James and Charles, who, at the time we are writing of, had retail premises at 64, St. James's Street, London. This firm had been established as Moore and Woodward in 1827 and became James Woodward in 1851, 'and Sons' being added to the title in 1872. We will encounter several patents taken out by James junior at various points in our narrative.

This trio do not exhaust the role of the gunmaking Woodwards. There was a Benjamin Woodward in Whittall Street, Birmingham, who marked his guns 'Maker to H. M. War Dept'.

Of the group comprising Woodward, Lang and Rigby guns, the Rigby is the least frequently encountered. Fortunately, the authors have access to a superb example, to examine and photograph. The mechanism for all three can be summed up as having a projection from the underlever that lifts the tumblers to full-cock. Any other differences, such as the Woodward and Rigby use of conventional sidelocks in place of the trigger plate action and the dummy plates of the Lang, would defy legal separation and this very point is made by Dr Walsh in *The Modern Sportsman's Gun and Rifle*.

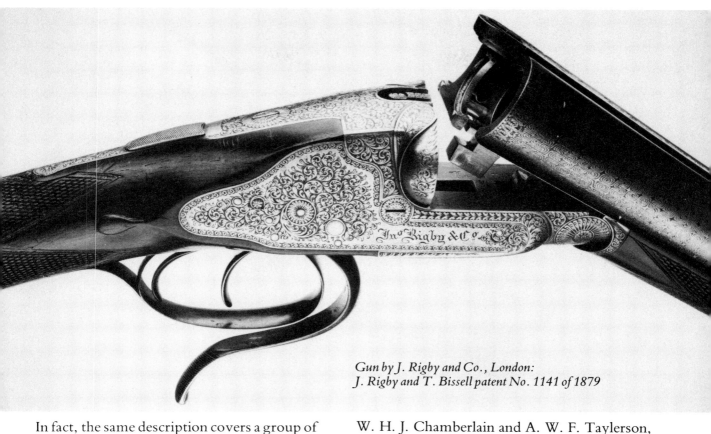

*Gun by J. Rigby and Co., London:*
*J. Rigby and T. Bissell patent No. 1141 of 1879*

In fact, the same description covers a group of less-known guns with equal accuracy: Lawden and Thomas's patent, No. 3291 of 1876; the provisional patent, No. 3573 of 1878, of Samuel Mathews; patent, No. 1128 of 1879, in the name of William Adams of Oxford Street, London; James Lang's patent, No. 1422 of 1880; and the patent, No. 13,688 of 1884, by John Gibson. All these conform to this description. (Incidentally, William Adams does not appear in the superbly researched book by W. H. J. Chamberlain and A. W. F. Taylerson, *Adams Revolvers* (1976), and we therefore assume that he was not a member of the revolver-making family.)

Of passing note is a provisional specification, No. 4647 of 1878, of W. Rogers in which a friction-relieving roller is added. Another provisional specification, No. 5002 of 1879, was granted to J. and W. Tolley for a cam in the action to ease the cocking motion in some way. The trigger plate underlever gun shown in

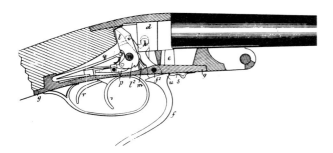

*T. Lawden and J. Thomas patent No. 3291 of 1876*

*F. Crutchley patent No. 3684 of 1879*

11

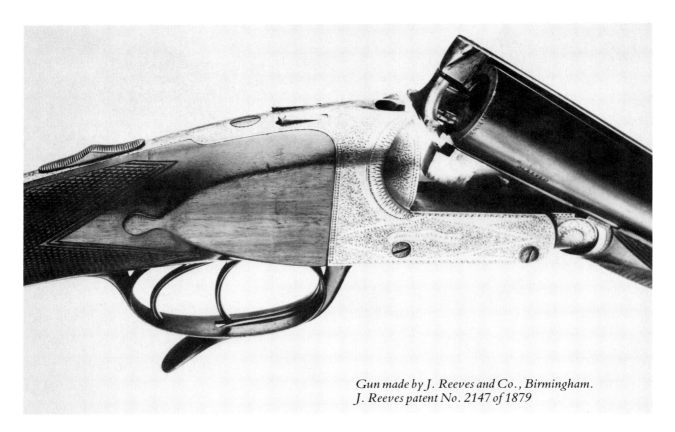

*Gun made by J. Reeves and Co., Birmingham.*
*J. Reeves patent No. 2147 of 1879*

Frederick Crutchley's patent, No. 3684 of 1879, resembles a simplified Lang lockwork and thus may possibly be mistaken for it.

A more distinctive trigger plate lever-cocked gun, from a construction point of view, is the John Reeves patent, No. 2147 of 1879. Here the lockwork is slotted into the bottom of the action more like an Anson and Deeley boxlock. We assume that this gun was made in at least token quantities as it is both illustrated in *The Gun and its Development* and an example has come our way.

Much more common, indeed found bearing the names of a host of lesser makers and retailers, is a gun now known to the collecting fraternity as the 'Spiral Spring Woodward'. This is perhaps the most original of all these Murcott-like guns and was in its day known as 'The Acme'; its modern nickname more accurately describes its mechanism. Mounted on each sidelock-like lockplate is a mechanism not unlike the bolt of a bolt-action rifle in that there is a plunger with an integral striker at its front. Around this 'bolt' is a spiral spring and the whole is covered by a tube-like internal cover. Projecting inwards from the plunger is a lug that is acted upon by a projection of the underlever which thus compresses the mainspring and forces the bolt back until it is caught by a sear. The patentee of this gun was Thomas Woodward and the relevant number is 651 of 1876.

Incidentally, very like the Spiral Spring Woodward is the design described in the provisional specification, No. 1329 of 1876, by Charles Price and William Harris. The specification gives Price's address as 16, Pitt Street, Southwark, and describes Harris as the manager of William Moore and Grey of 43, Old Bond Street, London.

Very much in the mould of the classic Murcott action is the cocking arrangement of one of

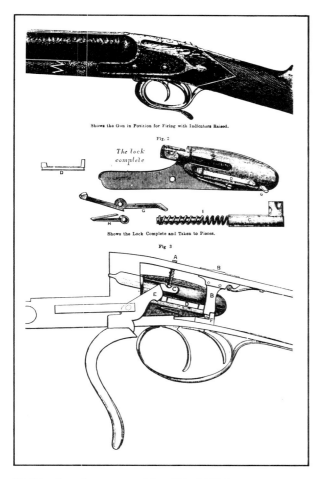

Shows the Gun in Position for Firing with Indicators Raised.

Fig. 2

The lock complete

Shows the Lock Complete and Taken to Pieces.

Fig 3

*T. Woodward gun patent No. 651 of 1876*

*Thomas Woodward's advertisement of 1884*

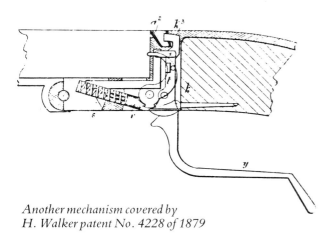

*Another mechanism covered by*
*H. Walker patent No. 4228 of 1879*

several guns included on the Henry Walker specification, No. 4228 of 1879. Here a sideways projection from the internal portion of the lever acts on an inward projection from the tumbler. The more distinctive part of this is the use of coil mainsprings, set in an oblique hole in the action acting on the tumblers via pistons.

A feature of British shotgun history is the patenting of gun designs that were obsolete when they appeared. For instance, a whole ten years later, Arthur Nouvelle of 36–38, Rue de Clery, Paris, patented, with the aid of the agents J. H. Johnson & Co., as No. 2563 of 1889, a species of trigger plate gun cocked by a push-forward, over-the-guard lever. This was no different to the original Murcott in that two inward projections from the tumblers are acted upon by the upward projections of the opening lever, the latter pivoted ahead of the tumblers.

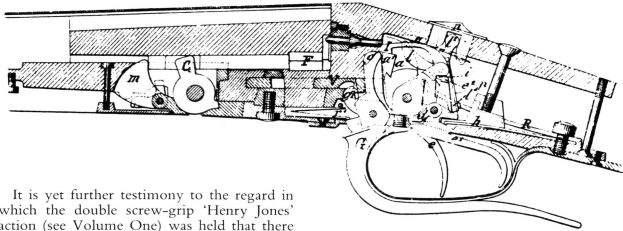

It is yet further testimony to the regard in which the double screw-grip 'Henry Jones' action (see Volume One) was held that there should be hammerless versions of it in which the long turning lever is used to cock the lock-work. It is the authors' view that the earliest of these is an uncommon variant of the Murcott gun, indeed the only example known to us is an action that was acquired (by IMC) as part of a 'box of junk' many years ago. In this action, a pair of rods run diagonally up and back from the turret and are turned by the underlever to the lockwork.

The Gibbs and Pitt patent, No. 284 of 1873, also describes a gun cocked by a turning under-bolt but this must be reckoned as a little-used

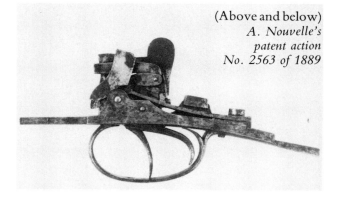

(Above and below)
*A. Nouvelle's
patent action
No. 2563 of 1889*

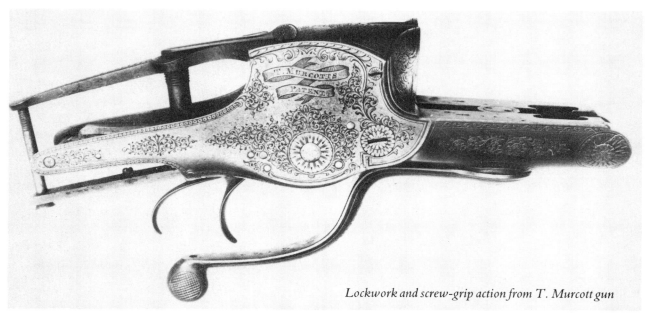

*Lockwork and screw-grip action from T. Murcott gun*

variant because very few specimens have ever come to our notice. The essential feature of this gun and indeed several others was to have a cocking rod that slid backwards from the locking turret into the head of the stock, there to cock the locks. This rod bears on a shoulder on the left-hand side of the turret so that, as the underlever is turned to the right, the cocking rod is forced backwards. The Gibbs and Pitt drawing shows this with the characteristic hinged lever to work the trigger plate action and also with a fixed cocking prong at its rear.

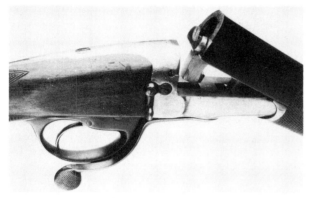

*Gun by G. Gibbs of Bristol: G. Gibbs and T. Pitt patent No. 284 of 1873, with turning underlever action*

The same idea for the cocking slide reappears as part of the H. Walker patent, No. 4294 of 1878. Here the slide forces back the bottom of the cocking lever pivoted high in the action head, as previously described.

It is one of the many anomalies of our story that because of Greener's *The Gun and its Development* – which has such a reputation and attracts a following among those interested in the mechanism of the sporting gun – those mechanisms he chose to describe in detail are well-known to present-day enthusiasts, whereas in some cases actual examples are not often seen. One of these is our next 'Henry Jones'-style hammerless gun that was patented, as No. 2993 of 1881, by Samuel Blakemore Allport.

Allport was to become one of the great names in late-nineteenth-century gunmaking, his greatness derived in large part from his work as Proof Master in the years 1892 to 1899.

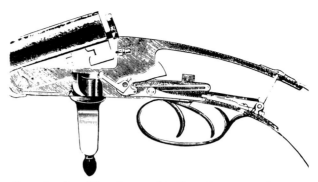

*Drawing from* The Gun and its Development *of S. B. Allport gun patent No. 2993 of 1881*

In the gun that Allport patented, and Greener describes, the characteristic quarter turn of the long and powerful Henry Jones lever is made to cock the lockwork via a second short L-shaped lever in the action. This has its long leg roughly horizontal and is pivoted about halfway along the short vertical leg on the same centre as the tumblers. The end of the long leg lies forwards and has there a roller which rides in a helical groove cut in the locking turret of the action so that, as this turret is turned by the underlever, the forward end of the cocking lever is raised. Resting on the short leg of the cocking lever are two inward projections from the front of the tumblers so the latter are rotated backwards and so are cocked. Greener's drawing (derived from the patent specification) and the only example of this gun the authors have been able to strip and examine indicate a trigger plate-style of action but there is no real reason why this cocking mechanism could not be applied to other forms of lockwork.

As if to illustrate the force with which ideas of this era are cross-linked there is tucked away in the specification, No. 873 of 1882 by John Dickson (the younger) and Andrew Graham Murray (which is mostly concerned with the classic three-barrel Dickson shotgun), a design that uses the sliding cocking rod of the earlier Dickson patent, No. 294 of 1880. Here it is worked by the barrels, for a cocking slide worked from the turret of a Henry Jones action; the rearward motion of the cocking slide is achieved by linking this to the left-hand side of the turret and so it is forced to the rear as the lever turns to the right.

Given the temper of the era we are describing, it is predictable that an inventor should use the Henry Jones action to pull forwards a cocking piece. This duly appears as part of Alexander Henry's patent, No. 5273 of 1882. This shows a V-shaped lever pivoted at its angle, which is to the right of the centreline of the gun. The forward limb of this V bears a projection from the Henry Jones turret so that – as this latter is turned in an anti-clockwise direction – when the gun, viewed from behind and above, is opened, so the rearward limb of the V moves forwards. Hinged to this is a two-legged slide, each leg of which engages with the bottom of the tumblers, if the locks have been fired, which are thus rotated backwards to cock.

*Gun by A. Henry built on its maker's patent No. 5273 of 1882*

So we come to the end of the underlever types. Most closely allied to these are guns that use a side lever to open, withdraw the locking-bolts and to cock the action. To form this sub-division is, to a degree, false because the actual position of this cocking lever could be varied to suit the preference of a customer or the whim of the gunmaker. Most, if not all, of the guns we know and describe as underlevers could have this lever curved around to one side of the action to produce a side lever and we are confident that some such will be found. Conversely these side lever guns could be made as underlevers. However, we have formed this sub-section of guns we know of, either through drawings or actual guns examined, as we feel that these are more likely to be encountered as side lever guns.

*An unpatented design for a sidelever-cocking hammerless gun by J. D. Dougall*

Four of these guns are very similar and can usefully be described together. The earliest patent is part of Joseph Mathews's specification, No. 3929 of 1878. Here we have a central cocking lever keyed onto a transverse spindle. This spindle also carries the tumblers which are free to rotate upon it. The cocking piece has slotted into it an upward projection from the barrel-bolt so that depressing the side lever, on the left-hand side of the gun, both cocks the locks and withdraws the barrel-bolts. The lockwork is shown as a conventional bar-action sidelock and the tumblers have inward projections on their heads by which they are cocked.

The Enos James gun, patent No. 4317 of 1879, is, again, a standard bar-action sidelock but with the tumbler pivoted fairly low on the lockplate. The tumblers share a common axle with the lever that withdraws the Purdey-bolt and this axle is continued to the outside of the lockplates where (on the left-hand side in the patent drawing) is fixed the opening lever. The tumblers are in part free to rotate on this axle but are forced to rotate backwards, as the external lever is depressed and the barrel-locking bolts withdraw, by two shoulders formed on the spindle which abut with corresponding shoulders on the tumblers. When the tumblers are at the full-cock position they are held by the sears but the shoulders which cocked them rotate away forwards as the side lever comes back to the up position and the barrel-locking-bolt moves forwards under the influence of a V snap spring set in the bottom of the action behind the spindle and bearing on a projection on the lever that works the locking-bolt. Thus the tumblers are free to rotate forwards when the sears free them as the trigger is squeezed to fire the gun.

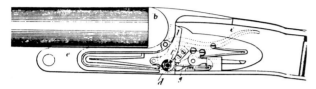

*E. James patent No. 4317 of 1879*

The foregoing description would seem also to cover the gun described in the patent, No. 278 of 1880, taken out by two London gunmakers, Thomas Southgate of Burton Crescent and Edward Harrison of The Strand. This is a provisional specification of which we have no knowledge but the description itself.

Thomas William Webley describes in his specification, No. 1860 of 1880, a trigger plate style of action, but, again, the tumblers are on the same axis as the side lever, this time drawn on the right of the gun. By virtue of the trigger plate layout the tumblers are set close together and are made to be pushed back by the locking-bolt as this is drawn to the rear. For convenience the mainsprings are set behind the tumblers and the whole mechanism bears a very strong resemblance to the Hughes action, patent No. 1290 of 1875.

A curious gun that falls within this sub-group is described in the specification, No. 4809 of 1879, in the name of Horatio Phillips, who was later to become well-known as the 'Gun Editor' of *The Field* and to have a somewhat chequered career. The lever-cocked gun in this specification is notable for no other reason than that there is no indication of how the mechanism is to be held cocked! The side lever is shown acting on a spring-loaded plunger that is carried on a vertical lever from the trigger plate that is pivoted top and bottom. Behind the head of this plunger is a rod around which is a coil spring.

The rod slides backwards through a guide behind the trigger work as the side lever forces it back in compressing the mainspring, but here the description stops and the drawing is no more explicit.

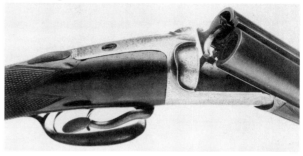

*Gun retailed by Stephen Grant with Phillips action patent No. 4809 of 1879*

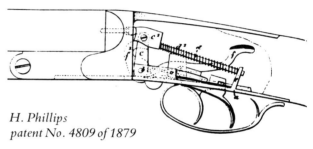

*H. Phillips patent No. 4809 of 1879*

Sound and practical as were the best of these various underlever and side lever designs, there were gun designers and sportsmen alike who sought the advantages of a hammerless gun with a top lever opening system. Today we regard the top lever as so natural and ordinary that we may perhaps lose sight of the fact that it was in the 1860s and early-1870s 'the new, modern system'. With all the lever-cocked guns, there exists the conflicting requirement that the mainspring needs to be strong to ensure a satisfactory blow is administered to the cartridge cap, but this very strength must not make the gun so fitted difficult to open. This requirement is made more acute if the opening lever is short; a point to bear in mind when looking at photographs or drawings of all lever-cocked guns, to see how the designer has achieved the maximum length of lever consistent with convenience and appearance of the gun so fitted.

(Above and below) *Birmingham-made gun:*
*G. Gibbs and T. Pitt patent No. 284 of 1873, retailed*
*by T. Horsley of York in 1884. Lock with barrel bolt,*
*spindle and top lever.*

As might be expected, just about every possible type of top lever motion was tried but the most numerous and certainly the most successful was the turning top lever. Here, again, we have an instance where the first in the field was also the most successful for a turning top lever was part of the Gibbs and Pitt patent, No. 284 of 1873. This variant has become known to present-day collectors as the 'second model', despite it being part of the original specification, but this tag recognises the fact that these turning top lever Gibbs and Pitt guns seem to be of a later vintage than the push-forward underlever models. These 'second model' guns are all bar-action sidelocks, in which the Purdey-bolt has a thickened rear portion which bears on inward projections on the tumblers so that the latter, as the gun is opened, are forced back to full-cock.

This is another gun action that will be found with any one of a whole host of 'makers' names, both London and provincial; but those presumably made within the span of the patent will have on the action flats the distinctive lozenge-

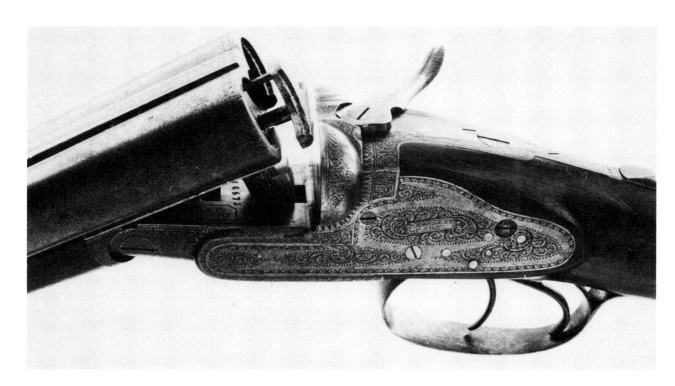

shaped stamp. Dr Walsh, in *The Modern Sportsman's Gun and Rifle*, tells us something of this design, which he criticises as being a gun with bar-action locks but lacking a top connection. While theoretically this gun has a weak action, the fact that large numbers have survived the 100-year interval is a more eloquent testimonial to the merits of the design. The basic outline of this mechanism is that of an extension on the rear of the Purdey-bolt to force back the tumblers. On close examination this proves to be an accurate description of some seven designs. Dr Walsh tells us that the Cogswell and Harrison 'Desideratum' was a true Gibbs and Pitt but there are patented designs as well.

| Name | Patent | Year |
|---|---|---|
| John Plumb Clabrough (from U.S. Patent 210,905 granted to Julius Bluemel in 1878) | 3611 | 1878 |
| William Hodgetts Tisdall | 2177 | 1879 |
| Frederick Crutchley | 3684 | 1879 |
| Henry Alfred Alexander Thorn | 499 | 1881 |
| Henry Tolley | 1515 | 1883 |
| William Monton, Edwin Brettel and William Bentley | 2116 | 1887 |
| Paul Brun-Latrige | 11,560 | 1888 |

Moreover, the J. and W. Tolley 'Perfection' gun answers this general description as well. This is not to imply that all these guns are identical, there are variations on how the top lever spindle is keyed on the double-bolt, and the purpose of the Monton, Brettel and Bentley is to reduce by almost one-third the angle through which the top lever had to swing. Also, in the case of the Brun-Latrige gun, one version is shown with novel lockwork. The V-shaped mainspring is fitted vertically, point uppermost, with its free forward end bearing directly on the back of the tumbler. But, aside from this, the most significant variations are in the safety arrangements (see Chapter Six).

Two guns which are slightly outside our sub-group bear investigation. One is the top lever version of the Scott patent, No. 3424 of 1874, which we always number as the carbon copy of the original Gibbs and Pitt. The other is a gun that, then as now, is of far greater importance if for no better reason than it is one of the most distinctive. One of the most elegant of all hammerless guns, the James MacNaughton is cocked by a Purdey-bolt worked by a turning top lever. Once again, the bolt does not act directly on the tumblers but with this trigger plate action each lock has a curved lifted lever pivoted at its rear and pushed up and back by the bolt on its rearward travel. In the beautifully-made lockwork that characterises these guns, the tumblers fit snugly into the curve of the lifter lever which raises them to full-cock. This gun, patented as No. 2848 of 1879 in Britain and as No. 264,723 of 1882 in the United States, was the classic MacNaughton gun.

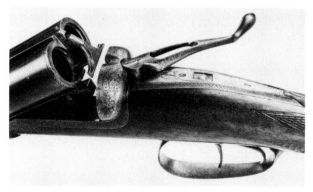

(Above and below) *Edinburgh bar-in-wood hammerless gun built by J. MacNaughton of Edinburgh. Stock removed from Edinburgh gun to show the trigger-plate lockwork*

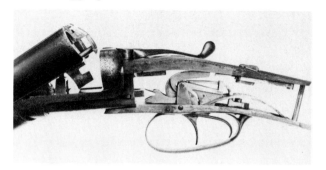

In this period there were, inevitably, detail changes but the most important of these was the production of a bar-in-wood version known as the 'Edinburgh Model' which we use to illustrate this gun. The choice of this illustration was particularly difficult as there were two other strong contenders: one was the more conventional model, without the bar-in-wood, with which the author (DJB) bagged his first Bob-White quail; the other was a very trim 28-bore version of this model that its owner found smothered in rust, with every spring in it broken, propping open a hen coop door.

It is a strange irony that we move from so svelte a gun to one which, in its patent drawings at least, is one of the most ugly – specification No. 4228 of 1879. It would be interesting to encounter one of these 'in the metal' simply to see if this lack of any line was merely the fault of the draftsman or if guns were really made looking like this. The patentee was Henry Walker (see Chapter Two). Once again we have a specification covering a multitude of ideas, but those that concern us here are hammerless guns. In these the tumblers have inward projections upon which bears the head of a lever, shaped like a capital letter T, which is set vertically in the head of, with its cross-piece across, the stock and pivoted on a transverse axle at the lower end of the upright limb. On the left-hand side of the top of the cross-piece is a small upward projection by which a rotating lever arrangement under the top strap, turned by the conventional top lever on the outside, pushes back the top of the T as the top lever is pushed to the right. This T-piece is linked to the underbolts so that they are withdrawn as the top lever is rotated. The patent drawing shows two distinct versions of this gun. One with conventional sidelocks, the other, which appears to be a species of boxlock with coil mainsprings, set forwards in the bar of the action.

A slightly earlier gun by Walker – that is distinctive if nothing else and unnecessarily complicated – is the top-lever-cocked hammerless. Part of patent No. 4294 of 1878, Walker's specification covers a variety of lever-cocked guns of which this top lever is the most unusual. The heart of the idea is to have a spindle inside the head of the action that shortens as the top lever turns. This upward motion is used via a bell crank lever to withdraw the barrel-locking bolt and cock the action. To provide this shortening action on the spindle the bottom is connected to the top by a pair of crossed levers and, since the top is free to rotate and the bottom is not, the desired motion is achieved. This is not the full extent of the complications: there is a compression spring in the spindle which is the snap spring for the action; and the whole spindle is hung on a pivot under the top strap so that as it turns and shortens the bottom swings to the rear. It is a matter of regret that a mechanism such as this is tucked away inside a gun and, providing it did not fail a user, it could be owned for years and remain undiscovered.

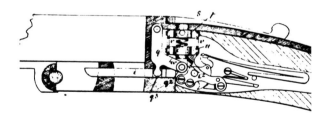

*Another variant covered by H. Walker patent No. 4294 of 1878*

Another variant on this general theme is found in the Bonehill and Matthews patent, No. 1952 of 1880. Christopher George Bonehill we will meet again, but all we know of William James Matthews is that he was a tool-maker. The gun they patented uses an L-shaped

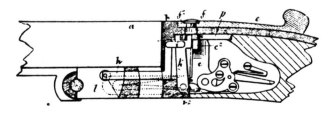

*Part of H. Walker patent No. 4228 of 1879*

cocking lever. This pivots crossways at its angle and is positioned so that the top of the lever is acted on by a cam under the top strap turned by the external top opening lever. As the top limb of the cocking lever is pushed back so the bottom forward end rises and this lifts the bottom limb of the C-shaped tumblers to the cocked position.

a sliding piece so that, as the top of the lever and the bolt are drawn back, this slide moves forwards. In so doing it bears on inward projections from the bottom of the tumblers and so these are forced to the full-cock position. The variant of this design is to dispense with the bottom slide and make the vertical lever with a forwards projection, a sort of backwards letter

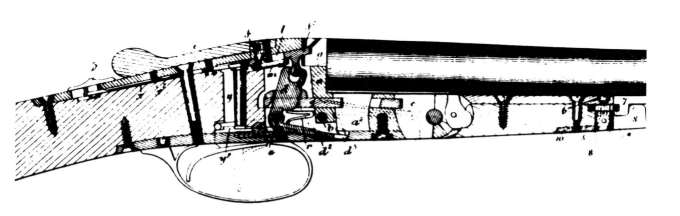

*C. G. Bonehill and W. J. Matthews patent No. 1952 of 1880*

Sharing the concept of a vertical cocking lever worked by a turning top lever, but which appears from its specification to be a handsome sidelock gun, is the Enos James specification, No. 2531 of 1881. We have already met Mr James and will encounter him again. Enos James and Company were one of the several firms who diversified their activities away from guns and into pedal cycles, but here we are concerned with their gunmaking activities. James's patent is, again, one with several variants. In the first of these a central vertical lever behind the standing-breech is hung on a transverse pivot just below its centrepoint. This pivot is also just at the bottom of the Purdey-bolt so that as the top of the vertical lever is drawn back so is the bolt. The very bottom of the lever is slotted into

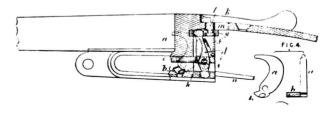

*E. James patent No. 2531 of 1881*

L, so that as the top is drawn back the forward projecting bottom portion lifts the bottoms of the tumblers.

We find yet another set of internal levers in the Thomas Woodward and Thomas Woodward, junior, specification, No. 3027 of 1881. On the vertical turning 'Scott' spindle is a transverse projection that is so positioned and formed that as the top lever is turned so this projection bears onto a cocking cam which again resembles a backwards L, this time pivoted at its angle on a transverse pivot so that as the top is pushed forwards so the back lifts the tumbler of the right-hand lock to full-cock. The left-hand lock is taken care of by having the cocking cam keyed onto the pivot which, at its left-hand end, has a lever to lift the left-hand tumbler.

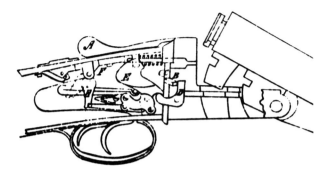

*T. and T. Woodward patent No. 3027 of 1881*

Another patent granted to this father and son combination fits neatly into our scheme at this point. No. 2344 of 1882 is stated to be an improvement on their patent, No. 651 of 1876, for the 'Spiral Spring Woodward' specification mentioned earlier. What is now proposed is to make the mechanism work by using a top lever. The vertical spindle which the top lever turns has a projection to the left. This withdraws the left-hand striker which has a projection that acts on the right-hand striker at the same time. However, in our understanding of the specification, the arrangement would mean that the left-hand lock had to be fired first. In addition to this unusual mechanism a novel form of sear is also proposed, a vertical rod around which is fitted a spiral spring. This rod has to be pushed up by the trigger blades to disengage the sear catch on the strikers, which were themselves rods with spiral mainsprings around them.

A gun which would appear to have at least a passing resemblance to the Woodward is that outlined in a provisional patent, No. 1463 of 1883. There are, unfortunately, no practical details included in this specification, which is of passing interest in that the men who obtained it were Thomas William Webley (who we

have already encountered) of Weaman Street, Birmingham, George Bouckley of Aston, Birmingham and Edwin Charles Hodges of Islington. We thus have a combined effort by the Birmingham and London trades.

An early and interesting gun, that has so far evaded our classification system, is that of Charles Henry Maleham and Thomas Mirfin. Maleham was the nephew and business successor to George Maleham whose business was long established in Sheffield. Thomas Mirfin was the foreman or manager of the firm's workshop and probably the real inventor of this gun. All that we know about him is that some years later he went out to Calcutta to work for the firm established by Joseph Manton's son. We have not as yet encountered a gun of this pattern, which we regard as one of the most appealing of the early hammerless guns. We first had an inkling of this design from an article which appeared in *The Field* in 1873. The most striking feature of the gun illustrated is the very long top lever. But there are also several novel features which we will return to presently. The heart of this mechanism is an internal slide under the top strap that is drawn back by the top lever. This movement, patent No. 940 of 1873, is achieved rather in the same way as the Westley Richards patent, No. 1572, of 1871. In both, the top lever is pivoted onto the internal slide but not fixed to the top strap. The forward end of the top lever has a broad shoulder which butts against a second shoulder formed as part of the top strap. As the top lever is pushed to the right, its right-hand shoulder bears against the fixed shoulder on the strap and so the pivot part of the lever, and hence the slide beneath, is drawn back. The snap spring is a small V-spring, set transversely under the top strap, with its free limb bearing on the rear of the internal slide. The forward end of this slide has two lateral projections which engage with recesses on the heavy firing pins and as these latter are drawn back so the locks are cocked. In addition the Purdey-bolt is linked to this slide to free the barrels for opening. The feature at which we hinted above is a loaded indicator of a type that reminds us how close we are to the era of the hammer gun, for these indicators are no less

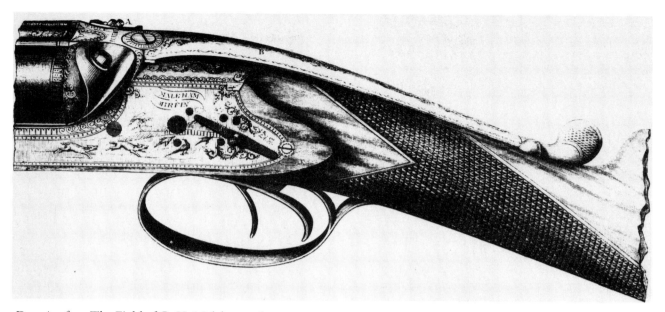

*Drawing from* The Field *of C. H. Maleham and T. Murfin gun patent No. 940 of 1873*

than dummy firing pins set in carved 'hammer gun' fences. The specification tells us that these pins were to be gold-plated and fitted with a coil spring so that, when no cartridge lay in the breech, the 'pin' would retract out of sight. The overall appearance of this gun is, therefore, of a hammer gun shorn of its hammers. (See also Chapter Six for a fuller discussion of loaded indicators.)

Our next top lever gun is relatively easily disposed of in that it is no more than a version of a mechanism we considered earlier as an under-lever type. Included in the Alexander Henry specification, No. 5273 of 1882, is the idea continuing the Scott spindle to the very bottom of the action where it would work a version of the cocking mechanism previously described.

To round off this section we have an unusual mechanism patented by another famous gun-maker. As patent No. 6787 of 1884, William Tranter of Birmingham protected a design for a top lever gun in which the rear of the locking-bolt pushed back an internal cocking lever that was hung on a transverse pivot just above the front of the trigger guard. The locks this lever

cocks are the most unusual feature since they have a coil spring round a striker rod, but with the cocking lever acting like a conventional tumbler in that the lock is controlled by a sear acting on the cocking lever. We have yet to encounter a specimen of this gun and suspect that it was overshadowed by the much better known, and indeed more sophisticated, 'Carlton' gun (see Chapter Four).

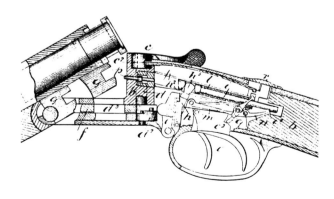

*W. Tranter patent No. 6787 of 1884*

Many times when searching through the diverse ideas deposited as the records of the Patent Office, we have paused and wondered whatever could have possessed a man that he expended effort and money protecting notions that, to be as kind as possible, are of dubious commercial value. Sometimes, it is true, these flights of fancy are to be found tucked in at the end of a specification and in these cases we imagine that the inventor was simply covering all possible eventualities and thereby getting better value for his patent fees. When such a claim is the first part of the specification, it is more baffling. This is certainly so regarding the Richard Ellis and Henry Scott patent, No. 2816 of 1879. Here the first claim and virtually the whole of the description in the provisional specification is for a hammerless gun that is both cocked and opened by a slide very like a conventional safety catch on the top strap of the gun. Moreover, this thumb piece is drawn little larger than a safety slide and there is no claim or clue as to supposed advantages of this idea. Essentially, the mechanism is very simple. The cocking lever is three-pronged rather like a capital letter E laid on its back and pivoted at its bottom. The two outside arms force back the tumblers as the centre limb is pulled back by the top slide. We believe something similar is also covered by part of the rather vague unillustrated provisional patent, No. 3573 of 1878, granted to Samuel Mathews of Birmingham.

But to return to the Ellis and Scott patent; the ironic fact about this is that the specification very fleetingly covers side or underlever versions which would be much more practical and, in addition, a barrel-cocked version that was to become moderately well-known and successful and which we shall consider with others of its ilk.

One of the more successful British shotguns of the 1860s was the William Powell push-up top lever design. This was to inspire further late-nineteenth-century designs for other gun actions (see Chapter Two). In addition to these, other designers took the idea and applied it to the cocking mechanism of the hammerless gun. In that they are thus a sept of the top lever clan, they demand our attention at this point.

The earliest is part of the Murcott patent of 1871. Here is drawn a version that has a top lever pivoted above and behind the tumblers with a hook-shaped forward portion that sweeps down over the heads of the tumblers so that as the top lever is pushed forwards and up the locks will be cocked, albeit not particularly easily. There is no indication of how this top lever is to work the barrel-locking bolts and we are thus inclined to suspect it is a 'make-weight' feature of this specification.

A feature of the Henry Walker patent, No. 700 of 1876, is that the drawing is minute. There are no less than 13 figures on a sheet of paper approximately the size of a page of this book – with a generous margin besides. What appears to be covered by one of these figures is a hammerless gun in which a vertical lever, pivoted at the bottom of the action on the trigger plate, has its top forced back by the internal portion of a push-up top lever. In turn, this lever would bear on one or both of

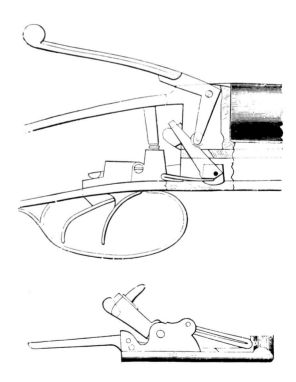

*J. Reeves patent No. 2147 of 1879.*
*Drawing from* The Gun and its Development

the tumblers, if they should be in the fired position, and raise them to full-cock.

This description could not be bettered for part of the John Reeves specification, No. 2147 of 1879. This we have previously encountered as a push-forward underlever type but, in addition, the patent drawing shows a push-up top lever version. The top lever is shown as an L-shape with a long limb lying along the top strap and the short one projecting down into the head of the action. This lever is hung on a transverse pivot at the angle and carries at the bottom of the short lever an anti-friction roller. As the external portion of the lever is pushed up, so the vertical internal cocking lever, which can be thought of as the remains of the push-forward underlever, is pushed back and hence, if necessary, the tumblers. This version is another of those described in *The Gun and its Development*, but the only example we have ever seen was of the underlever type previously described.

Another, slightly earlier, Walker patent, No. 4294 of 1878, also demonstrates the close affinity between the push-up top lever and the push-forward underlever. This is yet another idea where the downward projection of the top lever is linked to a vertical lever pivoted transversely at its bottom in the head of the stock. As the top lever is pushed up, the top of the internal

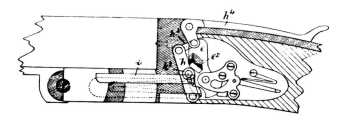

*Push-up top lever version of*
*H. Walker patent No. 4294 of 1878*

lever is drawn back and this motion both withdraws the locking-bolt and cocks the locks.

The one remaining possible motion for a top lever is to be pushed down into the head of the stock and while this has obvious disadvantages it was sufficiently attractive to gain some patents. Since the first is unillustrated we cannot be sure of all the practical details, but, in essence, the opening/cocking lever is shaped like a capital letter V with a crossways pivot at its bottom angle. If viewed from the right, the right-hand limb would have been shorter than the left, which projected from the top strap and was there turned backwards to form a thumb lever. When this was pushed down, the forward limb of the V would draw back the barrel-locking bolts while the rearward limb, via inward projecting studs, would force back the

*John Reeves advertisement published in 1876*

tumblers. This idea and variants of it are covered by a patent, No. 3883 of 1879, granted to William Middleditch Scott and John Tonks, a gun lockmaker of Aston.

Another design with a push-down top lever, patent No. 4258 of 1885, was obtained in Britain by William Phillips Thompson, acting as an agent for Andrew Hyde of Hatfield, Massachusetts. This, from its drawing, appears to be a single-barrel gun in which the top lever has first to be pushed up to retract firing pin and barrel-locking bolt and, at the same time, half-cock the lockwork; then a final squeeze down is necessary to bring the lock to full-cock. This is accomplished by a pair of levers on transverse pivots in the head of the stock. The one towards the front of the gun is vertical with its pivot at approximately its mid-point. Just above this it is slotted through a sliding firing pin so that, as the top of this vertical lever is pushed forwards, a curve on its rear, acting as a cam, withdraws the firing pin. While this is happening the bottom of the vertical lever will move to the rear and withdraw the barrel-locking bolt. This motion is given to the vertical lever by a horizontal lever which is also the thumb piece which lies partially exposed along the top strap of the gun and is pivoted almost at its front part. Pushing this thumb lever upwards pushes the vertical lever forwards and at the same time a downward projection levers back the hammer to half-cock.

The snap spring is a spiral spring in a recess in the standing-breech which is compressed as the vertical lever swings forwards. This, plus the weight of the lever, will return the horizontal lever to its rest position. The final bringing of the tumbler to full-cock is brought about by a squeeze down on the thumb lever when the rear of this lever bears on a spur on the rear of the tumbler. To lift the thumb lever clear of the tumbler there is a leaf spring under the top strap. Essentially a simple mechanism, but probably because it is so unlike a conventional action, it has claimed more than its fair share of space.

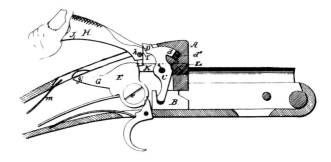

*W. P. Thompson (agent for A. Hyde) patent No. 4258 of 1885*

At this point we come to what was, frankly, one of the problems of preparing this work, a huge patent specification in the name of Andrew Wyley of Aston Manor, Birmingham, No. 2238 of 1874. In fact this is the middle of three specifications that this gentleman took out, the others being No. 863 of 1867 and No. 1754 of 1879. The first of these problems that we have is the sheer size of the specification. For instance, the 1874 specification has over 50 drawings covering a variety of single-shot rifles and pistols as well as several different shotguns. In addition, there are many references in the text of the later specifications back to the earlier ones. The only commercial use that was made of all this was a limited production of single-shot rifles marketed as the 'Webley–Wyley' rifle.

In Wyley's patent of 1874 there are drawn five different shotgun mechanisms, four of which are conventional pivot open-barrel, push-forward underlever, lever-cocked guns in which it is an upward extension of the opening lever that cocks the lockwork. In two of these we have an idea that is reminiscent of the French Robert gun of the 1830s, which had a striking head as part of its mainspring. In the Wyley design there is a species of tumbler, a broad V-lever hung on a stout pivot at its angle to transform the upward blow of the mainspring on one limb into a forward blow on the firing pin by the other. This lockwork is further unusual in that the function of a sear is performed by a notch on the actual mainspring that engages with another on a lever pivoted above the mainspring. This lever terminates at its lower end as a conventional trigger and drawing it back disengages the two notches. This gun is cocked by a backwards projection of the top of the opening lever that bears down on the free end of the mainspring as the gun is opened.

There is a variant of this idea that uses a mainspring lying in the action bar, with a small lever acting as a sear to release the mainspring head and so fire the lock, while a third variant is very much more conventional; a tumbler pivots on the same centre as the opening lever and is released by a sear, but still uses the intermediate lever between firing pin and tumbler.

The fourth pivot open shotgun drawn on the Wyley specification owes nothing to the three guns that precede it. However, we can consider it at this point because it is still an upward projection of the opening lever that cocks the lockwork. Now a short spur above the pivot point of the opening lever engages with, and forces back, a coil spring-loaded plunger set in the stock above the trigger work. A point which may be significant here is that the gun is shown as a single-barrel with no provision for working two such locks in parallel.

Many times we find guns, or groups of guns, which could be logically placed in more than one group, depending on the criteria used to establish a particular group. Now, for instance, we have a couple of designs which stand between the lever-cockers which compose this chapter and those guns cocked by the fall of the barrels that compose Chapter Four and, moreover, have parallels with the spring-cocked guns that we will consider separately as Chapter Five. The first is a patent, No. 881 of 1880, granted to David Bentley; the second a patent, No. 2505 of 1880, granted to Thomas Woodward and Thomas Woodward, junior, of 10, Steelhouse Lane, Birmingham. In these two designs it is the movement of the opening lever that raises the tumblers to full-cock but the movement of the barrels that compresses the

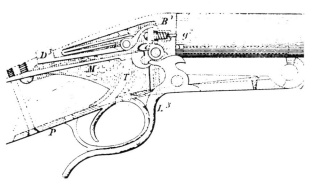

*A. Wyley patent No. 1754 of 1879*

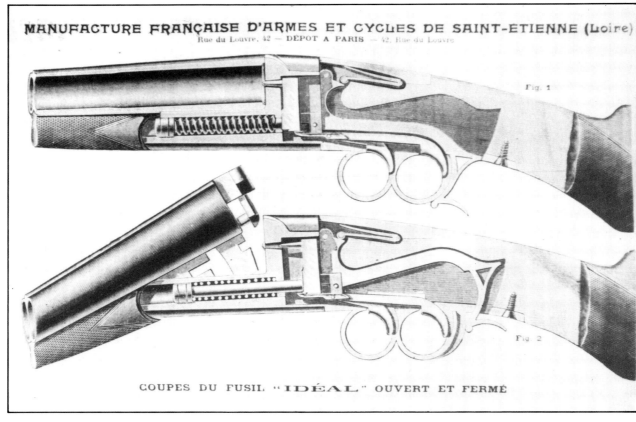

*Drawing from Manufrance catalogue of 1908 of 'The Ideal Gun',*
*P. Blachon and E. Mimarde patent No. 6936 of 1888*

mainsprings and so prepares the lockwork for firing. Since they perhaps are closest in concept to the spring-cockers we have included a fuller description at the end of Chapter Five.

To conclude what has been, of necessity, a long and tortuous chapter, we have retained a gun design which, viewed in terms of length of production, is by far the most successful of all the guns we have so far dealt with. The prime reason for its inclusion in this book is that it is the subject of a British patent, No. 6936 of 1888, derived from the French patent granted to Petrus Blachon and Etienne Mimarde, of 3, Place Villeboeuf, St Etienne, in central France. It was from this gunshop that the vast French organisation, Manufacture Française d'Armes et Cycles de Saint-Etienne – usually simply called 'Manufrance' – grew. Regrettably, it is beyond our scope to explore this very tempting

story. The point that we have to make is that this lever-cocked gun, the 'Ideal', was made in a variety of grades up to the very best as both shotgun and double rifle. Moreover, when the patent protection had expired, other firms in St Etienne took up the design, in the main to produce inexpensive guns. In later years Manufrance produced their 'Robust', a derivation of the Anson and Deeley boxlock, which became the cheaper gun in their range. The Ideal remained as the top of the range prestige gun, a role that it was well equipped to fill since the mechanics of the action permit the production of a very svelte, elegant gun.

One of the facets of this design that made such elegance possible is the simple stratagem of mounting the long cocking/opening lever within the action of the gun and having only a small fragment of it protruding to enable the user to rotate it through the necessary arc. The lever is pivoted high behind the standing-breech, just under the top strap and one limb of this projects vertically down to the barrel-bolt and lock mechanism. The other limb of the lever curves back and down in an arc from the pivot and, in the final manifestations of this gun, terminates as a short projection from the rear of the trigger guard which has to be pulled up to work the action. Pulling up on this limb of the lever caused the other limb to swing back as well which both cocked the action and withdrew the barrel-locking bolts. The locking mechanism we will consider with others, but the lockwork is equally ingenious. The striker is shaped like a letter U on its side with the top limb, the striker proper, shorter than the bottom limb which runs forwards into the bar of the action. Around

this limb is fitted a coil spring. This is compressed as the striker is drawn back by the opening lever and held back by a hook sear until this latter is released by the trigger, producing a mechanism that encroaches very little into the action bar and with no weakening transverse pivots. Given these advantages, a rounded bar can be used and lines reminiscent to British, or perhaps at this point we should say Scottish, eyes of the Dickson round action or Mac-Naughton trigger plate actions emerge – all three very handsome guns.

As a codicil that we are unable to explain, the Birmingham firm of Thomas Wild sold a gun they called 'The Triumph', apparently identical to the Manufrance Ideal, and publicised it in *The Sporting Goods' Review* of 1896. As to the facts of the case we can only wonder.

*Thomas Wild 'Triumph Gun': picture from*
Sporting Goods Review *1895*

# CHAPTER TWO

# The End of the Hammer Gun

It is very easy to survey the patents of the 1870s and see there so many specifications for hammerless guns of diverse type and thus be led to the belief that this style of gun was rapidly coming into fashion. Indeed, other writers taking a more wide-ranging view have given the impression that at this period the sportsmen of Britain were re-equipped with hammerless guns, much as an army would be issued with a new model of rifle. It is our view that nothing could be further from the truth. If surviving gunmakers' records are studied it is immediately apparent that, until say 1875, the building of a hammerless gun was a rarity. Even those makers whom we think of as pioneers of the hammerless gun were producing such guns in only relatively small numbers. For instance, Murcotts announced in April 1873 that they had made 100. Gunmakers' records of course, relate solely to guns being built and sold, so we see not only the first hammerless guns but the occasional pinfire and even the odd muzzle-loading gun. If we consider the more nebulous point of what sportsmen in the upper echelons of society were actually shooting with, we realise that the gun with external hammers held the stage on the stubbles and in the coverts of England and on the grouse moors of Scotland well into the

*A Royal Shooting Party, circa 1883, by courtesy of Her Majesty the Queen. Prince of Wales* (centre), *Prince Albert Victor* (third left), *Prince George* (second right), *Marquis of Hartington* (third right)

1880s. Indeed, all the inventions and patents for hammerless guns were behind-the-scenes preparations for the next act.

Conversely, it is from the same patent specifications that we see proof of the continuing omnipotence of the hammer shotgun. If we look instead at the patented inventions for barrel-locking mechanisms during our period we see that the greater part of these are drawn as external hammer guns. This does not mean that they were only built as such for, in practically every instance, it is possible to visualise the mechanism being used on a hammerless gun. So, while our classification is to this degree artificial, we nevertheless propose to use it if only to emphasise the continuing importance of the hammer gun.

Before we become embroiled with barrel-bolting mechanisms, there are three groups of inventions that are even more intimately bound up with the hammer gun and must be considered.

The invention of the rebound lock was one of the great milestones in the evolution of the external hammered shotgun. In general it was the Stanton patterns that were used, but it is yet further measure of the richness of our story that we find as a deposition in the British Patent Office, a rebound lock that was used by one of the greatest exponents of the American double-barrel shotgun, the communicator was no less than Wilber Fisk Parker. He was the son of Charles Parker, founder of the famous American company that bore his name. The agent who obtained the British patent, No. 180 of 1872, was Edward Thomas Hughes of the firm of Hughes & Son, Patent Agents of 123, Chancery Lane, London. In fact this design derives from the United States patent, No. 124,939 of 1872, granted to J. C. Dane. The essential feature of this lock was that it used, like the original Bardell and Powell, the sear spring to rotate the tumbler back the fraction of the turn necessary to lift the hammer off the firing pin and into the half-cock bent. The pressure of the sear spring could act in this way because the bottom of the tumbler is formed as a cam; the nose of the sear can then slide round it and so lift the tumbler back to the half-cock bent.

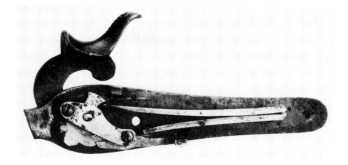

*The lock from an inexpensive Belgian gun on the same principle as the E. T. Hughes patent No. 180 of 1872, but in this example one spring is both mainspring and sear spring*

Inevitably, there were those who believed that the rebound lock was a mistake in that it could be claimed that it lessened the blow delivered to the firing pin. To satisfy this theory odd guns were built, late into the 1870s and beyond, that have non-rebound locks. To pander to those who would have the best of both worlds an optional rebound lock was devised though whether it saw use is another question. Essentially it is the 1867 pattern Stanton lock in which, in a bar-action lock, the upper limb of the mainspring is struck by a projection on the front of the tumbler so that the latter bounces back to half-cock. What was proposed by John Wallace Duncan was to have a lock with a fore-and aft-sliding T-piece. This pivoted on the lock plate, the T to lay on its side, so that when the T was in the rearward position, its head formed the connection between tumbler and mainspring and the lock would rebound. Pushing forward the T via an external stud removed this connection and the lock became a non-rebounder. The relevant specifications are provisional patent No. 4542 of 1875 and full patent No. 2581 of 1876.

The last of our three lock patents was in the name of John Stanton, No. 928 of 1877. This proposed no revision of the mechanism but, rather, the formation of a leg or bearing for the mainspring to act on, integral with the lockplate of a back-action lock. This, instead of acting on the bridle, was claimed to result in a sweeter-working, longer-lasting lock.

Emphasising the continuity of these designs as well as the continuing use, and indeed development of, the shotgun with external hammers is a further crop of inventions which tried to make such a gun safer, by mechanically retracting the firing pins. This crop fall neatly into two distinct groups: those which are worked by cocking the lock; and those which are operated when the locking-bolts are withdrawn as the gun is opened.

The first group, those worked by the locks, are patent No. 1512 of 1871 and patent No. 3552 of 1873, granted to John Sidney Heath and Joseph Thomas Roberts respectively. The Roberts patent is an unillustrated provisional and appears to be identical in principle to the earlier Heath specification. In both these, a vertical lever in the head of the stock was to be acted on at its bottom by the tumbler of the lock as this was drawn to full-cock. This would push the bottom of the lever forwards and, in turn, this would retract the firing pins.

The strikers retracted by the opening of the gun are a more numerous group, as befits an idea which is essentially sounder than the previous one. The great danger of loading with protruding strikers would not be avoided if it were necessary to cock the locks to retract the strikers, but would be totally obviated if the strikers retract as the locking-bolts are removed. Since there is little common ground between these mechanisms we once again must simply consider them in chronological sequence.

Thus, first is the patent, No. 2121 of 1872, granted to Robert Jones, gun manufacturer of Liverpool. This was part of a patent concerned with a treble-bolting Purdey-type bolt. However, from the rear of the bolt in the head of the stock two vertical extensions are formed. These engage with shoulders on the firing pins so that as the bolt is drawn back so, too, are the firing pins.

More complex is the whole mechanism patented by William Ansell, gun manufacturer of Birmingham, patent No. 2349 of 1872. As part of this action there is a vertical lever pivoted at about its mid-point set in the head of the stock. The lower end of this lever is slotted into the barrel-locking bolt so that it carries to the rear the bottom of the lever as the bolt is withdrawn. The top of the vertical lever, thus, is moved forwards and in doing so pushes forwards the inside ends of a pair of short levers set horizontally in the standing-breech hung on vertical pivots at their centres. The outer ends of this pair of levers are slotted into the firing pins so that, once again, as the bolt is withdrawn so the firing pins are retracted.

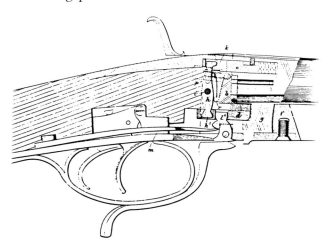

*W. Ansell patent No. 2349 of 1872*

Some parallel can be drawn between this and one aspect of the patent, No. 1268 of 1873, granted to that prolific patentee, William Middleditch Scott. This patent covers two methods of linking the top opening lever to the firing pins to retract them. One idea is to form on the top of the spindle, inside the standing-breech, a lever projecting to the left so that as the opening lever is pushed to the right to open the gun the spindle turns in a counter-clockwise direction and the left-hand firing pin is drawn back. To take care of the other firing pin, a small horizontal lever is set in the standing-breech, one end slotted into the firing pin and the inside end being pushed forwards by a shoulder on the spindle. The right-hand firing pin is also retracted.

The other part of this Scott patent uses a slide in the head of the stock. This slide is linked to the spindle so that, as this is turned counter-clockwise to open the gun, the slide moves to the left. This movement is utilised to retract the firing pins. Formed on the slide are a pair of curved inclines which act on bevels on the firing pins to retract them.

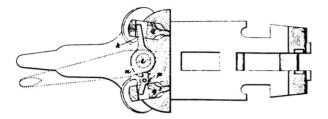

*W. M. Scott patent No. 1268 of 1873*

Another link between top lever and firing pins is part of the Alfred Burdett Hollis patent, No. 2128 of 1875. A slide in the top of the standing-breech is linked to the top lever. As the top lever turns it draws back the slide. Mounted on this slide are two small studs or projections which engage with slots in the firing pins which are drawn suitably large to accommodate this.

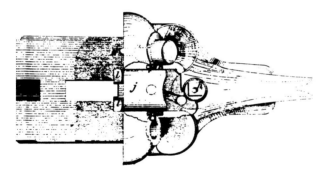

*A. Hollis patent No. 2128 of 1875*

Another use of inclines to retract firing pins is found in the patent, No. 3709 of 1875, granted to Henry Walker – a multitude of applications of the basic idea of using a rod sliding inside the standing-breech to act on a shaped slot in the firing pin. In all of these as the rod is forced into the firing pin the latter, by virtue of the shape of the slot formed in it, moves to the rear. The sliding rod is urged up in various ways by the locking-bolts of a variety of actions; most of these driving surfaces are themselves inclines.

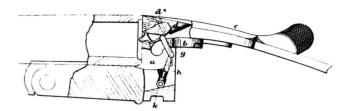

*H. Walker patent No. 3709 of 1875*

Finally, among the trimmings of the hammer gun, is a carry over from the 1860s, devices to proclaim the fact that a cartridge lay in the breech. These we call 'loaded indicators' (see Chapter Six).

We must now return from the gimmicks of the hammer gun and lay siege to the important question of the barrel-bolting mechanisms devised and patented in the twenty years, 1871 to 1890. Again, we get a strong sense of continuity with the period 1850 to 1870 (see Volume One). Two salient points need to be made at the very outset: first, continuing the trend of the 1860s, there are only two inert actions patented in the 1870s; second, and more importantly, the Purdey double-snap bolt, patent No. 1104 of 1863, was maintained for its maximum period. Thus we must regard some at least of the actions patented in the early 1870s as being attempts to equal, if not necessarily better, this action that we now regard as the one by which all others are judged.

The two inert actions are both modifications of the standard Henry Jones screw-grip action. The patentees of the first of these, patent No. 2119 of 1873, were Frederick Hargrave Grey and William Harris who both gave their address as 43, Old Bond Street, London. This design is very much in keeping with one of the trends of the time, the idea of extending the rear lump backwards into the standing-breech to secure a more advantageously placed locking site. This third bite is arranged by having a bolt hung on a transverse pivot almost at the top of the standing-breech and extending its bottom end downwards so that it projects through the bottom of the gun. Here it is in contact with a bevel formed on the top of the underlever; as the underlever turns to the right the bolt bottom swings backwards and thus all three bolts are worked by the one lever.

*F. H. Grey and W. Harris patent No. 2119 of 1873*

*The Greener Treble Gripfast Action: drawing from* Choke Bore Guns *by W. W. Greener*

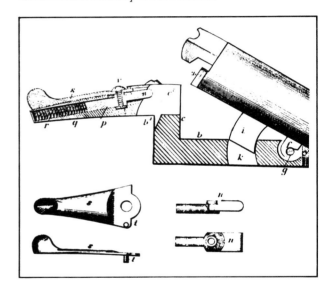

*Westley Richards patent No. 1572 of 1871*

Because it was invented by Greener, and therefore featured in his writings, the other inert action is certainly better known. This action is part of a patent, No. 3084, of 1873. It consists simply of a combination of the Greener cross-bolt with the screw-grip. To work the former from the latter a vertical spindle is mounted behind the standing-breech. This spindle is turned by a link from the turret of the screw-grip to a projection on the bottom of the spindle and this motion is transferred to the cross-bolt by a spur from the top of the spindle. In characteristic fashion Greener dubbed this mechanism his 'Treble Grip Fast' action and used it for a while on large calibre rifles as well as the larger bore shotguns.

One of the facts that our continuing research has uncovered is that the Westley Richards barrel top rib extension patent was both a master patent and maintained for its full span. This both explains why there were so few imitators of the idea and why it is after 1873, when the patent lapsed, that we see a few other users of the idea.

However, within the period of the master patent there is the Westley Richards patent, No. 1572 of 1871. This we regard as the culmination of the series of Westley Richards top extension patents. In fact, it is very much in the vein of the earlier Westley Richards top-bite patents. There is a broad-ended, almost triangular, top lever pivoted off centre at its forward right-hand corner. Pivoted onto this lever, but at its centreline, is a bolt that slides under the top strap. The snap spring is a coil spring fitted round a stem on the rear of the bolt. This barrel-locking action is one of the classics of the British gun trade and Messrs Westley Richards have probably made of the order of 2000 guns alone that use this action.

Beside such figures the rest of this sub-group are more than insignificant. Indeed, of the four remaining patents that we have to cover we know of only one actual shotgun: patent No. 1247 of 1875 granted to John Williams of

Liverpool. It is not surprising that the only gun of this type we have knowledge of is gun No. 7030 marked 'Williams and Powells patent Simplex' with the firm's address of 25, South Castle Street, Liverpool. The gun and the patent drawing are identical with a swing top lever pivoted on the top strap with a V-spring underneath. Ahead of the pivot the top lever has a forward facing extension into the standing-breech. This is the locking-bolt proper that swings over an extension from between the barrels that, as the gun closes, drops into a slot cut in the face of the breech. Also drawn on the patent and found on the gun is an extractor with twin external legs, one each side of the barrel lump, that are activated by their downward turned forward ends working in slots in the action bar. In all essentials the Cole and Melland patent of 1866. (See Volume One.)

*J. Williams patent No. 1247 of 1875*

While we are looking back at the patents of the previous decade, a version of the Samuel Mills patent, No. 1089 of 1878, is worthy of mention if only because it is an inferior copy of the Westley Richards 1864 and 1871 patents. The chief reason for its inferiority is that the top extension is a simple U-shape and therefore will not lock the standing-breech to the barrels in the way that a well-fitting doll's head will. Otherwise, the Mills is little more than a reshaping of the various parts with a broad top lever pivoted at one corner levering back a sliding bolt. The snap spring, like the Westley Richards, is a coil round a sliding rod.

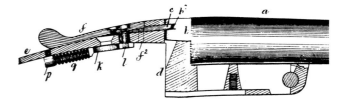

*S. Mills patent No. 1089 of 1878*

Even more like the Westley Richards action is the barrel-bolting mechanism in the Martin Wall Parsons patent, No. 1065 of 1879. Again, we have a bolt like the Mills patent but now we have a doll's head as well.

The penultimate member of this sub-group of barrel-bolting actions that depend solely on a top extension looks, at first glance, very like another Westley Richards; in fact, some unusual features set it apart. The top extension, it is true, is a doll's head, but the swinging top lever is arranged to stay in the open position until the gun closes. This is an idea which crops up on a variety of guns, perhaps the best known are the American Parker and Baker guns, the object being to make the gun easier to close by removing the need to compress the top lever spring or its equivalent for a second time. On the James F. Swinburn design, patent No. 4291 of 1880, this is achieved by having a small spring-loaded pawl or sear which engages with a bent cut in the head of the opening lever which is also the locking-bolt. When the top lever is in the fully open position with the barrels open, the top lever stays put. Then, as the barrels descend and the doll's head drops back into its recess, it disengages this sear and the top lever spring, a V-fitted point forwards in the underside of the top lever, can snap the bolt shut.

To conclude this sub-section there is a brief note in the patent, No. 3313 of 1881, of a top extension bolting system but while this is not known to us on a shotgun, the Michael Kaufman system, as patented by the agent W. E. Gedge, was used in some numbers on Webley drop-down revolvers.

If there is a type of barrel-locking mechanism that could be described as being characteristic of the 1870s it would be the style of action that has an extended rear lump projecting behind the

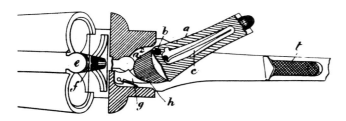

*J. Swinburn patent No. 4291 of 1880*

action face with a locking-bolt in the head of the stock. While it is true that the prototype of this was the Powell action of 1864 and the Thomas patent of 1870 (the 'Solid Self-Locking Vertical Grip'), we believe that it was the modest success of these two that prompted other inventors to explore this avenue.

The result was a small confusing group of very similar actions that all sought the improved efficiency of the rearward bolt sited as far as possible from the pivot. Because they are so alike, once again, the only description we feel logical is a chronological order of patent. First, then, is patent No. 3091 of 1871, granted to John Thomas. He describes himself on his patent specification as a gun and pistol maker of Birmingham but we can glimpse a little more of his career because in the *Birmingham Directory* for 1880 he advertises as a 'Birding Gun Action Maker and General Machinist to the Trade'. He

quotes his address as 66 and 67, Slaney Street, Birmingham and adds as a footnote that he was for eight years Working Manager to the late firm of Messrs Tipping and Lawden.

The Thomas patent of 1871 in a sense brings his patent of the previous year much more in line with the Powell because, curiously, in place of the earlier turning top lever the new mechanism uses a push-up top lever. It would seem probable that contemporary gun buyers felt, as we do, that this was a retrograde step for, whereas examples of the earlier design are relatively well-known, this later design is met with only very occasionally in our experience. The idea behind the patent is extremely simple. The locking-bolt slides back and forth in the head of the stock and is held forwards by a vertical V-spring fixed to the top strap. The locking-bolt is retracted, and the V-spring compressed, by a portion of the top lever that projects downwards and enters a slot in the bolt; as the rear of the top lever is raised and the lever swings about its transverse pivot the bolt is retracted. Incidentally, a modified version of this action appears in the specification for the lever-cocked hammerless gun, patent No. 3291 of 1876, that Thomas obtained in conjunction with T. T. Lawden.

Another inventor whose career had much in common with that of John Thomas was Henry Walker. As we have seen, Walker was a gunmaker in Birmingham but, before setting up on

*J. Thomas patent No. 3091 of 1871. Here used on a .450 express rifle built by Tipping and Lawden. (By courtesy of Christie, Manson and Woods Ltd)*

his own account, he had been working for another well-known Birmingham firm of gun-makers, Bentley and Playfair. Indeed, we suspect that the success of the invention we now come to consider may have had something to do with this. One of the incidentals of our story is the growth of the technique of advertising. While most of the inventions we describe would appear not to have been promoted in any other way than verbally (certainly, in most cases, no written material has come to our notice), Walker had his gun action described in editorials published by *The Field* and *Land and Water*, as well as inserting large advertisements in these papers. In addition, notices appeared in such unlikely sources as *The Standard*, *The Morning News*, *Birmingham Gazette* and *The Daily Post*. All this promotion took place in early 1872 and, about a year later, Walker took over No. 14, St Mary's Row, and thus established an independent business in the heart of the gun quarter of Birmingham.

All of this promotional activity was generated by the gun action that its inventor called 'Walker's Oscillating Gun'. In addition to the British patent, No. 445 of 1872, he also took out the same year a United States patent, No. 131,484. The essential feature of Walker's design is the rearwards extension of the rear barrel lump, held down by a bolt that swings to

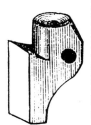
*Henry Walker's advertisement of 1872*

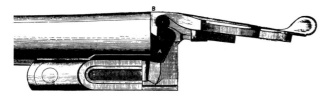

*H. Walker's patent gun No. 445 of 1872. Cut-away drawing from* The Field

and fro in the standing-breech. The strength of this action derives from the fact that the bolt was circle-jointed both onto the top of the barrel lump extension and, at its top, to the underside of its recess in the standing-breech. Interestingly, this bolt was not hung on a spindle. Instead, a stud with a rounded bottom to its head was to project from the top of the standing-breech. To work this bolt, top, side and underlever mechanisms were proposed. The turning top lever, which was the most important, drew back the top of the swinging bolt by a link from a turret under the top strap. The underlever had an upward projection that fitted into the bottom of the bolt; the forward-facing side lever, very reminiscent of a Needham action, drew back the bolt via a link from a downward internal projection from the transverse spindle that carried the opening lever. In addition to these features, there is an unusual variant in which the locking-bolt is hung at the top of the standing-breech and swings from side-to-side under the influence of an internal forward projection of the top lever. Finally, as it were, to leave no possible stone unturned, there is proposed a version where the pivot for the locking-bolt is moved to the bottom of the action and so, by inference at least, a whole new parallel family of designs could be covered by the patent. There is, too, what can reasonably be thought of as part of the patentee's later patent, No. 700 of 1876, in which a push-up top lever works, via a link, a swing bolt now pivoted under the top strap.

Very much like the Walker design is one of the parts of the patent, No. 1825 of 1872, granted to William S. Riley. Again, a swinging internal bolt is worked by a top lever. The only real difference is that part of the bolt extends

below the rear of the extended barrel lump and it is on this lower portion of the barrel-bolt that the V-snap spring bears.

Worthy only of the briefest mention is the provisional specification, No. 3257 of 1872, in the name of another Birmingham gun magnate, Francis Augustus Braendlin, which merely mentions the idea of an extruded rear lump.

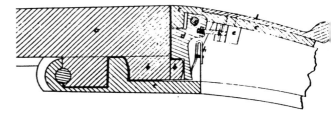

*Version of W. S. Riley patent No. 1825 of 1872*

In patent No. 1826 of 1873 there is an ingenious variation on the theme of the extended rear lump as a site for a single locking-bolt. The patentee is another Birmingham gun action-maker, Edward Crowley. Here we have another turning top lever but working a sliding bolt. This works at an angle to the centreline of the gun. Viewed from above and behind, the rear of the bolt is to the left of centre. The top lever is connected to this by an ordinary link arrangement and the snap spring is also conventionally sited under the top strap. The specification also covers another version in which a peg from the front of the top lever acts directly on the locking-bolt.

In that they employ a push-up top lever, the designs of Piddington and Hackett are two more patents that resemble the 1871 Thomas action and can logically be considered at this point.

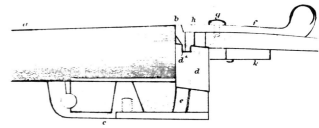

*E. Crowley patent No. 1826 of 1873*

The earlier patent, No. 1324 of 1872, is in the name of J. Piddington who was an agent for a member of one of the most respected gunmaking firms in Liège, Auguste Francotte of Mont St Martin. The mechanism is both simple and sturdy. The opening lever can be visualised as the long limb of a capital L, so positioned that the shorter limb is almost vertical in the head of the stock behind the standing-breech. This lever is pivoted at its angle; pushing up on the rear end of the longer exposed limb will move the bottom of the shoulder to the rear. The single sliding bolt is keyed onto this vertical lever and the snap spring is a leaf, fixed under the top strap, that carries on its forward end a friction-reducing roller via which it bears on the rear of the internal limb of the opening lever.

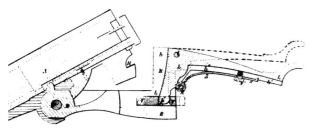

*J. Piddington (agent for A. Francotte) patent No. 1324 of 1872*

The later patent is also unknown to us as a gun. However, a part of the patent has become a very common fitting on British sporting shotguns and thus its inventor's name is well-known to devotees. In fact the first part of the George Hackett patent, No. 964 of 1878, is concerned with the barrel-bolting mechanism and the far better known fore-end fastening comes later. Like the Francotte action the opening lever is L-shaped but on the Hackett the internal leg is shorter and this is joined by a link to the vertical limb of the locking-bolt which is itself L-shaped. Again, the snap spring is a leaf, but now this acts on a shoulder on the opening lever just below its pivot.

There is in the patent records, as No. 3611 of 1878, a provisional specification in the name of John P. Clabrough of Clabrough Bros who were then in business at 8, Whittall Street,

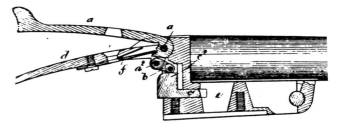

*G. Hackett patent No. 964 of 1878*

Birmingham. However, this design is described as a communication from Julius Bluemel who was at this period employed by J. P. Clabrough at his San Francisco shop. There is also a United States patent, No. 210,905 of 1878, on what appears to be the same gun. From this illustrated document we can better see the mechanism involved.

The single-bite is a sliding bolt that engages with the rear lump and the snap spring is a coil fitted round it. The rear end of the bolt is extended upwards and to the left and on this portion a lever bears. This is fitted to the bottom of a vertical spindle in the head of the stock, on top of which is the conventional top lever. So, pushing this to the right withdraws the barrel-bolt.

Another pair of patents, an echo of the previous decade, concern themselves with the idea of having a barrel-locking bolt that slid transversely across the action bar. It will be recalled that there was a minor vogue for such actions in the mid-1860s; we now have to consider these two stragglers which appear in the 1870s.

The first is a provisional patent, No. 825 of 1871, obtained by William Ansell. This does no more than outline the idea with neither illustration nor practical details. The other patentee is William Pountney who, we assume, is the same man who had patents on the same theme fourteen years before his patent No. 1970 of 1878. The 1878 specification, like the Hackett, is also concerned with fore-end fastenings (see Chapter Seven). The new bolt designed by Pountney was very simple. It had a small coil snap spring that was to be directly compressed between the thumb piece of the bolt and the action bar. We suspect the object was to permit the production of an inexpensive gun.

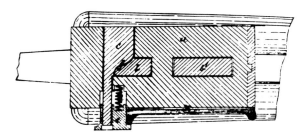

*W. Poutney patent No. 1970 of 1878*

Inevitably, we are left with a residue of snap action designs that fall outside the groups of single-bite action we have so far described. Since the only resemblance between most of these designs is that they are single-bite snap actions, we therefore believe that a chronological sequence by patent data is the only method of classification.

Some designs, old fashioned on the day they were patented, are yet more perplexing in that they appear in the name of a famous gunmaker. Just such a design, a decade late, is the subject of a patent, No. 1098 of 1871, granted to John Rigby who had then only recently opened London premises at 72, St James's Street, (1866). The firm, however, had been long established in Dublin (since 1735) as builders of the finest guns and rifles. Rigby's eminence as a scientific and practical rifleman was later to be officially recognised by his appointment as Superintendent of the Royal Small Arms Factory at Enfield. There it was his task to usher in the birth of the .303 service cartridge and the Enfield rifling system.

The action described in this specification consists of a push-forward underlever that projects into the gun as a hook-like barrel-locking bolt that engages with a bite on the rear barrel lump. The snap spring is a leaf spring fixed towards the front of the bottom of the action bar, with its free rear end bearing on a shoulder on the opening lever. The sole novelty of this action is that, because of the position of the bearing of the snap spring on the opening lever when the latter is in the fully open position, it would stay there until the descending barrel lump tripped it shut as the gun was closed. To do this there is a small

forward projection from the opening lever that, when the lever is in the open position, stands up in the lump slot and is thus pushed down by the barrel lump.

However, the most interesting point about this specification is that it also claims the idea of an insert barrel to convert a shotgun to a smaller gauge. (To the best of our knowledge this is the first time such an idea had appeared in print.)

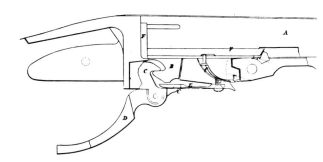

*J. Rigby patent No. 1098 of 1871*

Not surprisingly, the designs of the early 1870s have a strong affinity with those of the 1860s so it is as part of patent No. 1825 of 1872 we see revived the idea of a barrel-bolt mounted in the actual barrel lump. In this design, patented by W. S. Riley (then of 'The Eagle Gun Factory' in Stafford Street, Birmingham), we find a bolt standing in the rear lump with a V-spring between the two lumps to force it back into the action of the gun. To permit the gun so fitted to be opened, a cam on the bottom of a Scott-type spindle in the head of the action pushed the bolt forwards as the top lever swung over.

Such ideas from the previous decade, are present, too, in the patent of Samuel Allport, No. 3518 of 1872. Here we find the use of a vertical lever on a transverse pivot. This withdraws a sliding bolt that engages with a bite on the rear barrel lump, a description that could have been applied to a whole covey of guns in the 1860s. The novelty of this invention is a swinging top lever that works the vertical lever, the top of which fits into a slot in a flat piece of steel under the top strap. This is turned by, and turns on, a common centre with the top lever.

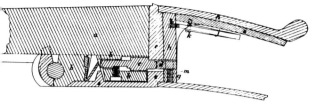

*W. S. Riley patent No. 1825 of 1872*

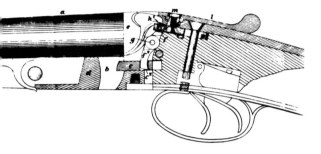

*S. B. Allport patent No. 3518 of 1872*

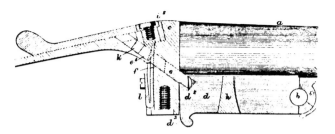

*R. Hill patent No. 1563 of 1873*

Street, Birmingham whose patent, No. 2396 of 1871, we are now concerned with was a maker to this level of the trade. (It is one of the odd quirks of collecting that, over the years, the authors had not encountered one of these actions, then four turned up in as many months, one of which is a rather dilapidated specimen. It is a conversion from a muzzle-loader, which may indicate another facet of the inventor's business.)

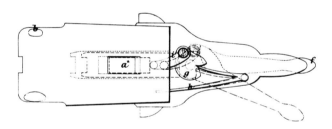

*J. Hall patent No. 2396 of 1871*

The snap spring is a V, fitted under the top strap, which bears on a shoulder on the flat, slotted piece of steel.

A feature that sets aside the final member of this group from most other guns is that it uses a bolt, sliding at an angle of about 45 degrees up into the head of the stock. In this the rear of the bolt is placed within the reach of an inclined stud mounted on a revolving turret, this being the underside of the forward end of the top lever. Thus, it is the top lever that acts directly on the locking-bolt while the snap spring, a vertical V, is mounted on the rear of the standing-breech and, again, acts directly on the locking-bolt. This relatively ingenious action, patent No. 1563 of 1873, is in the name of Richard Hill of Aston, Birmingham.

The idea, then, of an extended rear lump was one that enjoyed a modicum of support. Given this it is to be expected that improvements would appear, and one of the most logical lines of development would be to add an extra bite. In fact there are two such guns, the first of which we have only encountered emanating from lesser 'makers' and provincial dealers. From this we infer that John Hall of Lancaster

The extra bite on this action is on the rear of the front lump so that the action is really very like the classic Purdey double-bite. However, it is the extended rear lump that bears on the locking-bolt, the rear of which is extended upwards to provide the necessary bearing surface for this projection as it drops into the standing-breech. To connect the raised rear end of the bolt to the opening lever, the patent shows either a peg from the head of the top lever working in a slot on the top of the bolt, or a link to an internal lever that is rotated under the top strap by the external top lever. In the latter case, the snap spring is the usual V under the top strap.

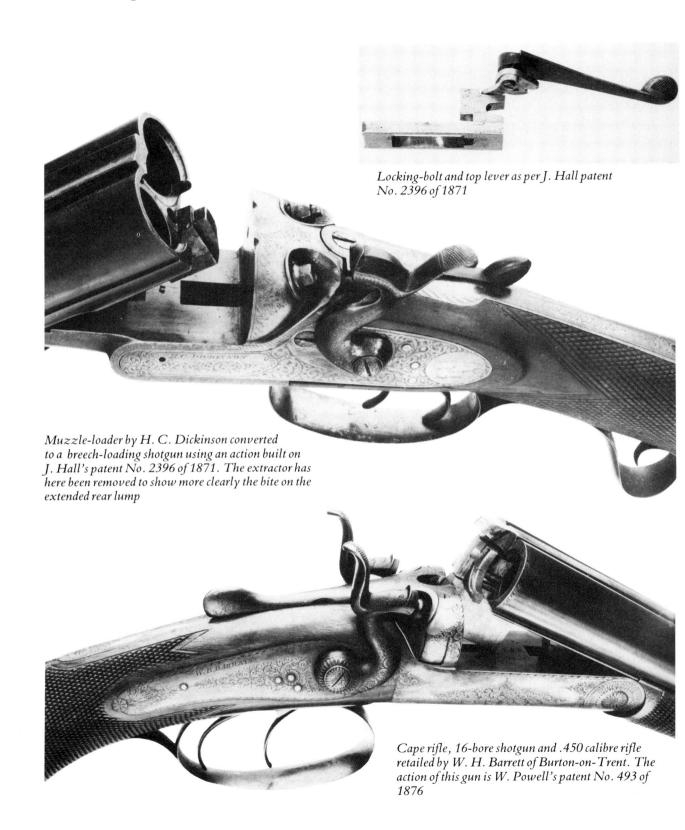

*Locking-bolt and top lever as per J. Hall patent No. 2396 of 1871*

*Muzzle-loader by H. C. Dickinson converted to a breech-loading shotgun using an action built on J. Hall's patent No. 2396 of 1871. The extractor has here been removed to show more clearly the bite on the extended rear lump*

*Cape rifle, 16-bore shotgun and .450 calibre rifle retailed by W. H. Barrett of Burton-on-Trent. The action of this gun is W. Powell's patent No. 493 of 1876*

One of the pioneers of the extended rear lump locking system was a firm of famous Birmingham gunmakers, William Powell and Son, who today trade from their long-established premises in Carrs Lane, Birmingham. While their original design, patent No. 1163 of 1864, was widely and apparently successfully used, they nevertheless felt it worthwhile to produce another action of this general type. This is covered by patent No. 493 of 1876. It has a square cross-bolt siding in the standing-breech, worked by a top lever which holds down the barrels by fitting over the rearward extension of the barrel lumps.

The stimulae that cause an inventor to produce a given invention are always a fascinating study. Chief among those in a trade such as British gunmaking in the nineteenth century, was the desire to evade another's patent while improving on the basic idea. However, another potent force impinged on the gun trade. This was the weekly pontification by Dr Walsh of *The Field*. As he advanced in years he became more trenchant in his views; one of his favourite hobby horses was the need for a top fastening or connection between the standing-breech and the barrels. It is now impossible for us to know exactly the influence that Dr Walsh exerted but we believe it to have been considerable. This might explain why the Powell patent uses a top extension with a hole cut into it which mates with a locking-bolt made solid with the standing-breech.

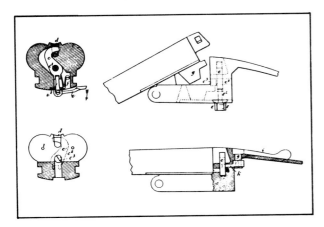

*Page from W. M. and M. Scott's patent No. 615 of 1876*

The final member of this group is the minor part of a patent of 1876, No. 615. We shall shortly consider the bulk of this specification, designed by William Middleditch Scott and his nephew, Martin Scott. Here we are concerned with an almost make-weight portion that uses a hook-shaped bolt, swinging on a longitudinal axis in the head of the action. The main locking site is evidently a massive top extension with a rectangular hole into which the hook bites. To trip this hook aside as the barrels close there is an extension on the rear lump that acts on an incline on the axis of the hook bolt. This extension lies behind the line of the action face, with the axis above it when the gun is closed. To open this odd mechanism there is either a top lever, which has a forward facing internal lever that rotates the hook bolt to the left, or a strange side lever that has to be twisted down about its longitudinal axis when an upward projection displaces the hook bolt. In all, an action that we do not expect ever to encounter.

There are two provisional specifications that, while the mechanisms they describe are of no real importance, are worthy of comment nevertheless, if only to remark on the trend that they illustrate. The two specifications, both dated 1871, are Nos. 929 and 2522. They are, too, both in the name of Edwin Charles Green of Cheltenham, though not for inventions of his own. He was acting as agent for Frederick J. Abbey and James H. Foster, gunmakers of Chicago. These specifications serve as a reminder of the two-way traffic that existed between the gunmakers of Britain and the United States. Neither of these provisional specifications is illustrated but they would appear to derive from the Abbey and Foster US patent, specification No. 114,081 of 1871, and our remarks are based on a study of this document. What it shows is a gun action with a short lever that projects down from the bottom of the action. This acts on an unremarkable single sliding bolt at the bottom of the standing-breech. The novelty of this patent derives from the additional bolts that it has. Formed in the top of the sliding bolt is a V-shaped slot with the point towards the rear of the gun. Into this V fit, what can best be described as the handles of a pair of scissors or pliers so that, as the underbolt slides to the rear, the handles are opened and with them the 'jaws' that lie in the top of the standing-breech. However, these upper parts are slotted into two round bolts that engage with a conventional top extension with a round hole in it.

Like the last action only in that it has a pair of locking-bolts working in opposing directions, is a treble-grip action patented by an inventor whose ideas crop up at many points of our story. In 1874 when Thomas Perkes obtained this patent, No. 2530, his address was 4, Duck Lane, Wardour Street, Soho, London. In many ways his action is very like the James Lang patent, No. 687 of 1870, but whereas this was a modification of the screw-grip to produce a triple snap bolt, this Perkes is best regarded as a triple-bite variation of the Purdey sliding bolt. Essentially, this is a very simple idea and uses a Scott spindle-type top lever arrangement to work a sliding bolt that can be thought of as a Purdey-bolt with part of the left-hand side removed. In this space the second bolt is fitted which also slides on the main bolt and is, again, worked by the top lever, but sliding in the opposite direction to the main bolt. Fixed at the bottom of the spindle is a transverse lever so that as one side moves forwards the other moves back and vice versa. There are no practical details in the specification as to how, or indeed if, the gun was to snap and in the absence of an actual gun to study we remain ignorant of this point.

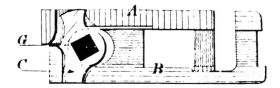

*T. Perkes patent No. 2530 of 1874*

As explained earlier, Messrs Westley Richards's top extension patent effectively barred that avenue of development for the 1860s. However, there were attempts to enjoy some of the advantages of this site by using other bolting methods. In the 1870s this was the path followed by William Ansell. In 1871, from his premises at 35, Fisher Street, Birmingham, he obtained a patent, No. 1174, which covered the idea of having a coil spring-loaded bolt under the top rib of the barrels. This bit back into the standing-breech and combined with another bolt that slid forwards into the rear barrel lump. To disengage the top bolt of this action, the user had to push forwards a thumb slide on the top of the action. The front end of this slide acted directly on the top bolt to displace it forwards and, at the same time, compressed the coil spring that lay in front of it. This was, surprisingly, the only snap spring in the action. This forwards motion at the top of the action was converted to a backwards thrust at the bottom by a vertical lever with a cross-wise pivot at its centre, set behind the standing-breech.

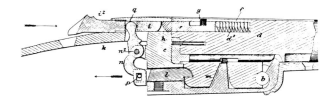

*W. Ansell patent No. 1174 of 1871*

Obviously, this patent was not the end of Ansell's exploration of this idea for, the following year, he obtained another patent, No. 2349, for a variety of improvements to an external hammer-style sporting gun. Among these is an action essentially the same as the 1871 patent but with every sign that a degree of rethinking had taken place in the interim. The most noticeable improvement is the abolition of the push-forward top slide in which the user had to compress the snap spring directly with no leverage to assist his thumb. In the improved version there is a push-forward underlever that acts as the bottom sliding bolt. This bolt in its turn pushes back the bottom of the internal lever, the top limb of which pushes in the barrel-bolt as before. Interestingly, there are now no less than three snap springs, one a coil in front of the top bolt, one a V acting on the internal lever and the third a leaf fitted round the trigger work and bearing on a spur formed on the rear of the internal portion of the underlever.

While we have yet to see a gun using either of these actions, we know a little more about the second variant than about some of its contemporaries. In both *The Field* and *Land and Water* in 1873 there appeared a woodcut engraving of a gun using this action. Two points about this illustration are curious: first, and most obvious, is the double perspective that the artist employed; second, the addition of a top lever. We hope that Ansell was not charged too much for this masterpiece, the purpose of which was to gain advertising coverage by way of the editorial section of these journals. In all fairness we must record that the gun on the patent drawing (which, as in most cases, we believe to have been drawn from an actual specimen) is a far more elegant illustration than the advertising block.

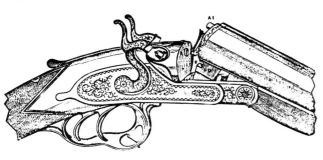

*W. Ansell's patent action No. 2349 of 1872. Copy of drawing from* Land and Water, *5 July 1873*

One way in which a top and bottom bolt could be produced was to have a piece of steel, shaped rather like a letter U, lying on its side with its open end forwards. This is the basis of Samuel Mathews' patent, No. 2579 of 1872, which contains three variants on this theme: first, a side lever in which an upward projection from the opening lever keys with the bolt to lever it back; second, two top levers – the first of these being a fairly conventional turning lever with a stud under its turret that withdraws the bolt; the third variant on the specification is, as is so often the case, the most bizarre. This is a push-in stud and now the barrel-bolt rocks about a central transverse pivot so that as the top lever is depressed the top bolt is withdrawn. To make use of this motion, which forces the bot-

tom bolt forwards, the bottom bolt bites on the front of the rear lump. We seriously doubt if such a contrivance ever appeared 'in the metal'.

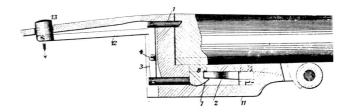

*S. Mathews patent No. 2579 of 1872*

The final member of this group, patent No. 2128 of 1875, is remarkable, first for a particularly fine patent drawing but also for its patentee, Alfred Burdett Hollis, who describes himself as a 'Commercial Representative of I. Hollis & Sons, Birmingham'. His grandfather and great uncle established the dynasty of Hollis gunmakers in Birmingham. These original partners separated to produce two parallel Hollis firms. Perhaps the best known of these firms was that of Isaac Hollis, who was, we believe, a second cousin of Alfred. It is an admitted limitation of our scheme of description that in it firms such as Hollis do not get the recognition that they deserve, for, dealing as we primarily are with inventions and innovations, we overlook the vast 'bread and butter' trade that Birmingham, in particular, carried on. It was this trade that produced thousands upon thousands of sound, honest but unremarkable sporting guns, rifles and pistols for what was then the British Empire and beyond. In furtherance of this trade Alfred Hollis travelled frequently, to North America, to Europe, Southern Russia and through the Middle East to Egypt. Ultimately, after a lot of effort, he was able to obtain an arms dealer's licence for the Bombay Presidency of India. On the strength of this he was able to build up a large trade in guns and ammunition of both British and American manufacture over the whole of the Indian subcontinent and beyond.

After this too brief detour we must return to a consideration of the patent that prompted it,

No. 2128 of 1875. Again we have a bolt engaging at two levels. The lower bolt engaged into a bite on the rear lump but the upper one now engaged with a lug formed on the rear of the extractor. To work this bolt were two forms of leverwork: first, a top lever with an internal link to the top of the bolt; second, a side lever which engaged with the bottom of the bolt. In addition to this, another claim for the top lever version is a slide in the top of the standing-breech. The prime purpose of this is to retract the firing pins, but formed on the front of this slide are two forward-projecting pins which engage with holes in the barrel breech face to produce a quadruple bolting system.

We have considered elsewhere (Chapter Four) the barrel-cocking aspect of the patent, No. 145 of 1883, by John Field Swinburn, gunmaker and Proof House Guardian of 16, and 17, Russell Street, Birmingham. The feature that we now have to consider of this boxlock gun is its barrel-bolting which is a combination of a swinging bite into a doll's-head top extension, with a sliding bolt into the rear of the sole barrel lump. The top bite is simply a forwards projection of the broad top lever, which pivoted to the right of the centre of the gun. This axle is a vertical rod that carries on its bottom end an inward-facing projection that in turn works the sliding bolt. The V-snap spring is another of those concealed under, and mounted in, the actual top lever.

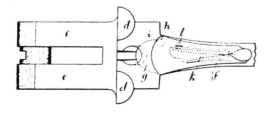

*J. Swinburn patent No. 145 of 1883*

In part, because it is so imprecise, a patent, No. 3318 of 1871, that lends itself to more than the usual amount of speculation is that of Seth John Wallis, 'gun manufacturer', of Spalding, near Lincoln. The main claim of this specification was that the appearance of a shotgun would be enhanced if the unsightly external opening levers were suppressed. To this end the trigger guard was to be made either to slide or pivot and this motion conveyed to the barrel-locking bolts. Now there is no possibility that Wallis could not have known that three years previously his fellow gunmaker, John Hanson, who had his shop at 244, High Street, Lincoln had produced just such a gun and covered it with a patent, No. 2657 of 1868. Our reason for describing the Wallis patent at this point is that the curiously faint drawing with it shows a lump fitted to each barrel. We therefore assume that there was a bolt that bit into both of these, but there are no details.

Also included in this patent is a lock with an internal striker, but with no internal means mentioned as to how it was to be cocked, and an elaborate system for demonstrating that a gun so fitted was loaded.

Amid all these actions, many of which are confusingly similar and known only as patent drawings, it is refreshing to find one that is both distinctive and known to have been used, albeit in small quantities. The idea of a lump on each barrel was not new. In 1874 George Jeffries of Norwich had obtained patent No. 3442, which harked back to the Smith, Townsend and Williams design of 1858 – one of the earliest indigenous breech-loading designs but with an inert action. The Jeffries is a snap action that has a sliding bolt; this engages with both lumps, the snap spring is a leaf fitted round the trigger work. A feature that many who handle the gun remark on is the short travel of the opening lever. This makes the gun peculiarly pleasant to use. However, the stumbling block for this idea is that it confers upon the guns that use it a very box-like action bar that is rather inelegant; this action is also encountered with two bites on each lump.

A double-bite action that is nothing if not ingenious is a Belgian invention that appears in the British patent records as No. 16,176 of 1888. This patent is in the names of Louis Jeusette, Dieudonne Henrard and Henri Henrard, all of Herstal, which is now a suburb of Liège in south-eastern Belgium. What they describe is to have two circular locking-bolts

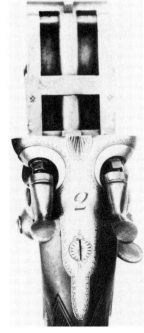

*Gun by George Jeffries of Norwich,*
*patent No. 3442 of 1874*

To conclude this sub-section we must, for the sake of completeness, mention two patents, Nos. 1817 of 1874 and 570 of 1883, in the name of W. R. Trevelyan of Emsworth in Hampshire. Both of these are brief and very imprecise and both seem to deal with the old idea of having two spring-loaded plugs made to fit into the chambers of a sporting gun to retain the barrels.

With these various double-bolting systems we believe it to be logical to include a small group that are in fact the Purdey double-bolt, but worked by leverwork other than the famous Scott spindle. Strictly speaking they do not belong at this point but we feel that they sit more happily here, where they all belong to the period after the expiry of the Purdey patent and, with two exceptions, are not the subject of direct patent protection.

Not necessarily the oldest in terms of when it was actually produced, but oldest in the sense that it is a derivative of a patent obtained in 1863, is the use by Horsley's of their pull-back top lever to work a Purdey-bolt. The discovery of an actual example of this combination underlines the fact that many, if not most, of the sliding single bolt snap actions encountered (see Volume One) could be built in this way and we would expect occasional hybrids of this type to occur. In the case of the Horsley action, it is not simply a substitution of the flat double-bolt for the round Horsley original. In this latter it is a coil spring round the bolt stem that is the snap spring. But, on the double-bolt version, the snap spring is a leaf, fitted round the trigger work, that is compressed by a sort of collar. This has a rearward projection that fits round the upright lever and is drawn to the rear by the external slide.

that bite into either side of a single hole on the rear lump. This is achieved by using the motion of either a top lever or turning underlever to turn a double-ended lever in this action. This arrangement is linked to, and displaces outwards, two slides working across the action that each carry a bolt. The top lever version is shown with a snap spring under the top strap but the underlever version is apparently inert.

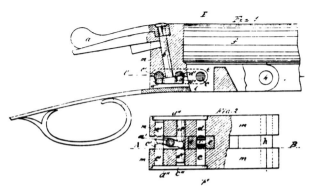

*J. Jeusette, D. Henrard and H. Henrard patent*
*No. 16,176 of 1888*

*The action of Thomas Horsley of York gun No. 3058*
*of 1888: Purdey bolt combined with Horsley top lever*

In contrast to this rarely encountered form, the side lever gun is one of the standard forms of the British shotgun which, incidentally, was much used by the firm of Thomas Horsley of York, as well as many others. The majority of the side lever Purdey-bolt guns have a lever on the right-hand side, running under the gun and pivoted on the trigger plate. Above the pivot is an upward projecting lever that engages with a slot in the rear of the double-bolt; the snap spring is usually very much as described for the Horsley pull-back top lever. The reason for the popularity of this style of lever is obvious: a gun so fitted can be very pleasant to use because the thrust of the right thumb acts to open the breech as the bolt is withdrawn from its bites.

There is also a version of the side lever gun made with the lever on the left of the action. This was not apparently made solely for left-handed users but with the thumb piece of the lever brought higher on the gun it is convenient for the right-hander to use it with very little alteration in the position of the right hand.

A good example of the sort of pitfalls that beset an attempt to write a definitive work on so variable a subject as nineteenth-century British sporting guns is provided by the rather battered remains of a gun at one time in the authors' (DJB) collection. At first glance it appeared to be an ordinary top lever action. The clue that this was not the case was that the top lever was pivoted rather further back than is usual. Part of the answer to the problem was a stamp on the action flats that read: 'Patent No. 3718 of 1877'. This patent was obtained by Christopher George Bonehill, the well-known Birmingham sporting gunmaker and military arms contractor. However, study of the specification reveals that the patent concerned a triple-bolting system based on the Purdey double-bolt. What was evidently done for this cheap-quality gun was to dispense with the third bite but retain the simple lever work. When the gun was stripped it was found that on the bottom of the top lever pivot pin, just under the top strap, was keyed a roughly oval flat piece of steel at the rear. This had a shoulder cut upon which bore a V-snap spring. Forward of the top lever pivot was cut a slightly curved slot. Into this fitted a stud, the termina-

tion of an upward rear projection of the double-bolt, and the slot was so positioned that, as the top lever was turned in the normal way, the bolt was withdrawn from the barrel bites. Taking a wider view of the lessons that this wreck of a gun taught, the probability exists that other actions were cheapened in this way even, possibly, to the extent of producing a single-bite snap action.

One of the great problems in identifying those cheaper guns produced by the Birmingham gun trade is that lever work will be found bearing no inscription or acknowledgement whatever and conforming to no patent in particular, but resembling several in various ways. This was an inevitability, when makers other than the patentee were free to make use of what had previously been protected by patent. An idea that became very popular, for the fairly obvious reasons of cheapness and ease of production, was to have the rear of the locking-bolt extended upwards towards the opening lever. Another variant on this theme was to extend the bolt first up and then back, as a sort of step, into this second level slot. Then to peg down, off-centre from the top lever, so that as this latter lever swings the bolt is drawn back. Such is the patent, No. 979 of 1875, in the name of Henry Job Altman.

As we will see later (Chapter Three) the mid-1870s saw the trade flirt with the notion of making a self-cocking hammer gun. One of the systems we will encounter is that of Thomas Bailey as described in his patent, No. 3240 of 1876. This shows an incline on the sliding bolts that forces up a diagonally-mounted rod that, in turn, lifts the hammers. There can be no doubt that a fair degree of force was needed to work the locking-bolt against the resistance of two fired locks, so a powerful lever was called for. What was chosen was none other than a Henry Jones-style lever over the trigger guard. Now, instead of working a screw-grip, there is an upward projection on the left side of the turret in the action. It is this projection that fits into a slot in the Purdey-bolt and forces it to the rear as the underlever is swung out to the right. The snap spring is a leaf, fitted to the back of the standing-breech, with its lower free end bearing on the back of the bolt. In all, this was a sound enough arrangement but, because of its use of a turning underlever, it would have been somewhat old-fashioned in 1876.

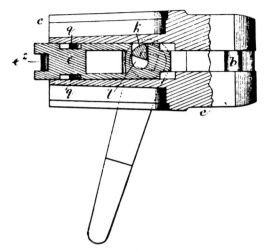

*T. Bailey patent No. 3240 of 1876*

As if to leave no possible stone unturned there is a trio of designs on the files of the Patent Office that use a push-down top lever to work the sliding Purdey-underbolt. The earliest of these is an unillustrated provisional specification, No. 4215 of 1877, obtained by W. S. Woodward. An L-shaped lever is hung on a transverse pivot at its angle and so positioned that one leg of the L projects down into the gun while the other limb lies forwards. Thus, as this forward limb is squeezed down the internal vertical limb swings to the rear and can be made to draw back the bolt.

In some ways very like the above is the gun shown in a patent, No. 11,625 of 1884, obtained by Walter Bentley of Ledsam Street, Birmingham. Here we have two L-shaped levers, pivoted as before but with one inside the gun and the other with a limb outside the gun and facing to the rear. This pair of levers is so arranged that pushing down on the rear of the external limb pushes forwards its internal limb. This, in turn, bears on the second lever to push forward and up on the top limb and so causes the other limb to move to the rear and draw back the bolt. The snap spring is a V, bearing on the actual bolt.

*Action of the gun built on W. Bentley patent No. 11,625 of 1884*

Without doubt, the most distinctive lever work that was applied to the Purdey-bolt within our period is the Jones and Taylor action, patent No. 7715 of 1885. This is another of those variants that Greener covered in *The Gun and its Development* and so the idea is well-known. As usual, Greener did not give any credit to, or indeed any idea of who were, the inventors and makers. What Robert Jones and Walter Taylor protected was the idea of producing an apparently leverless gun by concealing, within the gun itself, a set of rods and levers so when the comb of the stock was depressed the Purdey-bolt was withdrawn. To do this the front of the comb is the exposed limb of a bell-crank lever, pivoted transversely further back in the stock with a vertical lever extending downwards to the mid-line of the gun. Hinged to the bottom of this vertical limb is a rod that extends all the way forwards and is, in turn, hinged to the rear of the bolt. The snap spring is a stout coil, spring fitted between the rear of the bolt and an upward projection from the trigger plate, through which the rod slides. The rod through the stock also works the safety. A shoulder on the rod draws back a trigger blade blocking leg, connected directly to a conventional thumb slide on the top strap. When this top strap is pushed forwards the trigger blocking limb lies over a depression in the trigger blades so that they can now rise to lift the sears.

Robert Jones was apparently a working gunmaker. There are entries in the Liverpool directories which mention him, in the period between 1885 and 1919, at 38, Manchester Street. He called this establishment 'The Monarch Gun Works', where we presume guns of this design were built. A few have survived.

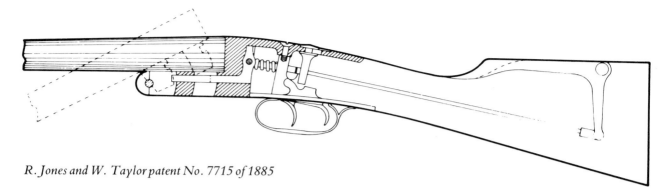

*R. Jones and W. Taylor patent No. 7715 of 1885*

Another novel scheme for working a double-bolt action is found in Enos James's patent, No. 4317 of 1879. In it he proposed an external vertical spindle on the right-hand side of the gun. A projection at its bottom back, to the mid-line of the gun, engaged with the bolt. On the top of this rod was fixed a top lever that also came back to the mid-line and, thence, turned to the rear of the gun.

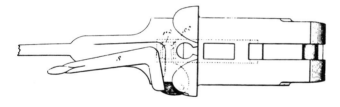

*E. James patent No. 4317 of 1879*

There can be no argument as to the soundness of the system of lever work for a sliding under-bolt, based on a roughly vertical spindle in the head of the stock. A turning top lever can be directly keyed to the upper end and widely spaced bearings, or indeed practically the whole

*H. Tolley patent No. 10,303 of 1886*

length of such a rod, can be supported. In recognition of its original patentee, William Middleditch Scott, who obtained patent No. 2752 of 1865, such a system is usually referred to as a 'Scott spindle'.

Various specifications, and part specifications, for minor modifications further confirm the quality of the basic idea. The first of these is a proposal by the original inventor to increase the travel of the underbolt or reduce the arc through which the top lever had to turn, by having the bottom of the spindle work an intermediate lever that, in its turn, acted on the bolt. This was the subject of patent No. 42 of 1872. Another idea was to retain a vertical spindle but to offset it to the right of the gun, the basis of George Jeffries's patent, No. 4351 of 1875. In the Henry Tolley patent, No. 10,303 of 1886, and the J. and J. G. Thomas patent, No. 14,348 also of 1886, there is a turning spindle, tilted so that the bottom is in front of the top. In all essentials the original idea of the Scott patent is rehashed in Job Cox's patent, No. 6148 of 1889.

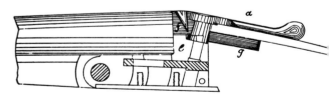

*J. and J. G. Thomas patent No. 14,348 of 1888*

As stated earlier, one of the great points about the Scott spindle is the excellence of the bearings that such a layout permits. On this basis we regard Henry Tolley's idea, in his patent No.

2663 of 1886, to be an inferior copy of the Scott. In this specification Tolley had a short vertical spindle that acted on an upward projection on the rear of the sliding bolt.

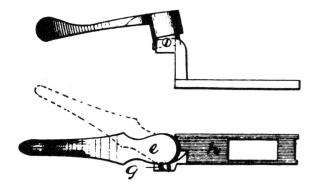

*H. Tolley patent No. 2663 of 1886*

It will come as no surprise to discover that there is a major sub-group of barrel-bolting mechanisms that have three locking sites or bites. By far the greater number of these use the Purdey double-bolt as their basis and add to this some form of extended top barrel rib. Two points should be borne in mind here: first, the influence of Dr Walsh that we remarked on earlier; second, the Purdey double-bite patent, No. 1104 of 1863, became public property on 2 May 1877, when its 14-year protection came to an end. Naturally, the greater number of additions to the double-bolt system occur after this date when no royalty payments could be demanded by the original patentees.

However, before we become embroiled with this group, one other idea should be mentioned.

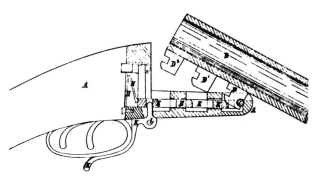

*R. Jones patent No. 2121 of 1872*

This is a triple-bolt produced by the obvious expedient of using a third barrel lump and forming in this a bite just like the Purdey. The patentee of this was Robert Jones of Liverpool, some of whose other ideas we have just considered. This patent, No. 2121 of 1872, was also concerned with retracting the firing pins of a hammer gun and the specification drawing is therefore of one such.

A widely encountered, and certainly the simplest realisation of this, idea of an additional bite is some form of doll's-head-type of extension that is not engaged by any sort of locking-bolt. Examples of these will be found in a variety of shapes. Some of the more elaborate, for instance a three-lobed clover leaf-type, are found on what were inexpensive guns. Such a combination of a cheap gun and complex shape inevitably means that the only use of such an extended rib was as a guide for the extractor for there was only the slimmest chance that, largely by happy accident, the top extension would fit sufficiently well into the standing-breech to add any strength to the combination.

By virtue of two patents, Nos. 3084 of 1873 and 3090 of 1874, we must consider Greener to be the pioneer of this type of addition to the Purdey system. In effect they are but a resurrection of his provisional patent, No. 1339 of 1867, married to the Purdey-bolt. With a characteristic lack of modesty Greener devotes several pages in most of his works on the shotgun to lauding the virtues, and recounting the deeds, of this action which he dubbed his 'Treble Wedge Fast'. More usefully, as part of this recital, he makes accessible results of a trial carried out with a specially constructed shotgun at the end of *The Field* Trial of Explosives in 1878.

We have been very fortunate in having access to the actual gun that was specially built for this trial. It is a side lever, single-bite, snap action double-barrel, 10-bore, with an additional loose cross-bolt that can be inserted or removed at will. To demonstrate the stability or otherwise of the breech fastening, fittings were provided so that a test piece of silver foil could be stretched above the rear of the barrels and the standing-breech. (It further adds to its unusual appearance that this gun is in the white with only a roughly shaped stock – just as it was at the trial over 100 years ago.) Despite what Greener claimed, this trial proved what subsequent experience has confirmed: on a full-sized, soundly-made gun firing normal charges, a top extension is not necessary for the silver foil only ruptured when overloads were fired with the top bolt missing.

*The 10-bore shotgun by W. W. Greener, with removable cross-bolt and support for silver foil, used in* The Field *trial to demonstrate the value of the top extension*

Be this as it may, Dr Walsh of *The Field* believed in the necessity of the top extension and the circulation of Greener's works was of such numbers that it behove other gunmakers to devise their own form of connection between breech and barrels. The most intelligible way to describe this, essentially, very narrow group of designs is to once again consider them in a chronological patent sequence. In this scheme the first one, occuring between the two Greeners, is a mechanism rather briefly described as part of W. R. Pape's patent, No. 1645 of 1874. It is a system of barrel-bolting that uses a bolt, shaped rather like a capital letter J, without its top piece and laid on its side so that the longer limb is at the bottom – effectively the normal

Purdey-bolt. The upper limb of the bolt is to engage with a projection from the breech face about halfway up the barrel face. To work this a link to a top lever is proposed with an ingenious idea, not described in detail, to have the lever so constructed that it will work if pushed either to the right or the left.

*W. R. Pape gun built on his patent action No. 1645 of 1874. On this example the top lever swings only to the right*

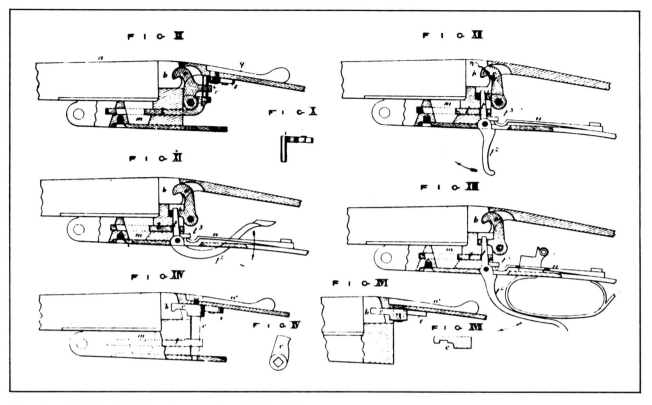

*Page from W. M. and M. Scott's patent No. 615 of 1876*

Following the second Greener specification is a vague provisional specification, No. 510 of 1875, obtained by the famous Birmingham gunmaker, William Palmer Jones. This simply mentions, without any details, the idea of a third bite.

Interestingly, our chronological sequence next produces two more William Middleditch Scott patents, No. 1902 of 1875 and No. 615 of 1876. These were obtained in conjunction with his nephew, Martin Scott, who is described as being a 'Gun Works Manager' – presumably for his co-patentee. In addition to a bolting system very like patent No. 1645 of 1874, there is the idea of having a hook bite pivoted transversely to engage in the head of the stock with the top extension. In one variant of this scheme the hook bolt is rotated backwards by a rearward projection, drawn back by an upward projection from the Purdey-bolt. In another scheme an underlever is shown, an internal upward

projection of which, above the pivot point, pushes back the hook. Yet a third method of working the same internal mechanism was to have a push-up top lever with, now, a downward limb to draw back both bolts.

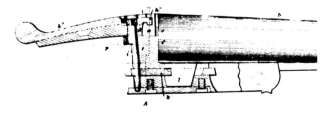

*W. Scott patent No. 1902 of 1875*

Much better known than the foregoing, chiefly we suspect because Dr Walsh chose to illustrate it in *The Modern Sportsman's Gun and Rifle*, is what we know as the 'Tolley Giant Grip'. This is part of Henry Tolley's specification, No. 461 of 1877, but Walsh shows it in his

*Anson and Deeley actioned gun by J. and W. Tolley*
*with 'Giant Grip' top extension. H. Tolley patent*
*No. 461 of 1877*

book as a J. and W. Tolley gun. The Giant Grip consists of a large barrel extension in plan view rectangular that drops into a suitable slot in the standing-breech. In the top extension is cut a slot, shaped like an inverted T, and the bolt that engages with this is, in plan, hook-shaped and pivoted on the same centre and worked by the top lever. The bolts that engage with the barrel lumps have an upward projection joined by a link to the internal portion of the top lever.

Very like the above are the bolts in the Joseph Tonks patent, No. 6673 of 1884.

By coincidence, in 1878 we find another patent obtained by two Americans, James Wentz Wilson and Isaac T. Milliken. Their gun is described, on specification No. 2293, as having a 'compound treble rotating grip and positive wedge fast action and quintriple compensating mechanism whereby all wear of the joints and grip of the locking mechanism may easily be taken up and compensated'!

Wilson describes himself as a 'civil engineer', while Milliken is listed as a 'gentleman'. Curiously, the United States patent, No.

241,466 of 1881, that equates to this British specification is solely in the Wilson name. It is also worthy of note that the British specification was not obtained by an agent and there exists a gun undoubtedly of British make covered by this patent. The inference must be that the patentees came to Britain, patented their invention and commissioned at least one gun of this design. We include it at this point by virtue of the claim made above to a treble-grip, but, in reality, the locking occurs on a top extension and on the rear lump. Incidentally, these two bites are both part of a sturdy through lump. The bolts that engage with these are both keyed to a conventional vertical spindle turned by a top lever. On the British patent drawing the bottom bite is a simple slot whilst the top is another slot but with a complex shape. On the American specification both bites are this shape, but on the actual gun neither are this form. However, it is probable that from the shape of the top bite on the British patent comes the claim to a triple-bite.

This complicated design has several other features. First, there is a pop-up pin in the bottom of the action which holds the locking-bolts in the open position, the pin is depressed by the descending lump as the gun closes. Then there is a sliding stop across the bar of the action that limits the arc through which the barrels pivot. To assemble the gun, the sliding stop has to be drawn back by the chequered grips, one each side of the action bar. Two leaf springs move it forwards so that it lies over a step formed on the front lump. Finally, the 'quintriple compensators' are sliding wedges controlled by set screws that work on the forend iron, the circle-jointed front of the rear lump and on both top and bottom bites. The final adjustment is a tapered hinge pin. All of these adjustments result in exposed screw heads, surely a gun tinkerer's delight!

*A 10-bore shotgun, patent No. 2293 of 1878, by James W. Wilson and Isaac T. Milliken*

The rest of this sub-section we will consider in strict chronological patent sequence. Firstly, an illustrated specification, No. 1902 of 1875 from William Middleditch Scott. Here we have, not surprisingly, the classic Scott spindle/ Purdey-bolt combination but keyed to the top of the spindle is a bite that thus swings in the top of the standing-breech. Variations on this theme are very commonly encountered, indeed three forms are shown on the Scott patent: the first is a simple projection with a down turn at its forward end; the second has a shape like a T, hung on its side with a cross-piece, now vertical; the third has two separate projections, one that bites into the rear, and the other into the bottom, of the top extension.

Very like that above is the top bolt in the Bonehill patent, No. 3718 of 1877, which we encountered earlier in the section on lever work

for the Purdey-bolt. The third bite shown on this patent in conjunction with the lever work previously described is, again, a forward extension of the conventional top lever which, in plan view, is a hook. This engages with a square, cut out of the top extension.

It is perhaps fitting that this section of additions to the Purdey-bolt should contain a patent, No. 397 of 1878, granted to the original patentee. Concerned with a top extension, not from the top of the breech ends but from a site just over halfway up the breech face, it is sometimes called a 'secret bite'. To engage with this the patent describes several bolts, some that are keyed to a version of a Scott spindle (and so swing in the standing-breech) and others that are sliding bolts cammed back by the spindle in just the same way that the double-underbolt is itself actuated.

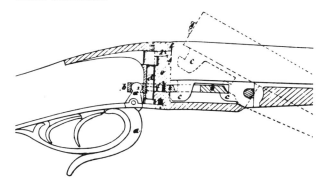

*J. Purdey patent No. 397 of 1878*

Later the same year the Liverpool gunmaker, William Richards, protected an unusual idea, patent No. 1085. This was to use the double Purdey-bolt, plus a top extension of the doll's-head-type and to have a third bite into the front of this extension. Also this year, 1878, there was another, relatively unremarkable triple-bit patent, No. 4980 of 1878, obtained by the Birmingham gunmaker, Samuel Mills. In this, a sliding top bolt is linked to the underbolt and together they are drawn back by a turning top lever. This description also covers part of the Richard Hill patent, No. 1728 of 1879.

An action that would seem to have a large 'Walsh content' is that covered by John Rigby and Thomas Bissell in their patent, No. 1141 of

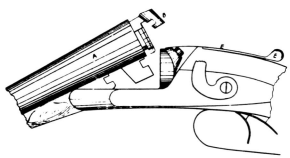

*W. Richards patent No. 1085 of 1878*

1879. In this, in addition to the Purdey-bolt, there is a vertical bolt very like Dr Walsh's worked from the Purdey-bolt via a bell-crank lever. It engages with a slot in the centre of a U-shaped top extension.

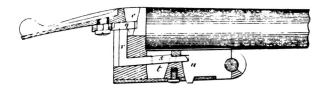

*R. Hill patent No. 1728 of 1879*

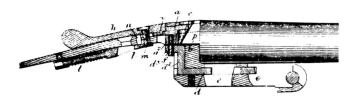

*S. Mills patent No. 4980 of 1878*

Because of their important position as makers to the trade, guns using the patents of the Webley company will be encountered frequently and often serve, as do those of their Birmingham rivals, Scotts, to give an indication of the true maker of the guns, no matter what name is on the rib. Two Webley patents concern us here. Relatively unimportant is No. 1511 of 1882. Here the idea of a bite into the top extension linked to the underbolt and drawn back by a top lever is described. Much more common is the Webley screw-grip, part of the patent, No.

3053 of 1882, of Thomas Webley and also Thomas Brain, a Birmingham gun action-filer. The top lever spindle has a thread formed on it and, with a matching thread as its bearing, the top lever causes both lever and spindle to rise. As the top lever is returned to its closed position it also retracts into the stock. This motion causes the forward portion of the top lever to bind

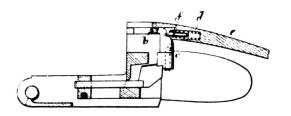

*T. W. Webley patent No. 1511 of 1882*

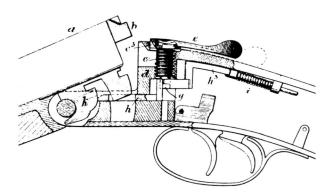

*T. W. Webley and T. Brain patent No. 3053 of 1882 showing screw-grip*

*Anson and Deeley actioned gun marked 'W. R. Leeson patent screw-grip'. Webley and Brain patent No. 3053 of 1882*

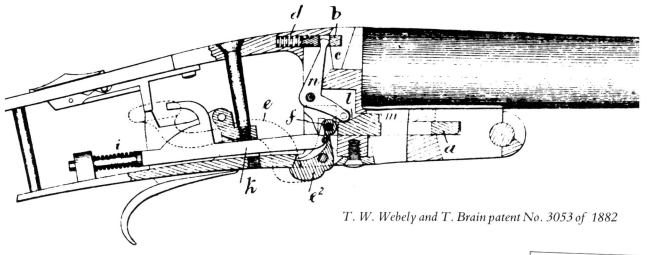

*T. W. Webely and T. Brain patent No. 3053 of 1882*

*Gun by Stephen Grant of London, using E.C. Hodges patent action No. 251 of 1871*

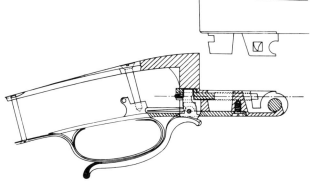

*J. Woodward and J. Emme patent No. 267 of 1872*

down on a stepped extension, while the rotation of the top lever spindle works the underbolts in the usual way.

Also on the same patent is another triple grip system. In this, the underbolt has an incline on its rear which raises the lower forward limb of a cranked lever set on a transverse pivot. The upper limb of this lever thus moves to the rear and carries with it a bolt that slides fore-and-aft in the top of the action that engages with a top extension.

To conclude this section of triple-bite actions, there are a pair of patents which can best be regarded as evasions of the Purdey. They are the Edwin Hodges patent, No. 251 of 1871, and the James Woodward and John Emme patent, No. 267 of 1872. In the former, two lateral projec-

tions are formed on the rear lump and the locking-bolt slides over these and engages with a bite cut into the rear of the front lump. In the latter, the reverse happens, in that the bite is cut into the rear lump and the two projections are on the front. The Hodges patent is usually seen on guns by Stephen Grant, when the action is marked 'Grant & Hodges Patent'.

It comes as something of a surprise to learn that the two patents covering the use of four locking-bolts are both designs patented by William Middleditch Scott. In a provisional patent, No. 3756 of 1873, Scott proposes having two cross-bolts work in opposition, so that they slide in from both sides of the standing-breech into a central top extension. In patent No. 186 of 1875 we have a similar arrangement;

but now there are two top extensions on the
outsides of the barrels into which the two cross-
bolts slide. These two bolts are worked by a
neat double-lever and incline arrangement from
the top lever. In both patents the two extra
bolts are the usual Purdey-bolt or, in the case of
patent 186, this double-top bolt is proposed
as the only bolting mechanism. (Many years
ago we were told of a gun that sounded as if it
were of this pattern, a hammerless shotgun
marked 'E. M. Reilly'.

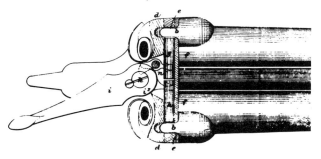

*W. M. Scott patent No. 186 of 1875*

To round off this chapter we have what we
would have expected to be the ultimate in
barrel-bolting systems for a drop-down shotgun
– no less than five bolts! Rather surprisingly –
since the probability exists that if all five bolts
were tightly fitted the guns would be impossible to open! – there are two patents, the first by
Scott, No. 2052 of 1874. The design is relatively
simple with a Scott spindle working a conventional Purdey-bolt and an inert doll's-head,
accounting for three of the bites. The final pair is
where the novelty lies. Fitted on the outside
tops of both barrels is a pair of short stout tubes
with closed forward ends which receive two
cylindrical sliding bolts. These are housed in
protrusions on the top of the standing-breech,
being worked by a V-shaped upward extension from the rear of the Purdey-bolt. Faced
with an aberration such as this, we can only
wonder that so practical and eminent a
gunmaker as Scott should have spent his money
thus.

To a degree less bizarre than the foregoing
is the idea protected as part of patent No. 4693
of 1883 by George Henry Needham of

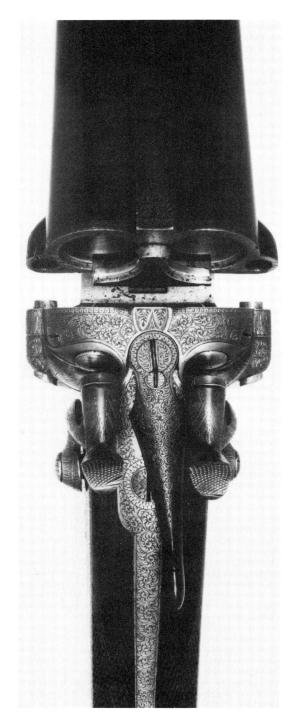

*W. M. Scott patent No. 2052 of 1874 on gun retailed
by Holland & Holland.* (Photograph courtesy of
Sotheby Parke Bernet and Co.)

Wandsworth, South London. He was a younger brother of Joseph Needham, who we shall encounter later in this work as the inventor of the first practical ejector mechanism. What George Henry proposed was to build a gun with a deep rearward extension from between the barrels of a side-by-side double-gun, and to cut into this a whole series of bites one above the other. These were to mate with a species of interrupted screw thread bolts, set vertically in the head of the stock and turned by the top lever. (In fact there are two versions on the patent, one with five, the other with six bites!)

So we come to the end of barrel-bolting systems. They represent a catalogue of inven-tion that borders on the incredible. When one reflects that all this ingenuity and the expense of patent protection was exhausted on just one aspect of the sporting shotgun then another glimpse is gained of the extraordinary inventiveness of the nineteenth-century British gun trade.

Creative though it was, the period 1871 to 1890 saw the end of inventiveness as regards the external hammer shotgun. However, in terms of numbers of guns built, albeit of increasingly cheaper grades as time went by, the hammer shotgun remained one of the staple articles of commerce for the British gun trade well into the period between the two world wars.

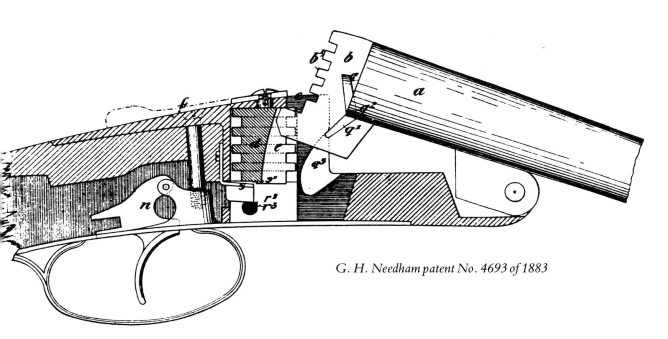

*G. H. Needham patent No. 4693 of 1883*

# CHAPTER THREE

# The Self-cocking Hammer Gun

Nothing resembling a change in the design of sporting guns ever happened without some degree of controversy. So it was that the hammerless gun attracted in its turn its own share. One of the strands of the argument surrounding this change was that a hammer gun was safer because a user was, or should have been, more aware of the state of his gun, be it cocked or not. In the main this resulted in a plethora of safety catches for hammerless guns. But there was another alternative: designers hoped to have the best of both worlds by making self-cocking hammer guns. On the one hand, the user would have the undoubted advantage of speed of manipulation of a self-cocking hammerless gun while, on the other, he retained the external hammers with all their claimed advantages.

The idea of an automatic self-cocking or half-cocking gun was not new. For instance, it was used by the Kalthoff family during the mid-seventeenth-century, both on the Continent and in Britain, in their repeating flintlock guns. The scheme was revived with Needham's patent, No. 1544 of 1862, which used automatic half-cocking, as did the Harrison patent, No. 271 of 1864. Finally, the idea of automatic half-cocking became almost universal with the adoption of the Stanton rebound locks. In the period 1871 to 1890 there is yet another patent which is very close to the rebound lock. What Thomas Tipping Lawden and John Thomas

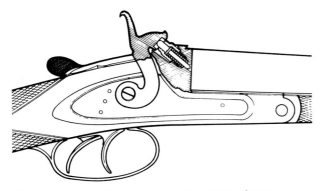

*T. Lawden and J. Thomas patent No. 3548 of 1874*

proposed in their patent, No. 3548 of 1874, was to have separate springs in the head of the stock. These forced back the firing pins which, in turn, pushed back the cocks to half-cock. Spiral or leaf springs are both mentioned in the specification.

In forming this group within our present two decades, we are at a peculiar disadvantage. Many of the actions we know as hammerless could be used to cock external hammers and so produce this type of gun. To resolve this point we have decided to include in this chapter only those guns that we know either from actual specimens or patent drawings as self-cocking hammer guns. But we are confident that examples exist of other self-cocking actions used in this way. Equally confusing is the fact that there are guns of this type that have internal strikers and use the 'hammers' as no more than cocking indicators. Such guns, at some time in their careers and in some instances, have been 'brought up to date' (possibly to make them more saleable) by having their cocking indicators removed.

The earliest gun in a chronological sequence illustrates the point of accurate delineation particularly well. Tucked away towards the end of the Gibbs and Pitt patent, No. 284 of 1873, there is a self-cocking hammer gun. (George Gibbs and Thomas Pitt appear to have been partners. They are listed in the Bristol street directories as 'Gibbs & Pitt, gunmakers' and in the 1885 directory they have two shops: one at 29, Corn Street, the other at 43, High Street. In the 1889 directory it would appear that the partnership had been dissolved for now we have Gibbs and Pitt in the High Street. Finally, in the 1890 directory, we find George Gibbs still in business as a gunmaker in Corn Street but now Thomas Pitt is listed as a 'Boot Wholesaler' at 4, Cotton Hill.) Their specification is mostly concerned with the lever-cocked hammerless gun that is widely seen and fairly well-documented in contemporary literature. The source also includes descriptions of a version of this action with

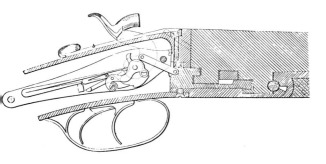

*G. Gibbs and T. Pitt patent No. 284 of 1873*

external cocking levers, similar to those often seen on the Gibbs-Farquharson rifles. So that, in effect, this specification covered the three possible variants: hammer, semi-hammerless and hammerless. To further complicate our task of description, there are two variations of the Gibbs and Pitt drawn on this specification. The first used what we regard as the conventional Gibbs and Pitt hinged rearward projection of the locking-bolt. This engages with the two notches in the tumblers as in the hammerless version, which the semi-hammerless essentially is. The true hammer gun is drawn with conventional back-action sidelocks and to cock these a T-shaped piece, hinged to the locking-bolt at its bottom, is formed so that the cross-piece pushes against a projection on the tumblers and so cocks the locks if they have been fired. Two versions of lever work are proposed, either a conventional top lever or a push-forward underlever.

Bearing some similarity with this, and also preserving our chronological scheme, are probably the two best-known British self-cocking hammer guns. They are an incredibly similar pair of designs, despite being the subject of separate patents produced by two of the, then, foremost London gunmakers, Langs and Woodwards. The similarity goes even further in that, under the respective patents, hammerless guns were also produced. The gun that Langs produced was covered by patent No. 1290 of 1875 taken out by Edwin Hughes. He gives his address as 36, Brook Street, Kennington Road, Lambeth. In fact, Hughes was the long serving manager of Langs. In a letter to *The Field*, in July 1886, Hughes recorded the fact that he had then been manager for Joseph Lang for 19 years.

The self-cocking hammer Lang is the one member of this group of which the present author (DJB) can claim first-hand knowledge, having owned one and shot fairly extensively with it. A pleasant gun to use, its mechanism worked easily and smoothly. After using a conventional hammer gun, finding the hammers at full cock immediately after closing the gun came as something of a surprise. It was the author's view, expressed by fellow shooters, that such a gun, unimproved with any safety catch except the facility to individually half-cock the locks, was dangerous, that was largely responsible for abandoning its use.

The mechanism of this gun is very simple. Stout studs project inwards from each tumbler and on these a portion of the underlever bears.

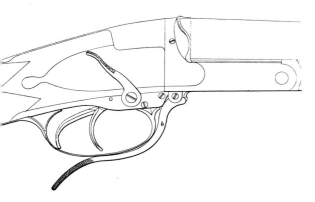

*Semi-hammerless version of G. Gibbs and T. Pitt patent No. 284 of 1873*

*Gun sold in 1877 by Joseph Lang and Sons London. E. Hughes patent No. 1290 of 1875*

61

As the outside portion of the underlever is pushed forwards and down, the locks are raised to full-cock. This gun shares, with all those that use a push-forward underlever or side lever, the illusion of being an assisted opener; the thrust of the user's hand serves to flick open the gun after the locking-bolts are withdrawn.

The Woodward gun uses the same lever layout except that there is a small lever between the main opening lever and the stud on the tumbler. The relevant patents are Nos. 117 and 600, both of 1876. In fact, No. 117 is a provisional specification but from our understanding of it, it would appear to relate to this gun. Both specifications are in the names of Thomas Southgate and James Woodward, the younger. Incidentally, a gun of this type was given by its makers to be a prize, actually the third, at *The Field* Trial of 1876: Choke versus Cylinder bores live pigeon match. In fact, two other guns were offered as prizes at this event: a gun by J. D. Dougall, which was the first prize; and a gun by Charles Maleham, which was the second. In all cases the winners were able to decide whether they wanted the guns choked or cylinder bored.

It is an indication of the relative popularity of this design that it was sold by makers other than the patentees. An example of this gun, by Jackson of Nottingham, is known to us and we suspect that this is probably not unique.

There is another self-cocking hammer gun that perhaps fits best at this point. The patentees are Thomas Tipping Lawden, of the firm of Tipping & Lawden, and his manager, John Thomas. In their specification, No. 3291 of 1876, they describe a push-forward underlever opening gun in which an upward projection of the underlever bears on a specially shaped tumbler to force the trigger plate lockwork back to cock. The mechanism of this gun is unusual: first, in the use of a trigger plate action with external hammers; second, a more subtle point, in the proposal of a sliding stop, either on the underside of the gun to limit the travel of the lever or on the top to limit the travel of the locking-bolt. Both of these stops would have the same effect that, by so limiting the rotation of the cocking lever, the locks would only be brought to half-cock; an interesting concept which can be thought of as taking its inspiration

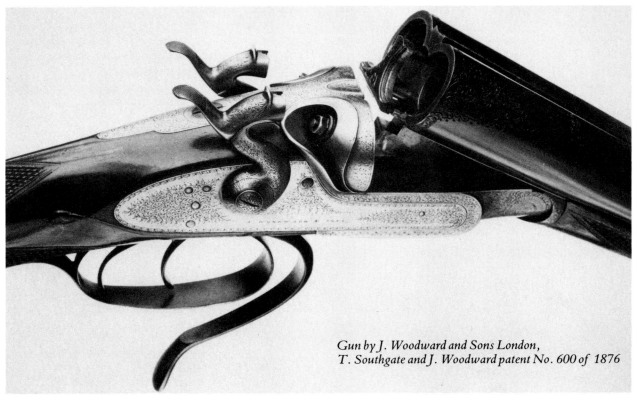

*Gun by J. Woodward and Sons London,*
*T. Southgate and J. Woodward patent No. 600 of 1876*

from a variety of sources. These two patentees had also obtained a provisional specification, No. 2235 of 1876, on the idea of converting the Thomas patent, No. 3091 of 1871 (with a lift up top lever), to a self-cocking hammer gun. But, as this idea languished as a provisional specification, we assume no serious use was made of it.

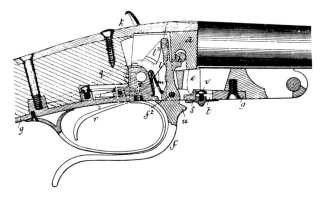

*T. Lawden and J. Thomas patent No. 3291 of 1876*

A different approach to this problem is contained in the patent No. 129 of 1876 of Thomas Perkes. The hammers themselves are lifted to full-cock by a bar that rises out of the head of the stock. To engage the hammers there is a cross-piece so that the lifter is essentially a capital letter T. The patent describes, and examples are seen of, two different methods of working this lifter. One scheme is to connect the bottom of the T to the opening lever which is either a push-forward underlever or a side lever, so that the lifter is raised as the barrel-bolts are withdrawn. The other plan is to pivot the lifter on the rear barrel lump so that, as the barrels drop, the T-piece is thrust up and back.

Another design that uses the same idea, of a lifter rising from the stock to act directly on the external hammers, is contained in the patent granted to Thomas Bailey, gunmaker, of Aston, Birmingham. The variation is to use a pair of spring-loaded pistons rather like over-sized firing pins which are forced upwards by an incline formed on the rear of the Purdey-bolt. As this latter is moved to the rear (by an under-lever as we have previously described), the cocking rods lift the hammers – the specification

*Gun by Holland & Holland using action covered by Thomas Perkes patent No. 129 of 1876.*
(Photograph courtesy of Geoffrey Boothroyd)

mentions only to half-cock but presumably it would be perfectly feasible for them to reach full-cock if the lockwork was so constructed. The relevant patent is No. 3240 of 1876.

An idea that arose from the Perkes patent, No. 129 of 1876, and which was borrowed by several other inventors, was to use the motion and leverage of the opening barrel, via some sort of a link, to cock the external hammers. Henry Tolley (whose relationship, if any, to James and William Tolley who traded as a separate firm in Birmingham and London, we have been unable to ascertain), uses a variant of this idea in part of his patent, No. 461 of 1877. What he proposes is to use a jointed slide fixed to the barrel lumps so that, as the barrels are opened, the slide is pulled forwards. As this happens its rear engages with a projection from the bottom of the tumbler which is thus rotated to full-cock. Also in the same specification is an idea to the same end that also works a link from the barrel lump, but this time acting on a sliding V-mainspring. This lies with its point forward as usual but on the open ends are two rollers. As the barrel is opened, the mainspring is drawn forwards and the upper limb lifts the tumbler which is also roughly in the shape of a V. When the full-cock position is reached the tumbler is held by the sear so that, as the barrels are closed and the mainspring forced backwards into the V in the tumbler, it is compressed ready to work the lock as the sear is released.

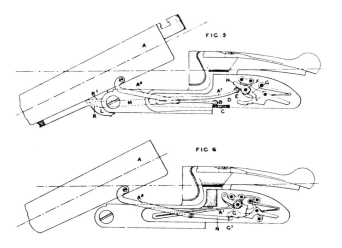

*H. Tolley patent No. 461 of 1877*

Another inventive Birmingham man, Samuel Mills, action-filer, used a link to the barrel lumps. He proposed in his patent, No. 1089 of 1878, to use a lever pivoted on the same centre as the tumblers of the lock and projecting forwards to engage with a second lever on the rear barrel lump. As the barrels were raised, so was the lever in the action, which picked up inward projections from the tumblers, if the locks had been fired, and so carried them back to full-cock.

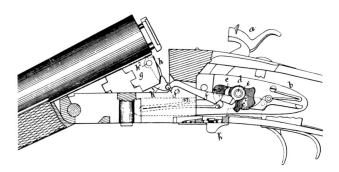

*S. Mills patent No. 1089 of 1878*

In essence, this is the same idea as Thomas Perkes used in a second patent, No. 1968 of 1878. Here we have a step on the rear lump that picks up a projecting toe on the bottom of the tumbler and raises the latter as the barrels are opened. This sporting gun would appear to have the proportions either of a small-bore, single-barrel, shotgun or a rook rifle, and it is in these classes that we suspect that examples of the mechanism will be found.

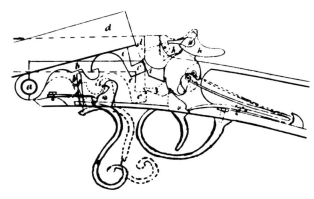

*T. Perkes patent No. 1968 of 1878*

We remarked earlier that the great problem, not to say potential pitfall, of this chapter was that most of the guns we describe elsewhere as hammerless guns could be made as self-cocking hammer guns. Our point is reinforced by the discovery of a patent on the idea of producing a self-cocking semi-hammerless gun. This patent, No. 17,037 of 1884, is in the name of David Bentley. He describes himself as a 'gun-maker' of Aston near Birmingham. His patent does not cover any lockwork or cocking mechanism but simply and solely the idea of having a curved slot in the lockplate in which the head of a hammer, shaped like a letter C, swings. Bentley specifically makes the point that any cocking mechanism could have this feature incorporated with it. Exactly how many were used is, of course, a moot point but the authors have seen or heard of three variants and believe there are more.

The gun which we know best is a magnificent lightweight 10-bore, marked 'Thomas Turner, Brook Street, London', which uses the Bentley semi-hammers in conjunction with the

*Gun by Thomas Turner of London, using D. Bentley's patent No. 17,037 of 1884*

conventional Gibbs and Pitt top lever-cocked action, usually seen as a hammerless gun. This combination was dubbed 'The Safest' by its retailer in advertisements of 1885.

But of all the self-cocking hammer designs, the most unusual is that for a gun which proposed to use the recoil from one cartridge to cock the lockwork for the next round. The gun is a single-loader, but it contains the seeds of the idea which was to become the recoil-operated repeater. The patent specification in question, No. 971 of 1877, was taken out by the agent William Robert Lake on behalf of Baron Richard Walterskirchen of Pressburg, Hun-

gary. The idea protected was to use a heelplate hinged at the top and held away from the stock at the bottom, and from the lower part of the heelplate to run a rod through the inside of the stock to the lockwork so as to cock the lock as the gun recoiled.

The self-cocking hammer shotgun, therefore, represents yet another of the variations that make the evolution of the British shotgun so fascinating. As is so often the case, the self-cocking hammer gun is an idea that has not been allowed to lapse into total obscurity. For, within the last decade, there has been a resurgence of interest in the hammer gun and the reappearance of self-cocking hammer guns. One of these, not a British gun it is true, is the 'Castore' or Castor from the Italian makers, Abbiatico and Salvinelli. They were previously known as 'Famars', an acronym of their Italian title, Fabbrica Armi Mario Abbiatico Remo Salvinelli. The Castore uses the basic Rogers sidelock action but with external hammers, thus bearing out our remarks at the beginning of this chapter. However, it is doubtless satisfying to the ghosts of Woodward, Hughes and the rest that the Castore has become a major part of Abbiatico and Salvinelli's strictly-limited, high-quality, production, so that their basic idea has been vindicated, in part at least.

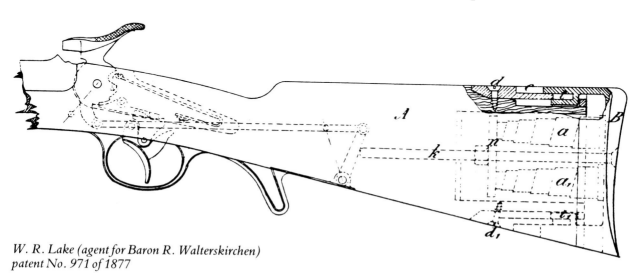

*W. R. Lake (agent for Baron R. Walterskirchen) patent No. 971 of 1877*

# CHAPTER FOUR

# The Barrel-cocking Hammerless Gun

From the commanding heights of hindsight it is easy to see the way any evolution (or revolution) turned out and to dismiss the result as inevitable. However, the outcome is never as clear-cut and obvious to those caught up in the actual event. So it was with the hammerless shotgun in the 1870s and 1880s. We have already explained those guns cocked by a lever other than the barrels and now must turn our attention to the other major division of the hammerless gun, those that use the weight and/or the leverage of the barrels to cock the lockwork.

In theory, the length of lever offered by the shotgun barrels of conventional length confers on the barrel-cockers an overwhelming advantage in the ease with which they could be manipulated. In practice, it is not convenient to grasp the barrels at the muzzle and so the leverage actually used is much less, but still more than the average lever-cocked gun. This potential was recognised by the various designers in and out of the gun trade and, in the period 1871 to 1890, slightly more barrel-cocked than lever-cocked guns were patented.

In order to explain this group in an intelligible fashion, we once more have to search for some form of classification and the scheme that we have chosen is to sub-divide them on the basis of how and from what site the motion of the barrels is transferred to the lockwork. But first we have abstracted and placed separately those guns in which it is the mainspring that actually raises the tumbler to full-cock. (See Chapter Five.)

A survey of the patent specifications reveals that two basic modes of transmitting the movement of the barrels to the locks were adopted: first, those in which the cocking arm met the barrels or forend iron at the knuckle or pivot of the barrels; second, those in which the barrel lump or other projection into the action bar was linked to the lockwork.

Our detailed consideration of the guns in this important group must start with the first member patented not so much for the practical use that was made of the mechanism but for the influence that it exerted on subsequent events. No. 1205 was patented by Joseph Needham of Piccadilly on 7 April 1874 and is one of the most important milestones in the evolution of the British sporting gun. Not only a barrel-cocked hammerless design, it also featured a working ejector mechanism. Even at this early date neither of these features was totally new. Even so, we remain convinced of the vital importance of Needham's gun and believe that neither it nor its inventor have received the recognition that is their due. Well over 100 years later, we have the advantage of a clearer perspective of the events but it is of interest to learn that Dr Walsh thought ejectors unnecessary. 'I confess that I cannot see the gain resulting from this arrangement, if a loader is employed he almost always has plenty of time . . .'. Greener, too, was loath to give credit to any rival even if, as in this case, he had bought out the firm in 1874 and was using a version of the ejector himself.

To appreciate the quality of this invention it is, as always, necessary to try and wipe away the knowledge of what happened afterwards and so to try and see it anew in its newborn context. If this is done then we can glimpse the calibre of the mind that conceived this simple (in the sense of using few parts) but effective mechanism. The ejector mechanism we must consider with those that it inspired but the reader is urged to skip to that section in order to capture an overall picture of the design.

The patent drawing shows a trigger plate gun but examples are more often seen in sidelock form. Description of one lock of the pair will suffice. The cocking lever is keyed onto the same spindle as the tumbler and extends forwards to end just in front of the action face. The rear barrel lump curves backwards so that it extends behind the breech end of the barrels and is thus reminiscent of the Needham hammer gun action. It is this rearward projection that lifts the cocking arm as the barrels pivot open.

*Gun by J. V. Needham built on J. Needham patent No. 1205 of 1874*

The cocking arm remains in the up position when the lock is cocked and is thus no impediment to the closing barrels.

An interesting feature of the patent for this gun is that it proposes to render a sear spring in the lock unnecessary by forming a projection on the sear so that, as the tumbler rotated backwards to full-cock, the back of the tumbler bore down on this projection. This in turn rotated the sear a few degrees so that the sear nose positively engaged with its bent in the bottom of the tumbler.

Another of the benefits of hindsight is that we recognise the foresightedness of those who developed, under licence, the pioneering Needham invention. The authors have encountered Churchill, Greener and both A. and C. Lancaster guns that we would place in this category. Closest to the original are the Churchill and Lancaster guns, characterised by a projection in front of the trigger guard that houses the downward extension on the rear lump necessary to carry the kicking lever.

The Charles Lancaster modification uses separate strikers and tumblers and rollers on light mainsprings to transmit their power to exceptionally heavy tumblers. Because these guns are built as back-action sidelocks the connectors between the tumblers and the ejectors are loose in the body of the gun and hook onto the tumblers as the locks are mounted. In later discussion of this action Dr Walsh was quick to point out that his unsuccessful hammer gun (see Volume One) embodied the same idea. But equally, the germ existed even earlier in the self half-cocking Cogswell and Needham pinfire and centrefire hammer guns. Such an argument can be endlessly, and fruitlessly, continued. What is in no doubt is that the Needham was the first British barrel-cocked hammerless sporting shotgun and it and its inventor can lay their claim to fame surely and squarely on this fact.

As always, the impact that the Needham invention had when it was introduced is now impossible to gauge. We can now only see it as the precursor of another of the very greatest

*Westley Richards gun with Anson and Deeley action patent No. 1756 of 1875*

landmarks in the history of the sporting shot-gun – the Anson and Deeley boxlock. The patent, No. 1756, was taken out in 1875 and the action, and minor modifications of it, have been and are manufactured around the world in every possible quality, from the very best to the very worst. In total numbers it is only rivalled by a few mass-produced repeating shotguns.

The two patentees of this invention were William Anson and John Deeley. It is a curious and, in a way, sad feature of our researches that while there are several obituaries, interviews and portraits of John Deeley, virtually nothing has so far come our way regarding William Anson. The total result of much searching is that he was the foreman in the Westley Richards & Co. Ltd., machine shop when the invention was patented on 11 May 1875 and that after-wards he set up in business on his own at 77, Slaney Street, Birmingham. He appears to have died in about 1890. This illustrates a pattern that repeats itself often: one of a pair of patentees is a more or less unknown artisan, while the other is a magnet of the gun trade. We have no doubt that in such cases as these the idea originated with the artisan who, lacking the necessary resources, took it to a man of means who obtained the necessary patent protection for a share in the profits.

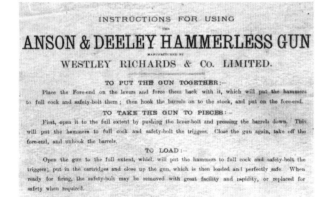

INSTRUCTIONS FOR USING

# ANSON & DEELEY HAMMERLESS GUN

MANUFACTURED BY

## WESTLEY RICHARDS & Co. LIMITED.

**TO PUT THE GUN TOGETHER:—**

Place the Fore-end on the levers and force them back with it, which will put the hammers to full cock and safety-bolt them; then hook the barrels on to the stock, and put on the fore-end.

**TO TAKE THE GUN TO PIECES:—**

First, open it to the full extent by pushing the lever-bolt and pressing the barrels down. This will put the hammers to full cock and safety-bolt the triggers. Close the gun again, take off the fore-end, and unhook the barrels.

**TO LOAD:—**

Open the gun to the full extent, which will put the hammers to full cock and safety-bolt the triggers; put in the cartridges and close up the gun, which is then loaded and perfectly safe. When ready for firing, the safety-bolt may be removed with great facility and rapidity, or replaced for safety when required.

*Label stuck inside case lid of Westley Richards gun, with Anson and Deeley action*

By 1875 John Deeley was, by his own efforts, just such a man of means. He was born in 1825, the son of a steel toy maker and started his working life at the age of eight and worked variously in the steel toy, brass casting and button industries of Birmingham. He joined Westley Richards in 1860 when he was 35 and in the interim had acquired a sound business education. From his obituary we learn that his first task for his new employers was to work at a balance sheet which on being audited was found to be perfect. It is a further measure of Deeley's ability that when Westley Richards himself retired from the active running of the firm in 1872 it was John Deeley who became managing director, a post he held until 1898. We can see that he managed his own affairs with equal skill: when Westley Richards was reorganised in 1899 it was revealed that John Deeley owned practically all the ordinary shares in the company – some £30,000 worth. Deeley was a generous supporter of many charities, whilst in his will he left a gross total of £16,079 plus 4000 ordinary shares in Westley Richards. In addition, he left 2000 of the ordinary shares, plus the first Anson and Deeley boxlock gun made, to his nephew, D. J. P. Haines.

So much for the patentees. Their invention shares with many other great ideas the considerable virtue of simplicity. This, and its consequent suitability for machine production which it doubtless owes to William Anson's training, set it fair for its subsequent success. We have already noted the lever-cocked version of this gun but since we regard this as something of an aberrant variant we will say no more about it.

The most noticeable feature of the patent drawings of the barrel-cocked version is that the cocking levers are part of the forend iron. They

*Westley Richards gun, with Anson and Deeley action. The forend is here removed to show the earliest pattern of cocking levers*

*A. W. W. Greener-made Anson and Deeley actioned gun, with cocking levers of modified shape*

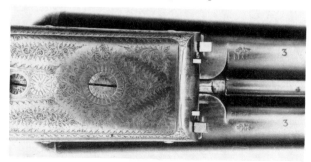

*Modern Webley gun, small cocking levers with separate ejector trips*

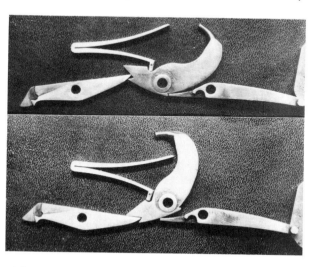

*The cocking lever, mainspring, tumbler and sear from Anson and Deeley gun, patent No. 1756 of 1875. The relative positions of limbs are: cocked (above); fired (below). In practice, the mainspring would be compressed in the action bar*

*Cogswell and Harrison gun with bottom plate removed to show solid knuckle. Anson and Deeley actioned gun*

project backwards into the action and under the toes of the tumblers, which are thus raised to the full-cock position as the barrels are depressed. However, on examples of what we regard as the classic Anson and Deeley, the cocking levers are pivoted in the body of the action on the same centre as the barrels and they project from the knuckle. The other characteristic feature of the patent drawing gun is that there are two separate safeties, one for each lock! These consist of a simple blocking device to stop the fall of the tumbler/striker. This is achieved by a transverse rod partly cut away and connected to an external lever. When the latter is in the horizontal position, the tumbler falls but when the external lever is swung to the vertically down position, the rod blocks the tumbler's path. A primitive method, to say the least, which was very soon abandoned.

We feel it is a fitting close to this sub-section to consider two further boxlock designs, one patented by William Anson together with John Deeley, the other by William Anson alone. The first is, in part and the second wholly, concerned with a modified cocking lever. The idea in both cases is that this should not project from the knuckle but instead a rearward extension from the forend should bear on the front bottom corner of the cocking lever. This being a right-angled triangle pivoted at its top corner, on a common centre with the barrels. That

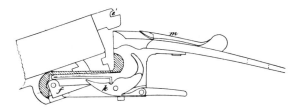

*W. Anson and J. Deeley patent No. 1833 of 1883*

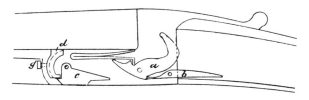

*W. Anson patent No. 4292 of 1884*

neither of these improvements is at all widely used merely serves to emphasise the quality of the original invention. The patents are respectively No. 1833 of 1883 and No. 4292 of 1884.

As an addendum we mention a gun patented by Edgar Harrison and, another Anson. Harrison, of 226, Strand, London, we have met before (he was the Harrison of Cogswell and Harrison) but of Edwin George Anson, gunmaker; Hayden Villas, Station Road, Harrow, we know virtually nothing. We do not know if he was related to William Anson. The patent, No. 14,444, obtained in 1887 by Harrison and Anson is essentially a classic Anson and Deeley gun with the pivot point of the cocking levers a little above and behind the barrel pivot. These are worked as usual by the forend but here, fitted into the forend under the ordinary iron, is a slide that doubles as a forend catch. In addition the slide slips under the noses of the cocking levers. The object of this invention is only obliquely mentioned in the specification, but seems to be to position the cocking lever more precisely and to eliminate any 'play' or sloppiness at this point.

One of the problems of the classic Anson and Deeley boxlock is simply that it is, just as its name says, a 'box' lock. This rectangular section of the action bar, imposed by cocking levers, is alien to the rounded good looks of other designs. This obviously concerned many gunmakers who sought, primarily by the way their guns were stocked, to mitigate or divert attention from this undesirable feature.

A more radical solution was proposed in the redesign of the Anson and Deeley, as contained in a patent, No. 7346 of 1887 obtained by Henry Smith. He was a gun action-maker of Price Street, Birmingham and the essential feature of his specification was to replace the twin cocking levers that cause the boxiness of the front of the action bar, where it is most noticeable, with a single cocking piece that serves both locks. This new cocking lever is T-shaped in plan view and pivoted transversely at the bottom of the upright on a common axis with the barrels. The forend iron is arranged to bear on the bottom of the T so that, as the gun is opened, the two ends of the cross-piece lift the tumblers to full-cock.

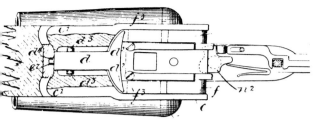

*H. Smith patent No 7346 of 1887*

*S. R. and W. Trulock patent No. 327 of 1882 (another version)*

As was inevitable, a gun action as good as the Anson and Deeley was immediately perceived to be spawned a crop of imitators. Four patents fall in this group, and all are unknown to us as actual guns. This may well be that externally they so closely resemble an Anson and Deeley that examples are passed over as 'boxlocks', or it may equally be that lawyers for Westley Richards were able to dissuade production of these on the grounds that they infringed the jealously guarded original Anson and Deeley patent. Certainly there are no legal battles recorded, but this could simply mean that patentees had no wish to take on the tough proposition represented by Westley Richards'.

Samuel, Richard and William Trulock (see Volume One), who all gave their addresses as 13, Parliament Street, Dublin, protected two ideas in their patent, No. 327 of 1882. The one that most closely resembles the Anson and Deeley is a boxlock design. In this the tumbler is elongated forwards, practically to the knuckle where its forward end is lifted by a backward projection from the forend iron as the barrels pivot open. The single leaf mainspring is situated behind the tumbler which has a backward projection on its head, and this bears down on the spring and compresses it as the tumbler is forced backwards. The other version of this gun is drawn as a sidelock or trigger plate. In this the

tumbler of the first design is altered to a cocking lever which forces back a more conventional tumbler.

Very similar to the boxlock version is the gun described in the provisional patent, No. 4977 of 1883, granted to E. Bled of Liège. In order to produce a very simple gunlock, the forend iron projects back into the action bar and under forward projections of the tumblers.

Something along these lines is probably also the subject of the provisional patent, No. 5843 of 1883, of Horatio Phillips. But lacking a drawing and having only a rather vague description, we cannot be sure.

Frederick Beesley's patent, No. 8657 of 1886, bears a very close resemblance to the Anson and Deeley. Used by the inventor and not sold to others of the trade, as so often was the case with Beesley's inventions, the only significant difference is the use of a slotted pivot on the cocking lever. As the tumbler came to full-cock it would be thrust back through a greater angle of arc so that, having this greater travel on firing, it would deliver a more certain blow to the cap. A point of identification, but of no significance to the principle involved, is that the cocking levers are joined by a transverse cross-piece across

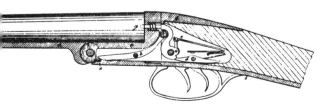

*S. R. and W. Trulock patent No. 327 of 1882*

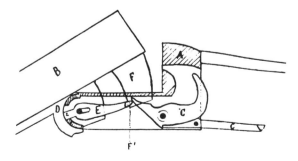

*F. Beesley patent No. 8657 of 1886*

their forward ends. In plan they are roughly U-shaped and probably work better as a result.

At this point it is also relevant to remark that drawn, but not claimed, in the Edgar Harrison ejector patents that we shall consider later are numerous variations on the Anson and Deeley. These variations act in precisely the same way, but with differently shaped parts.

A mechanism that we can only regard as a very close imitation of the Anson and Deeley, indeed in our estimation an infringement of the patent, is the Swinburn patent, No. 2711 of 1880. In this the cocking levers are permanently pivoted to the forend iron and, as the gun is assembled, slide back into the action bar with the rear ends slipping under the toes of the tumblers. Thereafter, the action is identical to that of the classic Anson and Deeley.

It is a further indication of the value of the lever through the knuckle type of action that we should find the much-used and important example, patent No. 397. This was obtained on 29 January 1881 by John Thomas Rogers and John Rogers. They style themselves 'gunmakers' on their patent but appear in the trade directories as gun action-filers of 78, Lower Tower Street, Birmingham. Their patent protected, what has become, the standard British gun trade sidelock action. As such it was used up and down the trade by those who did not have an invention of their own to foster. The result of this is that the enthusiast will encounter very few guns using this layout marked externally 'Rogers'. It is also a rarity to find the lock and lever work marked internally. We thus have a situation very like that regarding the Henry Jones double screw-grip action (see Volume One).

Like Henry Jones, the Rogers both worked for the trade but, unlike Jones, their patent was kept in force. The Rogers action therefore made money for its inventors. In addition to this, the Rogers exploited their invention in another way. We learn from their United States patent, No. 257,764 of 1882, that their invention was assigned to John P. Clabrough of Birmingham.

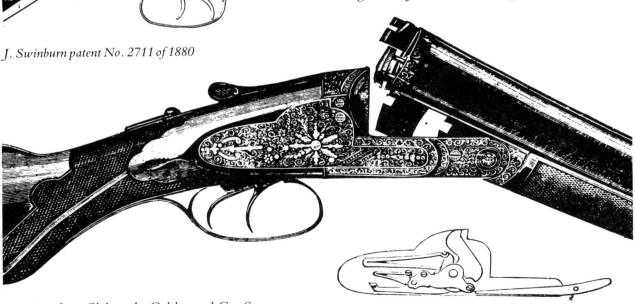

*J. Swinburn patent No. 2711 of 1880*

*Drawing from Clabrough, Golcher and Co. San Francisco catalogue of 1890 showing the gun built on J. T. and J. Rogers patent No. 397 of 1881*

Clabrough was a manufacturer who had built up an excellent trade with the United States, had a retail outlet in San Francisco in his own name and agencies with other dealers across the continent. Every indication suggests that he made extensive use of the Rogers action.

The mechanism uses a cocking lever pivoted just behind the joint pin. The forward end of this cocking lever lies in a slot cut in the knuckle, projects beyond it and bears on the underside of the barrels. The longer rear arm of the lever ends in the head of the stock, behind the action face, so that as the barrels are depressed the rear end of the lever rises and in so doing lifts the tumbler to the full-cock position. The patent drawing shows a back-action lock, as does the illustration in the Clabrough catalogue, but examples are found using bar-action sidelocks. This would alter the design to the extent that one of its features is the use of the lower limb of the mainspring as the sear spring.

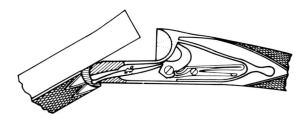

*T. Keight patent No. 6883 of 1884*

Leverwork like the Rogers does appear in a number of action patents, the legal validity of which must be questionable. For example, in 1884 patent No. 6883 was obtained by Thomas Keight who tells us on his patent that he was 'of, T. G. Styles & Co., Gun Manufacturers of Weaman Street, Birmingham'. The point of difference between the Keight and the Rogers actions, as patented, is that the former has a cocking lever that projects through the bottom of the knuckle. In fact, the two cocking levers are shown joined across their forward ends to produce an angular U-shaped member. This is hung on a slotted pivot so that the opening motion of the barrels thrusts back, as well as lifts, the tumblers. Like the Rogers, the Keight action is drawn with a back-action lock in which

the single spring does duty both as main and sear spring. In this case, however, the top limb acts directly on the tumbler with no intervening swivel.

Remarkably similar to the Keight is another gunlock reduced to its absolute essentials in the search for economy. William Charles McEntee, who traded as 'John Reeves & Co.' and John Hughes, his foreman, patented their design as No. 8314 of 1885. The only difference from the Keight is that one version uses a stout compression spring between the sear and a lifting arm to the tumbler as its sole spring.

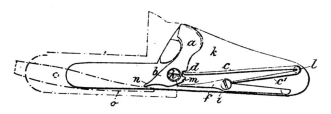

*W. C. McEntee and J. Hughes patent No. 8314 of 1885*

In patents No. 5834 of 1887 and No. 16,691 of 1888, obtained by Henry William Holland of 98, New Bond Street and John Robertson of 4, Dansey Yard, Wardour Street, lever and ejector work for bar-action sidelock guns is described. In the 1887 specification a simple lever, pivoted either on or behind the joint pin, lifts the tumblers as the barrels pivot open. In the 1888 version the lever has become compound with a short lever pivoted at the hinge pin, the rear end of which acts on the front of a second lever. The front of the front lever is therefore depressed and so the rear of the rear lever is also depressed.

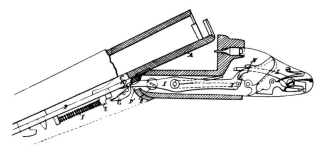

*H. Holland and J. Robertson patent No. 5834 of 1887*

Since the rear of the rear lever bears onto the tumbler, above and behind the latter's own axle, opening the barrels serves to cock the lockwork.

The simple Rogers lever reappears in no less than four more patent specifications: No. 2677 of 1888, James Lang and Arthur Jeffries; No. 10,084 of 1888, Thomas Perkes; No. 5159 of 1889, Thomas Woodward of Birmingham; and No. 20,979 of 1889, Frederick Beesley. All of these also concern ejector mechanisms, similarly with No. 12,178 of 1890 by Richard Trulock in which case the cocking lever also slightly slides back and forth. Apart from this, the differences between this group are nothing more than subtle variations in the shapes of the levers that would be both tedious and pointless to describe.

Also concerned, in part, with ejector work is an immense patent, No. 16,214 of 1886, by Edgar Harrison of 142, New Bond Street. This deals with the idea of cocking the lockwork with a series of levers and rods. Round the hinge pin is fitted a collar which is partially rotated as the barrels pivot open. To this collar is hinged a rod which is thrust back as the collar rotates. This rod in turn is hinged to a vertical lever pivoted at its bottom so that the arc described by the top of the lever is greater than the movement of the rod from the collar. This greater travel is transmitted by yet another rod to the breast of the tumbler so that the latter is cocked as the gun opens.

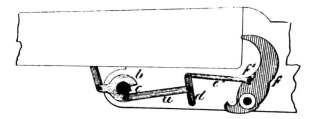

*E. Harrison patent No. 16,214 of 1886*

It is a recurring feature of guns patented by inventors outside the gun trade that their efforts show either originality or are more or less bizarre, depending on the point of view of the commentator. Certainly an ingenious

mechanism is the patent, No. 659 of 1886, obtained by William A'Court Granville Birkin, 'Gentleman', of Aspley Hall, Nottinghamshire. This uses a complex double-lever arrangement that first, as the gun opens, works a peculiar extractor mechanism that withdraws the cartridges almost half their length, doubtless to obviate the need for an ejector. Then, as the gun closes, this same set of levers cocks the action. The heart of this set-up is a three-armed lever pivoted transversely in the bar of the action, about halfway between the action face and the hinge pin. As the gun opens, a lever that projects back from the hinge, turning on the same centre, lifts the three-armed lever by its lower limb. This motion is used to enable the longer upper limb of the same lever to force back the extractor. However, as the gun reaches its fullest open position the three-armed lever slips out of engagement, both with the extractor and with the lever from the hinge pin, and at the same time is rotated slightly forwards by a leaf spring in the bar of the action; now the long top limb of the lever lies on the barrel flats. As the gun is closed, the barrels force this limb down and the third, rearward, limb lifts the tumblers to cock them. Finally, just before the barrels close completely, the long top limb slips back up into the extractor slot so that the tumblers are free to fall and the cycle can repeat.

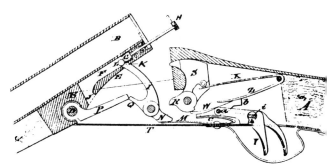

*W. Birkin patent No. 659 of 1886*

Certainly a wondrous creation and it is only a supposition that the inventor constructed an example for his own use, but if he did what a prize for a collector to find!

Before we leave the subject of strange extractors, completeness demands mention of patent

No. 7939 of 1884. This was obtained in Britain by the agent, A. M. Clark, for Norris O. Waymire of Garfield in Pawnee County, Kansas. This was to have a web, or fin-like, projection from the rear of the extractor that fitted, for greater stability, into a suitable slot cut between the barrels of a sporting gun.

Yet another group of guns fall naturally into place in a study of the barrel-cocked hammerless actions. It comprises those that use a rod or rods sliding in the action bar that are somehow forced back by the opening motion of the barrels; it is this motion and force that is used to cock the locks. Closer scrutiny of the various actions covered by this broad classification reveals that this mode was not without its problems. The chief of these was that the distance of travel of the cocking rods was probably not as great as might be desirable, and could not be as easily controlled, as with those barrel-cocked actions that used a lever where the alteration of pivot points and lever lengths could alter the travel of the cocking member at will. There is a patent, No. 14,626 of 1885, by gunmaker Edwin Green, to raise the pivot point of the barrels to obtain better leverage. But in those systems that used a simple cocking rod and a conventional hinge pin the designer was forced to steer a course between an action that was unpleasantly stiff to open, because the cocking rods could not exert much leverage on the tumbler, or the alternative of lightening the mainsprings with the attendant risk of misfires. Such a situation is very much the parallel of the lever-cocked actions. In fact, this present group sub-divides into those actions that use a simple sliding rod and those which combine the sliding rod with some sort of leverwork and thus overcome this cocking problem.

The first of this sub-division is found as part of Thomas Perkes's patent, No. 1968 of 1878. This specification, which we will encounter at several other points, is one of the more important steps in the evolution of the British shotgun. While guns built exactly as the patent drawing are not common, its relatively early date means that its features reappear in the inventions of others. The part that concerns us at this point is the use of a rod, running diag-

*T. Perkes patent No. 1968 of 1878*

onally up from the bottom of the front of the knuckle to the breast of the tumbler, so that as the barrels pivot open the forend iron bears on the forward end of this rod to force it backwards to cock the tumbler. It is perhaps worthy of mention that despite selling this patent to Messrs. W. & C. Scott of Birmingham, the same cocking rods appear in later ejector patents obtained by Perkes (which we deal with later).

The idea of, what we may call, a simple rod cocker reappears in the unillustrated provisional patent, No. 649 of 1879 granted to Henry Tolley. This specification would seem to cover a gun very like the Hackett and Belcher (that we will come to shortly). Later in the same year we find George Gibbs and Thomas Pitt of Bristol obtaining patent No. 3297. The immediate point of interest about this patent is how alike in style is this gun to the much more common lever-cocked Gibbs and Pitt guns. This is a further illustration of the phenomenon of 'house styles', yet another dimension to the pleasure of studying nineteenth-century British shotguns.

The action of this Gibbs and Pitt gun is very simple. A rod for each lock protrudes from the knuckle of the action bar below the level of the hinge pin. Each cocking rod has a shoulder at its exposed end that the bottom of the forend iron bears upon so that, as the gun is opened, the cocking rods are forced back and their rear ends in turn force back the tumblers of the back-action sidelocks to full cock. So that these cocking rods shall not impede the fall of the tumblers, a light coil spring is fitted round the rod. This forces the rod forwards as the gun is closed out of the way of the tumbler.

A cocking rod exactly as above, but without the return spring, is found on one of the variants in the Henry Walker gun, patent No. 1872 of 1881. But the rod was not always used on these guns. (The usual pattern of this gun we will return to with our consideration of the classic Scott hammerless gun.)

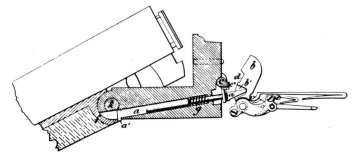

*G. Gibbs and T. Pitt patent No. 3297 of 1879*

*Underside of gun by J. Lang, built on patent No. 4916 of 1881 to show cocking piece*

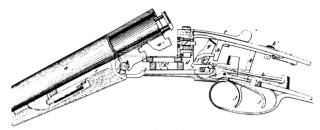

*J. Lang patent No. 4916 of 1881*

Still of the same general group, but rather different, is the sliding rod cocked gun described in James Lang's patent, No. 4916 of 1881. Typically for Lang guns of this era, it has a trigger plate action and the two-legged safety from earlier patents is also shown. On the insides of the tumblers, just above the pivot point, are two stout studs on which the cocking rod bears. This slides along the bottom of the action forced back by the bottom of the forend iron. At the rear end of the cocking slide is a stout hook-shaped upward projection. The inner curved surface of this hook acts on the studs on the tumblers and so cams back the tumblers as the slide moves to the rear. So that the cocking rod shall not impede the fall of the tumblers, another upward projection from it engages with the barrel-bolt and so the slide is carried forwards as the gun snaps shut.

One of the many problems that the vogue for ejector mechanisms created, and one which we will return to in Chapter Eleven, is that most of these designs added extra springs. All such springs needed to be compressed at some stage in the cycle of opening and closing a sporting gun. We suspect that this is the reason behind a patent granted to Thomas Perkes, who was very much a pioneer of ejector mechanisms, for hammerless guns that were cocked as the gun closed. In this patent, No. 3049 of 1883, the essence of the several designs drawn is that a rod is pushed back or drawn forwards by the closing of the gun and the lock is cocked before the gun is fully closed. The last few degrees of rotation of the barrels move the cocking rod a little further when an incline on the rod meets a suitable incline formed in the action and these two inclines, mating together, throw the cocking rod out of alignment with the tumbler and thus make it possible for the lock to fire. The

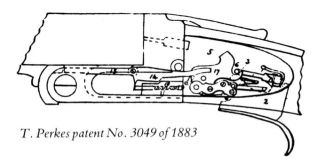

*T. Perkes patent No. 3049 of 1883*

patent shows no less than seven variations on this theme, some with coil springs to return the cocking rods to the rear to pick up the lockwork for the next time round.

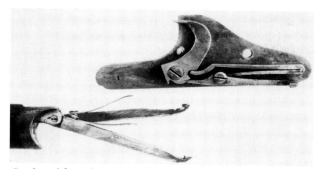

*Lock and forend with attached cocking levers from gun built on T. Keight patent No. 1657 of 1884*

Another rod cocker, but very different to the preceding designs, is found in the Thomas Keight patent, No. 1657 of 1884. This is of all the greater interest because he not only describes the mechanism that he has invented but tells us that what he had in mind was to enable a cheap hammerless gun to be produced. The search for mechanisms that were inexpensive to manufacture is a continuing theme in the history of the British shotgun. (The one example of this action that has come our way shows every possible sign of being a very low-priced product, but not at all to be despised on this account.) The most striking feature of the guns made in accordance with the drawing on Keight's patent is that they had pivoted cocking rods permanently fixed to the back of the forend iron. When the gun is taken apart, these two rods, which are about 4 inches long, are drawn like entrails from the knuckle of the action. Because the pivot point of the cocking rods is above that of the forend iron, as the barrels pivot down these rods are pulled forwards in the action. At their rear ends they have upward projecting hooks that engage with, and therefore pull forwards, the bottom of the fired tumblers. The lockwork of this gun betrays its cheap production, being reduced to an absolute minimum of parts with tumbler and striker made as one, as are the sear and mainsprings.

We alluded earlier to the George Hackett and Edward Belcher specification, No. 8851 of 1885. This may have been pre-empted by the Henry Tolley specification but whoever was the original inventor we now look on this system as one of some importance in the history of the sporting gun. What is drawn on the Hackett and Belcher specification is a gun with cocking rods extending from under the hinge pin back to the tumblers. Around these rods are fitted stout coil springs that are the mainsprings of the lock. The cocking rod is now hinged to the tumbler above the latter's pivot and the spring is compressed between a flange round the cocking rod, as the latter is forced back, and a shoulder in the action bar; so, when the sear releases the tumbler, the compressed coil spring forces the cocking rod forwards and pulls the tumbler with it. This system, and minor variants of it, have been re-invented and used many times. (Greener had a gun he called 'The Sovereign' that was like this but perhaps the most famous is the Winchester Model 21. At the time of writing the Winchester is the only high-quality side-by-side shotgun in production in the United States.)

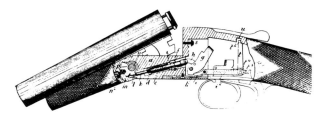

*G. Hackett and E. Belcher patent No. 8851 of 1885*

Another Henry Tolley design that, in its day, was well advertised and apparently made in some numbers was 'The Times' gun. It sold new for 8 guineas and was apparently a sound if not highly-finished gun. Embodied in this gun are two specifications, Nos. 2663 and 10,303, both of 1886 and both using the same slide cocking idea. Once again, the cocking slide is pushed back by the bottom of the forend iron, but there is only one central slide that travels along the outside bottom of the action bar. To the rear of this slide are hinged the two cocking rods proper that travel back and up through the action bar to the back-action sidelocks.

To preserve our sequence, we must here mention the patent, No. 12,402 of 1886, taken out by Edwin George Anson. This gun was cocked by a slide worked by the forend. However, this patent is really concerned with an ejector mechanism. (See Chapter Eleven.)

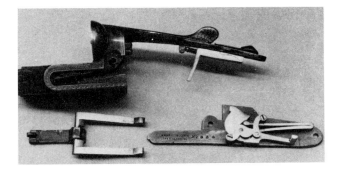

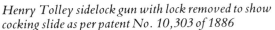

*Henry Tolley sidelock gun with lock removed to show cocking slide as per patent No. 10,303 of 1886*

We earlier discussed the problem of getting sufficient travel to a sliding rod and mentioned the solution of a rod and lever system. Bridging the gap between the rod and lever system and the simple sliding rod is another ingenious Scott design, patent No. 3859 of 1883. The patentees are Scott himself and Charles Proctor, gunmaker, of Handsworth, Staffordshire. To give greater travel to the cocking rods running up

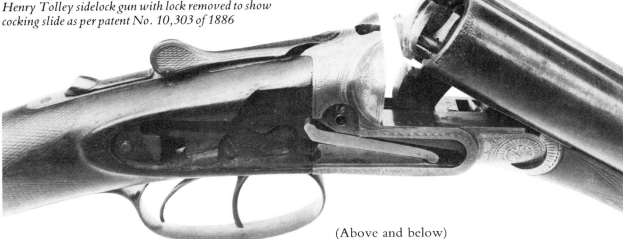

(Above and below)
*W. Scott and C. Proctor patent No. 3859 of 1883*

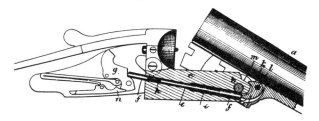

There is another barrel-cocker worked by a sliding rod in the action. This being part of an ejector specification, patent No. 19395 of 1890, in the name of John Ross. He was probably an outworker to the London gun trade as the specification records he was a 'gunmaker' of 26, Stewarts Road, Battersea. In this specification are a pair of horizontal rods pivoted on the tumblers. They run horizontally forwards to emerge from the knuckle as inclined faces that are forced back by the forend iron.

through the action bar, two cams are fitted in the rear of the forend iron. These cams ride over inclines, formed in the knuckle of the action bar, in such a way as to give the cocking rods an extra deep push through the action bar.

It is a remarkable feature of many of the inventors whose guns use slide and lever cocking systems that they are practically all, in their separate ways, famous gunmakers of the period. Fortunately, we can consider their inventions by patent date and are thus not required to devise any other order of precedence.

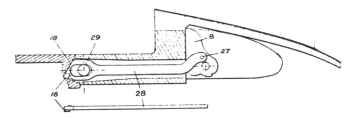

*Ross patent No. 19,395 of 1890*

Daniel Fraser of 18, Leith Walk, Edinburgh was probably better known as a rifle shot and rifle maker. He had been appreciated to Alexander Henry of 12, South Street, St Andrew's Street, Edinburgh and was, for most of his adult life, a member of The Queen's Edinburgh Rifle Volunteer Brigade and many times was a member of the Scottish Twenty. With regard to the gunmaking business that he carried on with his brother, the 9 December 1899 edition of *The Field* bore his declaration that: 'We will show our works in Easter Road and can submit convincing evidence that we produce all the weapons bearing our name from the raw material in every part.' On 13 December 1879 he obtained a patent, No. 5111, for a hammerless gun design. This had a slide, shown on his drawing on the outside of the bottom of the action bar, that was forced backwards by the bottom of the forend iron. The slide had, at its rear end, an upward sloping projection into the action where it worked the cocking mechanism. This latter consisted of two upright arms joined by their bottom ends by a transverse pivot so as to form a U-shape. In the middle of the pivot was a third, shorter, upright piece on which the slide works so that as the barrels opened the two cocking arms rotated backwards and so cocked the locks by bearing on the front of the

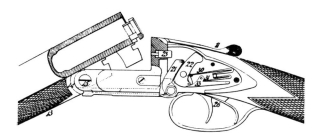

*D. Fraser patent No. 5111 of 1879*

tumblers. This motion was eased by the addition of an anti-friction roller on the top of each cocking arm.

Perhaps it is not by coincidence that just over a month later, on 23 January 1880, another Edinburgh gunmaker obtained a patent for a hammerless gun action that bears more than a passing resemblance to the preceding design. The patent, No. 294 of 1880, was granted to John Dickson (Tertius), grandson of the founder of this famous firm (and son of John Dickson, the younger) then in business at 63, Princes Street, Edinburgh. His mechanism has become famous as the basis of the 'Round Action' gun. It is a point to note that the original drawing shows a conventional back-action sidelock gun and not the trigger plate action we think of as the round action. (See Chapter Eight.)

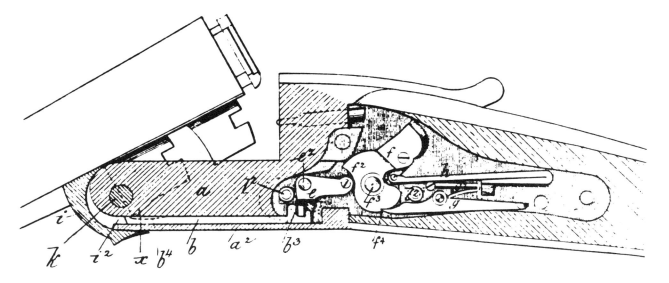

*J. Dickson patent No. 294 of 1880*

The Dickson cocking slide is worked by a downward projection of the front lump. This engages in a recess cut for it in the front of the wide slide that slides enclosed in the bottom of the action bar. The rear end of the slide opens out into a broad T-shape and each end of the cross-piece works a separate cocking lever. Essentially, each one of these is a right-angled triangle with the right-angle forwards and uppermost. At this point it is transversely pivoted and the bottom forward corner engages with the cocking slide so that, as the latter moves to the rear corner, the lever lifts the tumbler to full-cock.

While not famous in his own right, William Rogers was an employee of a renowned organisation, the Army and Navy Co-operative Society. At the date of his patent, 1882, this organisation was but eleven years old and owed its existence to the idea that by buying for cash its members could obtain high-quality merchandise of all sorts at a lower price than that offered by shops where the facility of extended credit was expected. ('The Army and Navy' was not in those days open to the general public but only to a membership governed by stringent rules. Those who were eligible for membership were in the broadest terms members of the Armed Forces and the Diplomatic Corps.)

It is probable that the gun department did not actually manufacture any of the guns, rifles, or pistols that the Co-operative sold. Repair and the alteration of members' guns was possibly offered, but all the evidence confirms that the shotguns were the products of the better class of Birmingham makers, who made for the trade, and of London outworkers, who made the very best Army and Navy guns.

So much for Rogers's employers. His gun, patent No. 3877, uses the opening motion of its barrels to work two levers pivoted on the same centre as the barrels. These levers, as his patent drawing and on the sole example of a mechanism that has come our way, are more in the nature of cheek pieces of the forward end of the bar and so the turning levers are not hidden inside the gun. To connect these turning levers to the lockwork there is a slide which has a hook on each end, the rearward one engaging with a

short leg on the bottom of the tumbler and the forward end hook fitting into the turning lever above the pivot. In this way, as the barrels and hence the cocking levers rotate, so the slide is drawn forwards and the lockwork cocked.

*Lock and action of gun built on W. Rogers action, patent No. 3877 of 1882*

In the same vein is the cocking mechanism proposed by Joseph Tonks of Malden, Massachusetts. His patent, No. 6673 of 1884, was obtained in Britain by the agent W. R. Lake. Two levers protrude from the knuckle of the action bar which are pivoted above the barrel pivot. The exposed ends of these levers engage with recesses cut in the back of the forend iron and so are turned as the barrels open. The bottom rear ends of the levers bear on rods sliding diagonally up through the action so that as the barrels pivot open the tumblers are pushed back to full-cock.

There are five more action patents that use this idea of the cranked lever to convert the

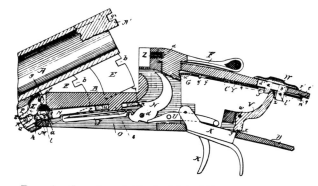

*Drawing from Joseph Tonks United States patent No. 333,795 of 1886, almost identical to British patent No. 6673 of 1884*

backward slide of a rod into a cocking motion of greater travel in the lockwork. Chronologically, the first patent, No. 2725 of 1886, is that in the name of William Palmer Jones of Bath Street, and Harry Alfred Smith of Whittall Street, both in Birmingham. The career of Jones is best left to his work with the try gun as this was certainly his greatest contribution to the sporting world. (See Chapter Thirteen.) The patent of 1886 uses a train of rod and levers to transmit the opening motion of the barrels back into the lockwork. From the knuckle emerge two short projections that engage with the forend iron so that as the barrels drop the projections rotate downwards. These cocking dogs are simply the exposed parts of two almost circular cams that rotate in the knuckle. Bearing on a flat on this cam is a horizontal rod that, in turn, bears on the bottom of a triangular lever hung at its top corner on a transverse pivot. The triangular shape is much exaggerated and the rear limb projects back into the lockwork, where the final corner lies under the toe of the tumbler. The latter is lifted to full-cock as the barrels open. The patent shows a flat spring fitted to the top of the cocking lever to ensure that it drops to permit the tumbler an uninterrupted fall.

The next patent on the same lines is that of William Ford. He was one of the foremost barrel-borers of Birmingham and founded a firm that still trades (1989). William Ford worked for a period in the Greener factory; a letter from Greener published in *Shooting Times* in 1886 infers that Ford learned his trade or at least sharpened his skill there. However, Ford came to the general notice of the sporting community as the aggrieved party in an unedifying public squabble and litigation with Lincoln Jeffries that was one sequel of *The Field* Trial in 1879.

The gun action covered by Ford's patent, No. 8841 of 1887, has a horizontally sliding rod, pushed back by a shoulder on the forend iron. The rear end of this rod, in turn, bears on the bottom of an L-shaped lever, pivoted at the top of its vertical limb so that the rearward thrust of the cocking rod is converted to an upward motion of the horizontal limb of the L. This, in turn, lifts the tumbler back to full-cock. (For illustration see Chapter Eleven.)

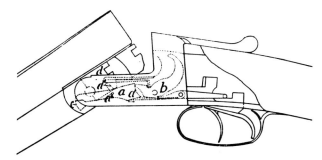

*W. Ford patent No. 2622 of 1888*

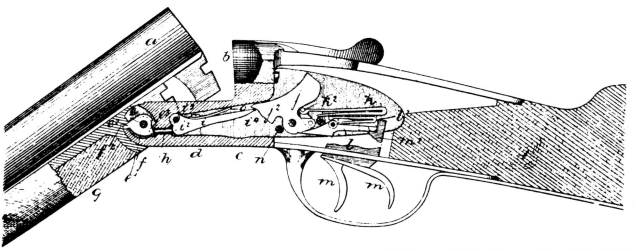

*W. Jones and H. Smith patent No. 2725 of 1886*

There is yet another Ford boxlock gun which might easily pass for an Anson and Deeley unless stripped. This patent, No. 2622 of 1888, shows emerging from the knuckle, two projections that could be mistaken for the cocking levers of an Anson and Deeley. But, unlike the latter, in this Ford design the cocking rods, as we must more accurately call them, slide back into the action as the gun opens. The rearward end of these cocking rods is an open C-shaped camming surface across which the toe of the tumbler, assisted by a friction-reducing roller, rides up so that the tumbler rotates backwards to cock. The patent of William Anson, No. 7274 of 1888, uses a layout similar to this but now the forend iron bears directly on the sliding rod and there is no return spring for the cocking lever.

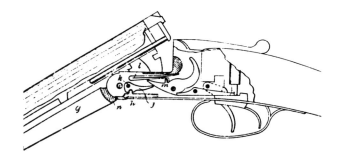

*J. Cox patent No. 6148 of 1889*

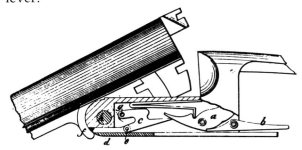

*W. Anson patent No. 7274 of 1888*

Yet another boxlock variant that conforms to this general sub-section is to be found tucked away in Job Cox's specification, No. 6148 of 1889. A slide on the bottom of the knuckle is pushed back by the forend iron and an upward projection from this slide is keyed into the bottom of a rocking lever below and behind its pivot so that, as the slide moves back, so the rear of the lever rises to lift the tumblers.

Reverting to our chronological sequence lends us to the important Greener patent, No. 930 of 1880. The patent is widely known from both Greener's writings and those of other contemporary authors, who, in many cases, used his engravings to illustrate their works. In addition, and probably in large part because of this publicity, Greener guns using this action, which was known as the 'Facile Princeps' (Easily the Chief), are fairly commonly met with.

*W. W. Greener's 'Facile Princeps' gun*

The importance of this gun lies in the fact that it precipitated legal action between the patentee and Robert Edward Couchman, who was a director of Westley Richards & Co. and a close friend of Westley Richards himself. Greener had taken out a licence on 24 May 1877 from Couchman to build sporting guns and double-rifles on the Anson and Deeley plan. Under the terms of this licence Greener agreed to pay a royalty of 15 shillings per gun or double-rifle, to render accounts of the numbers of such made and to submit his product for inspection and marking by the patent owner or his agent. Couchman's claim was that Greener's Facile Princeps action infringed the Anson and Deeley patent. He claimed £5,000 damages and, in addition, 15 shillings per Facile Princeps gun. In this attempt Couchman utterly failed, despite pursuing his case to the House of Lords, where he had the Attorney-General, Sir H. James, Q.C., M.P., plus a second Queen's Counsel, Mr Aston, appearing for him in addition to sundry other legal men.

To understand the basis for this judgement we have to look at the patent and compare it with the Anson and Deeley patent, No. 1756 of 1875. Greener's design used a sliding rod in the lower part of the front lump which was held to the rear by a backward projection from the forend iron. The tumblers of the Greener gun were, in side view, not unlike those of the Anson and Deeley. But, when seen from the bottom, they curved inwards in a pigeon-toed fashion so that both could be lifted by the single cocking stud which was the rear end of the sliding rod in later models. Earlier ones used a swivel catch pivoted on the forend lump and pushed back by the sliding rod.

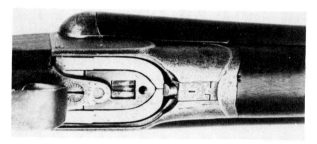

*W. W. Greener 'Facile Princeps' gun with bottom plate removed*

The House of Lords ruled that the two patents different fundamentally because, whereas the forend was essential to the working of the Anson and Deeley, it was merely desirable in the case of the Greener. On this point Couchman's case was dismissed. Greener was awarded costs, as had happened at the two previous hearings, so the total bill for Westley Richards & Co. must have been considerable.

These costs are merely a reflection on the vigour with which the case was pursued and are an indication of the richness of the prize that was sought, to wit a virtual master patent on the concept of using the fall of the barrels to cock the action. Greener had attempted to counter Couchman's claim by citing the Walsh self-cocking hammer gun of 1866 and the Needham action of 1874, but this tack was ruled inadmissable in that by taking out a licence he had accepted the goodness of the Anson and Deeley patent. In the event he won because his gun,

inspired though it might have been by the previous invention, differed sufficiently from it.

This whole affair has more than a passing resemblance to the Daw versus Eley litigation of 1864. In both cases an attempt was made to convert a patent for a particular idea into a valuable master patent on a general principle. In both instances the threat of litigation was sufficient to preserve the spurious master patent for a while but both ultimately came to grief when a challenger appeared who was rich enough to call the bluff. There can be no doubt that both Eley and Greener reaped just rewards for their successful challenges but they also benefited the whole of the trade by freeing it from unnecessary restraints.

Two other patents, neither as important as the Greener, but more intelligible can be considered at this point. Patent No. 4516 of 1882 is another granted to Greener for a different swivel catch on the front lump and this can usefully be thought of as a variant of the Facile Princeps. What sounds very like the latter mechanism is the subject of a note in the 'Abridgements of Patent Specifications, Class 119, Firearms', when in fact the actual patent specifications list No. 1576 of 1889 as 'Abandoned'. In the abridgements, which are thus our sole knowledge of this mechanism, the patentee is listed as 'H. Greener', possibly Henry Greener, William Wellington Greener's older brother.

Also very like the Facile Princeps is the cocking part of a patent, No. 17,792 of 1887, obtained for the dentist Robert Hampton, of Athens, Georgia, by the agent, A. J. Boult. Here again the tumblers are rotated by a swing catch on the barrel lump.

A sub-division of our present subject consists of those hammerless actions that harness the motion of the front lump, as the barrels pivot open to cock the lockwork in some way. Of these designs the most numerous are those that use an extension of the barrel-locking bolt as the cocking piece which is, of course, the essence of the Gibbs and Pitt lever-cocked system. Bearing this fact in mind, Greener's claim to have originated this group with his patent No. 1623 of 1877 is less than impressive. All that is added to the Gibbs and Pitt mechanism is a cam on the

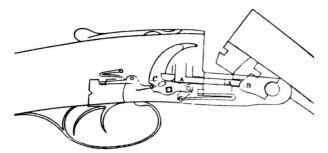

*W. W. Greener patent No. 1623 of 1887*

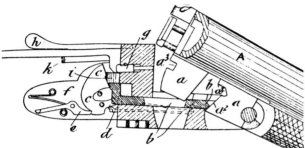

*R. Chaplain patent No. 4251 of 1886*

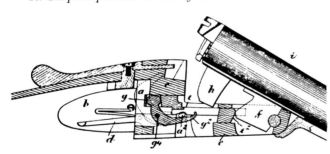

*E. James patent No. 4187 of 1882*

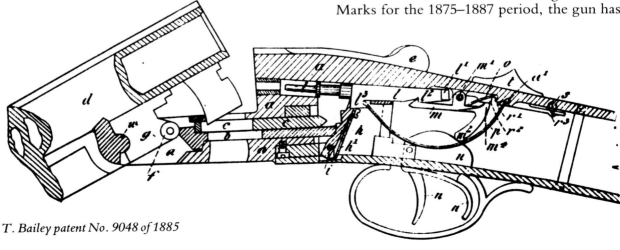

*T. Bailey patent No. 9048 of 1885*

rear of the front lump which forces back the Purdey-bolt as the gun opens. Nevertheless, this same idea with minor variations is to be found on five more patents of our period. First in line is that of Henry Hammond and Edwin Hammond. Their patent, No. 2886 of 1878, is but a provisional specification and therefore has no drawing. The John Williams patent, No. 2061 of 1882, has an incline on either side of the front lump that forces back a sliding cocking piece – the gun being drawn as a single barrel. While the Enos James patent, No. 4187 of 1882, uses the backwards motion of the bolt to work an intermediate cocking lever. This action can usefully be regarded as a barrel-cocked version of his earlier barrel-cocked action, No. 2531 of 1881. The gun drawn in Thomas Bailey's patent, No. 9048 of 1885, also uses the bolt motion, with the addition of a friction-reducing roller in the rear of the front lump. The novelty of this design is in the actual lockwork which is built on a stout top strap and uses what is a leaf spring powered bolt held back by a hook-like sear. The final patent in this group, No. 4251 of 1886, is that of Robert Chaplain, who gives his Birmingham address as 29½, Whittall Street.

To further complicate this point, and to bridge the seemingly finite division between barrel- and lever-cocked hammerless guns, there is a gun in the present author's (DJB) collection. Marked externally 'Geo. H. Daw & Co., 57, Threadneedle Street, London', but having the Gibbs and Pitt lozenge-shaped stamp on the action flats and Birmingham Proof Marks for the 1875–1887 period, the gun has a

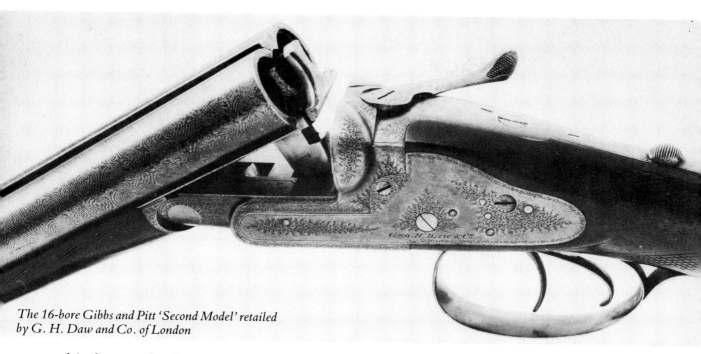

*The 16-bore Gibbs and Pitt 'Second Model' retailed by G. H. Daw and Co. of London*

rearward incline on the front lump. This will force back the barrel-bolt and cock the locks as the gun is opened. In addition, the top lever will perform the same office. In actual use what happens is that the effort of cocking the locks is divided between the user's two hands and makes for a very pleasant gun to use. In a second model Gibbs and Pitt gun examined, while there is a small incline on the rear of the front lump, the mechanism is so arranged that the locks are cocked before the barrels can be opened and all that the barrels can contribute is a slight help to the final motion of the barrel-bolt.

The rest of the guns in this sub-group are a more varied collection. Again, they are best

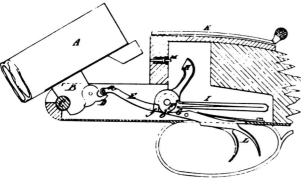

*J. Lang patent No. 545 of 1878*

considered in chronological order. On this scheme we encounter first the James Lang patent, No. 545 of 1878. Dr Walsh describes the version that cocks off the rear lump as 'Lang's Hammerless Gun No. 1'. On the patent specification is shown a lever, pivoted on the same centre as the tumbler that extends forwards to the front lump, which lifts and rotates the tumbler backwards as the gun opens and thus cocks the action.

A gun bearing a very close resemblance to the Lang is part of Thomas Perkes's patent, No. 1968 of 1878. Then at No. 4, Cleveland Street, Fitzroy Square, London, Perkes protected a gun that simply had forwards-extended toes on its tumblers; these were lifted by a rearward projection from the front lump. Greener notices this design and points out that, if the locks of this gun are tripped without the barrels in place, a special tool is necessary to recock them before the gun can be assembled – a feature that could in some circumstances be infuriating but in others be very valuable.

Very similar in principle to this is the Samuel Mills action, patent No. 4980 of 1878. Again, we have a tumbler and cocking lever on a common centre, the only real difference being that the barrel lump is solely used to work this

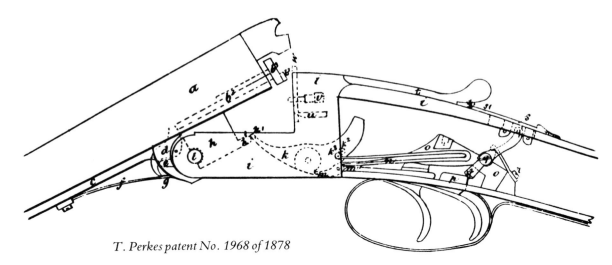

*T. Perkes patent No. 1968 of 1878*

lever and the barrel-locking is taken over by a doll's-head top extension with a bite into it. In its turn similar to the Mills is the John Field Swinburn patent, No. 145 of 1883. This design, too, has a cocking lever on the same centre as the tumblers, lifted by the rear of the lump as the barrels open. As drawn, this latter looks, externally, very like an Anson and Deeley and is, thus, yet another example of an uncommon gun that might be mistaken for a standard type on cursory examination.

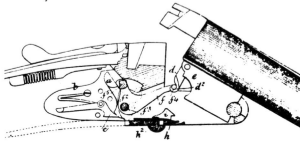

*S. Mills patent No. 4980 of 1878*

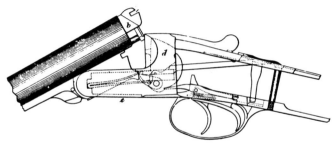

*J. Swinburn patent No. 145 of 1883*

To conclude this sub-section, we are left with three designs that resemble nothing so far considered and whose inventors are representative of the range of people who invented sporting gun actions in the last century.

In 1882, John Robertson was one of the highly-skilled outworkers so essential to the gun trade of London. From his workshop in George Yard, Wardour Street, Soho, emerged guns, 'stocked and screwed', of the highest quality that were to win for his customers, such as Grant, Lang and Holland, gold medals and awards that were a feature of Victorian exhibitions. After 1890, and so not part of this volume, John Robertson was to own the firm of Boss & Co. and it is in this later period that his most important contributions were made.

John Robertson's patent, No. 2833 of 1882, is concerned in the main with safety catches for the Anson and Deeley boxlock, but the specification also contains a hammerless action cocked by the front lump. This is arranged by having in the front lump a cam that, as the barrels pivot open, draws forwards two studs that project into the slot in the action bar. These studs are the forward ends of two cocking rods that, as they move forwards, pull on the bottom of the tumblers and rotate them to full-cock. Around this cocking rod is a spiral spring which acts as a mainspring and is compressed against a stop on the lockplate as the gun opens. This is very reminiscent of the earlier Scott design that we shall consider presently.

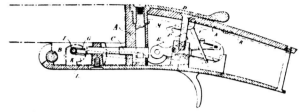

*J. Robertson patent No. 2833 of 1882*

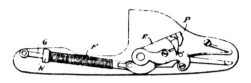

*J. Robertson detached lock, patent No. 2833 of 1882*

Just as the Robertson design harks back to the Scott then that of Joseph Samuel Pinder has something in common with the Murcott design of thirteen years before. On 1 January 1884, as patent No. 154, Pinder, who was a 'Lawn Tennis Outfitter' of 21, The Pavement, Lordship Lane, Dulwich, obtained protection of an idea for using the opening motion of the barrels to cock the lockwork. Probably this is best explained by likening it to a rod or link from the front lump that runs diagonally back through the action to the bottom of a shortened Murcott lever; as the barrels are opened the bottom of this lever is drawn forwards when the top of it forces back the tumblers to full-cock.

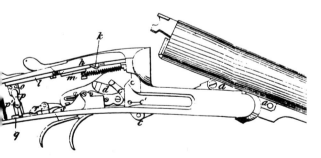

*J. Pinder patent No. 154 of 1884*

Another idea to harness the motion of the front lump is contained in patent No. 13,199 of 1884. The idea was something like the Robertson and the patent was obtained in Britain by the agent William Lake who was, in this instance, acting for Dresse Laloux et Cie of Liège. The cocking levers are pivoted at their forward ends on the same centre as the barrels and are lifted by projections that are picked up by two cam-shaped slots, one on each side of the front lump. The lockwork on this gun is a simplified back action side-lock that uses one spring for both sear and mainspring.

We now gather together yet another class of barrel-cocked hammerless guns, those in which the lockwork is linked to the rear lump.

From a designer's or inventor's point of view, the attraction of the rear lump as the source of the necessary force and motion to cock the lockwork of a sporting gun must lie in the fact that the lump is in close proximity to the lockwork and, at the same time, moves through a conveniently larger arc. Having said that, the fact remains that, while examples of some of the dozen patents that comprise this group are known, only one ever came near to rivalling the production figures of the Anson and Deeley boxlock or the Scott or Rogers sidelocks. The importance of this group lies in the fact that to it belongs the Needham design with which we opened this chapter. Normally, we would have followed this with a consideration of other actions that shared the same characteristic. However, we adopt a chronological sequence so that we describe early in the chapter the Anson and Deeley boxlock so as to further emphasise the towering importance of this Westley Richards action.

Now, having covered the Facile Princeps and those like it we must come back to the guns that cock off the rear lump. Closer study of these reveals that they fall naturally into two groups: the first (and smaller) consists of those guns in which the tumbler is lifted to full-cock directly by the rear lump; the second (and more numerous) uses an intermediate lever to convey the motion.

After the Needham the next of the directly-cocked guns patented was No. 950 of 1878. This was granted to Lionel Gye of 60, St. James's Street, London. The feature that is immediately noticeable on this gun is the protrusion in front of the trigger guard. This is necessary to house the downward extension of the rear lump that is the basis of this system. The lockwork is built on the trigger plate and each tumbler has a forward-facing limb that projects into the bulge on the underside of the action. On each side of the rear lump are pivoted transverse projections that slip under the tumblers and raise them to full-cock as the barrels open. Dr Walsh, in *The Modern Sportsman's Gun and Rifle*, tells us that production of Gye's gun ceased under threat of legal action from the Westley Richards firm, who claimed that it infringed their Anson and Deeley patent.

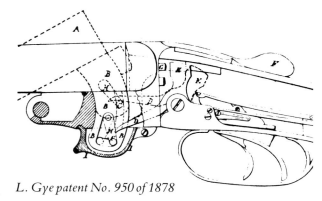

*L. Gye patent No. 950 of 1878*

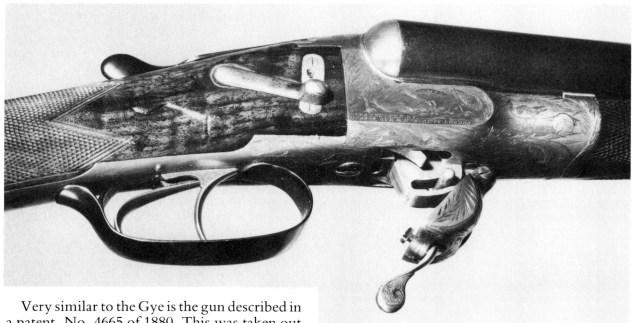

Very similar to the Gye is the gun described in a patent, No. 4665 of 1880. This was taken out by William Lake, once again for an inventor based in the United States. The inventor was David Kirkwood. In 1872 he emigrated to the United States where he set up in business in Boston with Henry Mortimer who was the son of Thomas Elsworth Mortimer. Kirkwood had been apprenticed to the latter in his home city of Edinburgh. Kirkwood's obituary, printed in the New York journal *Shooting and Fishing* in 1897, recorded that he was a fine rifle shot and deeply interested in all aspects of guns and shooting. Kirkwood before his death, assembled what was then considered to be the finest library of books on gunnery in the United States.

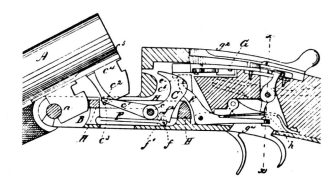

*W. Lake (agent for D. Kirkwood) patent No. 4665 of 1880*

The only real difference between Kirkwood's gun and the Gye is that the parts are so shaped that the bulbous and unsightly projection ahead of the trigger guard is eliminated.

Both of these guns used the barrel lumps to hold the barrels on face as well as cocking the action. In contrast, our next design uses the barrel lump as the pivot for the barrels, and to cock the action, but has a species of top extension to hold the barrels on face. This patent, No. 525 of 1881, is in the name of James Field Swinburn. He was a prominent Birmingham gunmaker with premises at 16 and 17, Russell Street. Perhaps the greatest claim to fame of Swinburn's company lies in the fact that it was the principal manufacturer of double-barrel, Jacob-pattern, muzzle-loading rifles. The Swinburn patent covers more than one design but the one that concerns us at this point can perhaps best be described as having tumblers like those of an Anson and Deeley boxlock, but with internal projections on their toes upon which the curved rear of the lump bears to lift them to full-cock.

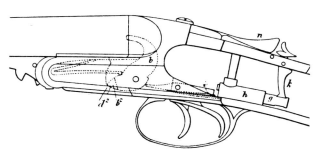

*J. Swinburn patent No. 525 of 1881*

The second group into which our present sub-division falls are those that use an intermediate lever to cock the action. The first of these patented is the design of James Lang of the firm of Joseph Lang. In his patent, No. 545 of 1878, he protected the idea of an L-shaped lever, pivoted at its angle on the same centre as the tumblers with its longer limb projecting forwards. This was lifted by a hook on the rear lump so that the shorter limb carried the heads of the tumblers back to cock. Again, Dr Walsh tells us that the Westley Richards firm were able

to persuade Langs, under the threat of litigation, to cease production of this model. Langs therefore turned to the underlever cocked gun described earlier. (See Chapter One.)

This same idea with minor modifications is also shown on James Lang's patent, No. 133 of 1879, when he also patented a safety system.

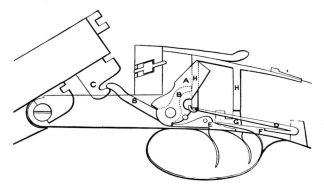

*J. Lang patent No. 133 of 1879*

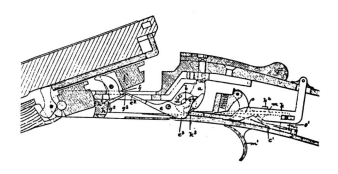

*C. G. Bonehill patent No. 2323 of 1878*

A very similar design to the Lang, though not smothered by threats from Westley Richards, patented as No. 2323 was that granted to Christopher George Bonehill. From what we know of him, we doubt if Bonehill would be easily frightened off and, moreover, he had the resources to conduct a legal action of considerable length if required to do so. In fact this patent, No. 2323 of 1878 formed the basis of one version of the 'Bonehill Interchangeable'. The latter, one of the most extensively-produced guns of the era, was almost totally made by machine and sold, by vitrue of its low cost and good reputation, in considerable numbers.

*C. G. Bonehill advertisement of 1887*

The C. G. Bonehill patent, No. 8471 of 1884, shows the cocking lever pivoted on the same pivot as the tumblers. There is, however, another very similar Bonehill patent gun, shown, but not claimed, in patent No. 7823 of 1888. Both of these actions have a hook on the bottom of the rear lump that lifts the cocking lever.

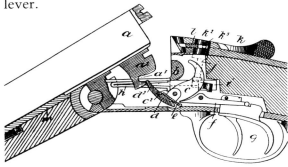

*C. G. Bonehill patent No. 8471 of 1884*

In the records of the Patent Office are superb drawings of gun actions previously unknown to us. In a sense these are, therefore, new guns. One of them is the ingenious action covered by a patent, No. 3929 of 1878, granted to Joseph Mathews who tells us that he was a gun action maker of Birmingham. Part of his specification concerns us at this point because, included in it, is a design for a hammerless gun that cocks as the barrels are opened, with the cocking mechanism linked to the rear lump. Instead of a directly-linked lever, a turning turret is set in the bottom of the gun behind the action face which perhaps can best be visualised by likening it to the locking turret of a Henry Jones screw-grip action gun. In the Mathews turret are cut two helical grooves and, in one of these, a stud projecting from the rear lump slides and so turns the turret as the gun is opened. In a second groove, in the rear of the turret, is the forward end of an L-shaped lever which is raised as the turret turns. Since the lever is pivoted on a cross-ways pivot at its angle, which it shares with the tumblers, raising the forward end pushes back the upright limb and it is this that raises the tumblers.

This is perhaps the most unusual action of the several that are included on the specification.

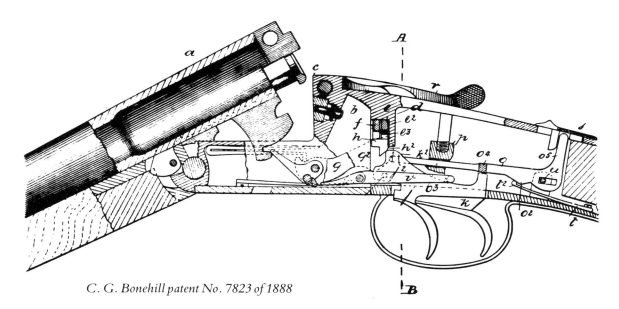

*C. G. Bonehill patent No. 7823 of 1888*

The one that may well have been thought more important, since it is the first claim to be made, is a much more conventional design in which the forward limb of the L-shaped cocking lever is lifted directly by the rear lump.

There is also some background information recorded on the next member of this sub-group which we know as the patent of Richard Ellis, gunmaker, and Henry Scott, gunlock and action-filer, both of Birmingham. The patent No. is 2816 of 1879. However, some three years later this same design was patented in the United States as No. 252,703 of 1882 in the name of Henry Scott only, with the note that it had been assigned to John P. Clabrough, whose career we noted earlier. The likelihood is that this gun was marketed for a period in Britain before the design was bought by Clabrough. This is certainly suggested by the existence of a gun in the authors' (DJB) collection, found in poor condition, bearing the stamp 'RE & Co. Patent 2816' and externally marked 'I. Hollis & Sons, London', but undoubtedly made in Birmingham, probably by the firm of Richard Ellis at 13, St. Mary's Row. Incidentally, this firm was later taken over along with W. & C. Scott and Sons by the famous P. Webley and Son to become the Webley and Scott Revolver and Arms Co. Ltd.

*A detached lock, the cocking piece and the action of a 16-bore gun by I. Hollis of Birmingham. Built on R. Ellis and H. Scott patent No. 2816 of 1879*

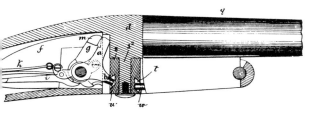

*J. Mathews patent No. 3929 of 1878*

The cocking levers of this action are pivoted under the breech face and are keyed onto a spindle that also carries a forward-facing lever. This is raised by the hook on the bottom of the rear lump as the barrels pivot open; the shoulders on the cocking levers force back the tumblers by acting on the shoulders formed on the inside of the tumblers.

Very similar in principle is the John Rogers patent, No. 2879 of 1879. Again we have an L-shaped lever that is lifted, in this case, by a sort of middle lump. The drawing shows what appears to be a trigger plate action.

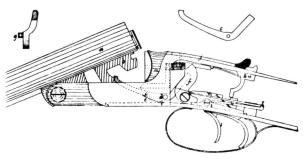

*J. Rogers patent No. 2879 of 1879*

Of minor importance in the context of the evolution of the British gun is a patent obtained by the agent Henry Harris Lake for Henry Allender of Detroit. This patent was for yet another mechanism using a lifting lever pivoted on the same centre as the tumblers and worked by the rear barrel lump. The greater interest of this patent, No. 10,903 of 1884, is that it also contains a single-trigger mechanism.

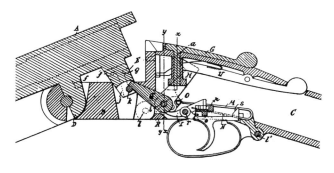

*H. H. Lake (agent for H. Allender) patent No. 10,903 of 1884*

Widely advertised in the sporting press of the day, and with a distinctive external appearance, William Tranter's gun was produced in quantity and today specimens are seen with fair regularity. With his patent, No. 1881 of 1882, Tranter, by this date a successful and prolific gun manufacturer with extensive premises on Lichfield Road, Birmingham, protected a somewhat complex but ingenious and interesting gun action and safety. Early the following year advertisements began to appear in *The Field* and elsewhere for 'The Carlton', offered for sale by Tranter's son-in-law, T. W. Watson, of 4, Pall Mall, London.

---

# THE CARLTON,
## A NEW
## HAMMERLESS GUN.

T. W. WATSON has the privilege of submitting this New Gun to the Public, and desires to call especial attention to the ease with which it is opened and closed. By a simple mechanical arrangement one half of the cocking is done when opening, the other half when closing, by which division both are rendered imperceptible, and the wear and strain similarly reduced. The safety is a new one, which by one movement bolts by a single piece the tumblers and the triggers, and the sear each having a separate fixing.

# T. W. WATSON,
## 4, PALL MALL, S.W.

---

*T. W. Watson's advertisement of 1883*

The mechanism of the Carlton can perhaps be best visualised if we liken the cocking lever to a continental figure 7, lying on its back with a pivot at the point that was its top angle and what was the upright limb pointing forwards. This forward limb is worked by a hook under the rear lump and, as the barrels open, the tumblers are lifted to full-cock (as is the way with the other guns in this section). The V-mainspring lies forwards in the gun, analogous to a bar-action lock, and the bottom limb is connected via a swivel so that, as the tumbler is cocked, so the bottom limb of the spring is raised and thus cramped. Then, as the barrels close, the bottom of the rear lump pushes down on the cocking lever and the second upright pulls down the top limb of the mainspring to complete the tensioning. It is the space required by this ingenious cocking lever that results in the distinctive 'box' that protrudes from these guns forward of the trigger guard. We wondered if this division of labour would be apparent as the gun is opened and closed but even being aware of what is going on inside, no trace of the 'double action' can be felt as the gun is manipulated.

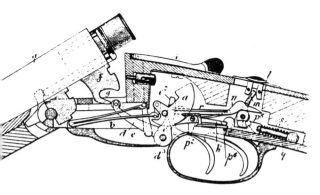

*W. Tranter patent No. 1881 of 1882*

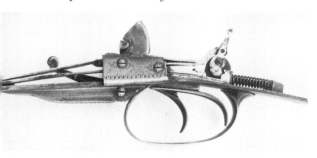

*Lockwork of gun built on W. Tranter patent No. 1881 of 1882*

It is a feature of this history that through the patents we can see how an inventor worked out more than one realisation of an idea. So it was that the Carlton was preceded in the patents by another William Tranter design, provisional patent No. 5395 of 1881. While this provisional patent is unillustrated we can understand the design better than many such because the description is more precise than many others: a gun that has a cocking piece shaped like a T, in which

the vertical stem lies in the action slot and is bent upwards in an arc. The forward end of the cocking piece is lifted by a hook on the rear lump so that the tumblers are cocked as the barrels open. The ingenious twist is that, as the barrels close, the rear lump now bears down on the stem of the T, both to move the cross-piece to permit the tumblers to fall and also to further compress the mainsprings, the top limbs of which are connected by links to the cocking lever.

Another similarity with the Carlton is the fact that this gun was to have a trigger plate action.

We suspect, but now will never know, that there were other variants of this idea. However, in 1885, Tranter, who was by then 69 years old, retired from active business and his premises were leased to George Kynoch and became known as 'The Kynoch Gun Factory'. Under this new regime production or assembly of the Carlton continued, which explains the existence of specimens marked 'Kynoch Gun Factory'. This organisation only lasted about five years and then it is believed that production of the gun ceased at the Lichfield Road Works. Watson's either arranged for fresh production or, much more likely, had stock in hand which they continued to advertise. (We believe that one of these guns was used in the testing department of the Kynoch Cartridge Factory for we have found a note indicating that after 100,000 rounds the original Tranter steel barrels were replaced by a set made of Bonehill 'three-bell' steel.)

Less distinctive than the Carlton but, we suspect, a well-used mechanism, is another part of David Bentley's and William Baker's patent, No. 5292 of 1883. This follows the general pattern of our sub-section, but with a straighter lever than some of the others. The only slightly-angled cocking lever is pivoted just under the breech face and acts on the conventional lockwork via a cross-piece, so that in plan view the lever is a T. Two interesting guns have come our way. Though unmarked we believe they both used this system: the first, a semi-hammerless gun using Bentley's patent, No. 17,037 of 1884; the other gun is a true hammerless but engraved 'Army & Navy Company Stores Ltd.'

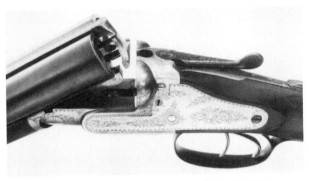

*D. Bentley and W. Baker patent No. 5292 of 1883, here used on gun by Chas. Osborne and Co.*

*D. Bentley and W. Baker patent No. 5292 of 1883*

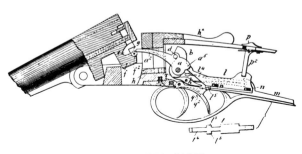

*L. Neuman patent No. 16,278 of 1888*

gunmakers in the United States. The Baker, the Lefever and the Savage/Stevens/Fox guns produced in vast quantities by The Savage Arms Corporation of West Field, Massachusetts, have all used the idea of a cocking lever worked by the rear barrel lump. So we must regard this idea as one of the classic mechanisms of the double-barrel hammerless sporting shotgun.

We have already noted the unevenness of William Wellington Greener's coverage of gun actions of this era. In earlier editions of *The Gun and its Development*, Greener includes a somewhat sarcastic description of a gun that we know of as a patent, No. 1065 of 1879, obtained by Morton Wall Parsons. Greener describes this inventor as a 'country gentleman'. Parsons quotes no profession on his patent specification, but gives his address as Brownsover, Warwick. However, from *The Gun and its Development* we gather the crumb of information that this gun was commercially produced by 'Messrs. Tolley' but, unfortunately, we are not told which of the two Tolley firms then in business in Birmingham was involved!

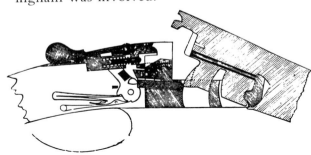

*W. Parsons patent No. 1065 of 1879*

The final member of this group is a more distinctive design patent by Lambert Neuman of Neuman Frères, Liège, as No. 16,278 of 1888. Here again we have a trigger plate action and the lever and tumbler pivoted on the same axle, but the cocking lever arcs forwards into a slot or hook in the top of the rear lump. This lever lifts the tumbler by means of a stud that picks up the head of the tumbler.

To conclude this sub-section we feel it is relevant to point out that the idea we have been describing has been extensively used by

The reason for Greener's tone is that he felt the Parsons gun used the same mode of cocking as was contained in his, Greener's, earlier patent, No. 1623 of 1877. This was marketed as 'The Club' gun, but the point of this thrust against the Patent Laws is somewhat blunted by the realisation that his own gun had itself been anticipated by the Gibbs and Pitt patent of 1874. In fact we are here at one of those points where the distinction between the barrel-cocked hammerless and those lever-cocked guns that use the barrel-locking bolt as the cocking slide come

to full-cock is as before but, because the tube and mainspring slide, the latter is not cocked as the gun is opened. In fact the cocking rod does not project from the end of the spring tube. It is the end of the tube that is hinged to the short internal lever, and the cam that the barrels turn is so shaped that, as the barrels close, the spring tube is drawn forward. In so doing, the mainspring is compressed, this time between a plunger on the forward end of the cocking rod and a shoulder on the rear end of the cocking tube.

The Scott patent, No. 5564 of 1884, differs from the preceding designs in that it specifies a mechanism for one lock only (the right one on the patent). What is shown is a cocking rod that runs forward from a projection on the tumbler to emerge at the top of the knuckle. Round this rod is a light coil spring which pushes it forward. The front end of the rod is partially cut away so that, in side view, it is missing its bottom half. On the remaining half bears the top limb of a lever that in side view is a U-shape, lying on its side with the upper limb longer than the lower. The whole is hung on a transverse pivot at its curved portion. The top limb of this lever is cut away on its top side. As the barrels close, the bottom of the top limb of the U-shaped lever bears on the front of the cocking rod and the lock cocks just before the gun shuts. At this point the lower limb engages with a stop on the knuckle which prevents it rotating further. Thus, the top limb of the U slips out of engagement with the cocking rod. The latter is then propelled forward by its coil spring out of

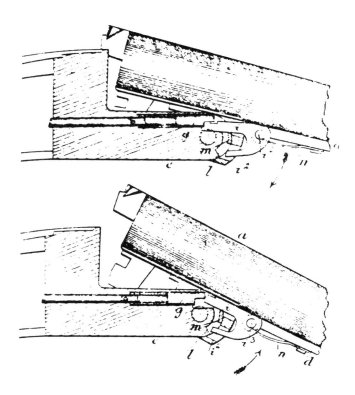

*The right-hand lockwork of W. M. Scott's patent No. 5564 of 1884*

the way of the tumbler and over the cut-away end of the U-shaped lever.

The foregoing represent those gun actions that use the motion of the barrels to cock their lockwork, with the exception of those that transmit this energy to the lockwork by some sort of spring. These we have abstracted to form a distinct chapter which follows directly.

# CHAPTER FIVE

# The Spring-cocked Hammerless Gun

The term 'spring-cocked' is strange to many enthusiasts. For our purposes it is useful, not least in that it enables us to hive off a manageable sub-group. We define 'spring-cocked' as a gun in which it is a spring, usually the mainspring of the lock, that raises the tumbler to full-cock. Essentially, there are two styles of this type of lock. The truest interpretations of the term 'spring-cocker' are those in which some of the energy stored in the spring is used to cock the lock. The other basic division of this class is comprised of those mechanisms that use the spring as a lever. We have included both forms in this chapter and would remark, as always, that the divisions formed are, to a degree, arbitrary and designs will be found that mingle the characteristics of both groups.

The credit for the first patent for a spring-cocked gun belongs to Henry Tolley. With his patent, No. 461 of 1877, he poses for us a minor dilemma as it is drawn as a spring-cocked external hammer gun. We feel, therefore, that it is more logical to place it with the other self-cocking hammer guns. (See Chapter Three.)

Returning to hammerless designs, we find that the first, in order of patent date, is a gun that uses the energy stored in the spring to cock the lock and also is the most famous and successful of the type. Not only this, its inventor was to be responsible, at least in part, for three of the patents that are covered in this chapter. We refer, of course, to Frederick Beesley and his patent, No. 31 of 1880, which has been made for just over 100 years by Messrs Purdey as their best-grade gun and rifle action. The prestige and importance of this patent are thus beyond question. In the period of its use it has been made in every standard calibre, from .410 up to 4-bore, of shotgun as well as seeing extensive service as a rifle action. Even more remarkable is the fact that, since its adoption, with the exception of the under-and-over guns, no other action has been used for a Purdey hammerless best shotgun. It was not, however, the first hammerless action that Purdey's used. There

are, for example, surviving examples of Gibbs and Pitt hammerless top lever guns built to the very highest standards.

So much for the actual use made of this action, what of the original patent specification? At first sight this looks complex, but the dozen or so drawings on it are all concerned with variations on the basic idea of using one limb of a V-mainspring to rotate the tumbler as the lock is fired. The other limb of the V is to cock the lockwork as the gun is opened and this same limb is to be acted upon by a slide or lever as the gun is closed, so that the spring is again put in compression ready to repeat the cycle. Curiously the action that Messrs Purdey actually use is the last one in the patent; normally the first claim is the more important mechanism. In this variant two cams are pivoted on the cross-pin. The upper surfaces of these cams are flat and abut onto the undersides of the barrels. The rear faces are curved and act on two sliding rods, one for each lock, that lie just under the action flats. At their rearward ends the sliding rods, via a short vertical lever, act on the top limb of the mainspring forcing it down into a state of compression as the gun is closed. The energy so stored in the mainspring can either rotate the tumbler or (if the lock is not tripped but instead the barrel-locking mechanism is operated) will reverse the cramping sequence just described and actively force open the barrels. So this

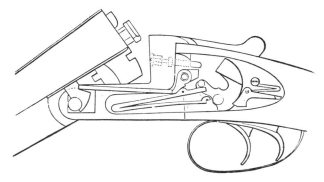

*F. Beesley's patent No. 31 of 1880, as used on the guns of James Purdey and Sons*

action is self-opening if either or both locks have not been fired and, even if they have, because the mainsprings retain a degree of compression.

Important as this action is in the context of its use by Purdey's, for its inventor it had another significance. We are told by Frederick Beesley's grand-daughters that it was the sale of this patent to Purdey's which helped their grand-father over a difficult patch early in his business career at 22, Queen Street, Edgware Road. His business appears to have prospered for he moved first to No. 85, Edgware Road and thence to 2, St James's Street, Pall Mall in the West End of London.

*Frederick Beesley in the doorway of his premises at No. 2, St James's Street, London*

We feel it likely that the freedom conferred by being his own master may have, in part, contributed to the series of important inventions that were to follow and which were to make Frederick Beesley a sort of unofficial 'inventor to the London Trade'. It is unfortunate that his

career has not been recorded in more detail. However, it is fascinating to speculate how an Oxfordshire farmer's son from Model Farm, Hampton Poyle came to be apprenticed at 15 years of age, with the firm of William Moore and Grey of Old Bond Street. When he went there, William Grey, Joseph Manton's old manager was still alive and so he would have been working with men who had known the Manton brothers. We can only imagine the stories that he was told as a lad, but these must have imbued him with a deep appreciation of the aura of the London gun trade.

From Moore and Grey he worked successively, and alas unrecordedly, for many of the top-flight London makers before going to Purdey's. All that his grandchildren could tell us of him as a man was that he was a perfectionist, which we feel comes over in a way in his patented ideas. As an off-shoot of this, as his business prospered, he furnished his home with fine antiques. Another facet of this trait was his impatience with incompetence of any sort in others. He was thus not an easy man to work for and so it fell, in later years, to his son, Herbert Phillip, who had a far better rapport with the staff, to organise the firm's annual outing to Brighton, with the inevitable 'bean feast' held at the Metropole Hotel. (Beesley's premises at St James's Street, were on the route of a variety of Royal Processions and seats were sold to all sorts of titled customers. Beesley's grand-daughters told us how they had been bounced on numerous noble knees on such occasions.)

In order of patent date, our survey of spring-cocked hammerless guns comes next to a patent, No. 3874 of 1883, taken out by Thomas Horsley of York and Charles Pryse of Birmingham. This is an unusual combination of patentees: a successful York maker with an equally successful Birmingham manufacturer. There must have been some reason for this partnership but it has been hidden by the mists of time. The Thomas Horsley involved is the son of the founder of the firm of that name then at 10, Coney Street, York, while Charles Pryse, also a son bearing the same name as his father, was in business at the time the patent was obtained at 84, Aston Street, Birmingham.

The gun they patented bears more than a passing resemblance to the Beesley/Purdey gun. The upper limb of the V-spring of a bar-action sidelock raises the tumbler to full-cock as the gun is opened and this limb of the spring also assists in the opening of the gun. However, the compressing/assisted-opening arrangement is entirely different in the Horsley and Pryse; they use a pair of rocking levers set-up so that, as the forward end of the foremost lever is depressed by the closing barrels, the rear end of the rear lever bears down on the top limb of the main-spring compressing it out of the path that the tumbler will take as it next falls.

*Gun built by Thomas Horsley of York, circa 1884, using his own and C. Pryse patent No. 3874 of 1883*

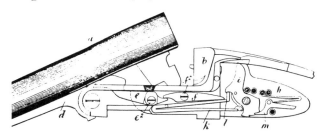

*T. Horsley and C. Pryse patent No. 3874 of 1883*

As to the number of these guns made, we believe it to have been very small. The Horsley records survive but the page that covers the patent date is missing and the brevity of the entries in subsequent pages is such that they contain no clue as to the type of hammerless gun referred to. However, in over ten years of special study of the Horsley firm we have encountered only one, albeit a magnificent specimen.

Our sole knowledge of our next gun is its British patent specification in the names of Edouard Bled and Edmond Richoux, who gave their address as 78, Rue Demours, Paris and their occupation as 'gentlemen'. The patent, No. 8591 of 1884, covers an ingenious sidelock mechanism composed of but four parts. However, what they lack in number is made up for in their complexity of shape. The main-spring is basically a V with its point to the rear, but the top limb is longer than the bottom and sweeps downwards in a gentle curve beyond the bottom limb. This extension hooks onto the back of the tumbler and flicks it up to fire the lock. The cramping lever is pivoted on the same centre as the tumbler and, at its forward end, has a right-angle projection that projects upwards through a slot in the action bar. The bottom limb of the mainspring bears on the rear of this cramping lever so that, as the barrels rise off the action flats, the rear limb of the cramping lever is forced down and since it is fitted into a wide slot in the tumbler, rotates the tumbler to the full-cock position. Then, as the gun is closed, the barrels force down the front of the cramping lever and the rear of this, therefore, rises to put the mainspring in compression ready to fire the lock.

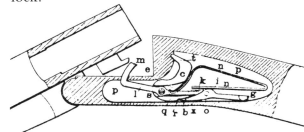

*E. Bled and E. Richoux patent No. 8591 of 1884*

It is surely indicative of the low level of interest in spring-cocked guns that we find the next patent almost a year later, No. 1467 of 1885. This ingenious action is patented in the name of a fairly prolific designer outside the gun trade, James William Smallman of Camphill Grange, Nuneaton, who was a mining engineer by profession. The layout of this gun action is basically as a boxlock with V-mainsprings with their points forwards. However, the forward ends of the springs are shown as being made as loops which fit over, and are fixed to, the ends of a transverse spindle. This is set across the bottom of the action just forward of halfway between the action face and the barrel pivot pin. On the centre of this spindle, where it can be acted upon by the forward barrel lump, is a cam, which is forced backwards as the barrel lump descends. This motion is transferred to the mainsprings and bends both limbs of the V, which compression fires the lock as the sear is released. However, when the lock is in the fired position the mainspring is still, to a degree, bowed. It is the straightening out of this residual compression as the barrels open and the cocking cam moves forward, that pushes back the tumbler to its full-cock position.

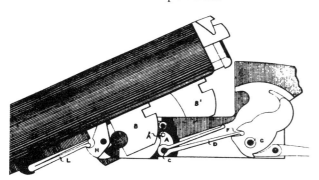

*J. Smallman patent No. 1467 of 1885*

Another spring-cocked boxlock is shown in patent No. 5049 of 1885. The patentees, two men very well known in the Birmingham gun trade, were John Deeley, the younger, and a gun action-maker, Frederick James Penn. What they patented can perhaps best be regarded as a spring-cocked Anson and Deeley boxlock but with the now familiar cramping lever projecting from the barrel flats. The projection was right forward by the knuckle, but the transverse pivot for this lever is back behind the action face. About halfway along the underside of this lever is a downward projection that bears on the top of the V-mainspring that lies point forward in the action bar. As the barrels pivot open, the upper limb of the mainspring is freed to rise and, as it does so, it lifts, via a link, the forward toe of the tumbler to the full-cock position.

Then, as the barrels close, the mainspring is cramped by the lever. Again, this was a gun action that saw little practical use.

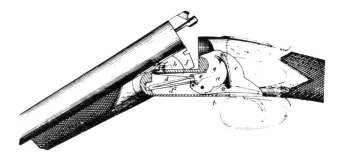

*J. Deeley and F. Penn patent No. 5049 of 1885*

Our final spring-cocked hammerless gun of this sub-group is very much a return to the Beesley/Purdey action. Indeed, from our understanding of the patent drawing, No. 2790 of 1889, we would go as far as to suggest that it very probably infringed the Beesley patent. The point is now academic. The patentee of this later design was Oliver Horton who, like many others, learned his trade in one of the centres of gun production and moved to the provinces to set up his own business. Having trained in Birmingham as a stocker, a trade which would prove a useful necessity in the provinces, he moved first to Whitehaven in Cumberland and thence to set up in business in Glasgow in 1863.

Shown on the drawings of the patent are two minor variants of the same theme. Both are boxlock guns with V-mainsprings, the points of which face forward. This acts just like the Beesley, with the upper limb used to lift the tumbler to full-cock as the barrels are raised; indeed, the spring would also aid this motion. In one version it is a sliding lever forced backwards and down by the closing barrels that compresses the mainspring; in the other it is a rod pushed back by the forend iron that, via a short lever and anti-friction roller, compresses the mainspring. It was probably fortunate for Horton that he never had to defend his patent in a court of law.

Designs can often be classified under more than one heading, in that they show similarities in more than one direction. This is no more than

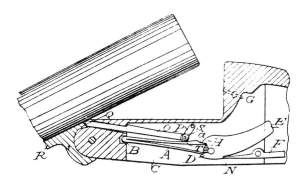

*O. Horton patent No. 2790 of 1889*

a reflection of the cross-fertilization of ideas that was then a feature of the British gun trade. For instance, we now describe a group of designs in which a spring, other than the mainspring, cocks the lockwork, but which, in so doing, also assists in opening the gun. Thus, the gun mechanisms in this group could equally be regarded as spring-openers or as spring-cockers.

It would seem that this idea was favoured by William Middleditch Scott, for we have two of his patents to this end. The first of these, No. 1320 of 1882, has in the bar of the action a sliding cocking rod. Round this rod a coil spring was fitted in such a way that, as the gun was closed,

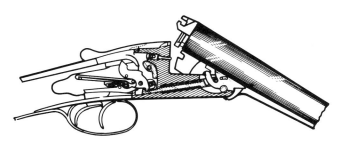

*W. M. Scott patent No. 1320 of 1882*

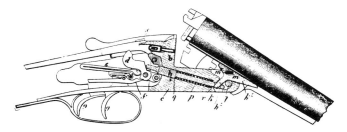

*W. M. Scott patent No. 1320 of 1882 (another version)*

this spring was compressed and this stored energy was used as the gun was opened to both cock the locks and assist the opening motion. Patent No. 1320 contains two variants on this idea. In one of these the act of opening the gun moves the cocking rod forwards, while in the other variation the cocking rod travels backwards as the gun opens. These two mechanisms differ in the site of the action of the cocking rod on the tumbler, and in the design of the lever in the knuckle which transmits the barrel motion to the cocking rod.

Another manifestation of this idea occurs as part of the Thomas Woodward patent, No. 2344 of 1882. A sliding cocking rod, running diagonally up through the bar of the action from the bottom of the back of the standing-breech to the top of the knuckle, has round it a coil spring. This spring is compressed as the gun is closed by the forend iron bearing on the forward end of the rod and, as this restraint is removed when the gun pivots open, this spring forces forward the cocking rod. The rear end of this has a hook-like projection that pulls forward the bottom of the tumbler and, thus, cocks the lock.

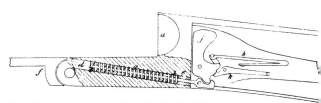

*T. Woodward patent No. 2344 of 1882*

The second Scott patent, No. 727 of 1883, is a provisional specification. The most interesting part is probably the information contained in it that the Scott firm had purchased Perkes's patent, No. 1968 of 1878, and that No. 727 of 1883 is a derivation of this. The Perkes idea was to have cocking rods sliding diagonally upwards from knuckle to lockwork. What 'Will' Scott proposed was to fit coil springs round these with a suitable collar so that, as the barrels were raised, the cocking rods would be forced back. To re-compress these springs two L-shaped levers were proposed, one for each lock, pivoted transversely in the action bar, the lower limbs slotting into the cocking rods, the upper and rear ends running out of the action flat so that the closing barrels would depress them.

It would seem that the idea of spring assistance was enjoying a vogue in Birmingham in 1883. Two more patents concerned with this idea were obtained by inhabitants of this centre of the British gun trade. David Bentley's provisional specification, No. 4867, sounds very like the Scott design just described but, in patent No. 5292, Bentley, now in conjunction with William Baker, a gunlock maker from Handsworth, Staffordshire, protects two more interesting ideas. The first of these is to fit a stout spring under the forend iron and make this spring act on a slide that bears on the knuckle of the gun above the pivot point. When the locking bolts are withdrawn, the compressed spring will tend to open the gun. Naturally, this spring has to be re-compressed as the gun is closed. The other scheme is very different and, significantly, is applied to the Rogers's patent No. 397 of 1881. What Bentley and Baker proposed was to fit a V-spring in the lock recess and under the cocking lever to raise the rear limb of the latter thereby assisting the opening and cocking of the gun so fitted.

All of these spring-assisted ideas are reminiscent of perpetual motion machines, in that, their designers find themselves faced with the fact that no machine can give out more work than has been put into it. We do not doubt, however, that the proposers of these various guns that were easy to open and yet stiff to close would claim that this was a preferable state of affairs. As is so often the case, history, in the shape of the gun buying and using public, takes a less enthusiastic view. While spring-assistance has not totally languished neither has it become widely applied and certainly not at the popular-priced end of the gun market.

The final sub-division of the spring-cocked guns that we have assembled are those that use the mainspring as a lever and it is a further tribute to Frederick Beesley that the first two that we encounter are designs of his, used by eminent gunmakers.

The first patent, No. 2813 of 1883, is in the name of James Woodward in addition to Frederick Beesley. At first glance the cocking mechanism looks like that of the 1880 patent used by Purdey's but made upside down. Closer inspection reveals that the explanation is not quite that simple. The heart of this action is a cam positioned under the lower, stronger limb of the mainspring. This cam is turned by a rod sliding along the bottom of the action, driven by a lever pivoted on the same centre as the barrels which is turned as the barrels are depressed. This part of the action is reminiscent of the classic Beesley/Purdey action. However, as the cocking cam rotates it lifts the bottom of the mainspring and this, in turn, forces back the tumbler to full-cock at the same time as the mainspring is compressed. Therefore, it could be said that this action only just falls within our definition of a spring-cocked gun.

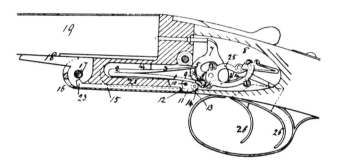

*J. Woodward and F. Beesley patent No. 2813 of 1883*

The action that is the epitome of a spring-cocked gun using its mainspring as a cocking lever is yet another Frederick Beesley design, patent No. 425 of 1884. In the list of Beesley designs in *Experts on Guns and Shooting* this patent is listed as being worked by its inventor and, indeed, guns of this design and of his make are known. But, in addition, it is also used, more extensively in the authors' experience, on guns bearing the name of Charles Lancaster. These are the so-called 'wrist breaker' actions which get their name from being so stiff to close. We can only assume that some sort of deal was struck between Henry Alfred Alexander Thorn ('Charles Lancaster') and Beesley.

In this design the mainspring cum cocking lever lies in a slot in the bar of the action and is pivoted on a transverse pivot, just ahead of the

*Charles Lancaster's 'Wrist Breaker'*

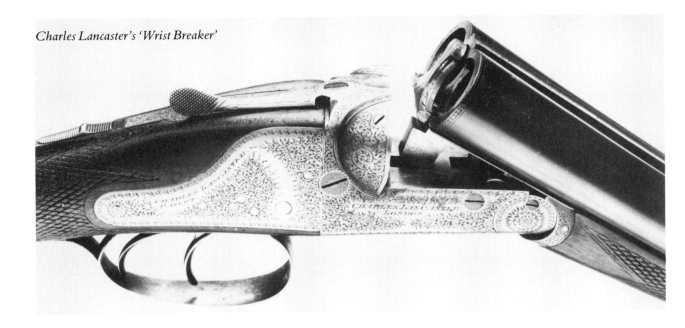

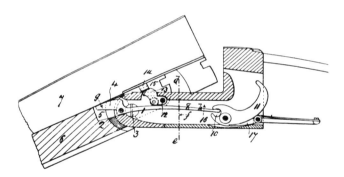

*F. Beesley patent No. 425 of 1884*

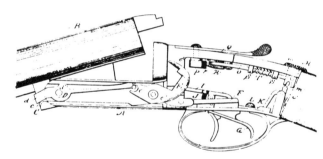

*J. Victor patent No. 9110 of 1884*

barrel pivot pin. The short forward end of this spring-lever projects through the knuckle and thus, as the barrels are depressed, the rear of the spring-lever rises and lifts the tumbler to full-cock. As the barrels close the spring-lever is, to a degree, cramped by the fact that the rear end is held up as the front is also raised. However, to increase the bend in the spring-lever, an additional cocking cam is used. This is pivoted above the mainspring and, when the barrels are raised, it projects through a slot cut in the action bar. Then, as the barrels close the cam bears down on the mainspring to increase its tension.

An action identical to the above, but without the cocking cams, is shown in a patent, No.

9110 of 1884, granted to Joseph Victor of Du Quoin, Illinois.

Another scheme to give adequate movement to a cocking lever/spring is found in the patent, No. 10,101 of 1884, of Henry Tolley of 65 and 66, Weaman Street, Birmingham. He proposed a U-shaped spring lying with its open end towards the rear of the gun; its upper limb was to be shorter than the lower and to have the barrel pivot pin in the angle of the U. The lower and longer limb of the spring was to be linked to the forward lower limb of a conventional C-shaped tumbler and the upper limb of the spring was to project forward from the barrel pivot and be permitted to rise out of the action flats. As the

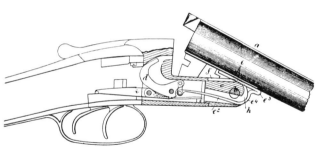

*H. Tolley patent No. 10,101 of 1884*

gun was opened the spring was rotated by the barrels and raised the tumbler to full-cock and then, as the gun was closed, the spring was bent and thus the lockwork made ready to fire.

An ideal much pursued in the evolution of the sporting shotgun during the nineteenth century was the simplification of the mechanism, by reducing the number of working parts. It is no surprise, therefore, to find Christopher George Bonehill's name cropping up at this point. He was deeply involved in the mass-production by machine-shop methods of sporting shotguns and indeed all sorts of firearms.

In patent No. 12,586 of 1884 we find Bonehill and his works manager, A. J. Simpson, collaborating on a design that would seem to derive from these roots. What is shown is a V-mainspring, the point of which projects through the knuckle of the action so that, as the

barrels drop down, the rear of the spring is twisted upwards. In doing so the upper limb of the spring lifts the C-shaped tumbler to the full-cock position while the bottom limb of the spring is raised by the bottom of the tumbler. Closing the gun forces the rear ends of the spring down and puts in tension the bottom limb in readiness to turn the tumbler when it is released by the sear.

Our final example of a gun action that uses its mainspring as a lever to cock the tumblers is another James Smallman design, patent No. 4437 of 1886. Not surprisingly, there is some degree of similarity between this and the earlier Smallman spring-cocked gun but the principles involved are different and so they are separated by our mode of classification. The central idea of this later Smallman invention is to fit the forward closed end of the V-mainspring to the moving pivot pin for the barrels and to make the barrels turn this pivot by making the front of the front lump a right-angled recess to fit over the square central portion of the hinge-pin. Now the upper limb of the mainspring bears on the top of its slot in the action bar while the bottom of the V is slightly longer and fits into a recess in the front of the boxlock-style tumbler. When the fired gun is opened, the barrels rotate the mainspring and its lower limb lifts the tumbler to full-cock. With the bottom limb of the mainspring held up as the barrels close, the

*C. G. Bonehill and A. Simpson patent No. 12,586 of 1884*

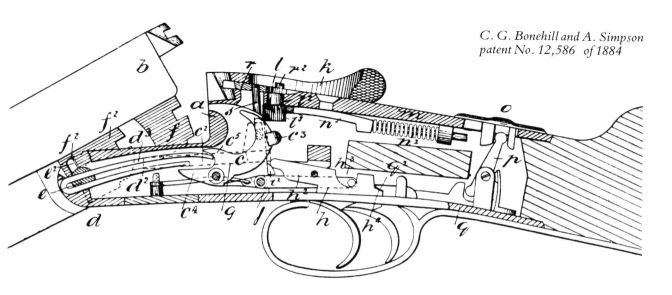

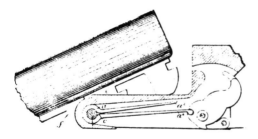

*J. Smallman patent No. 4437 of 1886, before mainspring is cramped*

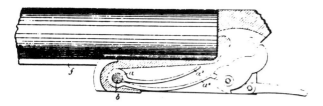

*J. Smallman patent No. 4437 of 1886, after mainspring is cramped*

limbs of the mainspring are bent to a bow shape and it is this tension that fires the lock as the sear is released.

At the beginning of this chapter we split the spring-cockers into those that used the energy of the spring and those that used the spring as a lever. We remarked that there were actions that, in a sense, bridged that gap. These consisted of three patents that show guns with sliding mainsprings which move fore and aft as part of the cock, fire, cock sequence of motions.

The first of this trio of actions is a patent, No. 4872 of 1881, granted to Hugh Adams Silver, merchant, and Walter Fletcher, gunmaker of Sun Court, Cornhill in the City of London. In this action the conventional V-mainspring, with its point forward, is drawn forward by a stud that projects laterally inwards from the top limb just behind the point. To engage with this stud, a slot is cut sloping backwards in the forward barrel lump and so the mainspring is drawn forward as the barrels open and forced backward as they close. Now the bottom of the tumbler has a smooth curve on it so that, as the mainspring is drawn forward, the top limb of the spring tends to rise. It is able to do so when it is in front of the pivot point of the tumbler and,

in so doing, rotates the tumbler to full-cock where it is held by the sear. Then, when the mainspring is driven back, it slides behind the pivot point of the tumbler and, at the same time, is compressed and is thus in a state and position to rotate the tumbler forward when the sear is released.

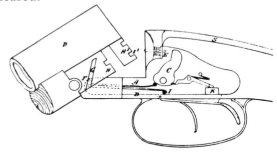

*H. Silver and W. Fletcher patent No. 4872 of 1881*

Another sliding spring action is that described in the patent, No. 3053 of 1882, by the famous Thomas William Webley and Thomas Brain. While it uses a sliding spring it has no other point of similarity with the preceding design. In this gun the spring is used as a push rod to force the tumbler back to full-cock. To cause the springs to slide there are two projections from the barrel flats that drop into the action bar, one under each barrel in side view between the barrel lumps. The mainspring is a conventional V, with its point forward and of such a length that in its forward position the point protrudes into the slot formed for the cocking lugs under the barrels. As the gun is opened, the cocking lug swings to the rear and so forces the mainspring back into the lock-work. The rear end of the bottom limb of the mainspring is fitted with an anti-friction roller and rides on the curve on the uppermost face of the tumbler and so pushes back the tumbler head to cock it. At the same time, the lower limb of the spring is forced up into tension by the rising bottom of the tumbler. If the gun is now closed it will not fire because the mainspring continues to bear on the tumbler behind and above its axis. To enable the spring to act it must bear in front of the axis of the tumbler. To move the spring to this position an external lever is provided which turns a transverse rod,

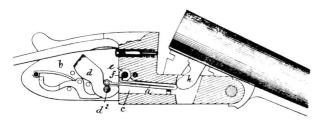

*T. Webley and T. Brain patent No. 3053 of 1882*

upon which flats are formed that act on the upturned end of the top limb of the mainspring. Therefore, this final part of the cocking cycle is also a very efficient safety device, for without its operation the gun locks simply cannot fire.

An action very like the preceding one is contained in James William Smallman's patent, No. 1281 of 1887. Here the V-mainspring has its point forward and when the lock is fired the mainspring protrudes through a slot in the knuckle of the action. To push it back there are, mounted on the forend iron, two fairly large anti-friction rollers that bear on the point of the spring as the gun pivots open. As the spring is forced back, its lower limb rotates the tumbler backwards while its upper limb slides along the top of its slot cut in the bar of the action. The latter is so shaped that, as the spring moves to the rear, the gap provided for it narrows and thus the spring is compressed. Also contained in this specification is an ejector mechanism. (See Chapter Eleven.)

Before we move on from those guns that use their mainsprings to cock their locks we should consider a very small sub-group outside this definition, but one yet more closely allied to the spring-cockers than to any other group. In terms of production, these patents are of no significance, but for the student of gun design they serve to demonstrate how thorough has been the exploration of every possible variation on the theme of the hammerless shotgun.

A patent in the name of David Bentley, which is a provisional specification, No. 881 of 1880, is one example of this sub-group. This is a lever-cocked hammerless gun of the Murcott type, with the top limbs of the V-mainsprings bearing, at their open ends, on levers which lie in open-topped slots in the bar of the action. The pressure of the mainspring is thus exerted on the barrel flats, assists the barrels to open and when these raise the mainsprings are untensioned. In this state there is the absolute minimum of resistance to the motion of the lever cocking the locks. Then as the barrels are closed the main-springs are cramped by the reverse of the process described above. An almost identical method of cramping the mainspring is de-scribed in two other provisional specifications, both of 1883, Nos. 687 and 3845, obtained by Thomas Woodward of Birmingham.

In another provisional specification, granted to William Tranter, there is a close parallel to the above designs. This patent, No. 2871 of 1881, describes a mechanism in which a lever, lying probably exposed in the top of the action bar, is so pivoted transversely and acted on by the V-mainspring underneath it that, as the gun is opened, the top limb of the mainspring lifts the forward end of the lever. The rear end of this lever thus cocks the lock and the forward end is depressed, cramping the spring, as the barrels close.

Thus we come to the end of our survey of the hammerless guns that use the motion of their barrels to cock their lockwork. At the end of each and every one of these chapters we are left with a feeling of wonder at the sheer volume of invention that is compressed into two decades. In the case of the barrel-cocked guns, we have both quality and quantity because it was in this period that most of the classic actions for side-by-side hammerless guns made their appearance. In the intervening century we can see how these British inventions have become the world-wide standard for the side-by-side double-barrel gun. The pity is that we know so very little of the men who designed them, but they could not hope for a better memorial.

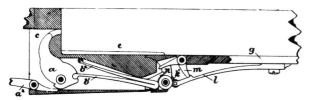

*J. Smallman patent No. 1281 of 1887*

# CHAPTER SIX

# The Safety

In the two decades with which we are concerned there are no less than 108 British patent specifications concerned wholly, or in part, with safety catches fitted to sporting shotguns. This remarkable fact, which further testifies to the ingenuity of the British gun trade, requires more than the usual background information if we are to understand the reasons for such a spate of material.

As we see it there are three prime reasons for this state of affairs. However, the relative importance of these is problematical and probably, in any case, variable.

First, and perhaps most obvious, are the regular pontifications of Dr Walsh in *The Field*. He had lost the thumb, forefinger and a portion of his left-hand when a muzzle-loading gun he was using had burst. This maimed left hand must surely have been a constant reminder of the dangers of the sporting gun and have played a significant part in shaping his thinking.

Then there is the less documented fact that the gun with concealed works was, to a large degree, new, novel and, in the minds of its users, untried. To assuage the natural apprehension of a potential purchaser, what better than an ingenious safety mechanism? If nothing more it would provide a good talking point for the salesman in the front shop.

Equally, these safeties may well have filled a definite need. What emerges from our researches into contemporary periodicals is that the expected etiquette of using a gun in the company of other sportsmen was very different in the 1880s to that of the 1980s. For instance, in *Land and Water*, on 6 November 1875, there was a report about a man who had died of tetanus after accidentally shooting himself. He had pulled a loaded gun by its muzzle out of his dog cart. What is absolutely amazing to us today is the editorial comment that introduced this item: 'Always carry a loaded gun half-cocked'! From this we can only infer that it was normal practice to carry fully-loaded guns in ways that we would consider the height of folly. This view is reinforced by correspondence in *The Field*, in 1894. A certain W. A. Adams wrote letters and even produced a small sketch to illustrate 'his' method of carrying a sporting gun in the field when it was not actually about to be used. This new idea was nothing more than carrying the gun broken over the user's arm! While Mr Adams was probably not the first man to think of this idea, the fact that *The Field* saw fit to use this material in this way would suggest that it was far from normal. Today we can only marvel at the fact that it had apparently taken over 30 years for this virtue of the snap action breech-loader to be appreciated.

*The drawing that accompanied a letter to* The Field, *10 November 1894, from W. A. Adams*

Against such a background, the appearance of a rash of safety catches is much more comprehensible. As always, when faced with such a collection of material and in order to describe it logically, we first have to devise some system of classification. What we propose is to sort these mechanisms primarily into their sites of action and, within this overall classification, form such sub-groups as is possible, with, as always, a rag-bag at the end of those that defy this, and, we suspect, any formal classification.

Far and away the largest group of designs is those in which the triggers are bolted by some sort of catch worked by the user moving a slide or lever on the top strap of the gun. What must be regarded as the archetype of both this group, and also the safety on the modern British shotgun, is that fitted to the Murcott shotguns and described in patent No. 1003 of 1871. Externally this consists of a lever, some 1½ inches long, that is fixed at its rear on a vertical pivot. Its front end swings from side-to-side, across the back portion of the wide flat rearward extension of the standing-breech. At both the left and the right end of its arc, the Murcott safety lever engages via a small projection under its forward end with a shallow depression bored in the top strap. On all the specimens examined, the left-hand depression is inlaid 'Lock'd' while there is no equivalent inscription on the right. The pivot for this external lever is a rod, set vertically above the trigger blades. The bottom end of the rod is flattened rather like a screwdriver. When the external lever is in the 'Lock'd' position, the flattened end of the vertical rod lies across the trigger blades and so prevents their movement; moving the external lever over to the right swings the rod so that, now, the trigger blades can rise either side of it.

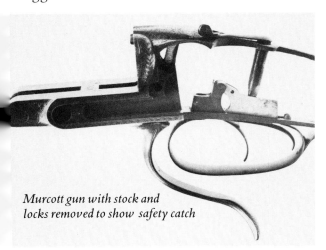

*Murcott gun with stock and locks removed to show safety catch*

It is, perhaps, fortunate that many of the ideas for safety catches are so similar that one description will cover several patented designs. Perhaps the simplest of the trigger-bolting mechanisms that followed the Murcott are those in which a thumb slide on the top strap was the visible part of an internal slide. This is seen in part of the: Bonehill patents, No. 2323 of 1878 and No. 7823 of 1888; the Rogers patent, No. 2879 of 1879; the Crutchley patent, No. 3684 of 1879; the Lang patent, No. 4916 of 1881; the Tolley patent, No. 10,303 of 1886; and the Neuman patent, No. 16,278 of 1888. In all these patents the internal slide at its rearmost position stands over an upward projection of the trigger blades. But, when the top slide is pushed forward the trigger blades can now rise behind the blocking limb. In the safety, part of the Richard Ellis and Henry Scott patent No. 2816 of 1879, this arrangement is reversed. The top slide has to be pulled back to move to the rear of the trigger blades that portion of the internal slide which checks their movement. However, on the guns known to the authors that use the Ellis and Scott action, this safety is not used. An ordinary push-forward type is fitted, consisting of a slide under the top strap, the front end of which is pushed to the rear by the rear of the barrel-locking bolt as the gun is opened. In this rearward position a vertical leg from the slide blocks the trigger blades.

Only very slightly more complex is the idea of bolting the trigger blades by the lower end of a vertical lever hung on a cross-wise pivot. The upper end of the lever is controlled by the usual thumb slide so that, as the slide is pushed forward, the lower limb of the lever swings to the rear and thus releases the triggers. With only the subtlest variation in the shape of the limbs, this idea crops up in the patents: Perkes's No. 1968 of 1878; Kirkwood's No. 4665 of 1880; Tonks's No. 6673 of 1884; Tranter's No. 6787 of 1884; Green's No. 14,626 of 1885; Brain's No. 10,487 of 1887; and Hampton's No. 17,792 of 1887.

There is another form of this popular idea. In this, the lower limb of the vertical lever works some sort of a slide or catch to bolt the triggers. Thus, in the William Anson patent, No. 4513 of 1876, the lever that the thumb slide works is bent at a right-angle to form an L-shape, pivoted at its angle with the lower limb forward. As the top slide moves forward the lower limb of the internal lever presses down. The patent describes two different rocking catches that swing on and off the trigger blades under the influence of this lever. In addition, this specification is also concerned with a grip safety that also works an internal rocking catch but, in the authors' experience, it is the top slide version that is most usually seen.

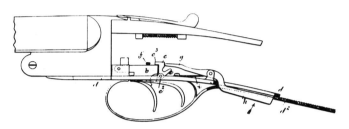

*W. Anson patent No. 4513 of 1876*

To continue chronologically, in Alexander Henry's patent, No. 5273 of 1882, the bolt that actually locks the triggers is a slide, hinged to the bottom of the vertical lever worked by the thumb slide. In the Joseph Pinder specification, No. 154 of 1884, the slide at the bottom of the vertical lever has a depression formed in its forward end that acts as a cam for a rocking catch set on a transverse pivot that in turn bolts the triggers.

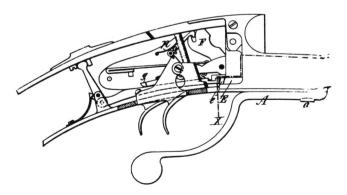

*A. Henry patent No. 5273 of 1882*

The final four patents in this sub-group are: Joseph Victor's No. 9110 of 1884; Bonehill and Simpson's No. 12,586 of 1884; H. Parsons's No. 15,763 of 1886; and the John Heath patent, No. 12,033 of 1888. All these have a slide on the inside of the trigger plate, moved back and forth by a vertical lever worked at its top end by a thumb slide. True, they differ subtly in the shape of these limbs and the rest of the mechanisms described in these specifications are very different, but as far as this feature is concerned, they are, for practical purposes, inseparable.

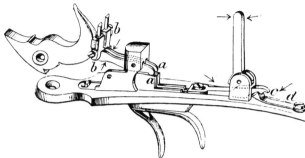

*J. Heath patent No. 12,033 of 1888*

Inevitably, we once again have a number of designs that, while they are trigger-bolting safeties, do not conform to any of the groups so far formed. For instance, in the Samuel Mathews provisional patent, No. 3573 of 1878, a trigger-bolting safety is mentioned but with no practical details or drawing.

In the James MacNaughton patent, No. 2848 of 1879, that covers the famous trigger-plate action gun, the safety is a turning top lever on the top strap, set just behind the opening lever. Internally, this is a miniature Scott spindle and Purdey-bolt arrangement with the bolt working into the triggers instead of the barrel lumps.

An unusual safety, but one that has a certain logic to it, is part of the Henry Tolley specification, No. 1515 of 1883. An ordinary trigger bolt is worked by a slide, consisting of a vertical limb that is simply slid over the trigger blades. The novelty lies in the fact that the slide under the top strap is continued forwards and becomes a sliding bolt that engages with the top extension as the safety is pushed forward to release the triggers. An ingenious way of providing extra barrel-locking just as it is needed.

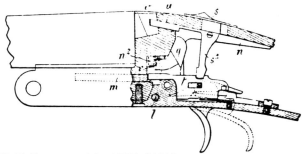

*H. Tolley patent No. 1515 of 1883*

*Detached Greener side lever safety catch*

A different idea, but one that we shall encounter again in this chapter, is that contained in a patent, No. 5459 of 1883, taken out in Britain by H. J. Haddan. He was acting as agent for John P. Burchard and Frank Novotuy of St Paul, Minnesota. In this, the top thumb slide controls an internal slide under the top strap. In its turn the internal slide moves a vertical plunger back and forth. The plunger is loose in its slot in the stock and its bottom rests on the trigger blades. In the rearward position, the top of the plunger bears on the underside of the top strap. However, when the thumb slide is pushed forwards the top of the plunger is brought into line with a notch, cut in the underside of the top strap, and into this the plunger rises as the triggers are squeezed.

There is a form of trigger-bolting that is well known, again, because it is a Greener product. But in this instance, the mechanism is found on a large number of guns as well as being described by Greener in the various books that he wrote. We refer, of course, to the side safety. As usually seen, this consists of a rod that is set across the head of the stock. In the rod there is a cut-out portion so that, in one position, the trigger blades are blocked while, in another, they are free to move. This transverse rod is controlled by an external lever, set flush into an escutcheon on the left-hand side of the stock. To hold the safe in either of its two positions, another pair of flats are cut on it and on these bears a little spring-loaded piston, mounted on the inside of the escutcheon. This mechanism is covered by Greener's patent, No. 1623 of 1877, and is non-automatic; it is often seen made automatic by linking it to the rear of the barrel-locking bolt.

Not surprisingly, there is another patent on the same idea. In a specification, No. 659 of 1886, by William A'Court Granville Birkin, the triggers are to be bolted by a rod with a flat, filed at its centre, that runs through the trigger blades. The latter have a slot like a keyhole cut in them so that they can move as normal when the flat portion of the safety rod is vertical. The safety is worked by a simple lever on the left outside end of the rod.

Another style of safety, pursued perhaps with less vigour than some, is to have a bolt on to the sear as a means of immobilising the mechanism of a sporting gun. The bulk of these guns use a thumb slide on the top strap. For our purposes we can form a small sub-group, composed of conventional guns so fitted.

In their patent, No. 1952 of 1880, Bonehill and Matthews describe the idea of having a vertical rod fitted by a transverse pivot to the tails of the sears. At the top, this rod is made to slip into holes in the top strap. To make the gun so fitted safe, a slide under the top slips into a

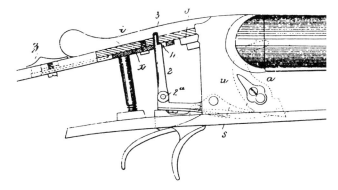

*C. G. Bonehill and W. J. Matthews patent No. 1952 of 1880*

notch cut in the vertical rod and so locks the sears.

Swinburn's patent, No. 4291 of 1880, has conventional sears bolted by a slide that runs back through the head of the stock with a yoke at its rear. The yoke blocks the sears when the slide is to the rear. To free the sears, the bolt has to be pushed forward by the thumb slide. The front end of the safety bolt is in line with the rear of the barrel-locking bolt so that, as the latter moves to the rear as the gun is opened, so the safety catch is applied.

Another Swinburn patent, No. 525 of 1881, locks the conventional sears with a slide that runs over their tails. The slide is worked by a lever, swinging back and forth pivoted in the top strap. The external upper end of this lever is formed as the thumb piece.

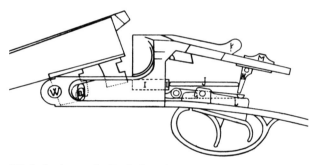

*W. Lake (agent for D. Laloux)*
*patent No. 13,199 of 1884*

An even more basic realisation of this idea is covered by the patent, No. 13,199 of 1884, granted to the agent William Lake for the Belgian company D. Laloux et Cie, of Liège. In this the safety bolt is simply a downward internal limb of the top slide.

More complex is the variant patented as part of Harry Alfred Smith's patent, No. 7346 of 1887. The top slide works an internal slide. This in turn acts on the top of the vertical lever, the bottom of which swings forwards to bolt the sears.

In our present group there emerges a sub-group of three unusual types of lockwork. All have safeties that bolt the sears. The earliest of these is the lever-cocked hammerless design of James Adsett described in his patent, No. 1981

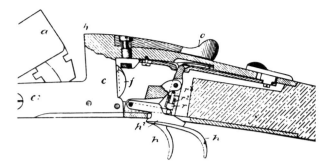

*H. Smith patent No. 7346 of 1887*

of 1877. The sear for this lockwork is a lever, pivoted just under the top strap at the top of the rear of the standing-breech. The lever runs backwards and then angles down to meet the trigger blades. The safety is a slide on the top strap, with a short leg projecting down into the lockwork which is so shaped and positioned as to block the upward movement of the sear.

It was the patent, No. 8851 of 1885, which, it will be recalled, covered the coil mainspring hammerless gun protected by Hackett and Belcher. In this a vertical rod is pivoted to the tail of the sear. The top of the rod is held to the rear by a light spring, in which position the vertical rod butts against the top strap. The action of the specially-shaped trigger blade is to push forward the top of the blocking rod when it can rise into a hole cut into the top strap and so permit the sear to pivot in the normal way.

The barrel-cocked gun that is covered by Thomas Bailey's patent, No. 9048 of 1885, has a sear that is another rocking lever under the top strap and, again, the safety is an inward projection from a thumb slide that holds down the rear of the lever.

Probably the most unusual lockwork of this little group is that of A. Bertrand contained in his patent, No. 14,874 of 1886. This lever-cocked gun had what was, in effect, an upside down trigger-plate action hung from the top strap. The sear for this is a lever, pivoted transversely at about its mid-point and, again, the safety is an internal projection from a top slide that in the safe position holds down the rear of the lever.

Safety catch designs are complex and interwoven. For example, one of the popular safety ideas was a bolt or block that was removed from the tumblers by the act of pulling the trigger, but a little group has a similar mode of operation working to a second sear. We admit that there is no answer to the conundrum of when does a catch become a sear? All we can offer is the fact that those we are about to describe have their safety at the same site as a sear would be found on a normal lock.

In his patent, No. 6624 of 1884, Swinburn describes such a safety as a 'blocking sear' and applies it to his trigger-plate actioned gun. The safety is pivoted above and just behind the sears proper and acts on shoulders formed on the insides of the tumblers.

Curiously, in patent No. 6943 of 1885 granted to T. Stead who was acting as an agent for Messrs D. & F. Moore of Brooklyn, we have again the idea of a second blocking sear. This time it is applied to an external hammer lock. The reasons for this are stated to be that, with this addition, the accidental jarring off of the mechanism is impossible. Be this as it may, the patent shows the blocking arm pivoted on the same centre as the true sear and acting like the Swinburn on an inward-projecting shoulder formed on the tumbler.

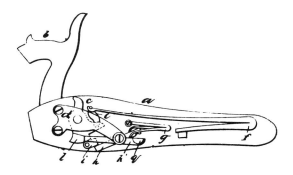

T. Stead (agent for D. and F. Moore) patent No. 6943 of 1885

Inevitably, we are left with a group of sear-bolting safeties that fall outside our grouping. It is probable that the earlier members of this group derive their individuality from the very fact that they are part of early hammerless actions, when the requirements of the sportsman were but dimly understood. For instance, the

safety on the lever-cocked Hodges gun, patent No. 1145 of 1878, is a slide on the trigger-guard strap. The latter works an internal slide that slips forwards over the sears of the trigger-plate action. Undoubtedly, this is an effective mechanism, but an inconvenient one.

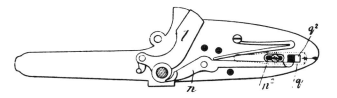

E. James patent No. 4317 of 1879

The same comment also applies to the side lever-cocked Enos James patent, No. 4317 of 1879. Here, on conventional bar-action side-locks, there is a separate slide on each lock plate to bolt the rear of the sears.

It is undeniable logic that, to prevent the lockwork of a hammerless sporting gun acting inadvertently, some sort of constraint should be applied to the hammers (or tumblers, as they are more correctly termed). The bulk of such ideas belong to the 1870s rather than later. So, it appears that this is an idea that was discarded as the hammerless gun blossomed. Like so many aspects of history there is probably no very simple answer to this but many of the designs that form the following group would certainly be far from convenient to use in the field.

The mechanisms that comprise this group fall, luckily, into two distinct sub-groups. Those that we will describe first are variants on the basic idea of having a rod of some sort across the lockwork, in front of the tumblers and below the strikers. In one position, cut-outs in this rod permit the tumblers to fall their full travel; in the other, or safe, position the rod bars the way.

Our description can further be simplified by considering, first, those rods that rotate to align or remove the tumbler blocks. The archetype of these, certainly as far as our survey is concerned, is found on guns built by Gibbs of Bristol on their Gibbs and Pitt patent, No. 284 of 1873. The original safety applied to these guns held the hammers at their tops by a bar that was pivoted on either side of the stout, inverted, U-section top strap that is a feature of the early Gibbs and Pitt. The dangerous failing of this idea was that, if the locks had jarred off, removing the safety catch would fire the gun. So, it is more usual to find early guns that have been remodelled by having this safety removed and the metal and woodwork made good. The replacement safety, hung on two brackets added to the rear of the action, is a notched bar so formed that in its safe position, if the tumblers should fall, not only will they be prevented from reaching the strikers, the bar will also lock tumbler and safety together, and the only way to free them is to recock the gun.

Very similar is the safety on the original Anson and Deeley boxlock patent, No. 1756 of 1875. Here, the novelty is that there is an individual safety for each lock. This consists of a turning rod that blocks the striker in the standing-breech. The strikers are, as usual in this design, part of the tumblers.

The final tumbler-bolting turning-rod safety is another Gibbs and Pitt design, this time contained in their patent, No. 3297 of 1879, which is concerned with a barrel-cocking action. In this, the safety has been made automatic by having the cocking rod for the left-hand lock rotate the safety spindle through 90 degrees to the safe position, at the same time as the cocking rod pushes back the tumblers. To do this, shoulders are formed on both cocking and safety rods. To remove the safety there is a side lever very like the original Gibbs and Pitt.

Slightly more numerous, but curiously all patented in a four-month period in 1879, are four minor variants on the idea of having a square rod slide from side-to-side in the action so that in one position the fall of the tumblers is blocked, but in another a cut-out portion permits their full travel. The four specifications are: provisional No. 649 in the name of H. Tolley; No. 769 by W. W. Greener; No. 1065 by M.

*The action of the fifty-first gun made under Gibbs and Pitt patent. Note the filled-in site of the original safety plus the replacement with the notch cut into the forward face of the tumbler*

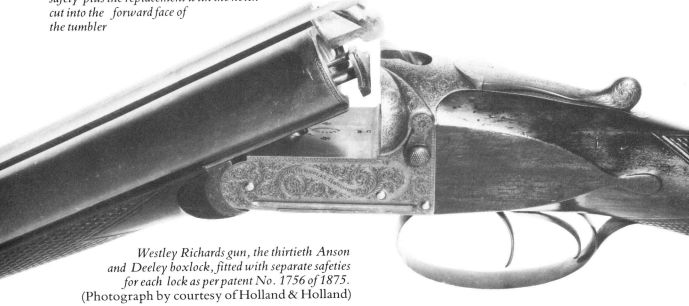

*Westley Richards gun, the thirtieth Anson and Deeley boxlock, fitted with separate safeties for each lock as per patent No. 1756 of 1875. (Photograph by courtesy of Holland & Holland)*

Parsons, and No. 2177 by W. Tisdall. From the designer's point of view, the fact that such a slide could be worked by the Scott spindle, or its equivalent, was obviously attractive but the inconvenience to the user who had to push in a stud on the right lockplate outweighed this.

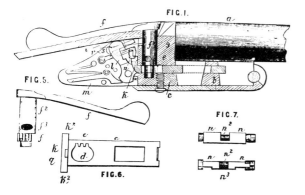

*Drawing from* The Field *of W. Tisdall 'Patent gun', patent No. 2177 of 1879*

It is, perhaps, not surprising that the idea of having a grip safety that worked on the tumblers should also have attracted some inventors.

The grip safety was an idea that was old even in 1871. As seen on muzzle-loaders (and earlier breech-loaders that were built one or more decades before our period) this device usually consists of a lever about 4 inches long, pivoted at its rear end to the rear of the trigger strap, with its free end just behind the trigger guard. As the gun is grasped in the normal act of firing, the forward end of the lever is squeezed up to the stock. Inside the gun this motion is used to work some sort of catch that releases the triggers as the grip is squeezed and automatically bolts them as the grip is released.

This is in the Tranter patent, No. 2871 of 1881, which is a provisional specification and simply mentions the idea of a grip safe working on the tumblers with no practical details. From the point of view of the relative positions of the components, the notion of a grip safe on the top strap has some merit and we find a quartet of designs that seek to exploit this advantage.

One of the very first safeties, patent No. 1512 of 1871, is that designed by John Sidney Heath. In this, a grip just in front of the comb of the stock, and pivoted up in the comb, is to be squeezed down. Then the forward end inside the stock pushes down the rear limb of a simple see-saw lever, transversely pivoted under the top strap. Thus, as the rear of this internal lever goes down its front rises. This motion is conveyed to another similar lever, so that, as the front of the rear internal lever goes up, the front of the front lever goes down and formed on this is a catch that is thereby removed from the head of the tumbler. We cannot but wonder if this Mr Heath was not in some way related to Mr Heath Robinson.

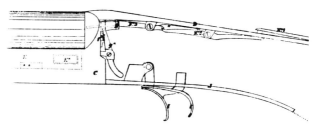

*J. Heath patent No. 1512 of 1871*

The final trio of top-grip tumbler-bolting safeties are sufficiently similar to share a description: in the A. Wyley patent, No. 2238 of 1874; the A. Leighs patent, No. 8620 of 1884; and the H. Allender patent, No. 10,903 of 1884, a lever pivoted under the top strap emerges at its rear as a stud. The latter has to be squeezed down to raise the hooked forward end of the lever clear of the heads of the tumblers. In all cases, a light spring is fitted to push up the stud.

To round off this group of tumbler-bolting safeties there is but one that uses a thumb slide to work a tumbler-bolt. This is mentioned in the provisional specification, No. 2886 of 1878, granted to Henry and Edwin Hammond, but no practical details are given.

Before we move on from the idea of a safety bolt that locked the tumblers we consider a group of mechanisms that are, essentially, different from those discussed so far but share the same basic concept. These designs have tumblers, restrained by some sort of lever work automatically operated by pulling the trigger. This idea, known as an 'intercepting sear or safety' has been widely applied to British guns of the higher qualities up until the present day.

The collaboration between Joseph Vernon Needham and George Hinton in their patent, No. 706 of 1879, demonstrates a fundamental aspect of this group of mechanisms. The pivot and lever lengths of the safety levers must be such that they magnify the movements of the trigger blade, so that the safety is displaced. The tumbler is then free to rotate before the sear is removed from its bent. Thus, this Needham and Hinton patent has a long forward-projecting lever (actually a part of the trigger blade) that curves forward to just behind the standing-breech of the gun. On the rear of the standing-breech are hung, on longitudinal pivots, a pair of L-shaped levers with the pivots through the angles. The front end of the extension of the trigger blade fits down into a slot in a horizontal limb; as the trigger is pulled the horizontal is drawn down and so the vertical limb of the L swings inward and out of the way of the tumbler. It is worthy of note that the patent drawing shows a classic Scott patent sidelock gun.

A very different manifestation of the same idea is found in the Webley patent, No. 1511 of 1882. To a conventional bar-action sidelock is added a sliding bolt that slips into a deep notch in the rear of the tumbler. To withdraw this bolt another right-angled lever is used, hung on the lockplate with its long limb down and its short limb to the rear, and so positioned that as the trigger blade rises the bolt is withdrawn before the sear is disengaged.

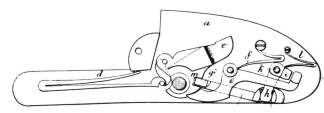

*T. Webely patent No. 1511 of 1882*

Relevant at this point is T. Woodward's patent, No. 687 of 1883. The brief provisional specification, covers a mechanism of this type but with no practical details.

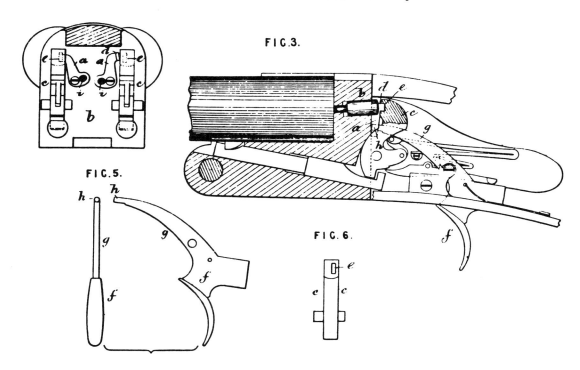

*J. Needham and G. Hinton patent No. 706 of 1879*

Yet another variant on this idea is contained in the specification, No. 1463 of 1883, in the names of Thomas William Webley, George Bouckley and Edwin Charles Hodges. Their idea was to have a sliding rod mounted outside, but fixed to, the trigger box. The rod was urged forwards by a spiral spring so that the forward end of the slide entered a slot in the tumbler axis and thereby prevented the latter rotating. To draw this slide back, an inward projection from the rear end was to fit into an inclined slot cut in the trigger blade.

In a curious way, part of the Henry Tolley patent, No. 1515 also of 1883, is this mechanism reversed. What is proposed is a slide that is fitted on the upper surface of the trigger plate. The front end of this slide has a small upward projection that fits under the breast of the tumbler and blocks its path. To permit the lock to fire, the slide is pushed forward by an incline cut in the trigger blade, acting on a lateral projection from the slide. To move the slide backwards, to reposition the block under the tumbler, the motive force is the force of the sear spring, acting via the sear, pressing down on the trigger blades that, in their turn, act on the slide via the incline cut in the trigger blades.

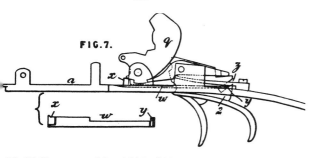

H. Tolley patent No. 1515 of 1883

Another realisation of this same basic idea is found in the patent, No. 3049, taken out by Thomas Perkes. This specification, and its attendant drawing, are rather vague. We suspect this was intentional. A hook is described on the rear of the head of a sidelock tumbler that is held by a bolt mounted on the lockplate. The latter, certainly in one version, swings on a vertical pivot. It has been our good fortune to have been shown a gun, almost certainly made

by Thomas Perkes, that uses this mechanism. To swing the locking-bolt there is formed on it a lateral projection, like the tail of a sear, that lies just behind the tail of the actual sear. The tail of the locking-bolt has, however, an incline on its underside upon which, as the trigger is squeezed, a raised rear portion of the trigger blade bears. The locking-bolt is, thus, swung aside before the lower forward portion of the trigger blade lifts the rear of the sear to trip the lock.

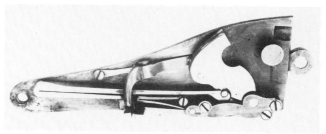

T. Perkes patent No. 3049 of 1883

Thus far all the mechanisms have been for sidelock guns but with patent No. 5405 of 1884 we have an intercepting safety for a boxlock gun in the name of James William Smallman. On the head of the tumbler is formed a transverse projection. To engage with this is a hooked head on yet another L-shaped lever. This is hung on a common centre with the triggers so that, as the horizontal limb is raised by the trigger, the safety catch is displaced.

J. Smallman patent No. 5405 of 1884

Our penultimate patented intercepting safe, No. 11,382 of 1884, is another specification that is vague to the point of being unintelligible. Its greatest interest lies in the fact that it is evidence of collaboration between Edgar Harrison and Frederick Beesley.

123

Of this whole group, the most widely encountered in contemporary magazine sources was what was known as 'Hollands Patent Safety Lock'. It is shown on Holland and Robertson's patent specification, No. 5834 of 1887, but appears to have been in use prior to this. The mechanism owes its importance to the fact that it was the lockwork of the current Holland and Holland 'Royal' gun (see Chapter Four). In this lock a blocking lever is pivoted above and behind the sear, with an inward lateral projection at its rear end that the trigger blade lifts. As the rear end of the lever is lifted so the forward end is depressed and, thus, a lateral projection on the front end of the lever is lowered out of the path of the tumbler.

In his preamble to patent No. 7823 of 1888, Christopher George Bonehill tells us that the object of the mechanism he is about to describe is intended to prevent the second lock of a double-barrel gun accidently jarring off as the first is fired. Despite this, we feel that this mechanism is more logically described at this point than with those others also concerned with the prevention of double discharge.

The gun drawn on this patent is a species of boxlock but is cocked via a lifter off the rear lump. In the cocked position the tumbler lies back in the action, where it is held both by a sear and by a sliding bolt that slides out from the centre of the action to a position across the head of the tumbler. The safety bolt for each lock has at the end, away from the tumbler, a light flat spring that slides it into the bolting position. To remove the bolt, the front top of the trigger blade over the pivot is raised to form a cam. This acts on a vertically sliding limb that Bonehill calls a 'pusher' and a shoulder on this, in turn, acts on an incline formed on the underside of the bolt. As the pusher rises, the bolt moves towards the mid-line of the gun and thus clears the path for the tumbler.

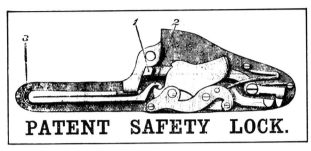

*Holland & Holland's patent safety lock from an advertisement for the 'Royal Hammerless Gun'*

A method of bolting the tumblers that is a form of safety catch, and yet very different from anything else we have in this sub-section, is another ingenious idea in the Needham patent, No. 4693 of 1883. What is proposed is a turning rod with suitable cut-outs set through the lower breasts of the tumbler. This principle is used in several other specifications. The novelty lies in the fact that to work this a detachable key is proposed so that the gun can be immoblised and made safe from meddlesome hands.

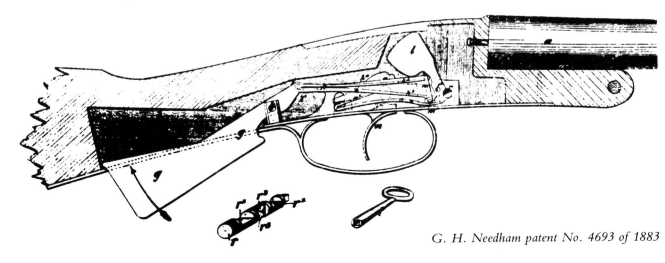

*G. H. Needham patent No. 4693 of 1883*

Another potential site for a safety mechanism is on the striker that transmits the blow of the tumbler to the cartridge cap. This would seem to be as good an idea as many others that form this chapter, but in actual fact it is very little used. In the two instances where it is employed it would seem that it derives as much from the peculiar type of lock that gun uses as from any inherent virtue of the notion. For instance, in the gun covered by J. and T. Adsett's patent, No. 574 of 1879 (see Chapter One), it will be recalled that a striker around which was the coil mainspring was one feature of the design. The safety on this gun is a turning rod, with two segments cut out of it, and so positioned in the standing-breech that, in one position, the rod blocks the path of the strikers. Alternatively, by rotating it through 90 degrees an external lever lines up the cut-out segments with the path of the striker and so will permit the gun to be fired.

A very similar idea for both striker and safety seems to be described in the provisional patent, No. 3466 of 1881, taken out by Robertson and Joyce.

Earlier in this chapter, we described the classic grip safety. Just such a set-up is in the patent, No. 13,400 of 1886, taken out for Jules Rochatte. To be fair, the external lever is a light leaf spring, but when this is squeezed, it rocks a small lever catch out of engagement with the trigger blades.

What may conveniently be regarded as a variant on this theme is found protected as patent No. 12,003 of 1889. In this the patentees, C. E. Batcock and H. W. Bateman, both engineers of Ponders End, Middlesex, propose a sliding bolt worked by a spiral spring to bite into slots in the rear of the trigger blades. To withdraw the bolt, it is connected to a slide working on the outside of the trigger strap. The rear portion of this slide is curved downward so that a user's hand will push it backward as the gun is grasped. From a user's point of view it is a scheme with obvious defects.

A form of grip safe is the idea of having a moveable heelplate that works a rod fitted through the stock. In some way, as the gun is pressed to a user's shoulder, the trigger work is freed. In terms of patent specifications this was a popular idea for we have no less than eleven full, or provisional, patents or parts of patents to consider. Despite all this, such devices are rarely found on surviving guns. The reason for this, we suspect, lies in the fact that many of this group of inventors were outside the gun trade and, of those that remain, several were foreign nationals with addresses scattered across Europe. Both of these groups would have had the greatest of problems in persuading the trade to adopt their ideas and pay them for so doing.

This state of affairs probably explains why G. H. Wilson of Camberwell did not pursue his provisional patent, No. 129 of 1872. So, we can only have a brief unexplained statement that a heelplate safety was envisaged.

Almost certainly, the best known of this group is the Greener patent No. 1623 of 1877. Once again, this device is widely known because its inventor featured it in his published works. The essential feature of Greener's mechanism is a heelplate hung on a transverse pivot, with the upper portion of the plate inside the stock. As the lower end is squeezed in, the portion above the pivot swings back. This motion draws back a rod, the front end of which

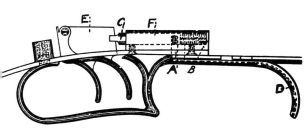

*C. Batcock and H. Bateman patent No. 12,003 of 1889*

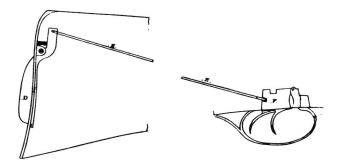

*W. Greener patent No. 1623 of 1877*

fits into a slot cut in the rear of the trigger blades.

It will be noted that the inward movement of the Greener heelplate is converted to a rearward movement of the locking-bolt. Four more of our group share this feature and thus we can conveniently consider these as a sub-group.

The patent of William Nokes, No. 2378 of 1881, tells ut that he was a 'metal roller and tube maker' of Chester Street, Aston, and shows a rod worked essentially like the Greener but engaging instead with the tumblers.

Another ingenious way of drawing back the locking-bolt as the heelplate is pressed in is contained in the patent, No. 1496 of 1888, granted to James Truscott. He was a watchmaker in business at 13, High Street, Tenby, Pembrokeshire. Truscott's heelplate was mounted on two longitudinal sliding rods, the forward ends of which, inside the stock, press forwards the ends of two vertical levers transversely pivoted in the stock. The upper sliding rod worked on the upper limb of the upper lever, the lower rod on the lower limb of the lower lever. The other limbs of the levers are joined by a pivot to the bolting-rod. This is drawn back as the heelplate moves forward. Like the Greener, the Truscott safety bolts the triggers.

A variation on this method of obtaining a backward motion to the locking-bolt is in the patent 18,164 of Robert Jentzsch of 3, Schwindgosse, Vienna. A heelplate is hinged at its top, pressing forward the top of the vertical lever just underneath it. The bottom limb of this lever draws back the locking-bolt. It is a curious fact that the same inventor obtained the previous patent, No. 18,163 of 1888. In this he proposed a locking mechanism, exactly like the lock found on a cupboard door, but one that engaged with the safety bolt so that the gun could be immobilised. In addition, there was a gravity catch on the safety rod that would lock it when the gun was in the vertical position. This would prevent accidental discharge, if the gun were stood against a wall, for example, but not an overhead shot, provided the gun was swung up with the butt against the user's shoulder from a roughly horizontal position. It is a further odd point of this specification that all these improvements

are drawn on a pinfire gun with what appears to be the classic forward-lever Lefaucheux action. (See Volume One.)

*R. B. Jentzsch patent No. 18,164 of 1888*

The balance of the heelplate grip safeties differ from those so far considered, in that, the safety catch in the action is released by the rod in the stock moving forward. In his patent, No. 5729 of 1882, Thomas Gilbert has a spring-loaded centre portion of the stock in an Anson and Deeley actioned boxlock gun. Over the triggerwork and sears is a sliding bar with cutouts. Either triggers or sears, or presumably both, are blocked when the slide is to the rear, and free when the slide is forwards.

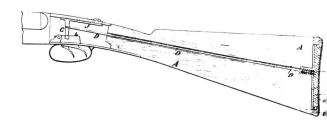

*H. Silver and W. Fletcher patent No. 12,329 of 1886*

Essentially, the same idea is repatented as No. 12,329 of 1886 by Silver and Fletcher, two men who seem to have been obsessed by safety catches. Their sliding bolt, on this occasion, runs under the top strap with one or more projections down into the lockwork to bolt triggers etc., when the slide is to the rear. Seemingly identical to this is the safety contained in patent No. 16,930 of 1884 granted to J. Bulloch and G. P. Appleyard.

Yet a fourth variation is found in the patent, No. 20,196 of 1890, granted to Louis Minèstre and Paul Pasquier of Rue Nyston, Liège. Here, the rod from the heelplate has a cross-piece at its forward end that fits into a slot in the trigger blades. The forward portion of this slot is deeper than the rear portion, so that when the safety rod is forwards the triggers are free to lift the sears.

It is something of a relief to have a totally different mode of using the forward-moving safety-rod. In George Henry Needham's patent, No. 4693 of 1883, the forward end of the rod pushes forward the top limb of an L-shaped lever that is transversely pivoted at its angle. This motion depresses the forward-facing lower limb of the lever which bears on, and thereby cramps, the top limb of a V-shaped mainspring. How practical it would be to cramp both mainsprings of a double-barrel gun in this way is a moot point.

The same patent also covers another realisation of the same principle; a species of grip safety so constructed that the act of gripping the gun cramped the mainspring. To do this there is a lever pivoted behind the triggers which rocks on a transverse pivot. The forward internal end of this lever is lowered by a user grasping the gun so the mainspring is bent down and tensioned.

There is an almost identical scheme patented the following year, 1884, as patent No. 11,898 by the agent S. P. Wilding for W. H. Whitney of East Brookfield, Massachusetts. Examples of these have not come to our notice and we suspect that the inconvenience of use outweighs the potential advantages of the idea.

Another design that has no close affinity with any other, though it was also a grip safety, is

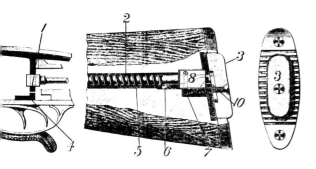

*Drawing from* The Field *of J. Bulloch and G. P. Appleyard patent No. 16,930 of 1884*

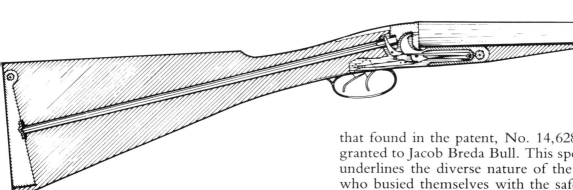

*G. H. Needham patent No. 4693 of 1883*

that found in the patent, No. 14,628 of 1884, granted to Jacob Breda Bull. This specification underlines the diverse nature of the patentees who busied themselves with the safety of the hammerless gun. Bull tells us that he was a newspaper editor of Christiania, Norway.

What he proposes is a stud on the top strap that the gun user has to hold down with the thumb of his right hand to permit the gun to fire. The specification also proposes a variety of ways in which this motion could be used. In one version, the inside of the thumb catch has an incline cut on it that works against another incline cut on the top of a vertical lever on a transverse pivot. The bottom of this lever swings to the rear, out of engagement with the trigger blades, as the stud is depressed. In the other variant the safety is some sort of bell-crank lever, still pivoted transversely, so that, pushing down on the top horizontal limb swings to the rear the vertical portion to free the trigger blades.

It is a tendency of human endeavour to believe that if one is a good idea, then two must be twice as good. In addition to the catalogue of safeties that bolt a gunlock at one site, there are yet more that act 'belt and braces fashion' at two sites. Looked at in chronological order, the first is patent No. 133 of 1879 in the name of James Lang. This is a somewhat unusual safety as it chooses to act at one of its blocking points on the mainspring of the gunlock. The other site is almost inevitably the trigger blade. This is the safety catch used on the trigger-plate lever-cocked Lang guns and so is met with reasonably often. Under the top strap is a slide with two downward projecting legs, one that blocks the triggers while the forward leg is poised over two inward-projecting points from the mainsprings. It is a fair comment on this action to report that on the example in the author's (DJB) collection, one of these mainspring projections has broken off.

*J. Lang patent No. 133 of 1879*

The slide is pushed back, applying the safety, by the top of the cocking lever pushing back on the front leg of the slide. The safe is taken off by a turning lever on the top strap that internally works a little cam acting on the slide. The patent also covers a simplified version that only bolts the triggers. The front limb of the slide is shorter, but is still pushed back by the head of the underlever.

The rest of the patents in this sub-group act on triggers and tumblers, and perhaps the best known of these is that of Silver and Fletcher, No. 4210 of 1880. This patent was featured in a series of lavish advertisements in the sporting press of the time and is a species of grip safety with the safety lever protruding through the top strap. Internally, this lever continues forward, just under the strap, and is hung on a transverse pivot above the trigger work. Forward of this pivot the lever divides into a Y-shape and is held down by a light leaf spring so that the tumblers are caught and held at full-cock. Behind the pivot pint of the safety lever is another lever, transversely pivoted under the top strap and passing obliquely forwards through a slot in the safety lever, so that, as the latter goes down, the vertical lever moves back. The position of this

(Above and on right) *S. and W. Silver and Co. advertisement of 1883*

vertical lever is such that, in its forward position, its bottom end is on the trigger blades. Grasping the external safety lever and squeezing it into the stock lifts the forward end out of engagement with the tumblers and moves the vertical lever back off the trigger blades.

There is a second Silver and Fletcher patent, No. 4872 of 1881, also concerned with a spring-cocked gun, that contains a safety mechanism very like the 1880 specification. Again, it is the triggers and tumblers that are bolted, but now by a slide that fits just above the trigger work. The slide is roughly T-shaped in that, at the front, there are sideways projections that engage with the tumblers and, about halfway down, the stem has a thickened part that, at 'safe', bears on the tops of the trigger blades. To move this slide, two sites for grip levers are proposed, one on the top of the stock, the other underneath. Squeezing in the underneath lever causes a wedge-shaped projection inside the stock to rise and the incline bears on a slot in the slide to force it to the rear. On the top lever version, there is an incline formed on the locking slide and a downward projection from the grip safe into the stock works on this. The underlever version is shown with a novel variation in the form of a thumb button which has to be drawn to the rear to permit the grip safe to work – a sort of safety on a safety catch.

Besides these two Silver and Fletcher designs there are four other less well-known mechanisms that share the same basic mode of action.

The earliest of these patented, No. 134 of 1879, is the design of those two famous names of nineteenth-century gunmaking, Henry Holland

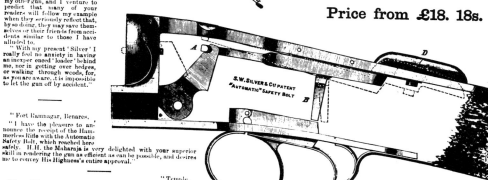

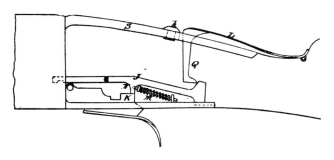

*H. Silver and W. Fletcher patent No. 4872 of 1881*

and Thomas Perkes. Their idea was to have a thumb slide on the top strap and by this to work a near vertical lever, transversely pivoted, so that as the top of the lever was pulled back, the bottom blocked the movement of the trigger blades. To this lever is pinned a slide that runs forward, so that, in its forward position it will catch the specially-shaped tumbler and prevent the latter from moving from the full-cock position. In addition, the shape of the projections on the forward end of the slide and the

recess on the tumbler are such that should the sear be accidently jarred off then slide and tumbler will lock together and only be released when the lockwork is recocked. In this way the potentially disastrous situation of a gun firing as the safety catch is operated is avoided.

A little later, in 1879, two more famous figures in the gun world, William Anson and John Deeley, obtained a patent, No. 907, for a device of this nature. Not surprisingly it is shown on one of their classic guns and, once again, there is a slide on the top strap working an internal lever. In this instance, however, the internal lever is a reversed L, pivoted transversely at its angle which is just above the trigger strap. Pulling back the thumb slide causes the forward lower end of the L-lever to rise. This motion makes a roughly T-shaped catch, pivoted at the bottom of the stem, flip forwards to bolt the trigger blades. Fitted to this catch is a rod running forwards, finally curving upwards behind the standing-breech to work the second tumbler catch. The tumbler catch is pivoted across the top of the rear of the standing-breech and for

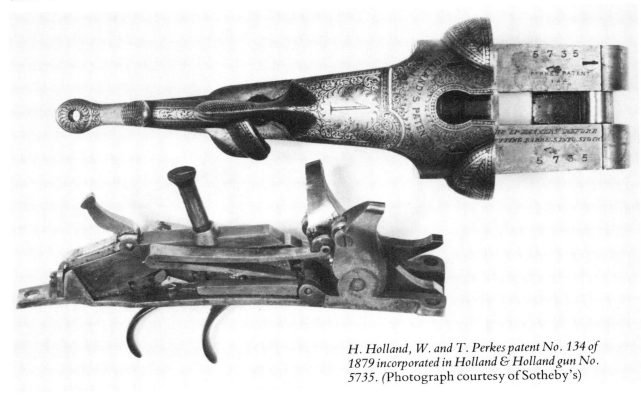

*H. Holland, W. and T. Perkes patent No. 134 of 1879 incorporated in Holland & Holland gun No. 5735. (Photograph courtesy of Sotheby's)*

each lock has a downward pawl-shaped catch which, when forward, lies in a bent cut in the rear of the head of the tumbler at full-cock. The pawl and bent are shaped to lock the mechanism if the tumbler should be jarred off. However, in the ordinary course of events, the pawl-catch is rotated back and up, out of the tumbler arc, by the rod from the trigger bolt moving backwards as the trigger bolt is taken off.

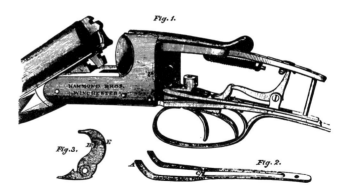

Drawing from The Field of H. and E. Hammond patent No. 4541 of 1882

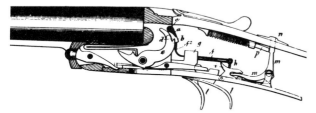

*W. Anson and J. Deeley patent No. 907 of 1879*

There remain a group of safety catches acting on both trigger and tumblers that differ from those just considered. This, by virtue of the fact that they combine a trigger-bolting catch with a second catch worked by the triggers that, in turn, remove the obstruction from the path of the tumblers. They can, thus, fairly be regarded as a combination of two of those groups previously considered.

In Webley's patent, No. 1860 of 1880, the trigger bolt is a simple internal downward projection from a thumb slide on the top strap. The tumbler interceptor is a lever, pivoted behind the tumbler, so that, as the rear end is raised by the trigger, the front end is lowered out of the tumbler's path.

In the H. and E. Hammond patent, No. 4541 of 1882, the trigger bolt is, for all purposes, identical to the Anson and Deeley patent No. 907 of 1879. The novelty lies in the tumbler catch, which is a long two-limbed spring, something like a tuning fork. It is fixed behind the triggers and curves forwards and up so that the free ends are halfway up behind the standing-breech. At the free end, each limb of this spring has an outward projection that engages with the tumbler head at full-cock. To permit the gun to fire, the trigger blades act on inward projections on the spring so as to lift the catch away from the tumblers.

Another variant on this theme is the patent, No. 15,209 of 1884, obtained by J. Darby, 'gun furniture and safety maker' of Loveday Street, Birmingham. Here, the trigger bolt is a slide moved back and forth by a side lever, and the tumbler bolt is a vertical slide that a projection of the trigger blade, forward from its pivot, pulls down as the trigger is squeezed.

The last member of this sub-group is another ingenious idea patented by Frederick Beesley, No. 14,488 of 1884. The trigger-bolting aspect of this design is a fairly ordinary slide that is pushed forwards by a thumb catch on the top strap. However, this slide also pushes forward two rods that run forwards to act on the short ends of two L-shaped levers, pivoted on vertical axes at their angles, with their shorter limbs towards the centreline of the gun and their longer limbs forwards. As the short limb of each lever is pushed forwards, its long limb swings outward and an upward projection on it blocks either the fall of the tumblers, or the movement of the mainsprings.

*F. Beesley patent No. 14,488 of 1884*

The final group of our formal classification of safety catches are those that act on the gun mechanism at three sites. Here again, we must sound a note of caution. Modifications during or after manufacture, which delete one or more of the methods of bolting, will appear to confound our classification. Description is aided by the fact that every one of these triple-bolting systems act simultaneously on the tumblers, sears and triggers. Three of the patents under consideration do this by a single sliding catch, of more or less complex shape, that in its forward position locks or blocks the three sites. As part of his patent, No. 1881 of 1882, perhaps better known as 'Watson's Carlton', William Tranter includes a safety of this type. The bolt of the Carlton safety is, in plan view, a Y-shape. The two prongs slide into slots on the rear of the tumblers while the stem, cut with suitable slots,

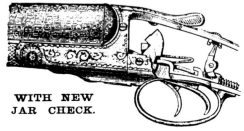

*T. W. Watson advertisement of 1883*

bolts triggers and sears. This slide is worked by a vertical lever that, in turn, is actuated by a thumb slide on the top strap. Very similar to the foregoing mechanism is Darby's safety that we only know as a rather generalised specification, No. 2224 of 1883. In this, an Anson and Deeley action is to have a slide of unspecified shape that is described as acting in the same way as the Carlton safety.

To conclude this group we have, not surprisingly, yet another Silver and Fletcher patent, No. 1064 of 1884. Here we have a sliding bolt that is, in side view, L-shaped with one limb under the top strap and the other projecting down into the action. This vertical limb is shaped at its bottom to fit over the trigger blades and the tails of the sears. The portion of the safety that slides under the top strap blocks the tumblers and, to do this, it is, in plan view, a Y-shape. The two arms of the Y are so positioned, and of such a thickness, that when they are in the forward position there would not be a sufficient space above the tumblers for the tumblers to rotate. When the safety slide is drawn to the rear by the thumb slide on the top strap, the tumblers now have clearance and the sears and triggers are simultaneously freed. However, as if to give point to our opening remarks, this patent specification also includes a simple trigger-bolting safe in which only the vertical limb described above is retained.

There is but one more safety that bolts triggers, sears and tumblers, but it is different and more complex than the other three. In 1882, William Anson obtained a patent, No. 4089, of this type, naturally concerned with the Anson and Deeley action. This safety is worked by the usual thumb slide on the top strap. Inside the gun this works a rocking lever, which is a

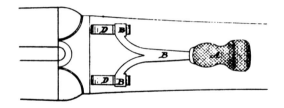

*H. Silver and W. Fletcher patent No. 1064 of 1884*

reversed L-shape, pivoted transversely at its angle just above the trigger plate. As the forward limb of this L rises, it rocks forwards a catch (pivoted just behind the triggers) that, in its forward position, impedes not only the trigger blades and the sear tails, but also the rear ends of a pair of levers, one for each lock, that are pivoted again on transverse pivots up in the angle between the top strap and the rear of the standing-breech. Both these levers sweep downwards in a gentle arc to the rear; each has formed on it a nose that catches with a suitable notch cut in the rear of the tumbler. In fact, this part of the safety is a second sear because of it, like the true sear, is disengaged by the rising trigger. Yet again, tucked away in the end of this specification, is a simpler safety, a simple slide to bolt triggers and sears worked by a vertical lever and top slide.

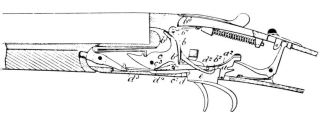

*W. Anson patent No. 4089 of 1882*

The standard Westley Richards safety would seem to derive from this patent, reduced to the rocking lever blocking the triggers.

While not in the ordinary sense of the term safety catches, but bearing a close affinity to them, are a small group of mechanisms designed to prevent one barrel of a double-gun being jarred off by the firing of the other. With trigger pulls of ordinary weight, and a properly designed and constructed lock, this should not happen and untold millions of guns have satisfactorily fired uncountable billions of cartridges without the benefit of such devices. Nevertheless, in the patent records of our period there are five such mechanisms which, for the sake of completeness, we must consider and we believe that they fit most logically at this point.

The first, and certainly the oddest, is the patent, No. 1917 of 1872, obtained by Seth John Wallis. The stated aims of this were: to prevent accidental double discharge; to prevent the user pulling the trigger of a previously discharged barrel; and to ensure that both barrels and locks received equal use and wear. To accomplish these ends, a single trigger is described which acts on an eight-toothed ratchet-wheel mounted vertically on transverse pivots that are carried on trunnions built up from the trigger plate. Each pull of the trigger rotates the ratchet-wheel by one-eighth of a revolution, causing it to engage alternately with 'sear-releaser discs', one on each side of the ratchet but on the same axle. To prepare this trigger mechanism for the subsequent shot, the trigger is spring-loaded and thus has to be released to swing forwards between shots. Viewed as a single trigger, this would have been a fatal defect, which may explain why, despite frequent advertisements offering the patent rights for sale, we have no evidence that it was ever adopted.

A further claim of this patent is a means of showing which barrel is the next to be fired. Either a projection from the sear-releaser disc was to protrude through the bottom of the trigger plate, or a similar projection was to push out a spring-loaded stud from a small box on the bottom of the trigger plate.

In part of Samuel Allport's patent, No. 2993 of 1881, he proposes a fan-shaped piece of metal pivoted on a vertical axle at its point. This to be so arranged that, as one trigger is pulled, the blade of the trigger displaces the fan piece laterally so that it blocks the other trigger blade. A mechanism that is almost identical, but acts instead on the sears, is contained in Swinburn's patent, No. 17,088 of 1884.

Also acting on the sears is a little device found in Greener's patent, No. 4516 of 1882. A U-shaped piece of steel is fitted, upside down and hung on a longitudinal pivot, to the rear of the action of a boxlock gun. As one sear rose, the other limb of the U pushed down on the other sear. A device exactly like this, but applied to a sidelock gun, was illustrated in the *Shooting Times* on 3 September 1884, credited to William S. Riley of The Eagle Gun Works, Vauxhall Street, Birmingham.

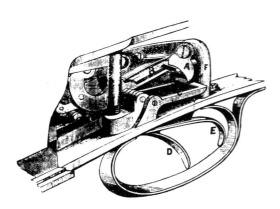

*Drawing from* Shooting Times, *5 September 1884, showing the W. S. Riley double-discharge preventer*

The final member of this quintet is part of a patent, No. 3606 of 1884, granted to John Henry Apted. Between the trigger blades, appears a little catch, rather like a capital letter T with an abbreviated head. This catch is pivoted at the bottom of the upright limb on a longitudinal axis and there are notches cut in the trigger blades so arranged that, as one trigger is pulled, the catch is displaced to the other side to lock that trigger. There is also a variation on this idea

In the overall pursuit of the ideal of safety, several inventors resurrected the idea, that had been used on hammer guns a decade or so previously, of providing some external indicator to announce a cartridge in the chamber. The first of these is part of the ingenious Adsett gun covered by the specification No. 574 of 1879. The idea was simply to have a spring-loaded pin that was pushed out from the side of the standing-breech if a cartridge was forcing back the firing pins. The latter had formed in them an inclined slot, so that, as they moved backwards the indicator pin was pushed out.

An idea that was protected (more accurately re-protected, if such were valid) by Henry and Edwin Hammond was part of patent No. 4541 of 1882. This was to use the head of a cartridge lying in the breech to push back a rod which, in turn, moved a shutter that exposed the word 'Loaded' set in gold on the top of the action. Essentially, this is the Horsley patent, No. 710 of 1868, though the Hammond specification is more subtle. It proposes means by which the tumbler of a gun, drawn as an Anson and Deeley boxlock, will push forward a small spring-loaded lever set vertically in the head of

*J. Adsett gun: J. and T. Adsett patent No. 574 of 1879*

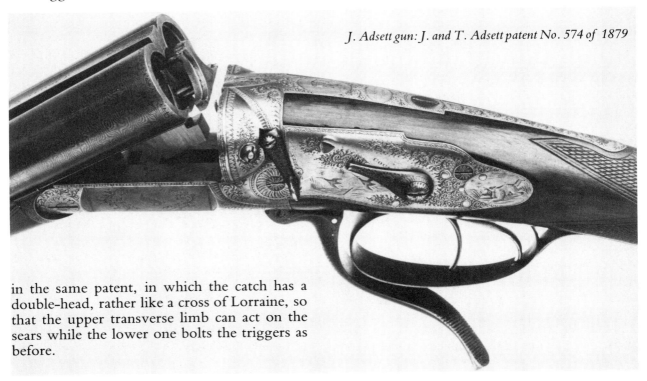

in the same patent, in which the catch has a double-head, rather like a cross of Lorraine, so that the upper transverse limb can act on the sears while the lower one bolts the triggers as before.

the stock, but fixed to the rear of the standing-breech. When the tumbler is down, another shutter on the outside is in a different position from that when the tumbler is cocked. All in all, a frail-looking set of mechanisms which we fear, if ever made, would be unlikely to survive in any but the most caring of hands.

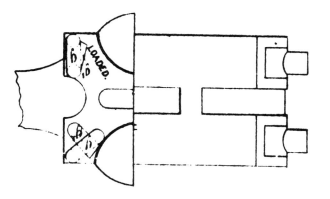

*H. and E. Hammond patent No. 4541 of 1882*

Another resurrected loaded-indicator is the subject of a patent, No. 1290 of 1886, by a Roumanian, Dr Georg Flaischen. His design covered the use of a lever, bent upwards at its forward end in a right-angle. The lever was to be fitted on the inside of the chamber in a gun barrel and pivoted at the rearward end so that, when a cartridge was in position, the forward end of the lever came up through a small hole and stood proud of the outside of the barrel. A small leaf spring serves to retract it. In all essentials, this is a resurrection of the Riley patent, No. 491 of 1866.

A very short step from the idea of a loaded-indicator is that of a cocking-indicator. Two

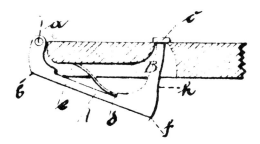

*G. Flaischen patent No. 1290 of 1886*

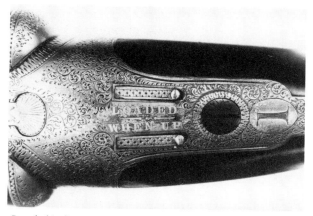

*Loaded indicators on a gun built on Reeves patent No. 2147 of 1879*

designs are seemingly quite close to the loaded-indicators that we have been considering and will serve as a bridge between the two. Part of the Reeves patent, No. 2147 of 1879, and the James patent, No. 2531 of 1881, both use the heads of the tumblers, when in the rearward or cocked position, to raise studs on the top strap of the gun. The difference between the two is slight. The Reeves indicator is a lever, bent at right-angles and pivoted on a transverse pivot at the angle, with one limb down into the body of the gun, where it is pushed back by the head of the tumbler, thereby raising the other limb of the lever lying along the top strap. The James patent is even simpler, in that, a spring-loaded stud with a sloped bottom is forced upward by the head of the tumbler as this comes to full-cock.

With a hammer gun the user can see the state of his locks. It was the aim of some inventors to preserve this facility on a hammerless gun. What was done was quite simply to provide windows, or portholes, through which the user could peer, if he were so minded, to view the works. Because they were one of the major makers to the trade, the most widely seen of such designs is the Scott patent, No. 3223 of 1875. A round porthole about seven-eighths of an inch in diameter is bored through the lock-plate in such a position that the heads of the cocked tumblers can be seen. To exclude water and dirt this hole is glazed with 'glass or other transparent substance'. On actual guns this

*Scott's patent crystal indicator: W. M. Scott patent No. 3223 of 1875*

window is smaller, about three-eighths of an inch is more normal. Guns of this style will be found bearing the names of fully half the upper end of the British gun trade of that time.

The same idea, but with a smaller porthole, is also to be seen on the Walsh patent hammerless gun, No. 5106 of 1878. (See Chapter Ten.)

The final example of this group is the rectangular window found in the top strap of the MacNaughton lever-cocked hammerless gun. Through this, the heads of the tumblers can be seen on the trigger-plate action. To enable this window to be used when the top lever was in the closed position, a wide slot was cut through the top lever. It is worthy of note that this slot was retained as a feature on some MacNaughton top straps long after the window had ceased to be incorporated.

An answer to this problem of making a sportsman aware of the state of his locks, which harks back to the hammer gun and thence ties in with the self-cocking hammer gun, was to place on the outside of the lockplate a lever, indicator or vestigial hammer which, since it was on the same spindle as the tumbler within the lock, would indicate the position of the latter. We are aware of four such indicators. They are respectively: the Gibbs and Pitt patent, No. 284 of 1873; the Adsett and Adsett patent, No. 574 of 1879; the Bonehill and Matthews patent, No. 1952 of 1880; and the James patent, No. 2531 of 1881. The first and last of this

quartet are drawn as having chequered thumb pieces, which would permit the lock to be lowered to half-cock and raised again to full-cock, just like a hammer gun. On the Adsett, and the Bonehill and Matthews, this indicator is a simple pointer which cannot be safely controlled by the user. It serves only to indicate the movements of the tumbler inside the gun.

(At this point, we should remark again on the Bentley patent, No. 17,037 of 1884, which we included in our self-cocking hammer gun section. Having examined closely a gun of this type we feel it a moot point if the external hammers could safely be manipulated by a sportsman with cold wet hands. So, the Bentley may more properly belong in the present section despite having the visible firing pins which caused us to place it with the self-cocking hammer guns.)

The idea behind the cocking-indicator has survived in sidelock hammerless guns right up to the present day. Instead of a lever, the indicator is now an engraved line or arrow on the external end of the tumbler spindle so that position can be ascertained at a glance.

Another link with the hammered sporting shotgun is provided by a gadget shown on the Ansell specification, No. 2349 of 1872. It is a repetition of the William Powell patent, No. 1055 of 1869, having the word 'Loaded' in gold letters on the head of a slightly enlarged firing pin.

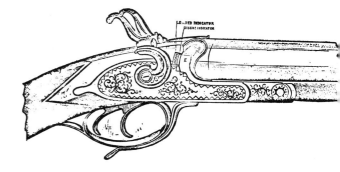

*Drawing from* Land and Water, *5 July 1873, showing W. Ansell gun with loaded indicators*

There are a few safeties that defy classification. The easiest of these to deal with is patent No. 14,444 of 1887, granted to Edgar Harrison and Edwin George Anson. The title of this is, 'An Improvement of cocking and making safe hammerless guns and rifles', but careful study reveals no trace of any safety mechanism described in the specification. (We mention this point for the benefit of any other researchers who should be so rash as to become embroiled with the patent specifications.)

A mechanism that we dealt with earlier (Chapter Four), is contained in Richard Hill's patent, No. 1728 of 1879. In this the projections from the barrel-flats that bore down on the cocking levers had to be slid aside to permit the cocking levers to rise as the tumblers fell. Truly a unique safety catch.

Another idea that stands alone is contained in the Joseph Needham patent, No. 5710 of 1882, an unillustrated provisional specification. This covers the idea of a safety catch of unspecified detail which was to be removed by a trigger, set ahead of the ordinary triggers in the guard. In some ways this was a good idea, but surely Joseph Needham should have realised the potential problems of such a device on his way to the Patent Office.

Likewise possessing a certain naive appeal is the idea protected by the London agent William Henry Beck for the Parisian gunmaker, Y. C. M. Tassel. In this patent, No. 5420 of 1881, it was proposed to fit two flaps like spaniels' ears which were to drop down to box-in the trigger guard. Amazingly, there is another patent on a very similar mechanism. In 1889 a Cambridge M.A., F. J. Candy of Fen Ditton, near Cambridge, obtained a patent, No. 18,275, on a collapsible box. One of the uses he foresaw for this was as a trigger-protecting safety.

There is one more patent at the very bottom of this rag-bag, not really a safety, but closely allied. The intention of this mechanism was to prevent a gun being opened until its safety catch was applied. However, the danger does not lie in opening a gun with the safety catch off, but in slamming it shut and jarring off the locks onto live cartridges. In most guns the safety catches are automatically applied as the gun is opened, so this contingency has been covered and would seem to be an elegant solution to the problem. However, James Hannay, a 'gentleman' of 33,

Porchester Terrace, London felt otherwise and invested in a patent, No. 1011 of 1885. From the familiar slide on the top strap, it was proposed to fit, inside the gun, a forward-facing limb. This was, in turn, to be pivoted to the top limb of an L-shaped lever and all arranged in such a way that, when the top slide was in its forward position, the lower limb of the L would block the path of the rear of the Purdey-bolt. Though sound in theory, this idea is yet another that would, in practice, collect more than its fair share of curses.

The opening paragraphs of this chapter included a tale from *Land and Water*. To help round off, we quote from the rival publication, *The Field*. In the issue of 9 April 1887, the following letter appeared.

---

**UNEXPECTED ADVANTAGE OF A SAFETY BOLT**
SIR: It may interest your readers to know that the British officers who were recently attacked by Arabs, when out shooting in the neighbourhood of the Pyramids, owe their lives to the fact that the Arabs could not fire the officers' hammerless guns.

The English papers omit to state that the Arabs intended to shoot their prisoners at once with the officers' breechloaders. Fortunately the safety bolt had been turned, so that, not understanding the action, they gave up the idea, determining to hang the officers, from which fate they were providentially rescued just in time.
Killingworth Hedges, C.E.
P. & O. SS Tanjore, Brindisi, March 31.

---

# CHAPTER SEVEN

# The Forend Fastener

It is a useful distinguishing feature of the two decades we are considering that, at that time, there came into wide use some sort of 'patent catch' to hold the forend of a shotgun in place. Indeed, in a shotgun that is completely conventional, the presence of such a fastener should suggest a date later than 1870 rather than before it. That is not to say this is an absolute rule. Such catches were made and used in the 1860s, but the vast majority belong to this later period. Equally, the use of the old cross-bolt did not abruptly cease. This simple arrangement, even then 200 years old, remained in diminishing use throughout our period.

The shortcomings of a cross-bolt fastening are obvious to all who have ever used one. If too loose it is insecure, if too tight it is difficult to take the gun apart. Most old shotguns with cross-bolts bear scars on their forends, where all sorts of unsuitable tools have been used to force the bolt out.

As with so many features of the sporting shotgun, the inspiration seems to be French. (See Volume One, Chapter One for a fuller discussion of this.) V. D. Majendie's account of the Paris Exhibition of 1867, in the *Illustrated London News* of 31 August 1867, seems to confirm our view:

> **M. Blanchard, in common with other French Makers, lays great stress upon his 'système de demontage' or facility for taking the gun to pieces . . . nearly every French gunmaker has been at pains to elaborate some ingenious contrivance specially with this view.**

The reader will probably be less than surprised to learn that there are 29 patents concerned with forend fasteners. Very commonly the fastener is only part of the patent and other aspects of the gun are covered in the remainder of these specifications. These designs have more than a passing resemblance to the various barrel-bolting mechanisms. We therefore start again with the inert mechanisms, i.e. those that do not feature a spring to snap the bolt shut.
snap the bolt shut.

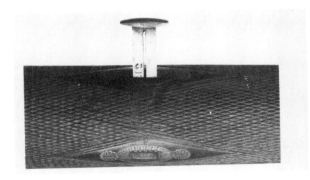

*The traditional cross-bolt and escutcheon fastening*

There are but two patents, both provisional specifications. The first, No. 1735 of 1878, is in the name of Frederick Thomas Baker of Fleet Street, London. This, like so many of its kind, is vague, but in this case we have the advantage of an actual example to study. In essence, it is the

*F. Baker patent No. 1735 of 1878 for a forend fastening*

Henry Jones screw-grip action born again as a forend fastener with the screw-grip worked by a flat bar on the underside of the forend. The bar has a knurled portion at each end to assist the user to grip it. Something similar may be described in part of another very vague provisional specification, No. 3756 of 1873, by Scott.

Aside from this there is one type of inert forend catch that will be encountered with reasonable frequency. Greener called it a 'grip' catch, but in fact it was patented in 1866 by

Charles Harvey of Wilkinson's. (See Volume One. Wilkinson's later became the Wilkinson Sword company we know today.) This is a resurrection of the Lefaucheux action, with a forward facing underlever that turned a screw-grip turret in the forend to engage with a bite on the barrel lump. This produced a sound, positive and neat mechanism that was favoured by some makers, notably Rigby's in London and Horsley in York. What sounds like a snap version of this is described in Samuel Mathews's provisional specification, No. 3573 of 1878. One of the advantages of this is that, as the lever is turned to the right on the upside down gun, the bite acts as a cam on the forend iron and raises the forend off the barrels. When the lever is at the full extent of its travel to the right, it becomes a convenient handle to grasp for the final removal of the forend.

*Grip forend from a Horsley gun (woodwork removed)*

If we turn, firstly, to the sliding snap-bolts, we find a remarkable state of affairs. Here we have ten patents obtained for a single idea. We cannot explain this situation, which is all the more curious in that the bulk of the patentees were working in Birmingham at the same period. We would, therefore, expect each to know of other inventions through the routine gossip of the trade.

The subject of this multiple, and therefore useless, protection is the scheme of having a push-rod that protrudes from the tip of the forend with a coil spring to hold the rod, and the locking-bolt fixed to it, in the forward position. In this position the locking-bolt engages with a bite cut in the rear of the forend loop and is freed by pushing in the rod. The patents on this are as follows:

No. 1825 of 1872 granted to **William Spinks Riley**
No. 3791 of 1872 granted to **William Anson**
No. 953 of 1873 granted to **Ebenezer Hollis**
No. 2193 of 1873 granted to **William Powell**
No. 3780 of 1875 granted to **John Bardell and Edward Blakemore**
No. 4215 of 1877 granted to **W. Woodward**
No. 3466 of 1881 granted to **Francis Robertson and John Joyce**
No. 14626 of 1885 granted to **Edwin Green**
No. 5224 of 1887 granted to **Job Cox**
No. 2563 of 1889 granted to **Arthur Nouvelle**

There are, it is true, variations in the way the spring is housed, but it would be a bold man who definitely ascribed an unmarked example. Despite this, the generic name 'Anson' is currently applied to all such fasteners. But for practical (and we suspect, legal) purposes, all these can be regarded as the same design.

*Anson-type, but unmarked, forend fastening from a Lang self-cocking hammer gun (woodwork removed)*

*W. Anson forend fastening (woodwork removed) patent No. 953 of 1873*

There are but two variants on this idea. Both are distinctive and one is tucked away in the Walker patent, No. 700 of 1876. A push-in forend stud works a sort of scissors-grip, via links fixed to the handles of the scissors. The other is a part of the patent, No. 4291 of 1880, granted to John Field Swinburn. In this, a push-in rod opens a pair of spring-loaded jaws.

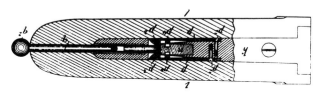

*J. Swinburn patent No. 4291 of 1880*

There is another group of forend fastener patents, somewhat like the 'Anson' type, which are also very much developments of a single theme. The concept was a forward-facing lever that terminated at the front of the forend as a finger grip of some sort. When this was pulled backwards and down, the lever pivoted about one-and-a-half inches back on a transverse pivot; an upward projection inside the forend thus moved in an arc forwards. This movement was then used to draw back a bolt to unlock the forend. There are five patents that, in part, involve this mechanism. They are as follows:

> **No. 953 of 1873 granted to Ebenezer Hollis**
> **No. 129 of 1876 granted to Thomas Perkes**
> **No. 615 of 1876 granted to William Middleditch and Martin Scott**
> **No. 1234 of 1876 granted to Jules François**
> **No. 4215 of 1877 granted to William Woodward**

*W. Scott patent No. 615 of 1876*

The differences between them are both minor and subtle. The Scott uses a coil spring and a rod

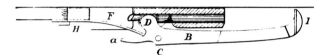

*E. Hollis patent No. 953 of 1873*

that is the forward end of the locking-bolt; both the Hollis and the Renette have a leaf spring bearing down on a shoulder of the opening lever behind the pivot.

Very similar to the above is the fastener that is the subject of a brief provisional specification, No. 2193 of 1873, in the name of William Powell, except that the pull-down lever is back from the tip of the forend. Resembling this closely is the fastener in the patent obtained in Britain by an agent for John Burchard and Frank Novotuy of St Paul, Minnesota. In the latter it is the vertical limb of an L-shaped lever that is the bite and this is withdrawn from the rear of the barrel-loop by a second lever so pivoted that when one is pulled down, the other end lifts the forward end of the L-shaped lever. This is patent No. 5459 of 1883. This description would also fit the mechanism very vaguely described in Scott's provisional specification, No. 712 of 1874.

Yet another scheme that attracted more than its share of patents was the sliding bolt that first appeared as part of the patent, No. 1422 of 1873, obtained by John Deeley and James Simeon Edge, the younger. The greater part of this patent is concerned with bolts that rotate (which we will consider in a moment), but there is one section devoted to the sliding bolt. The idea is to have a push-in stud, which is the bottom of an L-shaped lever, pivoted transversely at its angle. The motion thus given to the upright limb is used to move, forwards in the patent drawing, a locking-bolt. The snap spring shown is a leaf, lying above the lever and bearing down on it just behind the pivot point. In addition to this specification, there are two vague claims in a provisional patent, No. 3756 of 1873, in the name of W. M. Scott. These claims appear to describe the same, or a very similar, system. There is a gun in the author's (DJB) collection with a forend fastener of this type that has the Scott 'tower' trademark and the word 'Patent' on it. We therefore assume that it was made nominally, at least, under one or other of these provisional specifications and, further, that this is what Greener calls the 'key' forend fastener.

*W. Scott patent No. 3756 of 1873*

A widely found and distinctive catch is that consisting of an external chequered, circular, slightly-domed metal button that slides on an escutcheon, inset on the underside of the forend. Some examples have 'push' inlaid in gold. When the button is slid towards the muzzles of the gun, the forend is released because the portion of the bolt in the forend, which is connected directly to the external button, is slid out of engagement with a simple bite formed on the forend lump. The snap spring is a coil fitted round a guide rod and mounted on a small bracket fitted to the underside of the escutcheon. Part of the interest in this mechanism lies in the fact that it is not a patent, but a Registered Design: No. 5938 of 1877 granted to Charles Bland Homer of 31½, Lench Street, Birmingham, who is listed in the directories of the period as a 'gun finisher'.

*C. Homer registered design No. 5938 of 1877*

Similarly distinctive, and perhaps even better known, is the Hackett. This is one of those mechanisms which has no exterior evidence of its existence. It consists simply of a rod with a friction-reducing roller on its forward end that slides on two guides under the forend iron. Between these two guides, and working against

a shoulder on the rod, is a coil spring to force the rod forward so that it will snap into a bite on the rear of the forend loop as the forend is squeezed up to the barrels. To remove the forend, the user has to insert a finger tip behind a lip formed on the front of the forend and give a more or less gentle tug down. Then, by virtue of the roller end, the locking spring is slightly compressed, and the forend can be levered off. This mechanism is part of a patent, No. 964 of 1878, granted to George Hackett.

*G. Hackett patent No. 964 of 1878 (side view)*

Much less common, though somewhat similar, is a notion put forward as part of the William Pountney patent, No. 1970 of 1878. A spring-loaded stud, rather like a hammer-gun firing pin but with a blunt rounded nose, is mounted in the forend loop. From there it engages with a suitable notch in the forend iron. (Mounting and dismounting are as in the Hackett just described.)

By virtue of its patent date, yet another Scott takes priority in the group of designs that use a rotating forend catch. What is described in his patent, No. 1268 of 5 April 1873, is a lever, essentially triangular in shape, pivoted at its top corner on a transverse pivot. The bottom rear angle of this engages with an inclined bite on the front of the forend lump. The catch is disengaged by pushing up the front corner of the triangle. On the specification drawing, it is a push-in, spring-loaded stud on the underside of

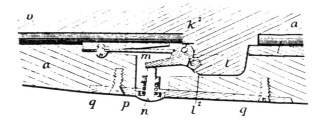

*W. Scott patent No. 1268 of 1873*

the forend that works the bolt, which has an additional leaf snap spring bearing down on its forward end.

Patented a mere fortnight later is a mechanism that has become one of the standard forend fasteners. We refer to the Deeley and Edge patent, No. 1422 of 19 April 1873, which, in developed and variant forms, is still in wide common use today. There are, in fact, four different fasteners included in this specification, one of which we have already considered, in that it is a sliding-bolt type. Contrary to how we now regard the Deeley and Edge mechanism, the basic version in the specification would seem to be for a push-in thumb-pivoted lever. Formed integrally with it is a hook bolt that engages with a bite on the rear of the forend lump. There is a pull-down lever version of this which uses a double-lever in tandem arrangement; pulling down the front of the front lever forces up the front of the rear lever and disengages the bolt as before.

effect, the first type rearranged to become a pull-down lever type. To do this, the bite is moved to the front of the forend lump and in front of the pivot of the lever. The snap spring also lies in front of the bite and is a leaf spring that lifts the lever up and back. The reason for this change is not difficult to understand, for the pull-down lever, like the push-forward under-lever gun action, has the great advantage that the force exerted on the lever is in the same direction as that needed to perform the next function, be it to remove the forend or to open the gun.

*The classic Deeley fastening: J. Deeley and J. Edge patent No. 1422 of 1873*

The final member of the Deeley and Edge patented quartet bears little resemblance to the rest. It is a rotating bolt, very like the original Lefaucheux action, except that its bite is on the front of the forend lump. The snap spring is a V, set above the lever and forwards of the bite so that it is compressed as the opening lever is rotated.

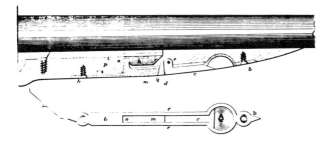

*J. Deeley and J. Edge patent No. 1422 of 1873*

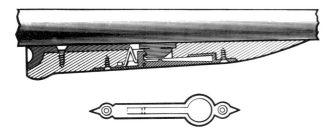

*J. Deeley and J. Edge patent No. 1422 of 1873 (squeeze-in lever version)*

The model most usually seen today, and what we all think of as the Deeley and Edge, is, in

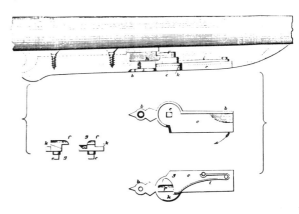

*J. Deeley and J. Edge patent No. 1422 of 1873 (turning lever version)*

Incidentally, a virtually identical mechanism is included as part of the Scott specification, No. 3223 of 1875. Another that sounds very similar is described in the provisional specification of Samuel Mathews, No. 3573 of 1878.

There is yet another patent on this principle, No. 984 of 1885, patented by Richard Redman and Samuel Whitehouse, both of Birmingham, which differs only in that the V snap spring is behind the bite instead of in front.

Before we leave the Deeley and Edge, it is appropriate to remark on another catch that may well be mistaken for it. This is the Thomas Bailey patent, No. 3240 of 1876. It shows an exterior lever, identical in form to the Deeley and Edge, but mounted in such a way that the lever is pushed forward and down. Internally it is another L-shaped lever, but pivoted this time at the top of the vertical limb so that the turning motion withdraws a catch formed in the angle of the L. The snap spring is shown as a leaf, bearing down on a shoulder at the top of the vertical limb just in front of the pivot.

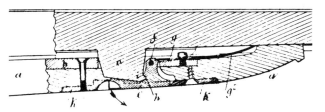

*T. Bailey patent No. 3240 of 1876*

Finally, there are three mechanisms that qualify as rotating snap types. One is a leaf spring version of the Hackett and part of the same patent, No. 964 of 1878. There is the friction-roller as before, but now it is mounted on a short lever pivoted on the underside of the forend iron. On the rear of this lever near its bottom is a short backward projection upon which a leaf spring bears down.

The other two rotating snap actions are part of the Bonehill patent, No. 2323 of 1878. Here it is either a spring-loaded hook or, on the version known to the author (DJB), a simple V-spring that engages, Hackett-like, with the forend lump. The simple V-spring is, perhaps, the simplest of all the fastenings.

*C. G. Bonehill patent No. 2323 of 1878*

The other rotating action Greener called a 'sugar tongs grip'. This consists of two sprung limbs, rather like a tuning fork with inward projections at each of the free ends, mounted on the underside of the forend iron so that the free ends can grip onto the forend loop.

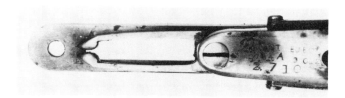

*'Sugar tongs' forend fastening on a Moore and Grey hammer ejector gun*

What could be thought of as one half of a pair of sugar tongs is part of Bonehill's specification, No. 8471 of 1884. Also in this patent is another design for a more distinctive forend catch. A rotating bite, fixed on a vertical pivot under the forend iron, is made to turn by a pull-down lever under the forend. The position of this lever behind its pivot (i.e. the rising point), has an incline on it that forces a stud on the bolt to one side. The snap spring is a leaf acting on the opening lever.

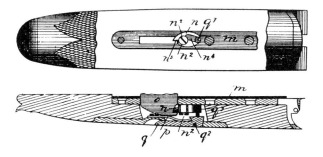

*C. G. Bonehill patent No. 8471 of 1884*

*Gun No. 2025 by Thomas Horsley of York
which has its forend hinged to the knuckle of the action*

There are times when it is inconvenient that a shotgun breaks down into three pieces and to overcome this a few inventors have produced guns that take down into two parts.

It was, at one time, almost universal on Continental guns for the forend to be hinged to the action. This idea was rarely used in Britain, but there is in the author's (DJB) collection a gun by Horsley of York that uses a cross-bolt to fix the barrels to the forend. This is, in turn, retained by two pins that slide in slots in the knuckle of the bar-in-wood action. This gun, No. 2025, can be accurately dated to 1871, but it is not known how many of such guns were made,

probably very few. The idea does not appear to have been patented.

Also in 1871, the idea of a permanently fitted forend appeared as part of the Westley Richards specification, No. 1572 of 1871. In this, the forend iron is formed with two curved rearward projections by which it is fixed to the outside of the narrow action bar. In typical Westley Richards style, the gun is drawn stocked bar-in-wood. Once again, this idea seems to have been little used.

There are more British patents of our period in which the forend is retained on the barrels. The first of these, provisional patent No. 585 of

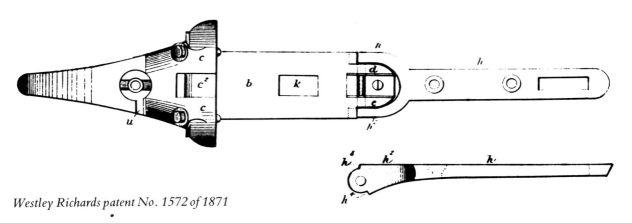

*Westley Richards patent No. 1572 of 1871*

1876 taken out by J. Johnson and R. Wayne, sounds so like the next that a single description will suffice. In No. 292 of 1877 in the name of Charles Osborne Ellis and Edward William Wilkinson (who traded as Charles Osborne & Co. in Birmingham) there is a transverse rod through the forend loop and under the metal part of the forend, the forend iron as it is termed. The forend, by virtue of suitable slots, is free to slide fore and aft. The catch that holds it in both positions is an ingenious arrangement that depends on a sloped step cut in the rear of the forend loop. Behind this, in the forend, is a horizontal arm on a transverse pivot. The rear end of the arm, nearest the butt of the gun, cams to the surface of the forend a push-in stud. The length of the arm is such that, when the forend is

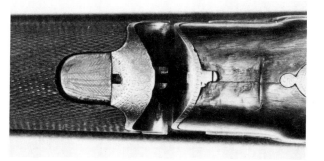

*C. Ellis and E. Wilkinson patent No. 292 of 1877*

in the rear position, the front of the arm bears on the wider upper portion of the forend iron. Then, if the button is squeezed in, this stop is removed and the forend is free to slide forwards until the front of the arm meets the narrower, lower portion of the forend iron. There is a V-spring that holds the front of the locking arm up so that the forend is held in both positions. It may be of passing interest to note at this point that Charles Osborne Ellis was the grandson of Charles Osborne and that William Edward Wilkinson had been apprenticed to Charles Osborne.

The final member of this group is a British patent, No. 1143 of 1878, obtained for Pierre Laffiteau and Louis Rieger of Paris by the agent A. P. Price. Here, to enable a gun with a fixed forend to be taken down, the bottom of the rear of the forend iron is made to hinge down as part of a snap catch.

As with all the groups we have considered, the harsh selection process of practical usage has decimated the ranks of the patented designs. In the case of the forend fasteners only two have survived, in the sense that they are used on British-made guns today, the push-rod 'Anson' or the lever-catch 'Deeley'. Why this should be so is debatable, especially as some of those designs abandoned appear to possess desirable characteristics.

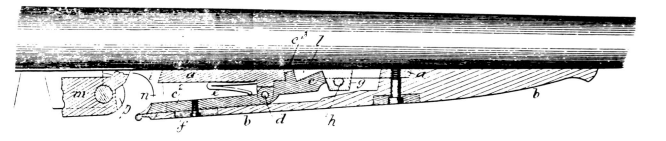

*C. Ellis and E. Wilkinson patent No. 292 of 1877 (patent drawing)*

# CHAPTER EIGHT

# Multi-barrels and Repeaters

Like so many ideas connected with guns and shooting, the idea of a gun with several barrels is a very old one. We have come to regard two barrels as 'the norm' and more than this as very unusual, but in fact all multi-barrel guns are of ancient lineage. Why this venerable idea was resurrected during the two decades we are concerned with can be summed up in one word – 'firepower'.

It is only a slight exaggeration to say that the history of firearms is all concerned with the quest for firepower. Certainly, the perfection and adoption, in turn, of breech-loading guns, the centrefire cartridge and the hammerless gun, leaving aside the other advantages of these developments, all contributed to the firepower at the sportsman's command. The need for this power arose from the 1860s onward when the mode of shooting known as 'driven' was generally adopted. When coupled with the artificial encouragement of game birds on a grand scale it made possible bags of game unheard of by earlier generations. Viewed in this light we can put into context the brief flirtation of British sportsmen and gunmakers with the multi-barrel shotgun, and with the repeating single-barrel as well.

However, the first example of a multi-barrel was probably not produced as a result of the forces outlined above as it was a French design. Somewhat surprisingly we have encountered two examples during our researches. The British specification, No. 921 of 1875, is in the name of Edwin Powley Alexander, consulting engineer and patent agent of 14, Southampton Buildings, Chancery Lane, London. However, the inventor was Jean-Baptiste Laine of Rue de Rivoli, Paris, who also obtained the French patent, No. 106,315 of 1875, to cover the same idea. This was to make a three-barrel hammer gun with either two barrels upon one or one upon two. The former is the main theme of the patent, but the examples we have seen have been of the latter. To fire these it was proposed to use the first trigger for the underneath barrels. The rear one, via a sort of single trigger mechanism in which the fall of the right-hand tumbler moves a lever laterally in the lockwork to permit the left-hand lock to be fired, was, in turn, to fire the top two barrels. The patent also refers to the use of three separate

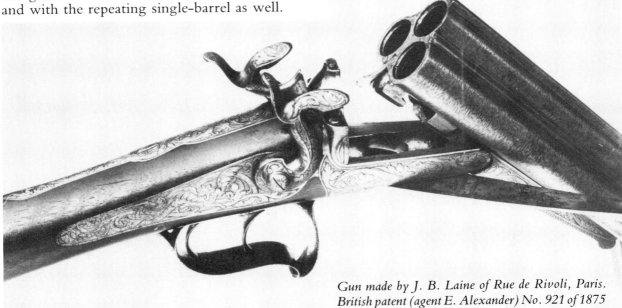

*Gun made by J. B. Laine of Rue de Rivoli, Paris. British patent (agent E. Alexander) No. 921 of 1875*

triggers or a more elaborate mechanism to fire all three, but gives no details. For the rest, this gun was shown as very conventional with a single-bite snap action, worked by a lever in front of the trigger guard. Again, those specimens we have seen differ, in that, they use the ordinary forward-facing lever, Lefaucheux action.

The quest for firepower by the British gun trade included a series of designs marketed by the London firm of Charles Lancaster. These are the famous four-barrel guns, the subject of three separate patents, which were made, in fact, as four separate types. The patentee in each case was Henry Alfred Alexander Thorn who was then well on his way to becoming one of the notables of the gun trade. Thorn was apprenticed for five years to Lancaster's, the firm run by Charles W. Lancaster, the eldest son of Charles Lancaster. The latter, a barrel borer by trade, had expanded his business to become one of London's top echelon of gunmakers. When Thorn was only just out of his apprenticeship, his master died

*Henry Alfred Alexander Thorn (portrait taken circa 1913)*

and, as was part of his agreement with the firm, the ex-apprentice bought the business. Under its new owner, who was active in gun trade organisations, an innovator in all aspects of gunmaking and, above all, very alive to the need for publicity of all sorts, the firm of Charles Lancaster became even more successful. This success was not, however, without its share of controversy and criticism, an almost inevitable consequence due to the very qualities that Thorn brought to his business.

*C. Lancaster four-barrel shotgun built on H. Thorn's patent No. 1242 of 1881*

The concept of a four-barrel gun was not new to Lancaster's. They, along with other makers, had produced muzzle-loading examples in which the barrels turned on a central pivot to bring the lower pair within the reach of the percussion hammers. The first of the breech-loading series (which corresponds to patent No. 1242 of 1881) was a hammerless gun in which the barrels were locked by a combination of a doll's-head top rib extension and a Henry Jones double grip underlever action. The novelty of the gun lies in its action which is essentially that of a double-action revolver. Double-action, in this context, means that the pull of the user's finger on the trigger first cocks the lock and then fires it. This was, and is, one of the standard revolving pistol actions and has the great advantage that such weapons can be managed easily by one hand in a mêlée. In the Thorn action, the trigger projected into the lockwork as a rod with an incline on its top, which fitted into a reversed

C-shaped recess in the tumbler. The slope of the trigger projection and the recess are so contrived that, as the trigger came to its rearmost position, the incline slipped out of the recess and the tumbler fell. This worked what can be best described as a firing rod, rotating on the head of which was the striker proper. The motion of this was controlled by a series of curved slots into which a spring-loaded stud projected. Each time the lock was cocked the firing rod was turned one quarter of a revolution. These slots were connected by straight slots which permitted the firing rod to go straight forward as the lock was fired.

This lockwork, but without the rotating striker feature, was also used by Lancaster's on rifles and heavy wildfowling guns but for use in a shotgun fired at moving targets, the weight and inevitable dragging nature of the trigger pull would have been disconcerting to a user accus-

tomed to conventional trigger work. So, we can well understand why, hard on the heels of this first model, came a successor. To overcome the problems outlined above, an ingenious lock that required the use of two fingers on separate triggers was introduced. Now, it was the second finger working the rear trigger that drew the lock to full-cock, from which position it was released by the front trigger and the forefinger. A variation on this was to have a lever lying along under the hand grip, connected to the trigger, so that a squeeze on this with the right hand would cock the lock. These modifications were the subject of the second patent, No. 213 of 1882.

In the third patent, No. 3089 of 1882, we see a radical simplification of the whole idea, indeed a reversion to combine hammers and conventional locks with a moveable nose to the tumbler. (We believe that the only gun of this type made was the example we were privileged to examine and photograph, in which the upper pair of barrels were rifled for a .500 rifle cartridge and lower ones for 16-bore shot cartridges. This 'Cape Rifle', as it was termed, was exhibited at

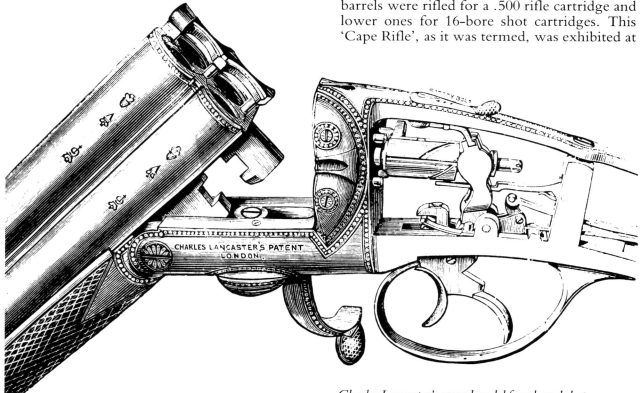

*Charles Lancaster's second model four-barrel shotgun. Drawing from* The Modern Sportsman's Gun and Rifle, *Vol I, by Dr J. H. Walsh*

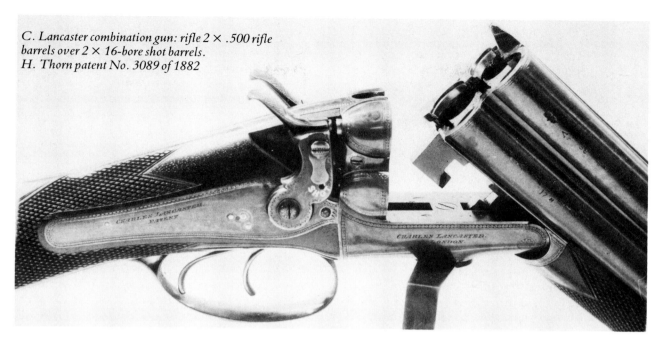

*C. Lancaster combination gun: rifle 2 × .500 rifle barrels over 2 × 16-bore shot barrels. H. Thorn patent No. 3089 of 1882*

The Sportsman's Exhibition held under the patronage of H.R.H. Prince Duleep Singh at the Agricultural Hall, London, in February 1882, where it reputedly generated a lot of interest.)

The final member of this quartet is not the subject of a patent specification but is, nevertheless, perhaps the most practical and useful gun of the four. Now an underlever, looking just like the cocking lever of a Winchester rifle, is fitted to the lockwork so that a second stroke of the lever is needed to cock for the third and fourth shots.

We have considered the four Lancaster guns as a series, which we feel is the only logical course,

but in so doing we have omitted another multi-barrel gun, the Dickson and Murray shotgun. We mentioned this gun earlier (see Chapter One) but must now retrace our steps. This three-barrel gun, subject of patent No. 873 of 1882 was designed by John Dickson the younger, 'gun-maker', and Andrew Graham Murray, 'advocate', both of Edinburgh. A 16-bore (it was the first of the 27 made by Dickson's of Edinburgh), it was built in 1882 for Murray, the co-patentee. It is, in all senses of the overworked term, a superb gun. The three barrels lie naturally and easily in the hand, the central barrel having the

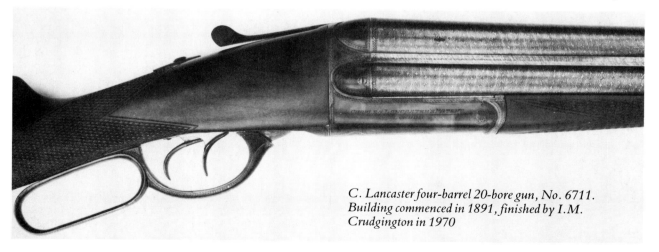

*C. Lancaster four-barrel 20-bore gun, No. 6711. Building commenced in 1891, finished by I.M. Crudgington in 1970*

*J. Dickson three-barrel shotgun (3 × 16-bore).*
*J. Dickson and A. Murray patent No. 873 of 1882*

character of a high, wide rib. Since it has a side-lever action, which creates the illusion of it being an easy opener, the thrust of the lever is carried on to assist in the breaking of the gun. The gun is simply a three-barrel version of the double-barrel gun described earlier.

While the Dickson and Murray was a practical sporting gun and all its barrels could be used equally at the covert side, the same could not be said of our final multi-barrel gun. This is, quite simply, a double-barrel hammer shotgun with a moveable nose on the right hammer which can be adjusted to strike a .360 smooth-bored barrel. In effect this is the essence of the patent that covers it, No. 17,732 of 1888 granted to William Palmer Jones. Also covered on the same principle are four-barrel guns in which the extra barrels are mounted directly above the barrels of a double-gun. It is one of the main points of the patent specification that, by means of this moveable nose, which had previously been patented by Thorn in 1882, the actions designed for

*Gun by W. P. Jones, Birmingham; patent No.*
*17,732 of 1888*

double-barrels could be used for three- and four-barrel guns. Also mentioned in the specification, but without practical details, are hammerless and single trigger versions. When made with a rifled small calibre barrel, this gun is said to have enjoyed considerable popularity in South America.

Thus we come to the end of the multi-barrel guns that belong to our present period. The idea was not laid to rest at this point, but was reintroduced in the decades that followed. However, discussion of that will have to await our next volume. In some ways the connection between the multi-barrel guns we have just considered and the repeating single-barrels that follow may be thought to be tenuous. However, the search for firepower gave birth to both and thus relates the two groups more firmly than might at first be apparent.

This section is composed of American inventions that were patented in Britain. (The Winchester Repeating Arms Company of New Haven, Connecticut, in particular, had a policy of protecting most of its designs in Britain. As a result, our consideration inevitably becomes a limited view of the evolution of the repeating shotgun in the United States.)

We begin with a gun that is rightly held to be one of the crucial designs in the history of firearms. It was, also, to point most forcefully in the direction which the repeating sporting shotgun was to take during the following century. That its inventor, Christopher M. Spencer, went bankrupt producing it is, alas, an almost inevitable part of the story, the familiar penalty of being in advance of the times. Spencer, along with Sylvester H. Roper, obtained a United States patent, No. 255,894 of 1882, and, via the agent W. R. Lake, British patent, No. 1636 of 1882, for a repeating single-barrel shotgun. The two enduring features of their design have proved to be a tubular magazine slung under the barrel and a sliding handle around this magazine which, via a pair of steel bars, works all the functions of the action except the actual firing, which is controlled by a normal trigger. The Spencer differs from most of the repeaters that were to follow it in that it uses a pivoted breechblock. Essentially, when viewed from the side, this breech-block can be thought of as a segment of a circle. In plan, the sides are parallel. This segment is pivoted at its apex, which is to the rear of the action, on a short transverse pivot across the top of the action.

Controlled by the sliding handle, but in fact activated by a very strong V-mainspring, the breech-block cycles through three positions. In its uppermost position, with the handle to the rear, it flings out the empty case which had previously been withdrawn from the chamber. Then as the 'pump' handle is thrust forwards, a fresh cartridge is pulled forwards into the chamber from the carrier in the lower half of the breech-block. The final part of the forward stroke lowers the breech-block, whereupon a cartridge is forced into the carrier from the magazine by a coil spring. The gun is then ready to fire. When the pump handle is drawn back, the breech-block is lowered and the spent case carried backwards out of the chamber to lie in a trough on the top of the block. At the same time the hammer is cocked. As the handle reaches the back of its stroke, the breech-block is released and flung upwards to the first position by the mainspring. The action may also be cocked by the reversed trigger in the front of the trigger guard.

This design is of particular interest because Thorn, of the Charles Lancaster firm, imported a batch of 70 of these actions in the white and fitted them with straight-hand stocks of British design, damascus barrels and probably magazine tubes as well. From a study of Lancaster records it would appear that this one and only batch sold slowly. The guns have two serial numbers: the Lancaster one on the outside of the bow of the trigger guard, and the Spencer one on the right-hand front of the action between the barrel and the magazine tube. One that has passed recently through the London auctions carried the Lancaster serial of 5547 and the Spencer number 1101. It is, thus, relatively early in the Spencer production runs and we are left speculating how Thorn came upon them so soon during the latter half of the 1880s.

Naturally, the introduction by one of London's premier makers of so radical a gun did not pass without contemporary comment. In his *Practical Hints on Shooting*, published in 1887, Basil Tozer ('20-Bore') comments that 'it handles far more pleasantly than any repeating gun we know of. In a hot corner, with a couple of such guns and a loader, nothing more could be desired.' Despite this, beyond a few letters to the sporting press,

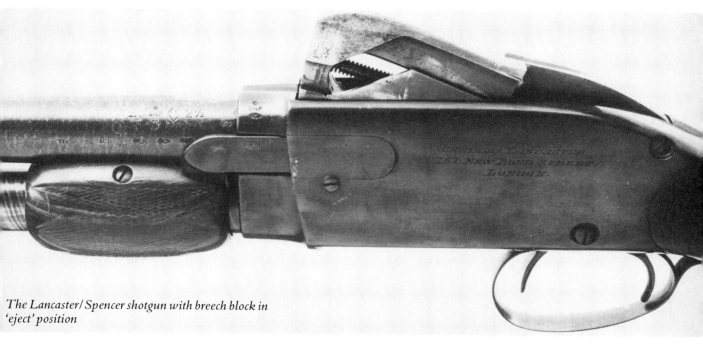

*The Lancaster/Spencer shotgun with breech block in 'eject' position*

this would seem to be the extent of the impact made by this experiment.

The rest of the repeating shotguns that we have to consider consist of a remarkable series. Not only are they in the name of one company, the Winchester Repeating Arms Company, but moreover, they are all the work of one designer, John Moses Browning. Browning was not a Winchester employee. He and several of his brothers owned and operated a small factory and a retail gun shop in Ogden, Utah. His father Jonathon was of the Mormon sect which permitted polygamy; he had three wives and John Moses had 10 brothers and 11 sisters. What is crucial is that the talents of John Moses Browning had been recognised by the Winchester management who had a gentlemen's agreement with him to buy all his rifle and shotgun designs. The majority of these were never produced on a commercial basis, but by means of their agreement with Browning the Winchester management was able to block one avenue of potential competition.

The first of the series of Browning designs that Winchester bought were rifles. One of these, patented in 1884, we know best as the Model 1886 lever action. It was put into production and more lever-action repeating rifles followed. In 1886, possibly as a result of the budding success of the Spencer previously described, came the U.S. patent, No. 336,287. From this derives the

British patent, No. 2283, also of 1886. Both patents relate to the lever-action repeating shotgun that Winchester marketed as their Model 1887.

Today, such a gun is an oddity. In 1887, however, the American shooting public, to whom 'lever action' and 'Winchester' were virtually synonymous terms, regarded the use of this action, with which they were very familiar, as entirely logical. Despite the superficial resemblance of this new gun to the earlier rifles, it was in no way a modification of a rifle action.

The action of the Winchester Model 1887 can best be described as a quarter of a circle pivoted at its centre and with the operating lever/trigger guard extending from its underside. To fill the magazine, the action is opened by pushing the underlever forward into an almost vertical position; the cartridges are fed down through the action and into the magazine tube. This latter has a capacity of four cartridges but one more can be held in the carrier in the action and yet another in the barrel chamber, so the total capacity of the gun is six cartridges.

When a cartridge has been fired, to eject the spent cases the underlever is depressed and the breech pivots, extracting the fired case fully from the chamber. As the breech reaches the limit of its travel, the spent case is flicked out through the top of the action by the fresh round coming up in the carrier. Also at this far extent of travel, the hammer is cocked. Since the hammer has an external spur, it can also be half-cocked and re-cocked by the thumb in the normal way if desired. Incidentally, there is a patent, No. 357 of 1889, granted to W. R. Miller for this hammer. As the underlever is brought up, a fresh round is fed into the chamber and the gun is ready to fire again. Actually the breech is not hung on a simple pivot but, as the lever goes down, the whole block moves about three-eighths of an inch forward and one-eighth down. It stays there through all the movement and only returns as the final locking motion of the block takes effect.

The standard '1887' had a 30-inch rolled steel barrel in the 12-bore version, or a 32-inch barrel in the 10-bore, each of which retailed for 25 dollars. Above this grade, various options were offered, for example 3 or 4 iron damascus

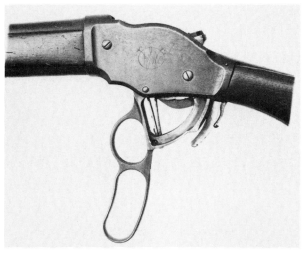

*Winchester model '87 shotgun*

barrels, the latter adding no less than 20 dollars to the price of the gun. Also available were better-grade walnut stocks which could, in addition, be chequered.

By the production standards of the Winchester Repeating Arms Company, this gun was only moderately successful. Some 65,000 guns were sold. In addition, there is the model 1901, a modification of the 1887 gun which, built only as a 10-bore, sold another 13,500 units.

Hard on the heels of this first Browning repeating shotgun patent came a trio of fresh designs. They were the subject of patent protection in both Britain and the United States. As if to emphasise the fertility of the inventive genius of Browning, there is within our period another design that was not patented in Britain and yet another gun in 1890, this time patented in both countries, which became the 1893 production model.

Browning learned the trade of gunsmithing from his father, though he would have been expected to be able to 'fix' the working guns of frontier America. However, he would have had no training in draftsmanship or design and as his talent blossomed John Browning realised his ideas in the way of many another practical man. Working from the roughest of sketches on the flaps of cartridge boxes and the like, by a process of 'file and fit', he produced his prototypes. Situated as he was, out in Utah, some 2,500 miles from the Winchester plant and the gun-making heart of the United States, he was, inevitably to a degree, hampered by not having access to ready-made components or rough forgings. Some of his prototypes had barrels that were cannibalised from commercially-made guns and, for raw material to produce the gun actions, he used the metal which came to Ogden as axles on railway rolling stock.

We must consider the Browning guns slightly out of the chronological order of their patent dates. First, the design mentioned earlier that was not patented in Britain, United States patent No. 376,576 of 1888. This is another lever-action design that has points in common with both the 'Model '87' and the gun we consider next, the subject of British patent No. 805 which derives from United States patent No. 356,271, both of 1887.

We mentioned earlier the pioneering success of the Spencer repeating shotgun. The Browning patent of 1887 shows very considerable Spencer influence and must be regarded as a derivation of the Spencer. Both the essential parts of the Spencer reappear, the pump-action and the breech-block transversely pivoted at the top rear corner of the receiver. However, there are two real points of difference between these two designs. Whereas with the Spencer it is a third position of the breech-block that ejects the spent case, in this Browning gun there is a separate ejecting arm, pivoted on the same pivot as the breech-block, that flicks the spent case off the top of the breech-block. The other differences lie in the lockwork. The Spencer, it will be recalled, used a rotating tumbler enclosed in the action; the Browning has a spring-loaded striker much more like a bolt-action, and a safety that blocks the movement of the sear controlled by a projection through the top strap.

This is one of the Browning designs that never saw commercial production and the two known examples of this gun are in the Winchester Museum, Cody, Wyoming, and the John M. Browning Firearms Museum, Union Station,

*J. M. Browning repeating shotgun; British patent (agent H. Lake) No. 805 of 1887. (Courtesy of Buffalo Bill Historical Center, Cody, Wyoming)*

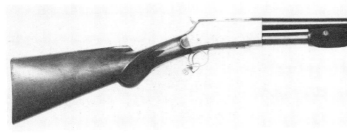

*J. M. Browning repeating shotgun; British patent (agent H. Lake) No. 9414 of 1886.* (Courtesy of Buffalo Bill Historical Center, Cody, Wyoming)

Ogden, Utah. Again, we can only speculate as to the reasons that lay behind the Winchester decision not to exploit this action. Possibly it was thought too like the Spencer but, more likely, the designs that we turn to next, some of which predate this Spencer-like gun, and which were to culminate in the Winchester Models '93 and '97, the latter being hugely successful, were rightly adjudged to have greater potential.

The three final Browning/Winchester shotgun actions that were patented prior to the end of 1890, we can, for our purposes, regard as variants of a single theme. The relevant British patents are Nos. 9411 and 9414 of 1886 and No. 19,156 of 1890 which correspond respectively to United States patent Nos. 345,881 and 345,882 of 1886 and 441,390 of 1890. In all of these we have a pump-action gun with a fore-and-aft sliding breech-block and an external hammer. The latter is rotated backwards to cock by the rearward sliding breech-block.

The points of difference between these three lie, firstly, in the mechanisms that raise the live cartridge from the level of the magazine to that of the barrel. In the first two what are, essentially, variants of a lever pivot on the same spindle as the hammer, projecting forwards under the fresh cartridge. These levers have a second limb that projects upwards into a partial slot in the bottom of the breech-block. When the latter has slid back to the correct position, and the spent case has been ejected, the live round is raised to lie ahead of the bolt ready to be pushed into the barrel chamber as the bolt is dragged forwards by the user working the pump handle. The patent of 1890 differs from this mode, in that, the carrier is now pivoted up behind the hammer and is far more robust-looking (more like a trough or gutter) and is worked by the slide rod directly, rather than indirectly, off the bolt.

Less importantly, the mainspring of the 1886 gun lies in the head of the stock behind the hammer, whereas in the 1890 gun the mainspring is forward and is part of the carrier.

However, there is another important feature in which the 1890 gun differs from the two patents of 1886. In the earlier guns the breech-block was unlocked by being made partially to rotate before it was forced backwards. This rotation was achieved by having a stud projecting from the bottom of the bolt that mated with an inclined slot cut in a flat piece of steel that slid underneath it. This slotted piece was the internal portion of the slide worked by the pump handle and it was by this stud, when it had reached the end of its travel, that the bolt was moved back and forth. While ingenious, it would seem that this was a weak feature of the design and it comes as no real surprise to find it abandoned on the 1890 gun.

On this mechanism the bolt does not rotate. It is locked by a shoulder on the top of the carrier coming up behind a shoulder on the bottom of the bolt, as the latter reaches its forward position. This was an altogether more robust set-up, as was proven by the longevity of gun that used it. In a sense, this later gun design is an amalgam of the bolt for the two 1886 guns, combined with the breech-block of the gun patented in 1887, that became the carrier and the breech-lock.

The 1890 patent gun, of which examples are in both the Winchester and Browning Museums, was to become the Winchester Model 1893. Just over 34,000 were sold before it was superceded by the model 1897 derived from it. One of the reasons for this brief run was that it had been found, with both the 1893 Winchester and the Spencer gun, that if the shooter was trying to shoot very rapidly, or if one of his cartridges were to hang fire for an instant, the situation could occur when the cartridge would explode outside the gun. One well-publicised incident of this nature happened to the exhibition and champion shooter, Dr Carver. On 17 June 1887 he was shooting with a Spencer at an exhibition at Ridgeway Park, Philadelphia. Part of his exhibition involved shooting from the hip. It appears that a cartridge hung fire and exploded as it was being ejected up out of the gun. The explosion blinded him for three days and he rightly considered he had had a miraculous escape from permanent injury.

Winchester's answer to this problem was to add an action slide lock that required the forend to move slightly forward, as would naturally

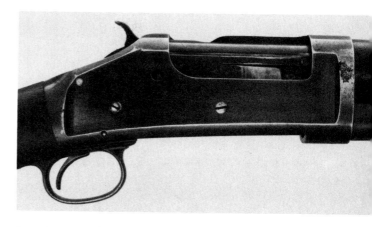

*Winchester Model '93 shotgun.* (Photograph courtesy of Geoffrey Boothroyd)

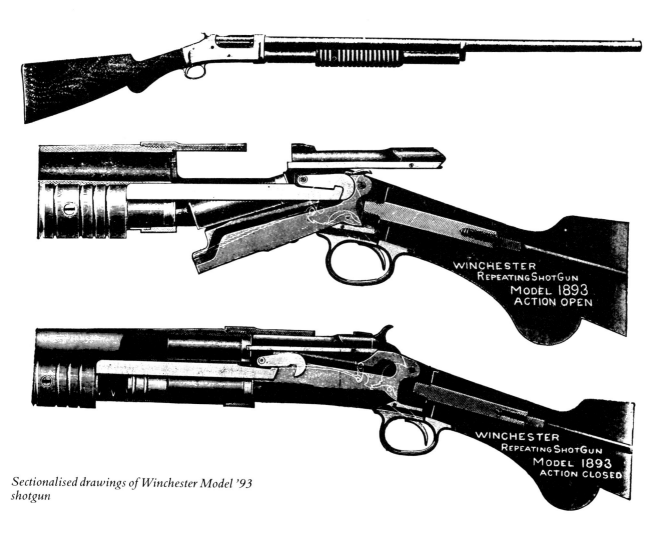

*Sectionalised drawings of Winchester Model '93 shotgun*

happen when the cartridge fired in the barrel and the gun recoiled, before the slide could be drawn back to eject and reload.

It is more relevant to our overall theme to consider briefly the reception of the repeating shotguns we have described (and of those that were to follow) by the British shooting public. The best documented is the Lancaster flirtation, but in addition to this, Spencers were also imported in their American form by Rigby's of London, again with no real impact. The Winchester 1893/1897 models were advertised at £5 (or even a little less) and were thus very competitively priced, only undercut by Belgian hammer guns and on a par with the cheapest British hammer guns such as the 'Farmers' gun made by Lewis of Birmingham. Even at this price they found relatively few takers. There is a story told in the author's (DJB) home village of an adventurous lad who made his way to the United States for a spell and who brought back a pump action repeating shotgun. The locals' response was to nickname the owner 'Yank', refer to his gun as a 'big heavy rattling thing' and look upon it as just another quirk of its owner, rather than something to be envied or copied, and it seems their views were shared by the great bulk of the shooting public.

So the manually-operated repeater has been largely ignored in Britain, which is in the sharpest possible contrast to the popularity it has enjoyed in its native land.

The multi-barrel, too, has remained an oddity with only token production, but despite, or perhaps because of this, it lends another facet to the story of the British shotgun.

# CHAPTER NINE

# Electrical Ignition

*The British electrical-ignition pioneer, the Bristol gunmaker Thomas Page-Wood, shown here with his wife*

In the period 1871–1890 there were patented in Britain no less than seven systems for electrically-ignited shotguns. The reasons for this flurry of activity are complex, but it is likely that the upsurge of interest in the practical utilisation of electrical power, a feature of the middle and later years of the nineteenth century, was a considerable stimulus. Certainly, all the electric-ignition systems that we have to consider bear more than a passing resemblance to an electric light bulb. In terms of size and power, an electric torch is perhaps a fairer comparison

but the principles involved are the same. Both in our guns and in the electric light bulb, the completion of an electrical circuit permits the flow of an electrical current. This causes an element or filament to glow and either give light or ignite a charge of powder.

Those concerned are listed below:

| Patentees | Patent | Date |
|---|---|---|
| Frederick Bertie Worsley Roberts and Benjamin Theophilus Moore of 11 Queen Victoria Street, London | 4019 | 1882 |
| Nelson Goodwin Green, 'Gentleman'. In part communicated by James P. Freeman and Joseph L. Galt of New York, United States | 6238 | 1882 |
| Edgar Abraham Monfort of New York, United States | 125 | 1883 |
| Henri Pieper, gun manufacturer, of Liège, Belgium | 1571 | 1883 |
| Thomas Page-Wood, gunmaker, of Bristol | 4786 | 1884 |
| John Andrews, solicitor, at 25 Broadhurst Gardens, Hampstead | 5249 | 1884 |
| Samuel Russell, physician, of Brooklyn, New York, United States | 14008 | 1884 |

The differences between all these patents are relatively minor; primarily ones of electrical circuitry and the internal layout of the cartridge. Our researches would seem to indicate that only two of these designs penetrated beyond the world of the Patent Office.

In the journal, *Shooting Times* – or, to give it its full name: *Wildfowlers' Illustrated Shooting Times, Sports and Kennel News* – of 24 August

1883, there appeared the following description of the Pieper gun and its cartridge, which we reproduce both for full coverage and to capture the true contemporary flavour contained in it.

We may state that the electric gun has passed the stage of mere theory, and it is now, in such sound working order, that it was practically, tried last week, before an influential committee of gunmakers and sportsmen, in the park of St Ouen. Mr. Pieper, of Liège, the inventor, himself superintended those experiments – which have been unanimously declared most satisfactory.

The gun itself is treble-bolted, and has all the appearance of an ordinary hammerless gun, but it has no locks, as it consists simply of stock and barrels, with the ordinary two triggers, and, of course, a trigger-guard. Inside the stock, two metal rods run from the heel-plate to what should be – in an ordinary gun – the striker-holes. These metal rods are isolated, by a ring of ivory, or of hardened gutta-percha, from contact with the metal breech, and each rod is touched by its corresponding trigger, whenever the said trigger is pulled, thus establishing the electric communication at will. So that, virtually, the gun cannot be discharged unless its stock is pressed against the shooter's shoulder, and the shooter pulls the trigger. Remove the gun from the shoulder, and no pulling of triggers can let it off, since the electric current is no longer existent. This is a very strong point in favour of the gun, which thus, it will be seen can only be fired when the stock is brought to the shooter's shoulder, and he simultaneously, pulls the trigger. In any other position, the gun is, necessarily, as harmless as a mere walking-stick, and no jarring of any sort can possibly fire

it off, since there is no communication, and no cap, and no fulminate in the cartridge.

We will now explain how the cartridge is made, and with this object in view, we append two cuts for its better elucidation. The cartridge, is a simple modification of Kynoch's well-known brass 'Perfect' case. Instead of a cap it contains a brass rod A, encased in India-rubber – see adjoining cut, (Fig. 1). This rod is fixed to the base of the case in a perfectly gas-tight manner, and it is made long enough to reach the powder wad, in any case, no matter how heavily the cartridge may be loaded. The rod A acts as a conductor for one of the currents from the accumulator. The other current is established by the mere fact of the shooter's left hand grasping either the barrel or the metallic breech of the gun. The base of the rod is isolated from the case by an India-rubber ring B. So that the current from the stock is established with A, through B, only when the gun is put against the shoulder and the trigger is pulled.

And now we come to the description of the powder wad – which plays so essential a part in the working of the gun.

This wad (see Fig. 2) is a waterproof cardboard one, and contains in its middle a brass ring B. This ring, when the wad is pushed home over the powder, fits on to that brass rod, which is an integral part of the base of brass case, as described already. The ring B is placed by means of a microscopic platinum wire, C, into communication with a small piece of brass, A, which folds over the wad, as shewn in the illustration. Virtually, therefore, the left hand, by grasping the gun barrels, communicates one current to the platinum wire C, on the wad through the piece of brass A, whilst the

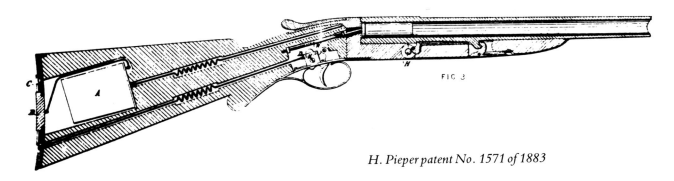

*H. Pieper patent No. 1571 of 1883*

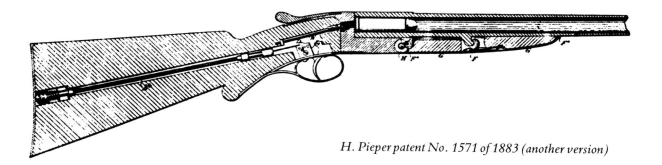

*H. Pieper patent No. 1571 of 1883 (another version)*

other current is sent on through the stock and brass rod in the cartridge case, on to the ring B, the junction of the two currents making the platinum wire red-hot, and thus instantaneously causing the explosion of the powder.

We have now only to explain how the current is produced, and our task will be accomplished. The accumulator weighs but three or four ounces, and is perfectly gas-proof and water-proof. Once loaded, it can supply sufficient electricity to last a fortnight without being seen to, and could produce 10,000 shots. This accumulator is made in the form of a watch, or of a purse, or of a pocket-book. To load it, it is sufficient to hang it, for a few minutes, inside a small box, to a hook in communication with a water and sulphate of zinc electric battery – which is very easily and simply attended to. Once loaded, the accumulator is practically

inexhaustible, at least for a fortnight. It may be carried in the shooter's pocket, or it may be fitted inside the stock of his gun, or in his cartridge belt, &c., &c. The cost of the cartridges is the same as that of ordinary cartridges. There is no escape of gas possible, no accident explosion can possibly occur, and the cartridges may be reloaded many times. Mr. Pieper shewed some which had been fired over 100 times. It had been suggested that possibly the piece of brass (A. Fig. 2) on the wad – which is to effect the communication of one current through the barrel, might not be occasionally touching the barrel, and thereby a miss-fire would be caused, but the inventor has proved conclusively that by placing a loaded cartridge near a small galvanic meter, the needle readily shews if the electric current is uninterrupted, therefore all cartridges could be thus tried by the makers, or cartridge loaders, before being issued to the public, and miss-fires should thus be a matter of impossibility.

We have endeavoured – to the best of our ability – to fully explain all details pertaining to this new invention. We understand its working perfectly well, and could readily build one ourselves; but should our explanations appear obscure in any way to any of our readers, we shall be most happy to explain to them viva voce, or through our 'Answers to Correspondents', any point which may require elucidation.

Meanwhile, we place ourselves at Mr. Pieper's disposal. If he will send us a specimen of his electric gun, we will give it an impartial and thorough trial, and will then duly inform our readers of the result. We could not say anything more to the point if we filled columns of our *Shooting Times*.

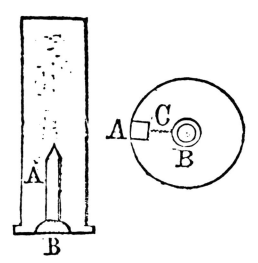

*H. Pieper cartridge as shown in 1883 article*

Sadly, Pieper did not comply with this request for a sample to try, so what seemed to be a marvellous avenue of research became another blind alley.

However, this was not the only contemporary reference to the Pieper gun and its cartridge. In the *Journal of the Royal United Services Institute* there is an account of a meeting held on 29 June 1883 at which the speaker was Lt-Col George V. Fosbery, V.C., who spoke on the subject of 'Magazine Rifles and Repeaters'. There is every indication that Pieper and Fosbery were close friends. At this meeting Fosbery took the opportunity of demonstrating to his distinguished audience a Pieper electrically-fired carbine. In the discussion that followed the meeting Capt McEvoy, also a friend of Fosbery's, had this to say of electrical ignition:

> In looking into the subject some years ago, I came to the conclusion that there was no safe way of employing electricity in connection with small-arms. I noticed that the cartridge fired today by our lecturer was fired by a low-tension current, and this involves the use of a piece of platinum wire. That is too expensive an arrangement, and unless the cartridges can be fired by a high-tension current, by a spark, I cannot for one moment imagine that the invention will present any feature of economy such as to make it generally applicable. Then if a high-tension current is employed there is very great danger of failure, or premature firing, as that character of electricity has a tendency to firing in the direction of any metallic attraction. I would therefore discard it as not being practicable. I was very much interested to see the success of that experiment, but I have no hesitation in saying if electricity is to be employed in small-arms, all that paraphernalia of insulation must be discarded, something simpler must be employed, and the great feature of safety must be looked to; when that is done we may have an electrical firing gun that will be available. At present it is in the stage of a toy, it is very taking, but it wants a good deal more to be done to it.

It is a feature of the list of electrical patents in our period that the bulk of the patentees were not British and that the majority were from the United States. Moreover, it would seem from the addresses of the Americans that New York was very much the centre of the development of the electrically-ignited shotgun. This view is further reinforced by a lecture that was delivered to the United Services Institute on Friday, 26 March 1886, by W. Syton. It would seem that the primary object of this gentleman's lecture was to promote the patent of Dr Russell (who we listed at the beginning of this chapter). In doing so Syton provided considerable valuable information on the practical testing that had been undertaken in the vicinity of New York.

Included in other reports published in the *Journal of the Royal United Services Institute* are two accounts of tests with military rifles converted to electric-ignition. In the first account, a 'Hotchkiss Military (Bolt) Rifle', and a 'Martini Rifle', were both fired by Capt S. A. Day, U.S. Army. But it is the second account that has the greatest bearing on our present theme. On 17 July 1885 a 5-hour test-firing programme was held at the Parker Bros. Arms Manufactury, Meriden, Connecticut. The guns used were a converted Colt double-barrel and a 'Harrington' double-barrel, both presumably hammerless guns. The Harrington fired brass-cased cartridges.

It was one of the features of the electrical-ignition cartridges of this era that the ignition system of the cartridge was not destroyed by the first use and, indeed, could be tested and reused. It was reckoned to have the same useful life as the brass case in which it was fitted: about 50 shots. There is no record of the number of rounds fired in this Parker test, but it must have been considerable as there is mention of the gun

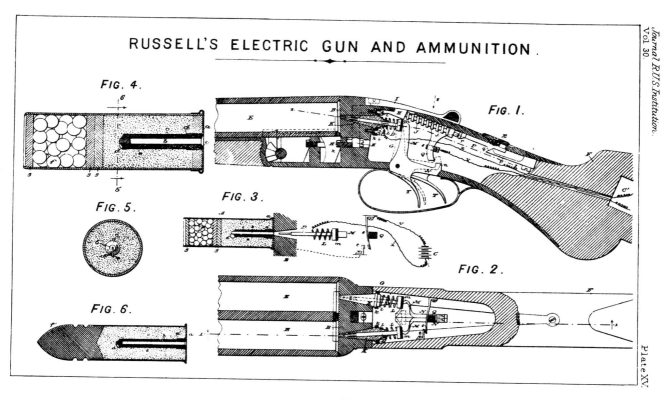

Journal RUS Institution.
Vol 30.

Plate XV.

*Drawing of S. Russell's gun from the* Journal of the Royal United Services Institution

barrels being dipped in water to cool them. In all this there was but one misfire, the result of a faulty cartridge. The report further records that the testers were: 'The Superintendent and Assistant of Manufactury, the Assembler and the Chief Salesman, who is a noted wing shot' and that shooting was at 'flying objects' and the 'guns never failed or flinched in their work'.

We must conclude from this trial, from the earlier Fosbery demonstration of the Pieper and from the shooting with the various rifles that the electrically-fired guns of our period were perfectly satisfactory ignition systems. This raises the question of why they received so little patronage. The answer is that they were competing against the highly-developed, widely distributed and understood percussion-ignition system. In such circumstances, it was not sufficient merely to equal the performance of the rival; real advantages would have had to be demonstrated to warrant the abandonment of the established system. For instance, if some very superior propellant had been devised that could only be electrically fired, or if electrical ignition had been demonstrated at about the same time as Dr Forsyth's first percussion gun, then it is possible that the history of sporting guns would have been very different. As it is, electrical ignition has only found practical use in weapons of war. This is demonstrated by its use in ordnance and warship guns, where it is desirable that the firing be under the control of a person away from the gun, and in aircraft-mounted weapons having exceedingly high rates of fire, possibly beyond the capabilities of a mechanical system.

None of the foregoing has, of course, prevented later inventors from reviving the whole idea of electrical ignition. It would be rash to exclude the possibility of electrical ignition's being adapted for sporting guns as a result of some future, unforeseen development.

# CHAPTER TEN

# Bizarre Actions

The increasing sophistication of the conventional shotgun was not to stifle the urge of those designers who dreamt of a radical revision of the mechanism of the sporting gun. Thus, the two decades produce yet another crop of mechanisms that cannot be reasonably included in any of the preceding sections.

It is impossible, with such a batch as we now turn to, to decide which is the oddest. A strong claim for this dubious honour could be made for our first example. The idea behind this was to make a gun that was easier to manipulate. In pursuit of this laudable end the designer produced a creation, to open which, the muzzle had to be raised, whereupon the breech-end of the barrel dropped through a slot in the action to protrude at the bottom! This description is just a little unfair to the inventor who envisaged his gun being turned upside down to open. As the barrel-bolts were disengaged, the barrel would drop open and the user, having recharged his piece, would then turn it the right way up when the barrel would snap shut. As is so often the case our knowledge of this gun and its inventor derives solely from the patent specification, No. 3327 of 1872. The patentee is Alfred Harris of Birmingham. The drawing that accompanies this specification shows a single-barrel gun with its barrel carried on two trunnions set some 3 inches forward of the breech face.

Further strong contenders for the dubious prize of most bizarre are two muzzle-loaders. The first, which we know as patent No. 2891 of 1871, concerns a system by which a percussion cap could be placed, via a removable plug, into the breech-end of a muzzle-loading gun. This percussion cap was to be fired by a pin that stood vertically, like that of a pinfire cartridge. The patentee was Jean Turon of Longueville, Lot et Garonne, France.

The other muzzle-loader, patent No. 3058 of 1871, by George Penton, used an underlever to cock the lockwork and a lever that had to be released from under the hand of the stock to fire the gun. The claimed virtue of this scheme was that it avoided the 'snatch' that can happen as a conventional trigger is pulled. In modern parlance this is a release trigger. What is amazing about the Penton specification is that there is no provision for any kind of safety catch!

In direct contrast to the preceding obscure designs is the Remington action that has become known as 'The Rolling Block'. This demands our attention because, on 23 April 1873,

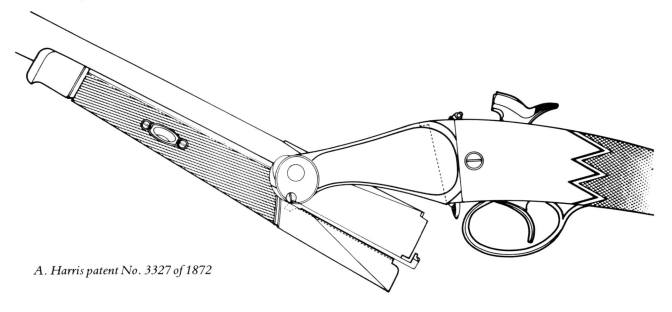

*A. Harris patent No. 3327 of 1872*

Samuel Remington obtained British patent No. 1465. The essential feature of the rolling-block action is that the breech-block and the relatively heavy hammer lock together at the instant of firing. Both are hung on stout transverse pivots which are, in turn, carried through the thick side walls of the action. This ingenious action is extremely strong. There is a story told that to test this feature the Belgian Proof House loaded a .50 inch calibre rifle with 750 grains of black powder and on top of this 40 bullets and two wads which completely filled the barrel. This load was then fired with no detriment to the rifle.

The Remington rolling-block is perhaps more correctly regarded as a family of designs, the subject of a string of American patents in the mid-1860s. In all, it was a highly successful mechanism used in vast number of single-shot rifles and, to a lesser degree, in pistols made by The Remington Arms Company, their Belgian licencees and, when the patents had expired, imitators in the United States.

Remington (and later Whitney) made a quantity of single-barrel shotguns of various calibres using this action. However, the rolling-block shotguns most often seen in Britain, certainly in the authors' experience, are Belgian-made, either built as such or conversions of obsolete military rifles.

We cannot leave this section without remarking on a gun that we discovered in the Royal Collection at Sandringham. This was a double-barrel shotgun with a rolling-block type action bearing the maker's name of 'Husqvarna, Sweden'. (For a full discussion see *The Royal Guns at Sandringham* (DJB).)

There is a group of designs that share one essential feature of the Remington design: the barrels do not pivot down to open. By virtue of its patent date the first of these is one part of a wide-ranging patent specification by Greener, No. 1623 of 1877. One aspect that is sketched, and briefly described, is an under-and-over gun with its barrels fixed in relation to the stock. To load there is a pivoting breech-block controlled by an underlever that is drawn as the Henry Jones pattern and not as the patentee calls it, a Lefaucheux type. Be this as it may, a stud on the head of this underlever causes the block to swing so that its front moves to the left as the lever is pulled to the right. The chambers are thus exposed and can be loaded as the situation demands.

Part of this specification concerns various improvements to cartridges. Perhaps the most interesting of these is to make up cartridges as pairs so that a double-gun could be loaded and emptied in a single motion. However, the inevitably fragile nature of the link between these

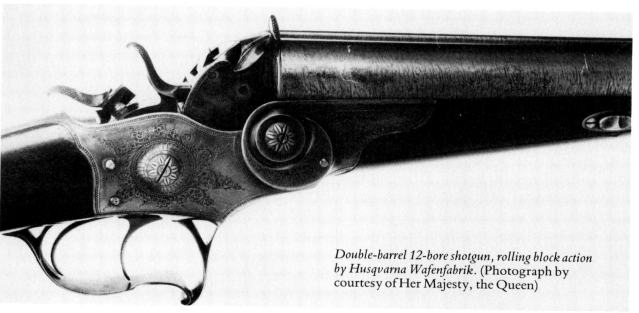

*Double-barrel 12-bore shotgun, rolling block action by Husqvarna Wafenfabrik.* (Photograph by courtesy of Her Majesty, the Queen)

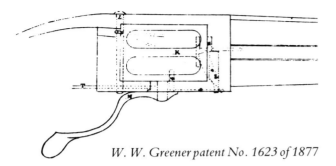

*W. W. Greener patent No. 1623 of 1877*

twins, the fact that they would only suit one chamber wall thickness and the point that very often only one barrel of a sporting gun is discharged, causes us to wonder why such 'improvements' were ever protected!

Similar thoughts are aroused by the specification of a certain John Titus Cooper, who described himself as a 'gentleman', of Linden House, Serpentine Road, Harborne, Staffordshire. The creation that he describes, in patent No. 12,869 of 1886, as a 'pocket fowling piece' is also a perfect poacher's tool. It is both concealable and simple and, hence, so cheap as to be almost disposable. Two versions are proposed, muzzle- and breech-loading. In the latter the barrel was to fit bayonet-fashion into the action. But the real novelty derives from the breech mechanism. What is shown is a sliding breech-block that, guided by a rod, slaps forward onto either percussion cap or firing pin under the influence of a stout elastic band. There is no other lock mechanism and it would appear that the block is simply drawn back and released by the user almost like a catapult.

In the *Shooting Times* of 11 May 1883, and only in this journal, there appeared a supplement devoted to 'the Gye Gun'. This publication is, we feel, of such interest not simply for its

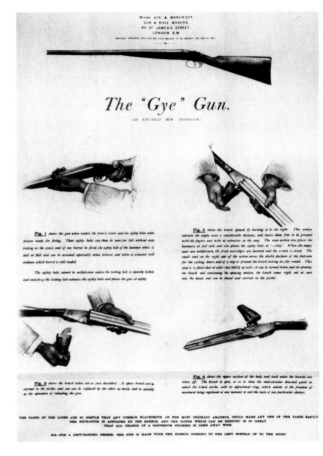

*A. Page supplement from the* Wildfowlers' Illustrated Shooting Times & Kennel News, *11 May 1883. (By permission of The British Library)*

content but also as an early example of more aggressive advertising in the gun trade. It stands as a description of this unusual British shotgun, for which Lionel Gye had obtained three patents, Nos. 4585 of 1881, and 1282 and 2746 of 1882, covering aspects of this mechanism.

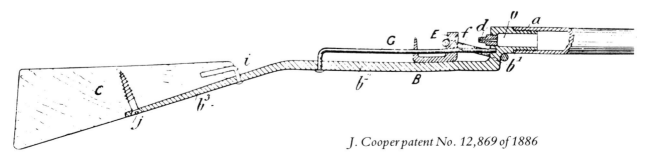

*J. Cooper patent No. 12,869 of 1886*

*Gye and Moncrieff's advertisement of 1883*

*L. Gye and L. Moncrieff gun, action partially open*

The background to Gye's firm is also unusual. The principals were both retired service
officers, Lionel Gye having served in the Royal
Artillery and Lynedoch Moncrieff in the Royal
Navy. In their advertisements they claimed that
their experience enabled them to offer the
soundest of guns as regards both design and
materials used.

More conventional, in that parallels can be
drawn to it, is a fixed-barrel gun. This patent,
No. 13,400 of 1886, is in the name of the patent
agent, William Henry Beck, who was acting for
a Jules Rochatte, a Parisian gunmaker. Naturally, this gun is also the subject of a French patent,
No. 175,516 of 1886. It is included at this point
by virtue of its tip-up breech mechanism and
fixed barrel. The basic idea behind this gun is to
pivot the breech-block on a pair of lugs that

project back from the top of the barrels like a top
extension. When the gun is closed for firing, the
breech-block is held down by a locking lug at its
rear, which is worked by a turning top lever.
But, in this case, the layout is the reverse of the
conventional; the thumb piece of the lever is in
front of the pivot, which is on the back of the
breech-block. As always, the locking mechanism is simply to hold the gun shut. The shock of
the discharge is resisted partly by the stout
pivots for the breech-block, but also by the fact
that the latter fits into a bed, analogous to the
action bar on a conventional gun. This similarity is enhanced by the projection. Like a barrel
lump it projects from the bottom of the breech-
block and fits into a recess in the bed.

The extractor of this gun is also novel. There
is a lever pivoted on the same centres as the

breech-block between the barrels, which, as the breech-block is flipped forward, forces the extractor and cartridges forwards. In view of the ingenuity that was applied to spring-powered ejectors, this is an example of a spring being used to retract the extractor. A coil spring fitted round the stem of the extractor is compressed as the breech-block is opened and so draws back the extractor as the breech-block is lowered.

It is, perhaps, fitting that the final member of this small sub-section should be the invention of Regis Darne. His name was to become all but synonymous with the fixed-barrel, double-barrel, sporting shotgun. Darne was based at No. 13, Rue du Bas-Tandy, St Etienne. The subject of his British patent, No. 6444 of 1890, was not the first fixed-barrel gun that he had designed and marketed, nor is it the classic 'Darne' with the sliding breech. The gun we now have to consider is sometimes called the 'model '87' from the date of its French patent and its year of introduction.

The essential and distinguishing feature of 'the '87 Darne' is a breech-block, pivoted at its rear, that tips backwards about this axis to reveal the breeches of the barrels. While they are the subject of but one patent specification, the ejector and non-ejector forms of this action are so different as to be almost two separate designs. The ejector model is, inevitably, the more complex of the two and the main thrust of the specification is directed towards it, probably indicating that Regis Darne considered it to be the most important part. For these reasons we will look at it first.

The breech-block is held down by a lug under the breech that requires the top lever to be turned a third of a turn. Then the lever, and with it the block, can be drawn back to lie over the small of the stock. Connected to the breech-block behind its opening pivot is a lever which, as the block is drawn back, is thrust forwards. This, acting first on the underside of the tumbler (if the latter has been fired), rotates it to full-cock. Connected to this cocking rod is another sliding in the bed of the action. This, too, is driven forwards by the motion of the breech-block. If the gun has not been fired, the extractor mechanism is operated by a short vertical lever on a transverse pivot, the bottom of which is pushed forwards by the sliding rod and, hence, the extractor draws the cartridges from the breech. If either barrel has been fired, a rod from the tumbler will have lowered the kicker lever so that, as the sliding rod continues on its way, a shoulder on it trips the extractor. The mechanism is so arranged that, as the breech-block is closed and the slide is drawn back, the bottom of the ejector kicker is pulled forwards and the ejector is cocked. One flat spring, lying longitudinally in the bed, serves both as main and ejector spring. This spring, when both percussion and ejector mechanisms are cocked, forms a very shallow U-profile.

The non-ejector Darne model 1887 is, by contrast, very much simpler. Instead of simply omitting the mechanism, two coil spring-powered plungers are built into the breech-block. These are cocked as the top lever is

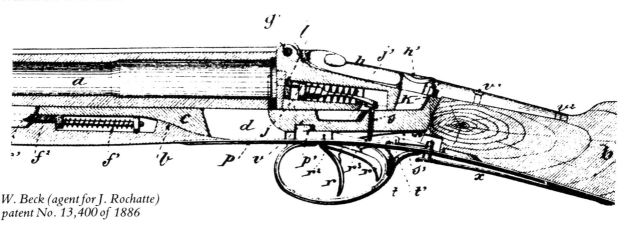

*W. Beck (agent for J. Rochatte)*
*patent No. 13,400 of 1886*

turned and are held by a simple rocking lever sear mounted in the breech-block.

Despite the great success they enjoyed, the rolling-block and the later Darne designs belong almost entirely to history. It is one of the fascinations of a study of the past that we, with the advantage of hindsight, can see more clearly than anyone alive in the 1890s which developments were significant and which were quirks of no consequence. Today we look back upon the few double-barrel guns in which the barrels were diposed one above the other as pointing one of the paths ahead, while in their time such guns were little more than curiosities. Not that the idea was new; even in 1873 when William Wellington Greener included such a design as part of his patent No. 3084 the status of the inclusion is debatable. As we have previously remarked, many of the patent drawings, in that they show minor features of the makers' style, could have been drawn from life. This Greener gun drawing has much more the quality of a sketch so we suspect that the inclusion of what is, essentially, a side-by-side double-gun turned on its side was little more than a make-weight – just one more application of the cross-bolt.

*Drawing, from* The Gun and its Development, *of W. Greener patent No. 3084 of 1873*

While the Greener side-opening under-and-over gun probably progressed little further, other makers made greater use of the idea. From our viewpoint, the most important of these was the firm of John Dickson of Edinburgh who, in 1888, marketed a gun of this type that was, essentially, their side-by-side gun with the mechanism turned through 90 degrees to the right. They took no patent on the gun, probably feeling that the Dickson and Murray patent for the side-by-side was sufficient. The remarkable feature of this story is that this supremely elegant gun was made in very small numbers for almost a hundred years and those who have used it claim that in use the unusual motion rapidly becomes second nature. We can only assume that its novelty was too great for the majority of potential buyers.

*Side-opening superimposed barrel, double-barrel gun by J. Dickson of Edinburgh.* (Courtesy of Christie, Manson and Woods)

From the arms centre of St Etienne, came an under-and-over of French design, patent No. 8667 of 1889. The patentee was Paul Brun-Latrige. The feature which first catches the eye is that the barrel pivot lies between the two barrels. The designer was thus faced with the problem of mating the standing-breech to the barrels. In fact, he saw fit to protect two solutions to this problem and, not content with this, two forms of lockwork as well. It is of interest to note that the lockwork specifications offer, to the problem of delivering a direct blow to the lower firing pin, two answers that have re-appeared in different guises down the years on under-and-over guns. The first set of lockwork described uses the classic V-spring back-action lock for the upper barrel and the same lockwork inverted for the lower. In this latter lock the sear engages with the head of the tumbler. The other lockwork is of the coil spring-loaded plunger-type, working between two vertical guides and, whereas the conventional locks were cocked by a push-forward underlever, the coil spring lock-work is cocked by a slide pushed back by the opening barrels.

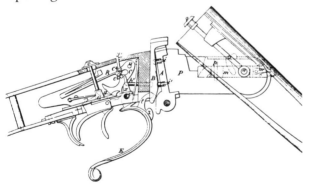

*P. Brun-Latrige patent No. 8667 of 1889*

On the V-spring lever-cocked gun there is a sort of double breech-block in which the rear portion is raised to permit the forward portion to fall back, thereby freeing the barrels to pivot. The coil-spring gun, by contrast, has a breech-block with a curved rear face hinged to the bottom of the bottom barrel so that, when the barrels have pivoted open, the breech-block can be opened to reload.

An ingenious feature of the two-piece breech-block is that it also locked the barrels shut and no other bolting device was necessary. The one-piece breech, however, has a cam worked by a slide that bears on the rear of the block to hold the barrels down.

An excellent example of a gun that appeared after its time is that patented by Capt Lomel of the Regiment of Pontoniniers from Avignon, France. It was a British patent, No. 1014 of 1875, and a gun, in many ways, very reminiscent of the Jeffries first model of 1862. Like the latter, the Lomel is a side-by-side gun in which the barrels are pivoted on a vertical axis, to the left of the barrels, which swing to the right to open. In common with the Jeffries, the Lomel has a dovetail tongue that engages with the action bar. Indeed, the only significant differences between the two are: firstly, the use of a simple single-bite snap-action on the Lomel (a push-forward underlever works a spring catch that retains the dovetail in the closed position); secondly, the rather quaint extractor of the Lomel (which is drawn as a pinfire). This extractor consists of a lever, pivoted below the barrels. It is shaped in the familiar fashion to engage with the cartridge rims, but continues and projects above the top rib to engage the cartridge pins but where it would also impede the user's line of sight. To overcome this draw-back, the projection is formed as a wide U, doubtless to double as a back sight! All this was 13 years after the Jeffries and when there were the clearest of indicators that the hammerless centrefire would form the next generation of sporting guns.

To combine a gun with some other implement has been the goal of many an inventor. A very popular choice has been the walking-stick gun, examples of which appear at irregular intervals from the early days of percussion ignition until the present day. One of these was the subject of a British patent within our period. The patent, No. 4825 of 1876, was obtained in Britain by A. M. Clark, who was acting as agent for Celestin Dumonthier of Paris. Unlike many patents, this gun, a 12 millimetre, was actually made and an example is preserved in the Museé International de la Chasse at Gien in

France (Inv. No. 634). The patent covers three versions of the gun, all of which were to have an outer sleeve to the barrel. This sleeve was to be pushed forward to reveal a loading port in the side of the barrel and drawn back to secure the cartridge. The variations are in the mode by which the gun was to be fired. One idea was to provide a ring on the rear end of the plunger/firing pin stem. Around the plunger was fitted a coil spring so that the user simply pulled back the plunger and released it to fire his walking stick. A more conventional approach was to have a similar plunger mechanism drawn back by a cord in the handle, but retained by a simple spring-loaded stud trigger. The stem of this had a hole through which the plunger could move when the trigger was depressed. The final version surely deserves some sort of prize in that it was to be fired by the user blowing the firing pin against the base of the cartridge pea-shooter fashion. To do this, part of the knob of the cane was to be removed to reveal the striker mechanism. We have, alas, been unable to trace any account of the use of this version, despite examples being known.

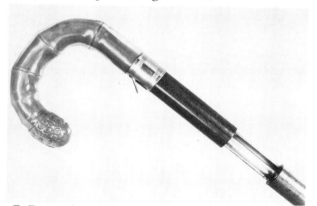

C. Dumonthier .410 walking-stick gun. British patent (agent A. M. Clark) No. 4825 of 1876

Some designs do tend to provoke the question as to why anyone would spend time and money protecting them by a patent specification, or, indeed, why they invented them at all. Very often these are the work of persons outside the gun trade and their pursuit of some bizarre idea can be dismissed as inexperience. Such an explanation is, however, no help when we find a curious idea protected by a gunmaker whose ideas had previously been sound. We are, thus, mystified by the provisional patent, No. 1590 of 1877, in the name of James Dalziel Dougall for a species of triggerless gun. To take the place of the triggers it is proposed to substitute push-in buttons or studs to be worked by the user's thumb and situated on the top of the stock.

There is no such problem, however, in perceiving the inspiration that lies behind the design of Messrs Cooper and Kriz of St Louis. Their British patent, No. 1215 of 1883, was obtained by the agent James McNally Cruikshank of Glasgow. Their design was for a repeating rifle with one or more barrels, set one above the other, sandwiched between the barrels of a conventional double-barrel shotgun. The magazine was to be in the head of the stock with the rifle cartridges carried almost upright with their bases uppermost. The mechanism was to be worked by a push–forward underlever that was also the trigger guard. The external hammers had adjustable noses so that they would strike either the firing pins for the shot or rifle barrel(s) and the spent rifle cartridges were to be ejected upwards between the hammers. Truly a gun for a hero in fiction.

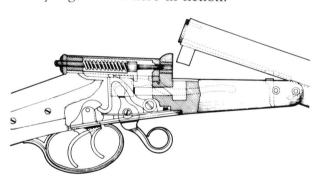

R. Piel patent No. 3549 of 1875

A pair of designs, both patented in Britain, are not only very alike but, being the inventions of Parisian gunmakers, may spring from a common root. The two inventors, Romain Piel and Eugène Gabriel Lefaucheux, patented their designs as, respectively, No. 3549 of 1875 and No. 1251 of 1877. These correspond to French patents, No. 109,892 of 1875 and No. 117,350 of

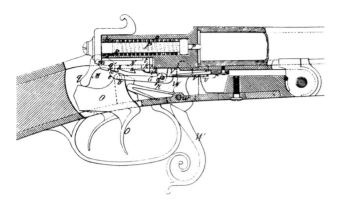

*J. H. Johnson (agent for E. Lefaucheux) patent No. 1251 of 1877*

1877. Both are concerned with pivot-open guns that have a plunger or captive-bolt lock mechanism mounted behind each barrel. They are thus reminiscent of the more common Dreyse-type German shotguns and share with these, and more normal bolt-action guns, the problem of extra inches of length imposed on them by this lockwork. The two French guns under consideration are also alike in that it is the rearward motion of the barrel locking-bolt that serves to cock the lock, if necessary, and both barrel-bolts are shown worked by a push-forward underlever in front of the trigger guard. In fact the only real difference between these two is the design of trigger work and sears necessary to fire the locks. The Piel gun was the most elegant and simple arrangement with a sear, shaped as an inverted U in side view, that is carried on a transverse pivot at the bottom of the forend leg. The sear nose that engages with the lock is a notch cut on the top of this arch. From here the sear curves downwards to end just in front of the pivot on which the trigger is hung. The trigger blade is an unusual shape in that it is formed to a hook-line shape that curves forward of the trigger pivot. Drawing back the trigger causes the front of the trigger blade to depress and so disengage the sear. The sear spring is a leaf fixed at the front and bearing up on the rear of the sear.

The sear arrangement on the Lefaucheux gun is worked by a conventional trigger blade, but with an intermediate right-angle or bell-crank lever transversely pivoted and so arranged that, as the trigger is pulled, the bottom limb of this lever is raised and, hence, the upper forward end is lowered. This then bears on the sear which is a simple lever pivoted at its forward end.

The problem with both of these French guns is that of what advantage their inventors could imagine they possessed. The Piel gun was advertised in Britain very briefly in January 1877 and was called by its inventor 'The Tassine Gun'.

In discussing the lever-cocked hammerless gun earlier (see Chapter One), we mentioned the patent specification of Andrew Wyley, No. 2238 of 1874. We return to it now, so as to deal with the unusual gun that it contains. This is nothing less than a resurrection of the idea of pivoting the barrels parallel to the axis of the bore and opening the gun by twisting the barrels to the right of the stock. Wyley was concerned with hammerless guns and arranged to cock them by using a cocking rod that slid parallel to the barrel-pivot. This was forced to the rear by an inclined surface acting as a cam as the barrels twisted open. In contrast to some of this inventor's other guns, conventional lockwork is shown and, since this gun is tucked away at the very end of the vast specification, it was probably something of a make-weight if such were needed in so vast a deposition.

Yet another gun that we never expect to encounter in the metal is that described in the patent, No. 6194 of 1882, taken out by James Hannay (see Chapter Six). His basic idea was to eliminate the necessity for working some sort of lever to unlock a drop-down spring gun. He proposed to so shape the bites and bolt that the latter would slide back as pressure was applied to force the barrels open. To this end, the mating surfaces of bite and bolt were to be in transverse section, curved so that the bites acted as cams to force back the bolt. This latter was to have on its rear end a stem that projected back beyond the lockwork to a guide fitted under the top strap behind the trigger work. Around this stem, and in front of the guide, is shown a spiral compression spring which, working between a collar on the bolt stem and the stop, forced the locking-bolt forward. As if this were not enough, there is a further complication proposed in the shape of a species of safety catch.

Let us here revert to the theme of what was unusual when it was proposed in the 1870s and 1880s, but which is now accepted and normal. An idea very like the under-and-over gun, in that, it was even then of some antiquity, was the notion of a single-trigger with a mechanism that would permit the user of the gun to fire successively both barrels of his gun. Throughout the 1890s a procession of these was patented but, within our period, there are two. The first is a little provisional specification, No. 4766 of 1882, granted to David Bentley and William Baker. Completeness demands we consider it here, but we shall have to re-examine it with those that followed for it was often quoted in the arguments and legal wrangles that centred upon the 'one-trigger mechanism', as the idiom of the day called it.

A point that was much argued in the 1890s was that, as it stood, the mechanism was unworkable. All that was proposed by Bentley and Baker were some means, not really specified, by which firing one lock aligns the trigger work in readiness to fire the second lock. Thus, no apparent provision is made for the involuntary pull that we all make when a shotgun or rifle recoils against our shoulders and we grip it to control it.

The second specification, while it is a single-trigger mechanism, has as its stated object the prevention of a sportsman repeatedly using one barrel of a double-gun to fire single shots. We are not told for what reason this was considered a bad practice, but to stop it a single-trigger mechanism is proposed. It was patented by Henry Allender of Detroit as British patent No. 10,903 of 1884 obtained by patent agent Henry Lake. The heart of this mechanism is a small disc pivoted on a central vertical pivot. From the circumference of the disc are cut square notches so that, in plan, the disc resembles a sort of sprocket. The notches are to be so arranged that an indentation is always opposite a tooth. The disc is so positioned in the gun that it lies below the sears and the mechanism is such that squeezing the trigger lifts the disc on its pivot and one of the teeth lifts a sear, while the other sear slides

through the opposite notch. By a method not fully described, the first portion of the movement of squeezing the trigger advances the disc one notch so as to align with the sear of the other barrel. So far so good in theory, but two points should be remarked on. Firstly, to fire a second shot, the trigger has first to be released and then re-pulled. Secondly, and much more a matter of conjecture, is how this mechanism would cope with the 'involuntary pull'. It is our belief that this would vary with how this pull was applied: if it were a simple continuation of the first pull, then all would be well, but if the trigger were sufficiently released and then re-pulled, the involuntary pull would fire the second barrel. We further suspect that this performance would vary with the individual using the gun and would possibly be further complicated by the type of load in the cartridge.

Among the delights of researching are the unexpected little discoveries and side issues that give scope for all sorts of speculation and discussion. For instance, in 1883 as patent No. 823, Frederick Beesley, then of Queen Street, Edgware Road, London obtained protection for a variety of ways of using some of the energy released when a cartridge is fired to recock the gun. Two methods are described. In the first, a rod from the heelplate ran forward and under the lockwork to work a crank lever. As the gun recoiled, the heelplate (which was carried on two lightly-sprung guides) pushed the rod forward and the tumbler was rotated backwards and cocked. The other idea was to have a sliding–block that partially supported the cartridge head, and so arranged that the cartridge case would push back the slide to recock the lock.

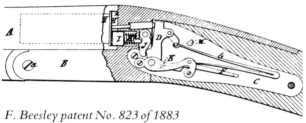

*F. Beesley patent No. 823 of 1883*

With these recoil-cocking ideas, as patented, the 'involuntary pull' would probably refire the lock as soon as it had been cocked. A single-trigger mechanism would be a probable cure. More serious problems would probably arise with the unsupported cartridge-head design, in which the ordinary ammunition of commerce would almost certainly burst.

To conclude this chapter, we describe a gun that its inventor offered to the shooting public as 'The Gun of the Future'. That we have included it at this point with a group of bizarre actions is an indication of the failure of the design. The inventor was none other than Dr Walsh, with whom we are well acquainted, and the gun is the subject of the British patent, No. 5106 of 1878. This is, in fact, the hammerless version of his earlier gun, patent No. 516 of 1866. But in sharp contrast to his earlier attitude, Dr Walsh used his position at *The Field* to attempt to boost his own invention. In the period 1878–1879 there are numerous mentions, all favourable, of his gun. The most lavish was a full-page feature, with drawings, in the issue of 15 February 1879, where the inventor sets out the criteria that he had sought to fulfil, namely strength of the action, safety of the lock,

*Dr J. H. Walsh's 'Gun of the Future'. An unmarked and unfinished example probably made by Greener*

*Drawing from* The Field *of complete engraved Walsh patent gun*

ease of loading, exclusion of water and explosive gas from lock and action, and freedom from wear and tear coupled with ease of tightening. To achieve these entirely laudable aims, Walsh retained the basic features of the hinge under the action-face with the locking-bolt sliding almost vertically in the head of the stock. To work the hammerless action the cocking cams now act within the head of the stock, and the safety is the only real addition. From the drawings it appears that there was to be a separate safety for each lock. These were to consist of an external level which, via a spindle, worked another and shorter lever inside the lockplate. The internal level and the tumbler were so shaped and placed that when the external lever was in the safe position the fall of the tumbler was blocked.

It is, we feel, much more a measure of Dr Walsh's stature in the shooting world, rather than the merits of *The Field* gun (the other title it was given) that three gunmakers proceeded to build the gun. Of these Messrs Bland, then of 106, The Strand, London, did the most with it, apparently selling limited numbers and devising improvements and alterations. First, they altered the opening lever to a push–up thumb lever on the lines of the famous Powell action and added a Lefaucheux-style lever-grip mechanism to ease the removal of the forend. Second, Blands completely revised the design, substituting a turning top lever to lower the locking-bolt and a conventional top slide to work the safety. Walsh described this final

modification in *The Modern Sportsman's Gun and Rifle.* The second maker who exploited the design was Green of Cheltenham. Correspondence in *The Field* indicates that he sold a few examples. The final maker of 'The Gun of the Future' was no less than Greener. In *The Field* we find a note, dated 1880, to the effect that Greener was building a prototype.

We are confident that we have found this gun. It came from Greener's collection and is an unfinished example, still in the white, but stocked in typical Greener fashion. That this prototype remained unfinished, and the fact that Walsh did not renew his patent in 1882 when the first three years had elapsed, both bear eloquent witness that those connected with the gun had realised that they were going down a blind alley. More than any other feature, the idea of putting the opening hinge under the face of the action produces an awkward gun. This feature is exaggerated by the far greater gape of the barrels. The result is that, even with the influence of both Dr Walsh and *The Field* behind it, this gun raised only a small ripple on the surface of the stream of gun progress and soon sank from sight.

In fact, the same could be said of practically all the guns we have included in this chapter. The Darne, and the Remington rolling-block are obvious exceptions and special cases. For the rest, perhaps the kindest thing that can be said of them is that they add new dimensions to the sporting gun of the mid-Victorian era and for this we should be grateful.

*Drawing from* The Field *of T. Bland's modification of the Walsh patent gun*

# CHAPTER ELEVEN

# The Ejector

An ejector is the mechanical means by which fired cartridge cases are discarded from a gun. Such a mechanism is now regarded as normal in a modern sporting gun, yet the ejector was another feature of shotgun design refined by our two turbulent decades of competitive invention.

The reason for the addition of an ejector to the mechanism of a shotgun was that it enhanced the firepower at the shooter's command. It is less easy to pinpoint where the inspiration came from. In common with so much of the story of firearms, previous use of similar ideas can be found. For instance, in the 1850s and 1860s, there was an interest in pinfire guns with slide-forward barrels, the so-called Bastin type. One of its features was that, in theory at least, the fired case was removed as the gun was opened to reload.

Though these guns would have doubtless exerted some influence on designers' thinking, a far more potent force, and one that has previously not been adequately stressed, was the carry over of ideas from developments then taking place in the design of the military rifle. For instance, the Martini and Soper rifle actions, to name but two, would have been the subject of much discussion in the early 1870s, because both, under ideal conditions, ejected their spent cases.

Before we become embroiled in a description of ejector mechanisms, let us identify those characteristics that an ejector mechanism should possess. Firstly, and basically, it should throw out of the gun only the spent case or cases. Secondly, and more subtly, the ejection should happen after the lockwork has been cocked, this to avoid a user finding himself with a reloaded but inoperative gun. Thirdly, this should happen faultlessly no matter whether the gun is eased or slammed open.

Like so many seemingly simple rules, these ideas are more easily stated than met and practical gunmakers are well aware of the perversity of ejectors. In fairness to the inventors we must not forget that today we see some of their creations after almost a century of wear, ill use and outright neglect, points that we are sure they would raise in their own defence if they were able to do so.

No matter where the inspiration came from, all sources are in remarkable agreement that the first pivot-open ejector sporting gun was that invented by Joseph Needham. He patented the design as No. 1205 of 1874. (In view of this it is all the more remarkable that no previous authors have seen fit to record anything of the man and very few have given even the briefest description of this first ejector gun. Since we regard this gun as being of the greatest importance, and have had the exceptional good fortune to contact Joseph Needham's nephew, a splendid old gentleman, born in 1890, we hope to give a fuller account.)

*Joseph Needham, inventor of the barrel-cocked hammerless ejector gun*

While we are sure that he was not unique in this respect, Joseph Needham is remembered as being a compulsive inventor with a long string of inventions, some of which he patented, and most of which were early in their field. Ideas as diverse as torpedoes, rotary engines and fountain pens bubbled forth and, more relevant to our theme, it is also claimed that he first produced the leather gun-case. To be told all this by a man who knew him while a portrait of 'Uncle Joe' looked down from the top of the parlour piano, was one of the great joys of our research. Perhaps to sharpen our perception of Joseph Needham as an inventor of gun mechanisms, it is relevant to our theme to recount the roll of his other, more important gun inventions. In 1852 he patented, No. 184, the needle-fire gun by which he could claim to have produced the first 'hammerless' gun. Then in 1862, as patent No. 1544, he produced the self half-cocking snap action.

*George Hinton when Mayor of Taunton*

Another interesting comment that his nephew made was that Uncle Joe, like some other inventors, tended to lose some interest in his creations once they were born. This snippet fitted with a story told to the author (IMC) about a man by the name of George Hinton. At the time of the invention of the ejector, Mr Hinton was working as a gunmaker in Birmingham, as we believe his father had before him. The story is that it was George Hinton who produced and made to work the early Needham ejector guns. From his profits in this endeavour, George Hinton was able to buy the gunmaking business of George Shepherd of 54, High Street, Taunton and move to the more congenial atmosphere of Somerset. In Taunton he entered local politics and in 1913 was mayor of his adopted town. It is from these archives that our portrait derives.

In the gun Joseph Needham designed, the ejector mechanism was an integral part of – and not, like the bulk of those that followed, an addition to – an existing action. The Needham action we described earlier (see Chapter Four), was, as well as being the pioneer ejector gun, also the first barrel-cocked hammerless gun. The crucial importance of this gun in the evolution of the British sporting gun cannot be overstated.

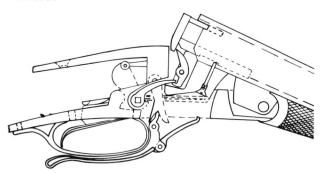

*J. Needham patent No. 1205 of 1874*

It will be recalled that, as patented, Needham's gun has a trigger-plate action set in the head of the stock. (See Chapter Four, page 64.) The cocking levers for this are keyed onto the same spindle as the tumblers and extend forward to be picked up and raised by the rear

**NEEDHAM'S**
**Ejector Hammerless Gun.**

IT ejects the exploded case or cases, is unique in its action and simplicity of construction; has been used for the past seven seasons with great success.

**Made as Illustrated above**
**FROM 25 GUINEAS.**

With the Top Lever Action, from 35 guineas.

Hammerless Guns, not Ejector, Best Shooting. Strongest made (Greener's Treble Wedge fast action), from 16 guineas.

**TRAP GUNS, WITH TOP LEVER ACTION,**
**13 GUINEAS**
(FULL CHOKE OR MODIFIED).

**KEEPERS' GUNS,**

With double Grip Action, made strong for hard work, Cylinder bore, £6 6s.

Choke Bored to give any pattern, 10s. 6d. per Barrel extra.

Do.   Do.   Top Lever Engraved, £7 7s.
Do.   Do.   10s. per Barrel extra.

Superior quality Choke Bore, Bar Locks, £10 10s.

**J. V. NEEDHAM,**
**GUNMAKER,**
(ESTABLISHED 1860)

**20a, Temple-st., New-st., Birmingham.**

*J. Needham advertisement of 1884*

lump as the barrels pivot open. On the rear face of the rear lump are cut two projections and it is the upper one of these that begins to lift the cocking levers. However, the length of the levers and the size of the projection are such that, just as the barrels gape sufficiently for the spent case to eject, the cocking lever slips off the top projection. It is forced sharply downwards by the partially-compressed mainspring to collide violently with the bottom projection on the rear barrel lump. Hinged in the rear lump are two reversed C-shaped ejector-levers. These work on transverse pivots at about their mid-point and it is on the bottom limb of each C that the cocking-lever strikes. The top of each ejector lever engages with one half of the extractor which Joseph Needham had split in half and so we have a selective ejector mechanism.

Today, Needham's ejector is part of history. All that has happened since overlays it, and we are perhaps apt to forget the importance that it once enjoyed. First it is vital to realise that this patent is one of the few that was maintained for the maximum spell of 14 years. That is to say it did not expire until 1888 and, aside from the use made of the whole patent or slight modifications of it, it contained protection of the idea of

*Gun by J. V. Needham of Birmingham built on J. Needham patent No. 1205 of 1874*

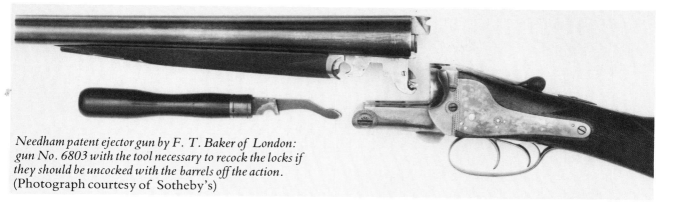

*Needham patent ejector gun by F. T. Baker of London: gun No. 6803 with the tool necessary to recock the locks if they should be uncocked with the barrels off the action. (Photograph courtesy of Sotheby's)*

fitting two semi-circular extractor rods together in a common hole. The so-called split-stem extractor proved to be perhaps the most valuable feature of the whole design, and on which Joseph Needham was able to charge 'heavy royalties'. (Our researches have yet to uncover the exact amount per gun but we recall the 15 shillings per gun that Westley Richards charged for their Anson and Deeley boxlock action. However, a story is told in the Needham family that in one year the royalties totalled £1,000 which, then, was some 20 times the cost of a 'Best London Gun'.)

The ejector work patented by Greener in his patent, No. 2003 of 1881, is, as stated on the specification, a combination of the Needham patent, No. 1205 of 1874, and Greener's own hammerless gun, the Facile Princeps, patent No. 930 of 1880. The tumblers of the Facile Princeps' action curve together at their lower forward ends and are lifted by a projection on the front lump to cock as the barrels pivot open. Now, in addition to being simply cocked as the gun opens, the toes of the tumblers work the kicking leverwork of the typical Needham ejector that has been transferred to the front lump.

As was normal, this design was well promoted by Greener in his various books on the sporting shotgun and, perhaps less well known today, in letters to the sporting press. An example of this is a letter published in *The Field* on 12 January 1895. Greener, writing from St Mary's Square, Birmingham on 9 January refers to:

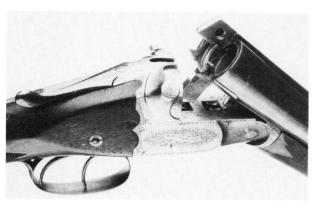

*W. Greener gun using patent ejector No. 2003 of 1881*

---

**THE BATTLE OF THE EJECTORS**

**Sir – In reference to Mr Deeley's letter about the 'Battle of the Ejectors', we do not consider he has made the matter quite clear. He says: 'Needham's gun was patented in 1874 and was well known and successful in 1880.' This particular ejector gun was never successful until the mechanism was improved upon by us in 1882. Between 1882 and 1884, 130 of these ejectors, with improved mechanism, were sold by us at high prices; and between 1884 and 1888, 510 were sold, making a total of 640 guns of this class in a space of six years. It was owing to the wonderful success of which our efforts attained with this ejector that others were induced to follow in our footsteps and to manufacture a weapon automatic in extracting the fired cases. Many of the ejectors made by us as far back as 1882 are in use at the present time and give entire satisfaction.**

---

By comparison with the Greener mainspring-powered ejector, the Ford is almost unknown.

Like its more famous competitor, this is a box-lock design that employs the 'slip off the step' idea of the Needham but in a different manifestation. To cock his gun, patent No. 8841 of 1887, William Ford used a sliding rod that was pushed back by the forend iron as the gun opened. The motion of this rod turns a bell-crank lever set in the bar of the action on a transverse pivot that in turn lifts the tumbler to full-cock. The essence of this design is to form a step in the cam that forces back the cocking lever. When the lock is partially cocked the cocking lever can slip forward before being raised again to the fully-cocked position. To use the jump thus produced in the cocking mechanism, a lever is set vertically on the front lump with its lower end bearing on the front of the bell-crank cocking piece. Thus, when the slip forward occurs, the top of the vertical lever jerks smartly backwards and so ejects the spent case. It follows that, if the lockwork remains at full-cock, the mainspring will remain confined.

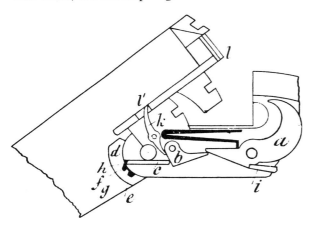

*W. Ford patent No. 8841 of 1887*

The final member of the mainspring-powered ejectors is to be found tucked away in the depths of one of Edgar Harrison's many ejector patents. As part of patent No. 13,591 of 1889, there is described a species of boxlock gun in which the front of the cocking lever bears on the bottom of the ejector tumbler as the gun pivots open. Thus the downward pressure of the mainspring on the toe of the lock tumbler becomes an upward thrust on the bottom of the

ejector tumbler. As the gun opens, the ejector tumbler is acted upon by a cam formed in the forend so that the top of the ejector cam moves to the rear. When the point at which the thrust of the cocking lever is being exerted moves to be in front of the transverse pivot of the ejector tumbler, the top of this tumbler is suddenly flicked back.

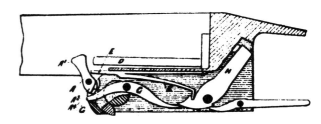

*E. Harrison patent No. 13,591 of 1889 (first version)*

We are well aware that we could be accused, by those whose business it is to make ejector mechanisms work, of taking a somewhat simplistic view of our subject. However, our concern is to explain how these mechanisms are *supposed* to work. While we must evade the technical problems of making ejectors work, it is important to be well aware of their existence, not least for the influence they had on designs of succeeding mechanisms.

It will be evident that if both barrels were made to eject with a common mechanism every time the barrels pivoted open, a simpler and cheaper-to-make gun would result. To restore the necessary degree of selectivity, some sort of impediment has to be placed in the way of the live cartridge so that a degree of complication is reintroduced and this could be argued to outweigh the advantages of the simplification. Nevertheless, there was a corps who felt that balance might be in favour of such a system for we are able to assemble a group of patents that share this characteristic.

It is certainly of interest that the first of these was patented by Joseph Needham as No. 2793 of 1875. We are tempted to wonder if he was despairing of solving the practical problems of his first ejector and was seeking a different path. Alternatively, this new patent may simply be

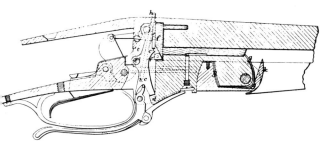

*J. Needham patent No. 2793 of 1875*

another manifestation of his restless urge to invent.

Needham's specification claims that the mechanism is an improvement of his first ejector patent, No. 1205 of 1874, but the ejector described in the later patent is totally different. The split-legged extractor has been abandoned and a separate ejector spring provided. This spring is shaped roughly like a letter U, and stands longitudinally in the slot for the front barrel lump. The rear limb of the U is fixed, while the front is free and is borne on by the front of the extractor leg. As the gun pivots open the extractor forces the limbs of the U apart. To enable sufficient tension to be given to the spring, the rear of the extractor has a small lever transversely pivoted on it. This is at rest when the gun is closed and projects horizontally to the rear. As the barrels rise, this lever rides up a slot, the bottom of which is so shaped that the lever is rotated until it hangs vertically down. When this lever rises above the top of the standing-breech, the ejector spring can now suddenly act on the extractor. It will be noted that there is no mention of any special provision for primary extraction. Presumably this was to take place against the ejector spring. More seriously, it would seem that the extractor would travel too far to the rear to eject the cartridges and, with no provision to draw it forwards, the gun could not be reclosed except by pushing in the extractor by hand. This second problem may explain why a modified form is also included on the specification. Now the ejector spring is a more complex shape but still fitted fore-and-aft in the action bar. This spring is fixed at its rear end with a loop in its

centre that continues forward to end as an upward projection just in front of the extractor. Just behind the upward projection is a shoulder on the spring that bears on a corresponding shoulder on the front of the front lump. Once again, as the gun is opened the ejector spring is tensioned, this time by the loop in it being tightened by the shoulder on the lump swinging forwards in an arc. Then, as the bottoms of the extractors clear the top of the standing-breech, the shoulder on the spring slips off the shoulder on the front lump; in theory, the upward projection of the spring forcibly strikes the rear of the extractor to eject the cartridges. Again, there is no mention of a primary extraction stage, but in this version the rearward travel of the extractor would not be so great as to prevent the closure of the gun.

In the absence of an actual gun of either design, these practical questions must remain unanswered. However, what is clear from the specification is that, in both versions, a pop-up pin on the standing-breech was to be used to arrest the ejection of the cartridge, or cartridges, that remained unfired. The retraction of these pins was effected by connecting them to the lower limb of the mainspring which lay forwards in the bar of the action.

The basic idea embodied in the second Needham ejector patent, which curiously provided a means by which the inventor's first patent could be evaded, had obvious attractions. We can assemble a manageable group of five patents, all of which share the idea of ejecting every time the gun is opened with some sort of pop-up pin to stop an unfired cartridge. It is significant that the first of this group, patent No. 1968 of 1878, is also the next ejector patent to the Needham in chronological sequence. This four-year gap is eloquent proof of the contemporary, low level of interest in the concept of the ejector shotgun.

Patent No. 1968 of 1878 is important in many ways, not least because its inventor was Thomas Perkes, then of 4, Cleveland Street, Fitzroy Square, made a series of highly-important contributions to the evolution of the ejector mechanism. Despite our researches, we know little about Perkes. As indicated earlier (see

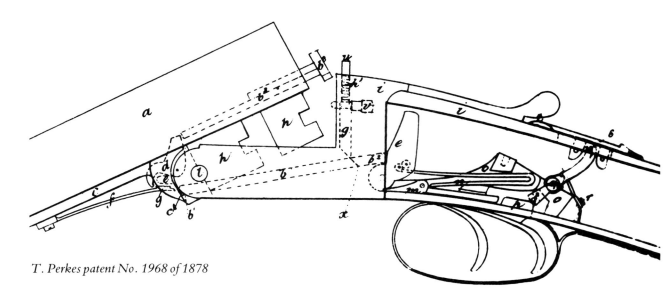

*T. Perkes patent No. 1968 of 1878*

Chapter Two) he had premises in Soho, but by this period had moved to 4, Cleveland Street, Fitzroy Square. He died, intestate, on 5 November 1922 and left an estate valued at less than £100. He had at least one son, who was for a period in partnership with him, but who at the time of his father's death had either left the gun trade or was working for someone else. The family simply fades into the suburbia of north-west London.

One claim to fame of this Perkes specification is that in it we see, for the first time, the use of the forend as the site for the ejector work. This idea was to be re-used by a whole host of inventors. Moreover, it is also the first use of the mechanism that, in gunmaking jargon, is referred to as an 'over centre ejector tumbler'. Other commentators have pointed out that the most familiar use of this idea is to be found in the ordinary folding pocket-knife where a single spring holds the blade both shut and open. While in practice the shape of the ejector tumbler can alter, the principles behind it can be appreciated by visualising a vertical lever swinging fore-and-aft on a transverse pivot. A leaf spring, also set fore-and-aft, bears up on the bottom of this lever. When the top of the lever lies to one side of the pivot the thrust of the spring on the bottom limb will tend to force the lever further in the same direction. However, if

the lever is forced in the opposite direction, so that its top passes over the pivot point, the upward thrust will cause the lever to rotate in the opposite direction and indeed, if free to do so, the lever will go over centre with a forceful flick. This mechanism was to become one of the classic ejector systems of the British sporting gun, but was known to posterity as 'The Southgate' after the patentee of a later version.

In the Perkes 1878 patent, the agent that rotates the ejector tumbler to its critical position is a cam formed on the knuckle of the action bar. It is so shaped that it both trips the ejector and, on the gun being closed, recompresses the ejector spring. The latter is drawn (and is probably more convenient) as a leaf spring, but a coil version is mentioned.

To make the arrangement selective, two pop-up pins are set in the top of the standing-breech. The patent describes how the bottoms of these pins are curved inwards towards the centreline of the gun. In one version these pins are raised by a rearward projection from the extractor that forces the bottoms apart as the gun is closed. To retract the pin, that is, to permit the ejector to throw out the spent case, the falling tumbler drives forward a slide in the standing-breech. The lower face of this slide has an incline formed upon it which forces down the stop pin. In another version, the interrupter pins are straight and set vertically in the standing-breech; at their bottom ends an incline bears against another incline cut on sliding cocking rods. Thus, when the cocking rod is in the rearward position, that is, the tumblers are cocked, the pins are held up. When the lock is fired the cocking rod moves forward and the interrupter pins are forced downward by a coil spring.

This patent is one of the milestones in the evolution of the sporting shotgun and contains, in addition to the mechanisms outlined above, two hammerless actions. It is a measure of the importance of this action that, after using the design on guns that he made for Holland and Holland, Perkes sold his patent rights to Messrs W. & C. Scott.

It is a further comment on the low contemporary regard in which the potential of the ejector was held that there is practically a five-year gap to the next patent, No. 1137 of 1883. This is also an interrupter, patented by William Nobbs, whose address in the Old Kent Road, London, obscures the fact that he was an employee of Messrs Purdey. Nobbs used another motion of the lockwork to operate his pop-up pins. To the sear of a bar-action sidelock hammerless gun he added an upward spur just above the pivot point. The top end of this spur works a slide, fitted to the lockplate, that moves back and forth. As the lock is fired, the spur moves this slide forward, and the underside of the tumbler holds the sear and its spur in this position until the lock is recocked. The forward end of the slide has a bevel on it so that, as it moves forwards, it pushes up a rod sliding vertically in the standing-breech. The top of this rod bears on the underside of the rear of a spring-loaded

rocking lever set in the top of the standing-breech. The forward end of the rocking lever carries the interrupter studs, which also act as cocking indicators. The actual ejector mechanism of this design is relatively unremarkable, with a coil spring round the stem of the extractor/ejector rod which is tripped by a lever on the knuckle as the barrels pivot open.

It was to be another three years before the great spate of ejectors was to come, but the trickle of patents begins to swell in 1883. Only three months after the previous patent we find another Thomas Perkes invention, patent No. 3049 of 1883. This covers several aspects of hammerless sporting guns, including another pop-up pin interrupted ejector. What is here proposed is a pair of pins sliding vertically in the standing-breech, each of which has to retract it an L-shaped lever that is pivoted transversely at its angle and behind the pin in such a way that the falling tumbler drives forwards one limb while the other retracts the interrupting pin. To hold the pins down, while the gun is opened and recocked, is, at the bottom end of each pin, a hook. These hooks are held by a T-shaped upward projection on the locking-bolt that engages with the pin when the bolt is to the rear. When the bolt is released and the gun recocked, a leaf spring bearing on the L-shaped lever raises

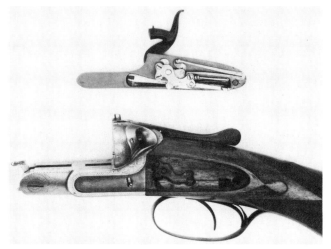

*Hammer ejector retailed by I. Hollis with T. Perkes patent No. 3049 of 1883 ejector mechanism.* (Photograph courtesy of Christie, Manson and Woods)

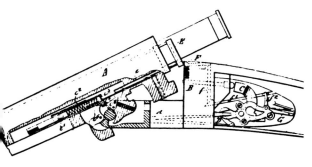

*W. Nobbs patent No. 1137 of 1883*

the 'stop pin', as Perkes called it. No details of the ejector mechanism are shown.

So far in this sub-section of non-selectively tripped ejector mechanisms we have a chronological sequence of the early ejectors, but now this ceases to be the case. With the upsurge of interest in the concept of an ejecting shotgun mechanism all sorts of different ideas had been tried before Thomas Woodward of Birmingham obtained his patent, No. 4920 of 1887. By the date of this patent, the concept of an interrupter was dated if not actually old-fashioned. What was covered by Woodward was the idea of fitting pop-up pins with coil springs in the bottom of their holes, and of retracting them by the front end of a rocking lever, the rear end of which was raised by the trigger blade.

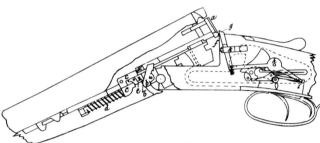

*T. Woodward patent No. 4920 of 1887*

Later in 1887, as patent No. 16,356, we have yet another variant on the idea of pop-up pins to stop the ejection of live cartridges. What Thomas Morton of 22, Cockspur Street, and

Edwin Hughes of 160, Lambeth Road (who were respectively owner and manager of the firm of Joseph Lang and Son of 22, Cockspur Street, London) proposed was to have in the standing-breech two spring-loaded vertically-sliding rods with forward projections on their bottoms. As the barrels closed, they pressed down on the forward projections so that, when closed, the gun had no unnecessary excretions. The position of the stop rods is such that, when the gun is fired, the firing pin in its forward position engages and locks down the stop permitting the spent case to be ejected. The ejector mechanism shown is a conventional sear and tumbler arrangement with a coil ejector spring working round a rod that bears on the back of the tumbler.

Another patent in this group, obsolescent when obtained, was No. 7813 of 1888, taken out by Isaac and Reuben Bullock, then located at 11, St Mary's Row, Birmingham. Their idea, shown on its specification as a hammer gun, was to have a stud on the centre of the extractor plate which, as the barrels closed, pushed the inner ends of a pair of transversely-set rocking levers in the standing-breech. The outer ends of these levers were formed as cartridge stops. In some way not specified, the stops were to be held up by the firing pins in the unfired position, but a slot was to be cut in the pins so that, when the firing pin was forward, a small spring retracted the stop lever into the slot.

*T. Morton and E. Hughes patent No. 16,356 of 1887*

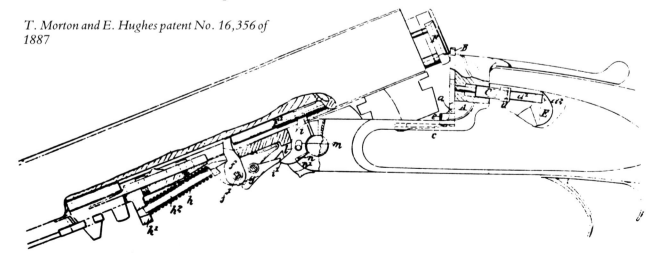

To round off this sub-section there are the related designs that, while the ejector mechanism trips each time the gun opens, use means other than an external pin to retain the unfired cartridge. There are but two of these, both the work of Birmingham gunmakers and both patented in 1887. As patent No. 7470, Isaac and Reuben Bullock again show on a hammer gun two stops mounted on the top extension. These stops swing laterally on fore-and-aft pivots and are splayed open by a spring-loaded stud that protrudes from the rear of the recess cut for the top extension in the standing-breech. Thus, the live cartridges are retained, and presumably these stops have to be moved aside with a fingernail if it is desired to remove a loaded cartridge from the breech. When the gun is fired, a spring-loaded pin is driven obliquely by the firing pin to push the stop off the cartridge rim.

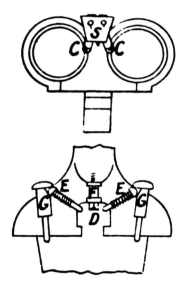

*I. and R. Bullock patent No. 7470 of 1887*

Like the preceding design, in that, it too has stops on the extractor and is drawn on its specification as a hammer gun, is the patent, No. 10,888 of 1887, in the name of William Henry Brighton of 13, Court, Price Street, Birmingham. It is more complex than the Bullock specification in that the stops are mounted on the extractor and slide up and down to retain or

release the cartridge in the barrel. As the gun is closed the stops are pushed down by a sort of spring-loaded flap, mounted under the rear of the top rib, and in this position the cartridges are retained. When a lock is fired the tumbler pushes forward a sliding rod with an incline on its forward end which in turn pushes up a second sliding rod, which is spring-loaded. The second vertical rod pushes up the appropriate cartridge stop and thus permits the spent case to be ejected. The actual ejector is a V-spring and tumbler arrangement in the forend.

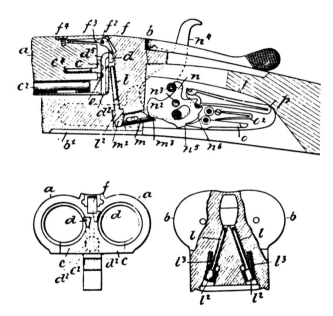

*W. Brighton patent No. 10,888 of 1887*

With the benefit of hindsight, we can view these interrupting ejectors more dispassionately than did their inventors. All of these mechanisms are, to a degree, fragile and their working includes an element of battering so, while odd examples are known, most of them are broken down.

Another small group of ejectors that share some of the features of the mechanisms just described, also provide a link with what, today, we regard as the conventional ejectors that followed. The five designs described are, on the one hand, all non-selectively tripped and, on the other, have a separate ejector mechanism for each barrel, the selectivity restored by some system of internal stops.

In the main these five designs were patented after those that formed our previous group and so, in a sense, we can regard them as the successors. This point is emphasised in our first design, patent No. 14,404 of 1886. The patentee, William Nobbs, claims that the new specification is an improvement on his previous patent, No. 1137 of 1883, which we have just considered. We are not told why No. 14,404 is an improvement, but we suspect it is that now all the mechanism is internal and so nothing disfigures the outside of the Purdey hammerless gun. What is described is a system of two interrupter pins sliding vertically in the front lump. To retract these, that is, to permit the ejectors to function, on either side a rod slides horizontally forward from the tumbler so that, as the gun opens, the interrupter rod is held down by a lateral projection from it catching on the slide from the tumbler. Very similar in principle is Edgar Harrison's patent, No. 16,214 of 1886, which is shown on its specification as an external hammer gun, and examples are seen as such.

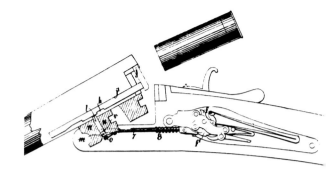

E. Harrison patent No. 16,214 of 1886

W. Harrison gun fitted with ejector mechanism covered by patent No. 16,214 of 1886

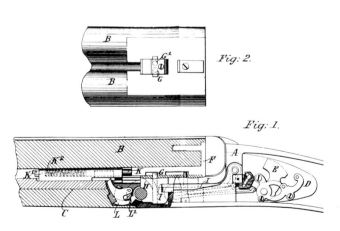

W. Nobbs patent No. 14,404 of 1886

The remaining three patents that comprise the rest of this group differ from the Nobbs and share the common principle of using some motion of the lockwork to raise the stop pins into position. These pins are withdrawn as the bar-

rels reach the limit of their opening travel so that the ejector spring can suddenly exert itself on the spent case. If the stop pin is not raised and the barrel not fired, the ejector spring pushes steadily back on the extractor and pushes out the loaded cartridge.

The three patents differ greatly in practical details, but it remains a curious fact that they were all patented in the early part of 1889 by men with Birmingham addresses. Taken chronologically, the first is the patent, No. 1249 of 1889, obtained by William Henry Brighton. His idea was to have a rod that slid diagonally down through the action bar from the tumbler, to protrude from the bottom of the knuckle when its lock had been fired. The ejector work is more complex than some, consisting of a V-spring and tumbler, but with the stop pin acting more like a sear, shaped like a letter J without its top bar, and free to slide up and down. When the lock has been fired, as the barrels pivot open, the forward end of the cocking lever rotates a cam pivoted behind the J piece and raises the latter so

*E. Harrison's advertisement of 1886*

that the toe of the J engages with a bent on the underside of the ejector tumbler. As the barrels pivot further, a second lever, also pivoted behind the J but above the cam that raised it, acts on a shoulder on the top of the knuckle to slide down the J and so release the ejector. If nothing more, this results in a complex drawing in the patent specification.

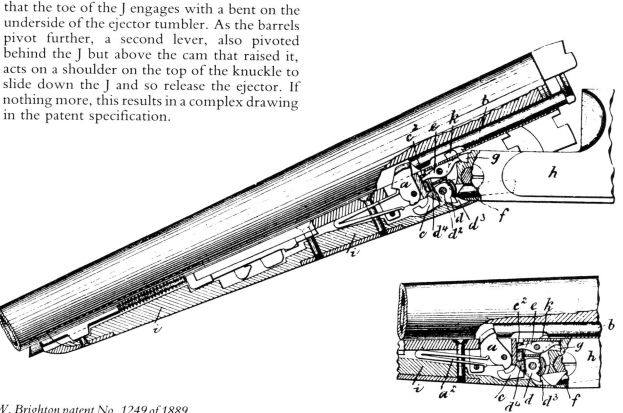

*W. Brighton patent No. 1249 of 1889*

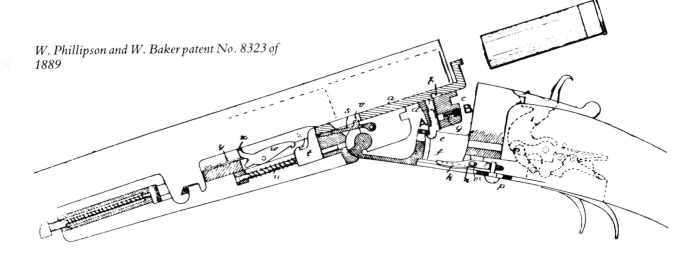

*W. Phillipson and W. Baker patent No. 8323 of 1889*

Much simpler is patent No. 8323 of 1889. This is in the joint names of William Phillipson of 78, Weaman Street, and William Baker of Smith Street, St George's, who quote their trades as respectively gun action manufacturer and gun lock maker. In their design a pair of vertically-sliding stop pins are mounted in the rear lump. These are raised by the forward ends of rocking levers in the bottom of the action. Exactly how the rear end of these levers is depressed, the patentees left deliberately open, but they mention the possible use of the motion of the trigger blades. The stop pins are withdrawn by forward projections on their lower ends catching under a lip formed on the front of the slot in the action bar cut for the rear lump.

The third member of this trio is, in the authors' experience at least, the most commonly met with. The patentee was Louis Edward Parfitt, who tells us on his specification, No. 9209 of 1889, that he was an engineer of Ashfield Road, Kings Heath. However, we find his ejector on some of the Bonehill guns and we are left to wonder what connection existed between inventor and user. One speculation is that the profession of 'engineer' points to Parfitt having been employed by Bonehill in his Belmont Works in Belmont Row, which was concerned with the making of guns by machine-shop methods.

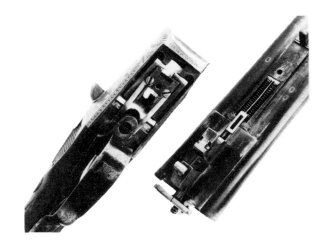

*C. G. Bonehill gun fitted with L. Parfitt patent ejector No. 9209 of 1889*

In the Parfitt ejector, the stop pins are mounted in the front lump and they are raised by the forward ends of rocking levers, pivoted in the bottom of the action bar. The forward ends of these levers turn inwards while their rears are depressed by the curved underside of the tumbler as it falls. Formed on the bottom of the holes in which the stop pins slide are two outward projections and, on the stop pins, are depressions. When they are in the down position, the lateral projections on the bottoms of the stop pins are flush with the sides of the lumps. In the up position, the toes of the stop pins project from the sides of the lump and are caught by suitable slots cut in the action bar.

A great advantage of the ejectors that we have come to call the internal stop pin or interrupter type is that, on extraction, the unfired cartridge is carried out the whole travel of the ejector and thus is easily removed, even with cold hands. The disadvantage that they share with all interrupters is that the pins are somewhat battered in use. In the words of an old man of the Birmingham gun trade when asked to comment on a Bonehill gun fitted with a Parfitt ejector, 'it's alright as long as you don't use it too much.'

We were diverted by the second Joseph Needham patent, and now must return to our chronological sequence and the designs that were to be the mainstream of ejector evolution. When we do this we first encounter a patent that became, for a time, perhaps the best known of all this group, not for the use made of it but because it was the central theme in the complex legal wrangle that became referred to as 'The Battle of the Ejectors'. Before we attempt to describe this important litigation, it is vital that we explain the patent over which it was fought.

In 1884 John Deeley the younger, son of the chairman of the Westley Richards company, worked in the firm as a designer and was also a very fine rifle shot. He obtained a patent, No. 14,526, for an ejector layout that used the split-stem extractor and had for its ejector-work a V-spring and tumbler arrangement. The tumbler was to be released by a sear that was tripped by the forward end of a rod that slid slightly

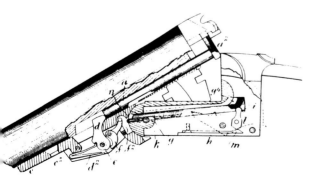

*J. Deeley patent No. 14,526 of 1884*

downwards from the tumbler to the knuckle. The patent drawing shows a boxlock gun.

In 1891 Westley Richards & Co. Ltd sued Thomas Perkes for the infringement of their patent, No. 14,526 of 1884. Perkes admitted that he had used parts of the specification, but claimed as his defence that the 1884 Deeley patent was invalid by reason of being anticipated in all its claims. This point he was able to sustain, both in the original hearing and in the Court of Appeal. Specifically, the tumbler powered by a V-spring and released by a sear was held to be the age-old gunlock. The position of this in the forend had been anticipated by Thomas Perkes's own patent, No. 1968 of 1878; and the sliding rods from tumbler to knuckle had been used on an unpatented gun mechanism, an example of which had been sold in 1882 by Messrs Rigby. This crucial gun had been sold to a Mr Medhurst who had taken it to America, but it had been returned to England in a broken-down state.

Not content with demolishing the 1884 Deeley patent, Perkes next applied to have this patent revoked and this started another and more complex legal process during which Messrs Westley Richards sought to amend their specification to produce from it a valid patent. Our account of this affair is, of necessity, much condensed and we would refer those who seek further information to the contemporary literature.

Two points, however, are much more relevant to our theme. The first of these is that while he won the battle, in a sense Thomas Perkes lost the war; in 1898 he was declared bankrupt, largely as a result of the expense of this litigation. In consequence, he relinquished his business at 15, Swallow Street, London to the control of his foreman, C. E. Andrews, and set up at 41, High Street, Eton, which enterprise was but short-lived. Secondly, and more importantly, if the criteria used to maul the 1884 Deeley patent were to have been applied to the multitude of patents we are concerned with a very wide swath indeed would be cut through them. This prompts us to echo the sentiments of William Wellington Greener as to the 'cruel fraud' of the Patent Office taking from inventors their hard-earned money in exchange for 'Patent Rights' which could prove to be as dubious as John Deeley's patent.

There are 16 further patents that use a slide from the tumbler to bring into operation selective ejectors fitted in the forend of the gun. We can consider these as a more or less chronological sequence.

We start with the patent, No. 7895 of 1885, granted to George Jeffries of Norwich. The drawing shows an external hammer gun in which the fall of the tumbler pushes forward a sliding rod fitted at a slight downward angle through the action bar. Probably because the 1874 Needham split-extractor patent was still in force, the extractor rods are separate flat slides fitted into slots that, in transverse vertical section, have a dovetail shape on the undersides of the breech-ends of the barrels. A neat point is the use of a friction-reducing roller on the rear end of each of these to ease their passage down the action-face as the gun was closed. The actual ejector work is the usual rod and coil spring set-up, but it lacks a conventional sear. Instead, the nose of the tripping rod lifts the ejector rod over a shoulder in the forend and so permits ejection to take place.

Conveniently, the next specification, No. 3400 of 1886, is another by George Jeffries. Naturally, there is a degree of resemblance between them. Again, we have an external hammer gun with the oblique ejector tripping rod, but now the ejectors are carried on a pair of circular-section rods and the friction-reducer has been eliminated. The actual ejector work is here a leaf spring working an over-centre ejector tumbler.

It is a minor point of interest that yet another hammer ejector is contained in part of the Charles Osborne Ellis and William Wilkinson patent, No. 7222 of 1887. These two, of 12 and 13, Whittall Street, Birmingham, were prolific makers for the trade, so this ejector work could be found on guns bearing a wide variety of "makers' " names. Like the two Jeffries patents, the Ellis-Wilkinson has a rod worked off the tumbler, but now it is used to trip a very conventional sear to an ejector that is an unremarkable coil-spring and rod arrangement.

The Thomas Brain patent, No. 10,487 of 1887, is one of those wide-ranging, value-for-money rag-bags that were beloved of certain inventors. One part of it is an ejector mechan-

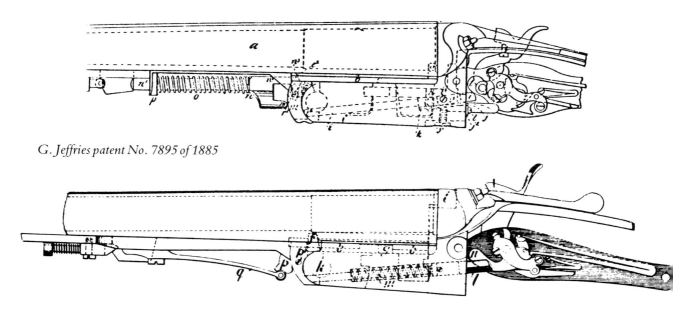

G. *Jeffries patent No. 7895 of 1885*

G. *Jeffries patent No. 3400 of 1886*

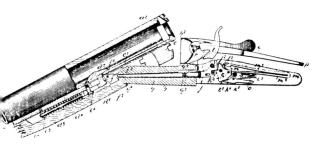

*C. Ellis and E. Wilkinson patent No. 7222 of 1887*

ism shown on a species of boxlock gun. We include it at this point because the tripping-slide, which is shaped like a reversed letter L, is moved forwards by the toe of the tumbler striking an incline cut on the rear of the vertical limb. The actual ejector is another coil spring round a rod, and the sear is a rocking lever on a transverse pivot.

Yet another sliding ejector trip is found in the patent, No. 11,623 of 1887, in the name of those two famous and prolific London inventors, Henry William Holland and John Robertson. Their drawing shows a bar-action sidelock gun in which a small inward projection on the breast

of the tumbler works in, and acts upon, a curved slot in the tripping slide so that, as the tumbler falls, the slide moves forward. Also covered by this specification is a modification of this idea that substitutes a transverse projection from the front of an extended trigger blade for the original projection on the tumbler. The virtue of this is that the blow delivered by the tumbler is not weakened by the extra function of moving the ejector slide. Both these versions are shown with coiled spring and rocking sear ejector work.

We depart briefly here from our chronological approach to consider together two patents, both in the name of Thomas Perkes. The specifications in question are No. 12,176 of 1887 and 10,084 of 1888. Protected by these two patents are both varieties of ejector work and an even greater variety of means by which this could be tripped, so there is a large number of possible permutations that could be said to be covered by either patent. Among these are some ideas for a rod pushed forwards by the tumbler. In patent No. 12,176 there are four such. First, a curved slot is cut in the tumbler of a boxlock gun so that, as this tumbler falls, it pushes forwards via

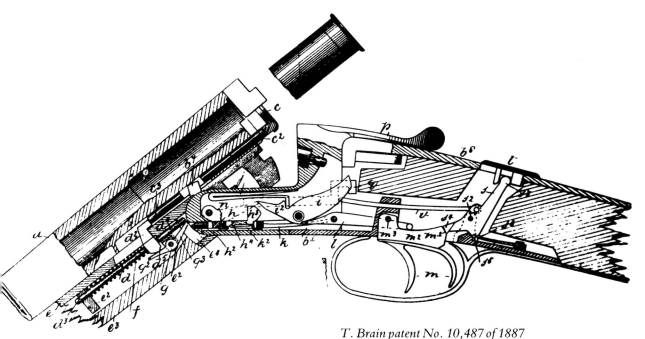

*T. Brain patent No. 10,487 of 1887*

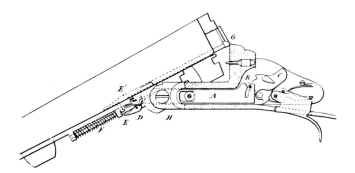

*H. Holland and J. Robertson patent No. 11,623 of 1887*

a lateral stud the tripping rod. Another links the
tumbler to the rod by a bell-crank lever. The
remaining two are different in that they employ
a coil spring-loaded ejector trip, which is released rather than pushed forward. In one, the
lock end of the rod is flexible to permit tumbler
and rod to reunite. As a variation of this idea
there is a mechanism in which the lock sear is
extended forwards so that, as it is lowered, it
releases a spring-loaded ejector trip rod. In all
these, the ejector work is a tumbler, powered by
a flat spring released by a rocking sear, but with
subtle variations in shape which may be significant or merely draftsmen's deviations.

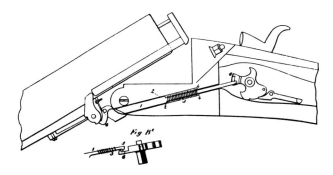

*T. Perkes patent No. 12,176 of 1887. First version*

In patent 10,084 there is but one push forward
rod, simply pushed by the breast of the tumbler,
but there is a host of other tripping rods which
we will consider with others of their type.
However, the actual ejector work is an interesting variant on the V-spring and tumbler idea.

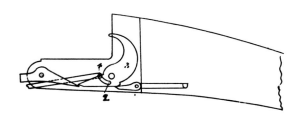

*T. Perkes patent No. 12,176 of 1887. Second version*

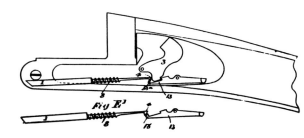

*T. Perkes patent No. 12,176 of 1887. Third version*

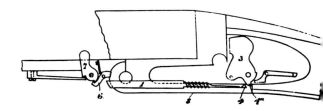

*T. Perkes patent No. 12,176 of 1887. Fourth version*

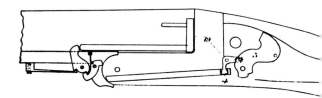

*T. Perkes patent No. 12,176 of 1887. Fifth version*

The bottom limb of the spring is extended to the
rear so that it acts as a sear.

We move on to a somewhat simpler specification, No. 2677 of 1888. This was granted to
James Lang and Arthur Jeffries. Lang we have
met before; Jeffries, too, was a London gun-

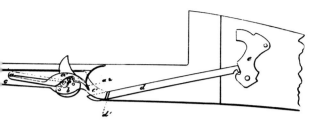

*T. Perkes patent No. 10,084 of 1884*

maker, located at 91, Tyneham Road, Battersea, possibly a son of George Jeffries of Norwich. Their ejector trip slide has at its rear end an upward-curved hook-like projection, the inside of which is acted on by a lateral projection from the tumbler so that the slide is pushed forward as the tumbler falls, and drawn back as it is cocked. Tripped by this slide is an unusual ejector that has a combined spring and striker. This is roughly U-shaped and is compressed by squeezing the limbs together. The forward end is fixed and the rear acts on the ejector rod. The rocking sear that trips this engages with a bent, formed on the underside of the top of the rear limb.

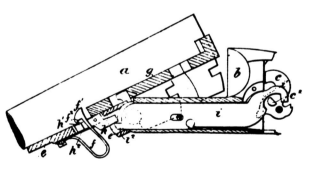

*J. Lang and A. Jeffries patent No. 2677 of 1888*

An important ejector was that patented in 1888 as No. 3100 by William Wem, gunmaker, of 21, Rothwell Buildings, Tottenham Court Road, London. In this, studs on the tumblers work horizontally back-and-forth, a pair of exceedingly thin slides through the bar of the action. When the slides are forwards they push aside equally light stops from engagement with the ejector tumbler. When the stops are in place, the tumblers working on a cam on the knuckle

have sufficient freedom of movement to push the ejector rods to act as extractor; when the stops are out, then the same cam trips the ejector. Probably the most valuable idea in this specification is to have, on the knuckle, a bar or projection that forces back the ejector-tumbler as the gun closes, instead of using the motion of the ejectors as they are forced back by the action face.

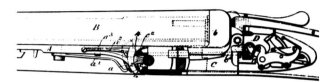

*W. Wem patent No. 3100 of 1888*

The importance of this invention is that it is the ejector work usually found on the Beesley-designed Purdey hammerless gun. In this application, the apparent problem of the very thin ejector tripping rods is overcome by the fact that they are supported along their entire length in accurately cut guide slots. On the Purdey gun the ejector is an over-centre tumbler of the Perkes/Southgate type.

We have previously noted an ejector, patented by Louis Edward Parfitt, that was extensively used on Bonehill guns. The first ejector patented by Parfitt, No. 9872 of 1888, is an interesting variant on the idea of tripping the ejector work with a slide from the tumbler. What is shown on the drawing of this invention is a boxlock gun, the underside of the tumbler of which bears on, and forces forwards as it rotates, a rod with a coil spring around it mounted in the bottom of the action bar. The ejector work, which is contained in a metal box set in the forend, consists of a single stout coil spring that drives a plunger to the rear every time the gun is opened. To do this there is a conventional rocking sear that is tripped by a fixed projection from the knuckle. On the plunger are pinned two flat slides that work up and down; it is the function of the slide in the action to bear down on the rear of a rocking lever to lift one of these slides. In the raised position, the slide on the

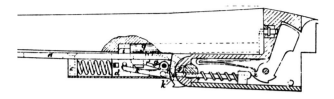

*L. Parfitt patent No. 9872 of 1888*

plunger will strike the ejector as the gun opens.

As we remarked earlier, the idea of using the fall of the tumblers as a means of moving the ejector trip is a very attractive one. However, some of the applications of this idea involve such radical re-design of the ejector work that to consider them chronologically with the previous group would be both unhelpful and artificial.

This is true of a singular ejector mechanism, patent No. 16,307 of 1884, by Thomas Southgate which occupies a position in a grey area between the true ejectors and the extractors. What is protected is the idea of having the tumbler, as it falls, push forward a slide on the inside of the lockplate of a back-action lock. The front of this slide is to bear on another slide and push this diagonally forwards so that its front end moves into a slot cut in the face of the standing-breech. In this position, the second slide would intercept the rearward limb of one of the ejectors (which are a pair of L-shapes pivoted at their angles in the bottom of the rear lump) with the upper limb of the L the actual extractor.

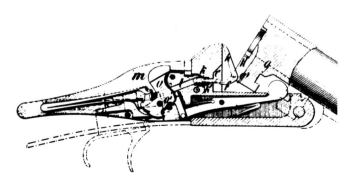

*T. Southgate patent No. 16,307 of 1884*

The action of this mechanism is very dependent on the vigour, even the knack, with which the gun is opened and, lacking any means of primary extraction, the system would be even more at the mercy of the size and condition of the spent cartridge case.

In the patent, No. 5966 of 1889, obtained by two action-makers, Thomas and Joseph Green, who both quote Weaman Row, Birmingham, as their address, we have another radical revision of the ejector mechanism. Firstly, they proposed to mount their ejector under the breech-ends of the barrels, with a separate ejector rod for each barrel of a double-barrel gun. This ejector is another of those in which it is the fall of the lock-tumbler that, in a sense, cocks the ejector mechanism. Mounted on transverse pivots under the rear of the barrels are rocking levers that have inclines filed on their front and rear ends. On the rear incline, a slide from the tumbler acts when the tumbler has fallen so that the front of the rocking lever is raised. Part of the front is an upward projection that engages with the stem of the extractor or ejector. The latter has a coil spring under compression in front of it which is compressed as the barrels are closed and the extractors forced back. To release the ejector there is a slide working against a stop on the knuckle so that, as the barrels pivot open, the slide moves rearwards. On its rear end is an incline that works on the incline on the front of the rocking lever, to lower the forward end out of engagement with the ejector rod if the lock-work has not been tripped. This arrangement, in conjunction with a stop on the knuckle, will act as a simple extractor.

As if to illustrate, yet again, the fine divisions of our subject, there are two patented ejectors that use the tumbler spindle as the agent that moves the slide that trips the ejector. The idea protected was to file a flat on the projecting end of the tumbler spindle, so that this flat acts as a shoulder and pushes forward the tripping rod as the lock is fired. The two specifications are Nos. 12,314 of 1889 and 662 of 1890, both in the name of Thomas Southgate. He was, as we have seen, one of the top London gunmakers and was then located at 6, Bruton Crescent, London. What makes his two specifications important is that

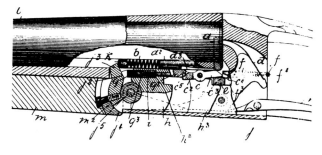

*T. and J. Green patent No. 5966 of 1889*

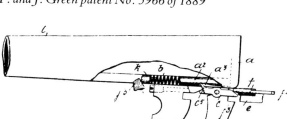

*T. and J. Green patent No. 5966 of 1889 (detail of ejector work)*

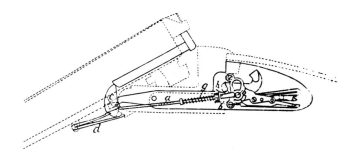

*T. Southgate patent No. 662 of 1890*

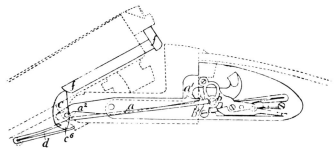

*T. Southgate patent No. 12,314 of 1889*

they represent the patent protection for one of the classic ejectors of the British shotgun, the over-centre tumbler usually referred to simply as 'The Southgate'. It was also known, more rarely, as the 'two-piece' ejector since it consists of simply the tumbler and the V-spring that powers it. The two patents differ merely in the addition to the second model of a coil spring round the ejector tripping rod.

We cannot avoid, in a sense, dismembering a gun where the entire mechanism forms the subject of a patent. In such a gun, we have to consider each aspect with other mechanisms of its type. Such, then, is the fate of the design of Arthur Nouvelle's British patent No. 2563 of 1889. It will be recalled from our description of the lockwork and safeties on this gun that it is a lever-cocked trigger plate design. The ejector

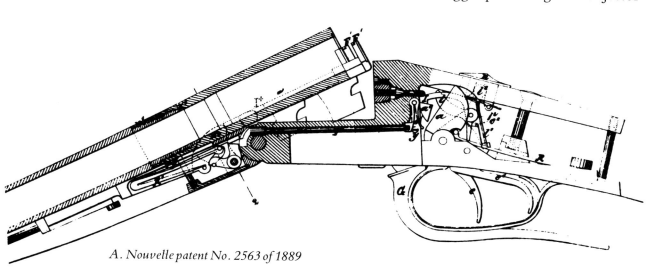

*A. Nouvelle patent No. 2563 of 1889*

work is a perfectly conventional V-spring and tumbler design that is tripped by the inturned forward ends of a pair of rods that run just under the action flats and are driven forwards by the fall of the tumblers.

The background to Nouvelle's invention is such that, in all likelihood, it was disregarded by the British gun trade. However, we cannot dismiss in the same way the ideas contained in a pair of patents, Nos. 14,886 and 19,395 of 1890, granted to John Ross of London. As with so many others, the two Ross patent specifications contain a whole family of ejectors, with two types of ejector work and several ways of tripping them, on which a large number of permutations is possible. The ejector work is unconventional in both patents. The earlier one shows ejector sears hung on vertical pivots, while the later patent has sears on longitudinal pivots. To activate these sears, both patents have sliding limbs in the bar of the action. In patent No. 19,395 it is the fall of the tumbler that pushes them forwards, while in No. 14,886 it is the unusual idea of having a stud on the cocking lever that engages with a slot in the ejector-tripping slide to move it into position.

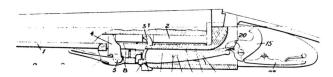

*J. Ross patent No. 14,886 of 1890*

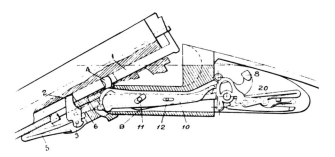

*J. Ross patent No. 19,395 of 1890*

Another twist to our tale is provided by William Baker. His idea was to make it possible for a gun user to bolt the ejector-tripping slides and so immobilise the ejector work of the gun. The details of this are covered by his patent, No. 17,292 of 1890, which shows a boxlock gun with ejector-tripping slides that are pushed forwards by projections on the bottom of the tumblers, as the latter reach the full-cock position. To force these slides to the rear, their forward ends are so shaped that the forend iron cams them back as the gun is closed. To bolt the tripping slides, there is a sliding catch working across the inside of the underside of the action bar, controlled by an external button. In order that bolting the ejector slide does not also prevent the gun being re-cocked, the rear of the tripping slide is formed as a sort of pair of spring tongs that can slip over the tumbler projection. The ejector work is, again, a sliding rod with a coil compression spring. The novelty of it lies in the fact that the long ejector sear pivots at the forward end of the ejector box, thus giving its bent a greater travel at the rear.

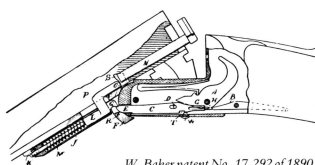

*W. Baker patent No. 17,292 of 1890*

Occasionally, a touch of, what we suspect is, unintentional humour enlivens the dry jargon of the patent specifications. By the date of Edgar Harrison's patent, No. 20,234 of 1890, there had been something like 80 individual patent specifications covering easily three times that number of ejector mechanisms. The introduction to Harrison's specification blandly says, 'a number of devices have been invented whereby on opening the gun the cartridge or cartridges which have been fired are ejected'. Following this gem, Harrison adds two more ideas to the mass that preceded it. The one that concerns us at this point has an ejector-tripping rod with, at its rear end, a pivoted catch. As the lock tumbler was being re-cocked, the catch on the rear of the rod engaged, for part of the travel of the tumbler, with a shoulder formed on the underside of the tumbler. Thus, the ejector-tripping rod was pushed forward, but before the tumbler reached full-cock, the rod slipped out of engagement with the tumbler to permit the latter to fall again. No specific ejector work is mentioned, but the drawings show several of Harrison's previously-patented ejector mechanisms.

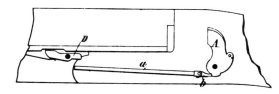

*E. Harrison patent No. 20,234 of 1890*

From outside the gun trade we have our final specification, No. 20,880 of 1890, on the much-patented idea of a slide from the tumbler to trip the ejectors. George Lilleyman, 'gentleman', of 31, Manor Road, Stoke Newington, Middlesex, thought it worth spending his money to protect the idea of forming on the rear end of the ejector-tripping slide a second lower limb. This was to act in conjunction with a stud formed in the action bar. This second limb was thin enough to act as a spring catch and had two flats or steps on it. When the slide is to the rear, the lower step bears against the stop, but when the tumbler falls its action is to push the lower slide limb down and forwards, so that it is the second step that now bears against the stop. As the gun opens, it first ejects then, as the tumblers are

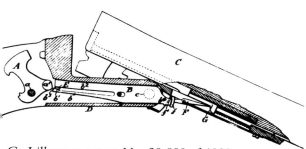

*G. Lilleyman patent No. 20,880 of 1890*

re-cocked, it is a shoulder on the ejector sear bearing on the tripping slide that forces it to the rear.

It is but a short step between using the fall of the tumbler of the gunlock to push forward a slide that, in turn, trips the ejector work, to using the fall of the tumbler to depress the rear end of a rocking lever that performs the same function. This short gap is bridged by Richard Trulock of Dublin with his patent, No. 12,178 of 1890. Here, the part that trips the ejector both pivots and slides as the tumbler falls. What is shown in the patent specification drawing is a nose-like projection on the front of the tumbler working a lever with a slot-pivot, practically at the hinge-pin, so the exposed forward end of this lever moves outwards through a small arc as the lock tumbler falls. The ejector lock shown is a variant on the V-spring and tumbler type, in which the ejector tumbler is worked by a second tumbler that is, in turn, acted on by the ejector spring.

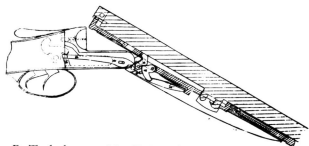

*R. Trulock patent No. 12,178 of 1890*

We can now progress to those ejectors that are tripped by a lever controlled by the fall of the tumbler. An unusual idea is the patent, No. 1880 of 1889, in the names of John Rogers, gun action-filer of 52, White Head Road, Aston, and John Rogers, junior, also a gun action-filer of 198, Frederick Road, Aston, then 'near Birmingham' but now well swallowed up by the metropolis. Their proposal was to have levers set on vertical pivots in the rear barrel lump, with the levers exposed on the barrel flats. In the standing-breech what are, in effect, a couple of extra firing pins are so placed that, as the tumbler pushes each firing pin forward, its forward end pushes outward the rear end of the appropriate tripping lever. Thus, the forward end moves inwards and a shoulder on it is disengaged from the stem of the ejector. This is, thus, permitted to move to its fullest extent when tripped by a suitable means not specified on the patent.

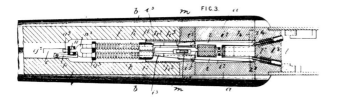

*J. and J. Rogers patent No. 1880 of 1889*

John Rogers, junior, also obtained patent No. 8915 of 1889 on much more conventional basic ejector work. Here the levers that trip the ejectors are depressed by a forward extension of the sear and a nose on the tumbler. Further novelty lies in the fact that to lock these levers in place Rogers proposed laterally-projecting studs from the barrel locking-bolt. The ejector tripping rods were held rigid while the bolt was in the rear position and the gun was open.

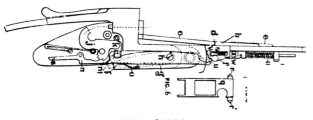

*J. Rogers patent No. 8915 of 1889*

The most basic of all this group is part of Charles Rosson's patent, No. 15,313 of 1889. Part of this patent shows a hammer gun in which the tumblers inside the lock are shaped to depress the rear ends of a pair of rocking levers. These run forward through the action bar and are hung on transverse pivots at about their mid-points. The forward ends of these levers are the ejector trips.

An ingenious ejector, tripped as the lock mechanism moves beyond its full-cock position, was devised by the action-maker Job Cox

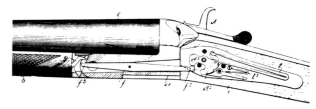

*C. Rosson patent No. 15,313 of 1889*

of 23, Clarendon Street, Aston. In his patent No. 6148 of 1889, Cox proposed an L-shaped lever, transversely pivoted at its angle, which was positioned in the forward lower end of the action bar of a boxlock gun. On the tumbler is a stud that lifts the rear lower limb of the lever as the tumbler rotates backwards to full-cock. Thus, the forward end of the L-shaped lever moves forwards and so pushes forwards a slide mounted on the forend. The front of this slide is bevelled so that it, in turn, pushes down the rear of a spring catch that releases the ejector work.

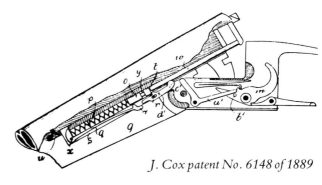

*J. Cox patent No. 6148 of 1889*

What can be regarded as a combination of the later two groups, in that, the tumbler moves a lever that works a slide to trip the ejector is found in the superb and distinctive hammerless guns made by Dickson's of Edinburgh. The ejector work of some of these is based on the two patents, Nos. 9399 and 10,621 that were taken out in 1887 in the name of John Dickson. It will be recalled that the so-called 'round action' Dickson hammerless gun is a trigger-plate action in the head of the stock. What was protected in the 1887 patents was the idea of having a small rocking lever, set ahead of the tumblers, so that a toe on the front of the tumbler lifted the rear of the rocking lever as the tumbler pivoted back to its full-cock position. The ejector mechanism consists of two sliding rods under the barrel breeches, each having, at its rear end, an upward projection to catch the cartridge rim. At their forward ends, these rods are acted on by kickers, the upper ends of a pair of levers transversely pivoted in the front of the action bar. In the action bar, two rods with coil springs around them run backwards to the lock-work so that, as the gun is closed, the extractor is forced back by the action face. In its turn, the face forces forward the kickers which, in their turn, push back the rods in the action bar and thereby compress the coil springs. In patent No. 9399, the rear ends of the rods in the action and the rocking lever in the lockwork have, where they mate, hooks formed so that lever and rod catch and hold until the tumbler, as it reaches full-cock, trips the ejector.

In the later specification this point is slightly modified: now the rod in the action is in two parts, the rear pivoting on the front end. At the rear, the rod has a shoulder; when it is in the rearward position, the shoulder engages with the rim of the hole in which it slides. The action of the tumbler is now to lift the rod out of this engagement.

An advantage of these designs is that, by eschewing the forend as a housing for the ejector mechanism, the weight of the ejector work is kept more to the rear of the gun, to the benefit of its handling qualities.

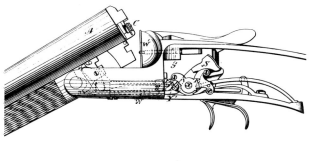

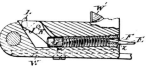

*J. Dickson patent No. 10,621 of 1887*

A more complex, indeed a refreshingly different, ejector is contained in William Brighton's patent, No. 2830 of 1890. In this a cocking rod, set diagonally up through the action bar of a sidelock gun, bears at its forward end on a swinging lever that is carried on a transverse pivot on the top of the knuckle. The bottom of this lever has a forward projection that, when the gun has been fired, projects further forwards and, as the barrels pivot open, bears on the bottom of a rocking lever or cam set in the forend. Since the pivot of this lever in the forend is at the front end of the lever, rotating it as the gun opens causes the rear end to

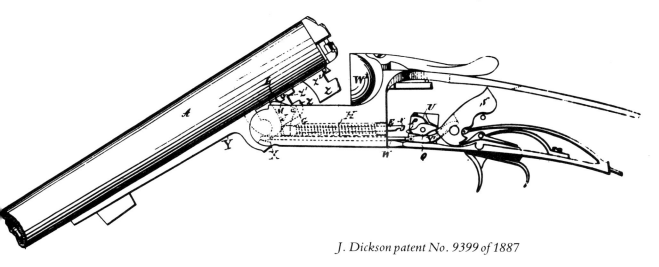

*J. Dickson patent No. 9399 of 1887*

rise and this, in turn, lifts the upper rear of the forend lever. The ejector stem is in two separate parts. The front part has a notch cut in its rear end and is acted on by both a coil spring at its front and a leaf spring from above. This leaf spring is to force the rear end down and the notch into engagement with a suitable shoulder, when the ejector rod is in its forward cocked position. It is the function of the cam to lift this notch out of engagement with its shoulder and thus to trip the mechanism.

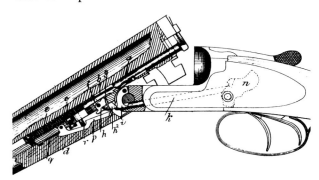

*W. Brighton patent No. 2830 of 1890*

It is a feature of many barrel-cocking hammerless sporting guns that some form of cocking lever extends from the tumblers to the knuckle of the action bar. This resembles strongly the slides and levers from the tumblers that we have just considered as a means of tripping ejector work. The problem of attempting to combine the two functions, that of cocking lever or rod and ejector trip, is that while the fall of the tumbler alters the position of the cocking member, as the gun is opened (and thereby, usually, re-cocked), the cocking member returns to its cocked position. Thus, it does not provide a means by which the fired barrel could be differentiated at a point in the cycle where the spent cartridge should be ejected.

What happens in many of them is that the movement of the cocking piece moves a portion of the ejector work, usually the sear, into engagement in such a way that, when the gun is opened, it will trip and the ejector will work.

Giving further emphasis to his creative ability Thomas Perkes is first in this group with the patent, No. 10,679 of 1886. As usual, there are a variety of renderings of the basic idea which is to have a V-spring and tumbler ejector mechanism, with a toe-like projection from the tumbler that, as the gun pivots open, first bears on the projecting cocking rod. The ejector tumbler is rotated backwards and its spring is thereby compressed. Further rotation and/or the cocking rod moving backwards, causes the toe of the tumbler to slip off the cocking rod and so the ejector trips.

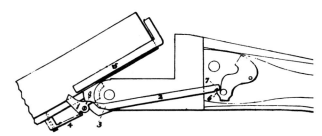

*T. Perkes patent No. 10,679 of 1886*

As part of his massive patent specification, No. 16,214 of 1886, Edgar Harrison describes a means by which the cocking lever is used as an ejector trip. The basic action of the gun in question was to have a cocking lever pivoted on the same centre as the joint pin, but to increase the travel of his lever by pivoting it onto a vertical lever in the action bar and from the top of this second lever, which was pivoted at its lower end, to take a third lever to the breast of the tumbler. To provide a trip for the ejector work, this third lever is continued forwards and has a slight upward projection at its forward end which, when the lock has been fired, is rocked up into engagement with the stem of the ejector. The ejector is thus restrained until the projection slips out of the ejector stem, which happens when the barrels have sufficiently gaped for the spent cases to clear the standing breech.

In his patent, No. 2294 of 1888, Thomas Webley of the famous Birmingham firm of this name, actually claims the use of the cocking lever as the ejector trip as one of the features of his design. This can be thought of as basically a classic Rogers action in which the rocking lever is also permitted to slide to a small degree.

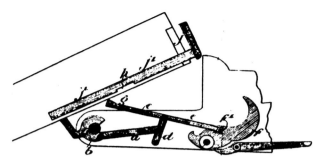

*E. Harrison patent No. 16,214 of 1886*

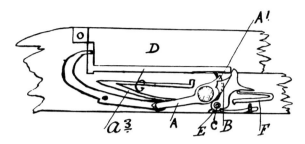

*R. Paulson patent No. 5672 of 1888*

When a particular lock has been fired, its cocking lever is further forwards than when not fired, and this position is maintained until the gun is reclosed. Thus there is a trip for the ejector work, which is an ordinary rocking sear and coil spring arrangement. To move the cocking rod back and forth, there is a spring-loaded cam built into the breast of the tumbler.

In Richard Paulson's patent, No. 5672 of 1888, the fall of the tumbler raises the front of the cocking lever in a gun that is a derivation of the Anson and Deeley boxlock. The ejector

tumbler is mounted on a transverse pivot, the hole in the tumbler being such that the tumbler can rock from side-to-side as well as pivot back-and-forth in the usual way. All we are told is that, when the cocking lever is in the fired position, the ejector tumbler is rocked so that it lines up with the extractor stem. On how this was to trip, and on any other details, the specification is deficient.

While it is true that most of the inventions we are considering are ingenious, some have an almost cunning streak to them. One that strikes

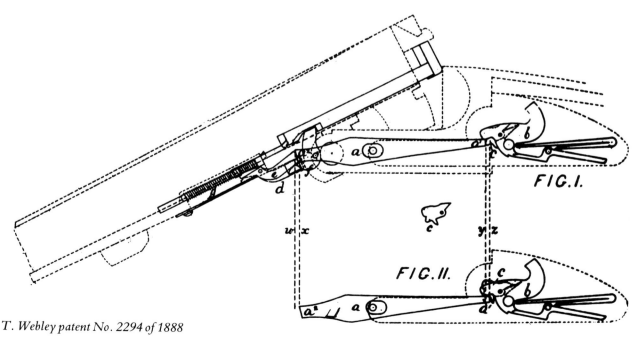

*T. Webley patent No. 2294 of 1888*

us in this way is contained in the patent, No. 9348 of 1888, granted to William Ford of 23, Loveday Street, Birmingham and James Clifford, a gun action-maker, of 6, Greaves Place, Moland Street, also in Birmingham. On the specification are shown two versions of this ejector, fitted either to the boxlock action that William Ford had patented as No. 2622 of 1888 and which we considered earlier, or to a standard Anson and Deeley action. This ejector is essentially a rocking sear that releases a striker that is a rod with a coil spring round it. The point of the patent is the idea of having two sears for each ejector. On the Ford patent gun, one of these is tripped (as the lock is fired) by the cocking lever sliding bodily forwards. The second sear is tripped on a projection on the knuckle of the action when the barrels are fully open. In realisation, this ejector is more complex than implied by the description above in that, to release the first sear, there is a rocking lever, the rear end of which is depressed by the front of the cocking lever. Thus, as the front of the lever travels down, its front end lifts the front of the first sear and so disengages the rear end of this sear.

On the Anson and Deeley version, the fall of the tumbler pushes forward a slide that is part of

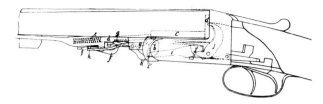

*W. Ford and J. Clifford patent No. 9348 of 1888*

the cocking lever and on this slide the first sear trips directly, the intermediate lever being dispensed with. Further opening of the barrels trips the final sear as before.

The gun shown on the first part of Charles Henry Maleham's patent, No. 9677 of 1888, is a typical Anson and Deeley boxlock modified to have a lateral projection on the cocking lever below and, in the fired position, slightly in front of the pivot of this lever. As the lock is fired, this projection pushes forwards onto a lever, set vertically in the knuckle of the action. The top end of this lever curves slightly forwards. As it moves forward it bears on one corner of the ejector sear, which is roughly triangular in side view. The ejector sear is thus rocked forward so that its other top corner engages with the bent on the ejector-tumbler, in readiness to be tripped by the bottom corner of the sear coming

*Gun, using ejector covered by Ford and Clifford patent No. 9348 of 1888*

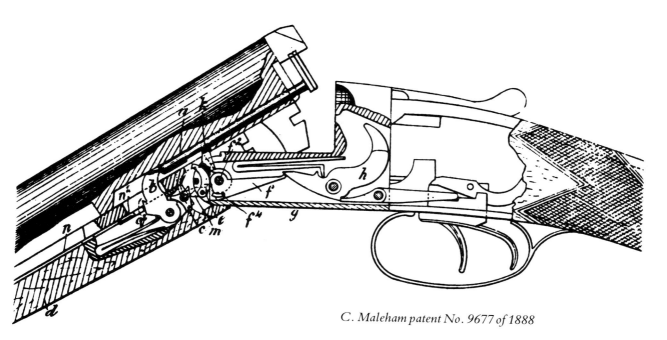

*C. Maleham patent No. 9677 of 1888*

into contact with the lower end of the arming-lever as the gun pivots open.

A subtle variation on our theme is provided by a complex patent, No. 16,691 of 1888 in the names of Henry William Holland and John Robertson. They propose to use a conventional rocking sear to release an ejector kicker that is a coil spring round a rod. The novelty of this patent lies in the idea of using the slightly raised position that the cocking lever adopts (when the lock is fired) to bear on a lateral projection from the ejector sear. This rotates the sear slightly so that, as the gun opens, the sear will be tripped by catching in a recess formed in the knuckle of the action.

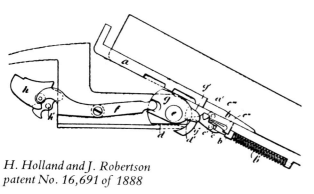

*H. Holland and J. Robertson*
*patent No. 16,691 of 1888*

*Charles Henry Maleham in his Sheffield shop*

Yet another use of the upward motion of the cocking lever of a fired hammerless gunlock is found in the variations proposed in Edgar Harrison's patent, No. 18,157 of 1888. In this he covers the idea of using this motion to lift the rocking ejector sear into engagement with the ejector stem. In fact, the patent shows three variations on this theme with boxlock guns and a further two on sidelocks.

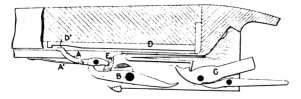

*E. Harrison patent No. 18,157 of 1888*

Essentially similar, but more complex in realisation, is the ejector mechanism in the patent, No. 5077 of 1889, of William Brighton. He describes sears mounted on vertical pivots to control a V-spring and tumbler ejector mechanism. To push these sears into engagement, the cocking rod of a sidelock gun as it moves forwards bears on and rotates a cam that turns on a transverse pivot in the forend. The cam and sear work together through their reciprocally-inclined adjoining faces so that the rotation in a vertical plane of the cam is translated to motion in a horizontal plane by the sear. To disengage this sear, it has a rearward projection that works

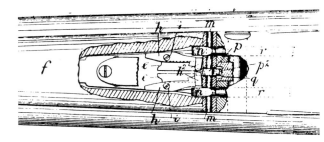

*W. Brighton patent No. 5077 of 1889*

in a sloping slot cut in the knuckle of the forend.

A similar, but simpler idea, probably intended for an inexpensive gun, is that patented as No. 5159 of 1889 by Thomas Woodward of 7, Bath Street, Birmingham. Shown on a sidelock gun of the Rogers type is an ejector work, of the coil spring and rod variety, with a rotating sear that is lifted into engagement by the upward motion of the cocking lever, which projects from the knuckle into the forend. The sear is tripped by a projection from the knuckle as the gun opens.

It might be thought that, by now, this particular small patch had been so well combed and covered with patent specifications that no other inventor would bother with it, but still they came. As patent No. 9062 of 1889, James William Smallman protected an ejector mechanism in which the sear is engaged by the cocking rod as a sidelock gun is fired. In side view this sear is T-shaped and is pivoted transversely at the point where the limbs cross. The

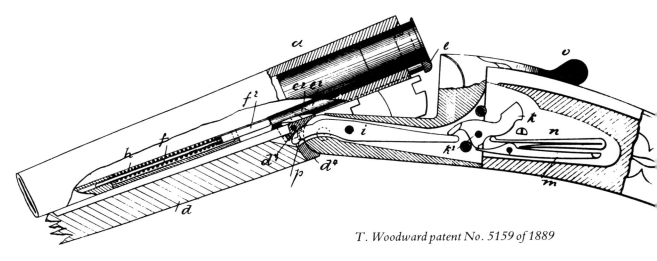

*T. Woodward patent No. 5159 of 1889*

bottom of the upright limb is curved backwards and on it the front end of the cocking rod bears (when the lock is fired) which slightly rotates the sear. This motion serves to lift the forward end of the horizontal limb to engage with the ejector tumbler. When the gun is opened in this condition, the ejector is tripped by the third limb of the sear coming into contact with a projection on the knuckle. The patent also describes variants on this idea in which an Anson and Deeley boxlock-type gun has a sliding mainspring to work the same ejector sear.

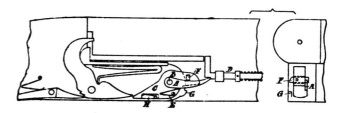

*C. Maleham patent No. 13,158 of 1889*

1889, is that the drawings that accompany it are, while adequate, crude by the standards of typical patent specifications. Study of the text reveals no agent's name and we thus wonder if by this date Beesley felt that he had learned sufficient of the technique of obtaining a patent to dispense with the services of the draftsman and patent agent, and so save himself their fees.

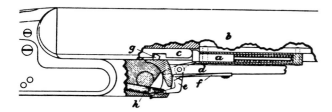

*J. Smallman patent No. 9062 of 1889*

Penultimate in this sub-section, is Charles Henry Maleham's patent, No. 13,158 of 1889, which again covers the idea of using the movement of the cocking limb to position the ejector sear. In the boxlock version shown in his specification, the sear is spring-loaded and pivoted onto the cocking lever which has a lateral projection to act as a stop to control the sear. When the gun has been fired and the front of the cocking lever is in the up position, the sear can rise into engagement with the ejector tumbler. The ejector work is of the rod and coil spring type. As the gun is opened, the cocking lever rotates and carries the tumbler to full-cock. Then, as the barrels rotate further, one end of the sear stop (which is a short lever on a longitudinal pivot) comes into contact with a projection on the knuckle. This causes the other end of the sear stop lever to push down and so release the sear. The patent also covers sidelock versions of this idea, in which the L-shaped ejector sear is a rocking lever actuated by a cocking rod but no other practical details are given.

The most immediately noticeable feature of the Frederick Beesley patent, No. 20,979 of

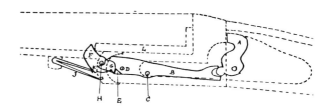

*F. Beesley patent No. 20,979 of 1889*

What is contained in this specification is cover for an ingeniously simple ejector. The tumbler is of the over-centre variety and is powered by a V-spring. To rotate the ejector tumbler the few degrees necessary for the over-centre position to be passed, there is a lateral projection from the front of the cocking lever which, when the latter is in the up, fired position, bears on the curved face of the front of the ejector tumbler. So, as the barrels pivot open, the ejector tumbler is rotated.

At this point we feel it logical to include a design that does not conform strictly to the group we have just described. Nevertheless it is more akin to them than to any other group. The patentee of this gun was Samuel Blakemore Allport, who was, at this date, 1890, both master of the Birmingham Proof House and also in business at 50, Whittall Street. His patent, No. 2760, covers the idea of having a small downward projection on the underside of the cocking lever of an Anson and Deeley box lock at the point where the lever pivots. As the lock is fired the rear limb of the cocking lever is depressed, thus swinging the downward projection forwards. This movement is used to push forward a rod on the underside of the knuckle that trips the ejector as the barrels pivot open. The ejector work is shown as a conventional coil spring and kicker, and the ejector sear is a simple rocking lever on the rear of the ejector box.

When an Anson and Deeley boxlock gun is fired, the mainspring moves forward. Given this, it is but a minor modification to fit a forward projection to the front end of this spring, so that the projection stands proud of the knuckle when the lock is fired, and to use this as the trip for the ejector mechanism. In essence, this description covers several ejector patents of our period. However, the real importance of this idea derives from the fact that, in the shape of the Deeley ejector, it has become one of the abiding standard ejector mechanisms. In fact, the Deeley ejector is covered in two very similar patents in the names of three members of the Westley Richards firm. The first specification, No. 4289 of 1886 is in the name of John Deeley, the younger; the second, No. 6913 of 1888, is claimed by Frederick James Penn and John Deeley, the elder. These two patents are so similar that separate descriptions would be merely repetitious. In both, the ejector mechanism is a tumbler worked by a V-spring and released by a sear behind it that is tripped by the projection from the mainspring. The only differences would seem to be in subtle variations in the shape of the parts.

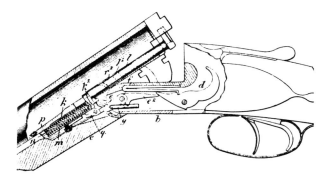

*S. Allport patent No. 2760 of 1890*

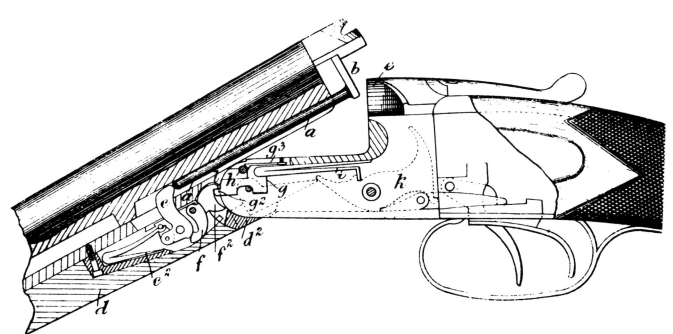

*J. Deeley patent No. 4289 of 1886*

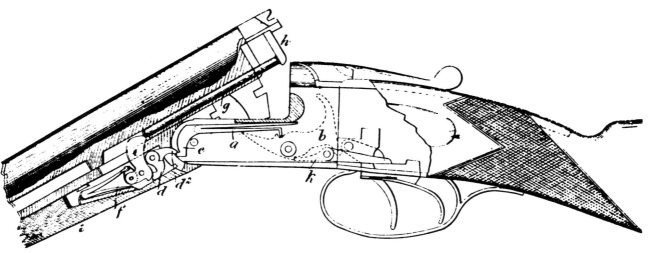

*F. Penn and J. Deeley patent No. 6913 of 1888*

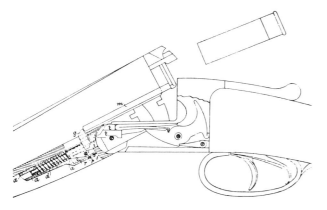

*Deeley ejector, patent No. 4289 of 1886, with the associated mainspring and ejector trip*

This remark is, for practical purposes, also true of five other specifications. For instance, in patent No. 14,964 of 1886, obtained by the agent W. H. Beck for the famous gunmaker Auguste Francotte of Liège, we have an almost identical tripping device to release a coil-spring ejector. A very similar mechanism forms part of the Charles Ellis and Edward Wilkinson patent, No. 7222 of 1887, a lateral projection from an Anson and Deeley mainspring tht engages with a slide that, in turn, trips the ejector. In this case the ejector work is a coil spring around a rod released by a rocking sear.

In the patent, No. 4697 of 1889, James Smallman uses a coil spring fitted round a rod as the ejector work. In his patent, No. 12,008 of 1889,

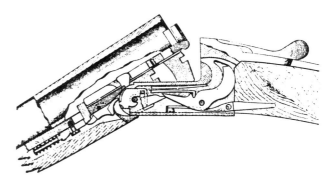

*W. Beck (agent for A. Francotte) patent No. 14,964 of 1886*

*C. Ellis and E. Wilkinson patent No. 7222 of 1887*

William Brighton dispenses with an intermediate lever (or sear) between the ejector tumbler and the tripping nose on the mainspring. Instead the projection from the latter acts directly on the tumbler.

More slight alterations on this theme are to be found elsewhere in the patent literature. For instance, one idea contained in the Charles Henry Maleham patent, No. 9677 of 1888, was to use the forward travel of the mainspring (as an Anson and Deeley boxlock was fired) to engage it directly with the ejector sear. If the lock had been fired, the triangular ejector sear is rocked forward, in which position, as the gun pivots open, it will impinge on a projection on the knuckle and be tripped out of engagement with the ejector tumbler. Also shown in this specification is a variant that uses a rod from a sidelock tumbler for the same purpose.

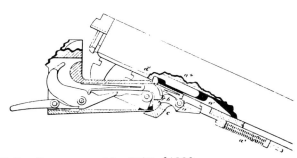

*J. Smallman patent No. 4697 of 1889*

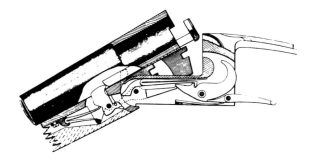

*W. Brighton patent No. 12,008 of 1889*

Also harnessing the movement of an Anson and Deeley mainspring, but using the movement in a different way, is the mechanism covered in Edgar Harrison's patent, No. 11,550

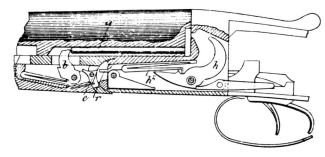

*C. Maleham patent No. 9677 of 1888*

of 1888. In this the ejector sear, which is a rocking lever on a transverse pivot, is made to engage with the extractor stem by the rear end of the sear being forced downwards by the mainspring sliding over it. From this state, the ejector will trip as the barrels are opened and the rear end of the sear bears on a shoulder formed on the knuckle of the action.

Another Edgar Harrison patent, No. 13,591 of 1889, has three different ejector mechanisms. The one powered by the mainspring we have already considered. There is another mechanism that uses the forward motion of the main-

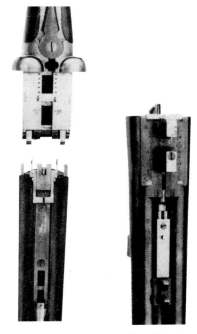

*Cogswell and Harrison gun with E. Harrison patent No. 11,550 of 1888*

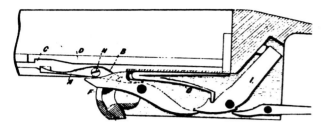

*E. Harrison patent No. 11,550 of 1888*

spring to engage the ejector sear. It would appear that the sear is a lever pivoted above and in front of the ejector tumbler and that the action of the extension of the mainspring is to push the rear of the ejector sear downwards and so into the bent. The sear is tripped by a projection on the knuckle of the action bar. The third ejector covered by this Harrison patent uses the forward motion from the mainspring to push the ejector tumbler forward and, thus, over-centre. If the lock has not been fired, the ejector spring, shown as a leaf-spring lying forwards of the ejector tumbler in the forend, again helps ease out the live cartridge, but if the lock has been fired, the ejector tumbler does not move until its bottom is eased forward by a cam in the

knuckle. Then, when it has passed the centre, the ejector spring is able to flick it round.

Yet another mode of using the forward action of the Anson and Deeley mainspring was patented by William Phillipson and William Baker, as No. 18,781 of 1889. This was to have the mainspring push forward a slide, or rock forward a tumbler, that would act like a sear and hold up the ejector tumbler until the gun had pivoted open sufficiently for the spent cases to clear the standing-breech. Then the locking slide was to be withdrawn from, or rocked out of, engagement with the ejector tumbler by a shoulder formed on the inside of the action bar. In the version that used the sliding stop, this member was to be formed as an L-shape, mounted with the short limb vertical upon a stud projecting from the cocking lever. In addition, a slot is formed longitudinally in the cocking lever, and a corresponding ridge on the ejector slide works in this, so that the cocking lever and slide pivot in unison. The version that used the rocking ejector tumbler catch is somewhat simpler, in that the catch is, roughly speaking, a square pivoted at its lower rear corner. The mainspring pushes forward on the upper rear corner and thus rocks the upper forwards corner out of the arc of the knuckle

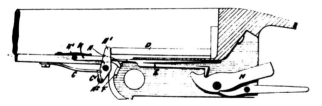

*E. Harrison patent No. 13,591 of 1889*

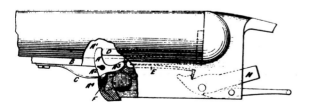

*E. Harrison patent No. 13,591 of 1889. Alternative version*

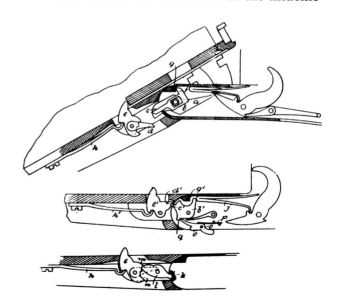

*W. Phillipson and W. Baker patent No. 18,781 of 1889*

and under the nose of the ejector tumbler. As the gun opens, the rocking catch and the tumbler pivot together for a while, until the barrels are clear of the standing-breech, when the catch is arrested by the internal shoulder and the ejector tumbler disengages. On this version, there is also the provision for a thumb slide (under the front of the forend) that works an internal stop, by which means the ejector can be made inoperative by holding up the rocking ejector tumbler catch.

This Phillipson and Baker patent has yet another feature. Instead of having the ejector spring cocked by the ejectors being forced forwards, by bearing on the face of the standing-breech as the gun closes, a short rocking lever is mounted in the forend. One end of this lever mates with the ejector tumbler, the other with a notch in the knuckle. By this means the ejector tumbler is not only cocked, but as the gun opens, if unfired, the loaded cartridge is extracted, if fired, the primary extraction is effected.

Patent No. 1281 of 1887 differs from those just considered in that the lock mechanism is not the classic Anson and Deeley. Instead, James Smallman proposes a spring-cocked boxlock of his own design which we considered earlier with others of that ilk. However, to trip his ejector mechanism, he describes a forward projection from the mainspring. The rights to this particular patent were assigned by the inventor to the three Birmingham gunmakers, W. M. Scott, C. O. Ellis and E. W. Wilkinson.

In the Smallman gun, the V-mainspring fits diagonally in the action bar, with its front end at the bottom. From the top limb at the front of the mainspring a spur projects forwards and slightly upwards through the knuckle to catch the ejector sear as the gun pivots open. This sear is shown as a V-shape, pivoted upside down at its angle, so that as the rear limb is caught, the front limb is swung forwards. This motion serves to disengage the sear from a lateral projection from the ejector spring, which is a V with a friction-reducing roller on its free end that bears on the bottom of the ejector tumbler. Two modifications are proposed on this basic design. In one there is an intermediate swinging catch between mainspring and ejector sear; in the other, cocking rods of the Scott hammerless gun type work a modified swinging catch.

As ordinarily constructed, the mainspring of a sidelock gun does not exhibit the same convenient forward movement that the preceding boxlock guns harnessed to trip their ejectors. However, as a V-mainspring releases its stored energy, it opens its prongs. On a sidelock gun, this movement is used to move a rod to trip an ejector as part of the Thomas Perkes patent, No. 12,176 of 1887. What he proposes is to form a stud that projects laterally from the lower limb of the mainspring and to fit this stud to an upward projection of a rod that slides back and forth in the bottom of the action bar. In the upward projection is formed an inclined slot so that the up-and-down motion of the lower limb

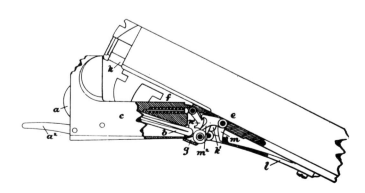

*J. Smallman patent No. 1281 of 1887*

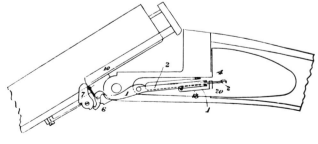

*T. Perkes patent No. 12,176 of 1887*

of the spring is converted to a back-and-forth motion of the ejector tripping rod.

Another motion that a sidelock mainspring can be made to perform is to rock back-and-forth and this movement can be accentuated if the peg that locates the spring is set rather more to the rear than is usual. Part of Edgar Harrison's patent, No. 20,234 of 1890, uses this method to produce an upward motion of the front of the mainspring to raise the rear of a rocking lever set in the forward end of the action bar. Thus, when the gunlock is fired, the front end of this rocking lever is depressed. This in turn forces down the rear end of a rocking sear set in the forend, so that the front end engages with the ejector stem. Then, as the gun is opened, the rear end of the sear is caught by a stop on the knuckle and the ejector is tripped. This, of course, can only happen if the sear has previously been engaged.

Practically every possible moving part of a gunlock has attracted some inventor as a means by which he could trip his 'perfect ejector'. If the trigger is linked to the ejector trip directly, the energy that is required to move the parts is not abstracted from the mainspring.

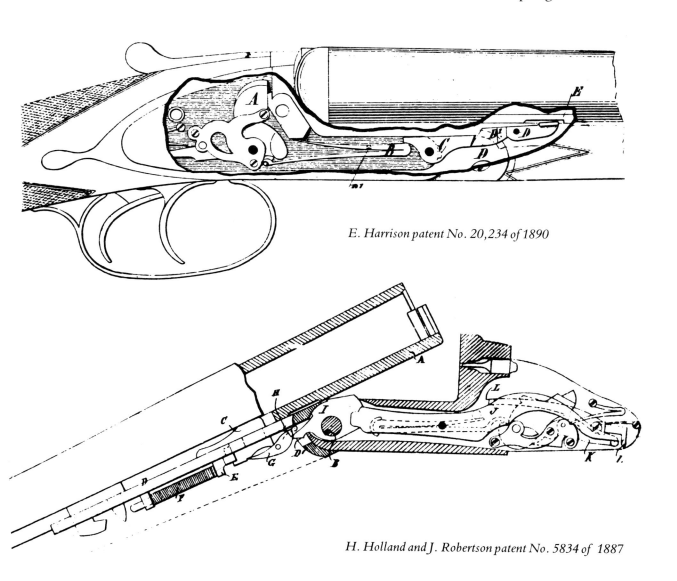

E. Harrison patent No. 20,234 of 1890

H. Holland and J. Robertson patent No. 5834 of 1887

Thus we can perceive the ideas behind Henry William Holland's and John Robertson's patent, No. 5834 of 1887. A rocking lever lies in the action bar and is hung on a transverse pivot just forward of the plane of the action face. The rear end of this lever arches backwards so that its rear end lies alongside the tail of the lock sear so that, as the trigger is pulled, the rear end of the rocking lever is raised. The consequent lowering of the front end depresses the rear of a second, short lever pivoted on the joint-pin. It is the front of this second lever that protrudes from the knuckle to trip the ejector work. The latter consists of a rocking sear that releases a coil spring and rod arrangement.

The main concern of Charles Rosson's patent, No. 15,313 of 1889, is to have a wider lock sear on a boxlock gun and to use part of this width to depress the rear of a rocking lever in the bar of the action. When the forward end of this lever is in the up position, it trips a conventional rocking sear out of engagement with an equally ordinary coil spring and rod ejector, but when the tripping lever is down, it does not meet the sear.

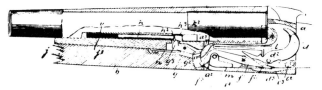

*C. Rosson patent No. 15,313 of 1889*

We see the same idea, of using another moving part to position the ejector tripping slide, in S. A. Grant's patent, No. 4360 of 1888. This time a vertical lever in the head of the stock converts the rearward movement of the locking-bolt, as the gun is opened, to the forward movement of an ejector trip. To make this mechanism selective, the vertical lever is made as a light spring and its sideways position is controlled by a cam on the tumbler. In one version it disengages the bolt, in another it engages the slide.

At this point two designs fit more easily than anywhere else. What they are concerned with is the idea of both simplifying and, in some ways,

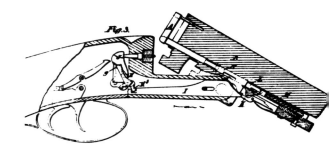

*S. A. Grant patent No. 4360 of 1888*

making more versatile, an ejector mechanism by making it non-automatic. A user of such a gun has to push a catch each time it is necessary to eject the cartridge case.

The first of these patents, No. 4446 of 1886, was obtained in Britain by the agent B. J. B. Mills for George D. Potter of Chicago. We strongly suspect that its American origins may be explained by the prevalence of cartridge-reloading in what was, then, a remote, relatively poor country that teemed with game and wildfowl. What is shown on the specification is a loop-spring (in the forend) bearing on a vertical lever hung on a transverse pivot. The upper end of the lever bears on the rear of the extractor leg, while its lower end is restrained by a hook catch. Part of this catch emerges from the bottom of the forend as a lightly sprung spring-loaded catch. Squeezing in this catch releases the ejector.

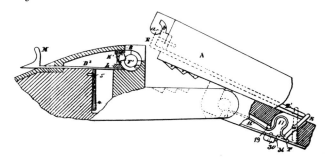

*B. Mills, agent for G. Potter, patent No. 4446 of 1886*

The other manifestation of this idea, patent No. 13,857 of 1888, was taken out by the two Birmingham men Job Cox and Joseph Dallaway. We have already met Cox and all we know of Dalloway is that he was a gun action-maker located at 1, Aston Church Road, Washwood Heath. Their ejector, which is otherwise a conventional split-stem worked by two coil springs in the forend, is controlled by a pair of levers. The levers lie beside the springs and are hung on vertical pivots near their centres. The rear end of each lever projects inwards as a catch to hold the ejector rod and both forward ends are acted upon by studs that emerge on the sides of the forend.

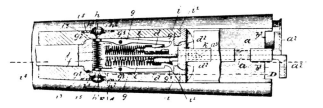

*J. Dalloway and J. Cox patent No. 13,857 of 1888*

Of dubious efficacy is an unusual and simple ejector mechanism, patented as No. 15,299 of 1884, by William Anson. On this specification he now gives his address as 'Small Heath', Birmingham. What he proposes is to fit a leaf-spring to the bottom of the face of the extractor and to control it by a rocking catch fitted to the underside of a doll's-head top extension. The rear end of the rocking catch is raised by a rod that runs up through the standing-breech from the sear of the boxlock action. The front of the rocking catch would thus hold back the ejector spring, but the shape of the front of the catch is such that when the pressure of the extractor is relieved, as the gun starts to close, the catch slips out of engagement with the spring and the spent case is ejected. Also covered by the same patent and, in the authors' experience, more common, is a variant of this idea where selectivity is achieved by catches on the ejector plate. These are swung down out of engagement with the cartridge heads by pins driven forwards by the fall of the tumblers.

Modifications to this idea were protected by William Anson in his provisional patent, No. 16,138 of 1886, where he proposes a notch cut in the chamber-rim. Into this the cartridge, as it

*W. Anson patent No. 15,299 of 1884*

fired, would expand and slightly bind. So, as the extractor stem moved backwards as the gun opened, the spring in the extractor face would be put in tension until it could overcome the artificial resistance of the cartridge binding in the chamber. That this idea was not pursued beyond a provisional patent is silent testimony of its unreliability.

As with all our classifications, there remains a residue of patent specifications that do not really belong in any of the groups we have formed and so again we have to form a 'various' group at the end. Taken in chronological order, we begin with a little mechanism tucked away at the end of Webley's specification, No. 5143 of 1881, which was principally concerned with revolving pistols. What is shown in the drawings, but not explained in the text, is a C-shaped lever, pivoted at its middle onto the front barrel lump with a small V-spring bearing on its rear limb, and its front end on the extractor stem. This lever is so shaped that, when the extractor stem has been pushed back by, for instance, a cam on the knuckle as the gun is opened, the end of the C-shaped lever can slip behind it and the spring

211

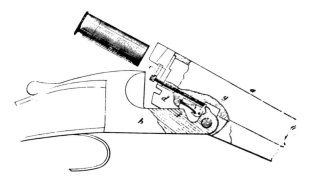

*T. Webley patent No. 5143 of 1881*

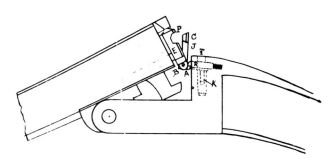

*H. Parsons patent No. 7205 of 1886*

thus flicks out the extractor. It is a puzzling feature that it is not in any way selective, unless it was expected to work only on a spent case.

Much closer to our group is a patent, No. 7205 of 1886, for a singular design by another well-known member of the gun trade. Henry Parsons, gun barrel maker of 2, Court Hanley Street, Birmingham, is perhaps best remembered as the patentee of the chopper-lump barrel. His trade mark, a little hammer with one

pointed face will be found on the chopper-lump damascus barrels fitted to guns bearing a variety of makers' names. What Parsons proposed was a much-simplified ejector system. A conventional extractor is used, but each half of the head has a separtely-pivoted face and each of these has a rearward projection that fits on to a vertical slot cut in the front of the standing-breech. The idea is that, when the gun is fired, along with the firing-pin a stud is urged forwards into

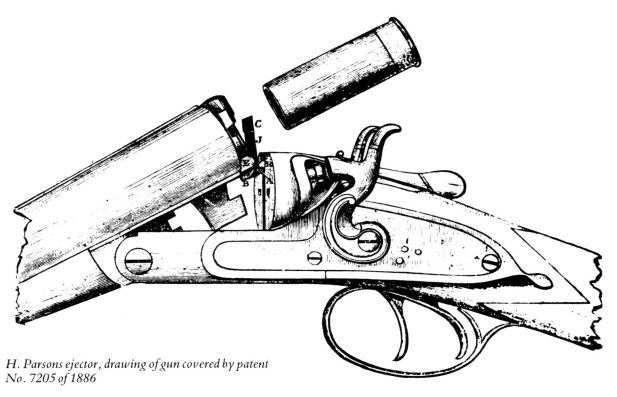

*H. Parsons ejector, drawing of gun covered by patent No. 7205 of 1886*

this slot so that when the gun is opened, the rearward projection from the extractor trips on this stud and flips out the spent case.

We know this mechanism better than many because its inventor organised a little publicity on it by sending an account of its mechanism to both *Land and Water* and *The Field*. His account is an almost verbatim repeat of his patent specification, and he had an attractive engraving made to illustrate his remarks.

It is a remarkable feature of this section on unusual and singular ejectors that most of them were patented by well-known figures in the gun trade. Yet another instance of this phenomenon is the patent, No. 12,402 of 1886, in the name of Edwin George Anson. In this, the spring and kicker of the ejector mechanism are both mounted in the cocking slide of, on the patent specification at least, a back-action sidelock gun. When the gun tumbler falls, the slide, which is hinged onto the breast of the tumbler, moves forward and the gun is re-cocked by a projection on the forend iron that forces back the slide as the gun is opened. Also, as the gun is being opened, the forward end of the extractor rod, which has a downwards projection, is pulling forwards the ejector kicker by the upward projection of the front of the latter. This compresses the coil ejector spring, which is fitted round the kicker, between the collar at the end of the ejector rod and the front of the cocking slide. The collar at the rear of the kicker has a downward projection that butts against a second sear, pivoted behind the tumbler, and the bottom of the tumbler bears on this second sear. Formed on the bottom of the tumbler is a

swelling that acts as a cam, so that, as the tumbler reaches full-cock, the second (or ejector) sear is depressed out of engagement with the rear of the kicker. The coil spring is thus enabled to drive the kicker and extractor rod to the rear and thus, in the words of the specification, 'the empty case (is) flirted from the open back end of the barrel'.

An ejector that should provide no problems of identification, if one ever comes to light, is the subject of a patent, No. 3413 of 1889, granted to Robert Jones and Walter Taylor of 'Monarch Gun Works, Manchester Street, Liverpool'. The ejector work, again, uses the back-and-forth motion of an Anson and Deeley mainspring, but here any resemblance to any other ejector ceases. Mounted on the front lump are a pair of V-springs with their points downwards and their open ends fitted into a slot between the barrels. On the bottom end of the spring is a lateral projection, over which the lock mainspring slides when the gun is fired. The V-ejector spring is, thus, held down as the gun opens and the rear limb of the spring slips off a shoulder in the tip of its slot and expends itself, in one version of the patent, against the upper extractor guide. In another version, the same mechanism on a slightly-reduced scale, works on the lower extractor rod.

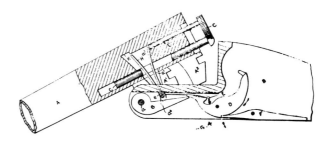

*R. Jones and W. Taylor patent No. 3413 of 1889*

To round off this chapter, we have three ejectors that have so far evaded our classification because they are concerned with the contents of the ejector box rather than the tripping mechanism.

Most of the ejectors that we have considered so far are re-cocked by the extractor being

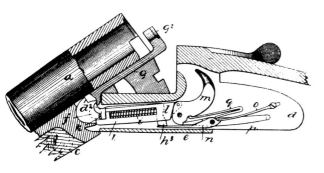

*E. G. Anson patent No. 12,402 of 1886*

forced forwards by the action face as the gun is closed. Thus, in comparison with a non-ejector gun, they will close more stiffly. To overcome this defect, Thomas Perkes, in his patent No. 2784 of 1889, proposed to apply the idea of a rebound lock to the ejector, so that the ejector tumbler would rebound from either a separate spring or a limb of the main ejector spring. Within this idea, there is a range of variants, some with a coil and V-spring, some with a V and a leaf-spring, some with two Vs and some with two coils. In each of these, as the ejector tumbler comes to the eject position, a limb or projection from it compresses a spring which has then to rotate back again.

the V-ejector spring, is raised and the ejector spring compressed. The third limb of the lever, which projects upwards, acts as the extractor cam.

The improved ejector work proposed by James MacNaughton, of 26, Hanover Square, Edinburgh, had at least the virtue of being original. His idea was to make a more effective ejector by keeping the ejector hammers always in contact with the stem of the extractor. There was, thus, no blow delivered to them, the motion being more in the nature of a sharp push which, to quote the specification, 'enables the first and best part of the motion to be got out of the (ejector) springs and the chances of breakage

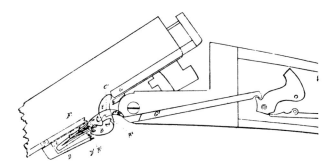

*T. Perkes patent No. 2784 of 1889*

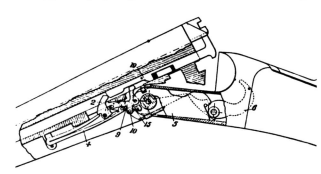

*J. Ross patent No. 1955 of 1890*

The object of John Ross's patent, No. 1955 of 1890, was also to ease the closing of a hammerless ejector gun by devising an ejector mechanism that was cocked as the gun was opened. Ross, of 26, Stewart Lane, Battersea Park Road London, omits to mention that, as a normal hammerless gun is opened (if it has been fired), the mainsprings also have to be compressed and in the absence of an actual sample of this mechanism, the success or otherwise of this idea must remain a moot point. What we can be sure of are the details of the patented mechanism. The heart of this lies in a three-legged lever, roughly T-shaped and lying on its side, pivoted transversely just about where the two limbs join, and located in the rear of the forend. The limb that projects downwards has a friction-reducing roller at its end which rides over a projecting cam on the knuckle. Thus, the forward limb, which is linked to the lower limb of

by concussion are diminished'. The details of how this aim was to be achieved are in patent No. 7759 of 1890. The nub of the idea was to mount the ejector work on a slide in the forend and move the slide back-and-forth by linking it to the extractor cam, so that the ejector work actually moved with the extractor. Beyond this, the ejector is conventional with a rocking sear releasing ejector hammers that are rods with coil springs round them. The nightmare thought about this idea is that, if it had become popular, it could, at a single stroke, have at least doubled the number of ejector variants; we are thankful that it did not!

# CHAPTER TWELVE

# The Choke-bore and other Modifications to the Internal Form of the Barrel

We have up to now concerned ourselves solely with the evolution of shotgun mechanism and cartridges and have ignored the ballistic performance of the combination for the simple reason that this had remained virtually consistent. This state of affairs was upset during our period 1871–1890 and, therefore, we have to consider developments that were of vital, but different, importance to gunmaker and sportsman alike.

The idea that, by modifying the internal form of the gun barrel, a charge of shot could be held closer together in flight, and so be effective at a greater range, was an exceedingly old one. Means to this end have many times been invented, by accident or design, forgotten and reinvented anew, with the result that there have been many who could claim, in all honesty and sincerity, to have been the 'original and true inventor'.

This point was discussed in the readers' letters column of *The Field* in April 1875. In an attempt to resolve the problem, A. J. Lane, who wrote under the nom-de-plume 'One who has fired upwards of 20,000 trial shots at marks', offered a challenge cup to the value of 10 guineas, or the cash, to 'the English gunmaker who can satisfactorily prove either his being the original inventor or the first user in this country of the system' (choke-bored barrel). On the basis of his patent, No. 1501 of 1866, the prize, as cash, went to W. R. Pape of Newcastle. As a result, Pape made great play in his advertisements that he was 'The inventor of the choke bore'.

Both in the search for material for *The Gun and its Development*, and to clip the wings of Pape, Greener researched this point in some depth and produced evidence of a M. de Marolles (who is presumably G. F. Magne du Marrolles) and his book, *La Chasse au Fusil (Hunting with the Gun)*, published in 1788. In this Marolles describes cutting shallow rings in the bore just inside the muzzle of a gun to prevent the shot scattering. Also mentioned by Greener is another book, *Vieux Chasseur (The Old Hunter)*, by Theophilus Deyeux and published in 1835, in which guns with constricted muzzles are described.

It is perhaps surprising that Greener missed one source that our own researches have revealed. Why Greener should have omitted this is a puzzle as he would certainly have been aware of the lead that directed us to this unusual source. In the correspondence column of *The Field*, 26 November 1898, there appeared a letter from John Rigby which drew readers' attention to a passage in a novel written by the, then, celebrated novelist, Maria Edgeworth. The novel, *Ormond*, was published in 1817. In this we read, of one of her main characters, that:

> **He had contrived and executed a tool for enlarging the barrel of a gun in any particular part so as to increase its effect in adding to the force of the discharge, and in preventing the shot from scattering too widely.**

It is believed that the character in question was modelled to a large degree on Miss Edgeworth's father and that he had travelled widely on the Continent. So this trail, if trail it be, cannot be followed backwards. However, the passage quoted above is an accurate description of the process that produces what we now call a recess-choke.

It is with considerable interest, therefore, that we note from Joseph Long's book, *American Wildfowl Shooting* (1879), that in 1827 choke-boring was practised by a certain Jeremiah Smith of Smithfield, Rhode Island. That Smith drew his inspiration from *Ormond* can be no more than a tempting, if attractive, speculation. Unfortunately for this theory, Long goes on to explain that the recess-choke was not, in his opinion, the true choke. Long claims that the recess-choke was invented by Robert M. Faburn, who obtained United States patent No. 128,379 of 1872. Having been mistaken in his attempts to discover the nature of the choke-bore in the workshop of J. L. Johnson, a gun-smith in a township then called Young America, in the state of Illinois, Johnson had been told of the secret by a friend and shooting companion of Joseph Long's, Fred Kimble, who had obtained his first choke-bore gun via Long from the Boston gunmaker Joseph Tonks, who, along with others in the same city, apparently knew of the choke-bore. If Long's account be true it would effectively destroy the earlier made claim that Fred Kimble invented the choke-bore. Long goes on to explain that Robert Faburn, having made a supply of expanding-bits to cut his recess-choke, peddled them around the Western American gun trade with the result that the users started to issue advertisements to describe the wonderful results that they were obtaining. These claims spilled over and got caught up with a correspondence that was running in the columns of the American journal, *Turf, Field and Farm*. The editor of this paper (no doubt mindful of the kudos which had accrued to his London counterpart, Dr Walsh of *The Field* as a result of similar ventures) arranged a trial to test the various claims.

Both Greener and Long tell how, having had his guns soundly beaten in the *Turf, Field and Farm* trial, Greener set out to discover the reason and so introduced the choke-bore to Britain. We suspect this is something of a simplification of the story. On the basis of the correspondence to *The Field* of 13 February 1875, there are reasonable grounds for believing that E. C. Green of Cheltenham knew of, and was using, a system of boring that produced denser shot patterns in 1868 or possibly even earlier. A correspondent, 'Junius', wrote that Green, in 1869, claimed to be able to produce guns able to 'beat any of my London guns by 30%' and, in fact, had made good his boast. However, there are no other statistics quoted in this or other correspondence upon which we can base any more definite conclusions.

That Green, too, learned of the system in America would seem to be a reasonable suggestion, as he evidently did a useful trade with that country. His agents, at a slightly later date, were

G. and A. Hayden of Jacksonville, Illinois and Green certainly brought in other American ideas including, in 1875, the Sturtevant all-brass cartridge case. In addition, he had acted as agent for Abbey and Foster of Chicago in the matter of the patent for their breech-loading system. (See Chapter Two.)

In spite of all this, the honour of popularising the choke-bore in Britain belongs, without doubt, to Greener. Indeed, we feel that this was his greatest contribution to the development of the British shotgun and it is right that at this point we should sketch something of his biography and background.

He was born at Felling-on-Tyne, near Newcastle in 1834 and was the second of William Greener's four sons. In the year that William Wellington was born his father published *The Gun*, and we can see that William Greener was

*William Wellington Greener, 1834–1921*

an ardent admirer of 'The Iron Duke' for not only did he give the name Wellington to his son, he also dedicated his book to 'The Prince of Waterloo'.

At the age of 17, William Wellington suffered a serious attack of measles which left him almost blind and it says much for his strength of purpose that, in spite of so grave a disability, he achieved so much. As is common with the blind and very poorly sighted, he cultivated his sense of touch, and an obituary notes that he was respected and not a little feared by his workmen in that he could, by touch, detect flaws in their work.

William Wellington's earlier working life was spent in his father's employment. William Greener had worked for John Manton in London before setting up his own business in Newcastle-upon-Tyne in 1829. From there, in 1844, he had moved to Birmingham. It is interesting in view of later events that William Wellington was trained as a barrel-borer (perhaps this was the one trade that he could master with his poor sight), but he ultimately became responsible for the outworkers that his father employed. Possibly also as a result of his handicap, we are assured by his descendants that William Wellington had a great aversion to being photographed, which explains why so few portraits of him exist.

However, in 1864 father and son parted company and William Wellington set up a rival business. That there was enmity between the two we can gauge by the fact that William Wellington advertised that he had no connection with his father's establishment. Like many another parting, the reasons behind it were probably complex, but one recorded point of contention was that the father had no time for the, then, new breech-loading guns that his son rightly perceived to be the way forwards.

Though there are several patents bearing his name on the files of the Patent Office, the adoption and development of the choke-bore illustrates what was perhaps Greener's greatest ability, which was to perceive the value in the inventions of others and refine and market the result. As part of this marketing, he followed the precedent set by his father and wrote books

on gunmaking and shooting. His first work was *Modern Breechloaders*, published in 1871, based in some part on material inherited from his father, who had died in 1869. He followed this with *Choke Bore Guns and how to load for all kinds of game* in 1876 and, in 1881, published the first edition of his great work, *The Gun and its Development*. This ran to nine editions, the last one being published in 1910. In addition to the English language edition, Riling notes French and Russian translations. Today there are reproduction copies of the ninth edition. Then, in 1888, came *Modern Shotguns*, even more widely translated than before. Riling notes German, Spanish and Italian editions. In 1892 came *The Breechloader and How to Use it*. His last three books were all about the use of rifles and were: *Sharp Shooting for Sport and War*, published in 1900; *The British Miniature Rifle*, 1908; and *Sharp Shooting for War and Defence*, 1914.

With all these works we can see that part of their purpose was to popularise Greener products and to project Greener ideas. As such they must be approached with caution by a modern enthusiast seeking a balanced view of gunmaking and development. Providing this aspect is kept very firmly in mind, they are of the greatest value to all students of gunnery and we acknowledge that *The Gun and its Development*, in particular, has been and continues to be of the greatest use to us in our researches.

So much for the man: now we must return to our theme and his claim to fame. Popularisation of the choke-bore can be accurately dated as beginning with an announcement in *The Field* of December 1874.

The text of this has been reproduced before, but we feel that its importance to our theme justifies its reappearance at this point. Given the fiercely competitive state of the British gun trade and the propensity of British sportsmen to express their views in print, it is not surprising that this advertisement stirred up a hornet's nest of debate comparable to, or even greater than, that generated by the introduction of the breech-loader not 20 years earlier. Without doubt, Dr Walsh at *The Field* realised the potential of this for the commercial success of his

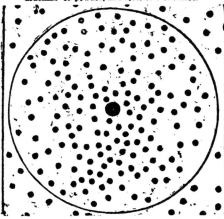
*W. Greener advertisement of 1874*

paper and managed affairs accordingly by organising another '*Field* Trial'. The story is told in most minute detail in Greener's *Choke Bore Guns* and parts are also to be found in Walsh's *The Modern Sportsman's Gun and Rifle*. (The conditions of the trial were published in *The Field* on 13 March 1875.

To supervise the 1875 trial, a committee composed of Col G. L. Goodlake, V.C., and Messrs E. B. Cox, A. J. Lane, W. Lort and E. O. Partridge was assembled. Col Goodlake also brought two corporals of The Guards as his assistants.

The outcome of much effort resulted in Greener's guns winning all three choked-bore classes (8-, 12- and 20-bore) and the coveted silver cup for the most important class, the 12-bore. The final class, which was that termed as 'English' boring, was won by Thomas Turner. He admitted that his gun carried a five-thousandth of an inch constriction in the muzzle, upon which, under the humid conditions of the trial, black powder fouling built up to form a virtual choke constriction, which produced a denser pattern than some of the guns entered as choke-bores.

Greener, therefore, emerged from this trial with a vastly-enhanced reputation which was in contrast to that of W. R. Pape, whose conduct was lamentable. During the shooting of English bores, the markers behind the iron-faced wooden butts complained that one gun was balling its charge to the extent of punching holes in the backstop. The gun was shown to be one of Pape's, and it was disqualified. Subsequently, wads were found that had been hollowed out to carry more shot which was, presumably, intended to concentrate the pattern. If this were not enough, Robert Davison of Morpeth (who, it later emerged, was a front-man for Pape to enable him to enter an extra batch of guns) complained of the veracity of the scoring after the time for such questions had passed and the paper targets had been virtually discarded as rubbish. Not unreasonably, the recount was not permitted and, as a result, heated words were exchanged both at the trial and in print afterwards, with the offer of taking the matter to Law. In fact, nothing ever came of it except that

Pape was branded by Dr Walsh in *The Field* as a very poor loser and the stage was thus set for the acrimony that was to mark so much of Pape's subsequent utterings in the sporting press.

Not unexpectedly, the view was expressed that the slight muzzle-constriction that constituted the choke-bore would be fairly rapidly worn away and, to elucidate this point, a subsidiary trial was undertaken after the main patterning trial. This came to be known as 'The Wear and Tear Trial'. For this, three guns (made respectively by Greener, Maleham and Baker) that had been tested in the previous trial, were loaned by their makers, who also supplied 2,500 cartridges with each gun. These cartridges were fired into a pit in batches of 200 a day on two days a week, after which the guns were cleaned. Only oil, turpentine and tow (or similar vegetable cleaner) were permitted and only a quarter of an hour was to be spent cleaning. The guns were locked up between firing sessions and, after each 200 cartridges, the guns were tested for pattern and penetration as before. As we today would confidently predict, there was no significant alteration in the shooting of any of the guns.

In the wake of this evidence that choke-bored guns did, in fact, achieve what was claimed for them, the discussion then turned to the question of how these guns performed in the hands of shooters on stubble and moors and in the coverts. The readers' letters column of *The Field* at this period contains reams of anecdotes on this subject and, in an attempt to arrive at a more objective appraisal, yet another trial was arranged. This took place on 21 July 1876. The idea was to have two teams of shooters, 'choke' versus 'cylinder' bores, to shoot against each other on the same day, under the 'Gun Club Rules' adopted by Walsh, at live pigeons released from traps.

Unfortunately, for all the care and effort that had gone into this project and before the first shot had been fired, the trial had been debased to such a degree that the results likely to be obtained were of no practical value. What the formers of the trial rules had overlooked was that, about a year earlier, the rules of the Gun Club had been altered to permit the use of what were called 'Concentrators'. These were either open-ended cylinders of card that enclosed the shot-charge within the cartridge-case (rather like the present-day plastic shot-cup, but open at the bottom), or copper-wire mesh containers into which the shot was packed with bone-dust and held together by a thin paper case. When subjected to the stresses of firing, the shot

*Drawing from* The Field *of the 25-guinea cup donated by* The Field *to the winner of the 1876* Field Trial

escaped from its container. It is only safe to fire a concentrator in a cylinder-bored gun, where it can increase the density of the pattern thrown to approximately the level of a half-choke. As the trial was about to start, it was discovered that the 'cylinder' side was proposing to use these devices and the organisers objected to this. However, the 'smooth-bore' squad, as the cylinder-bored shooters were termed, sensed that they had both a good chance of winning and of embarrassing Dr Walsh, so they insisted that he abide by the rules he had produced. In the event, the cyclinder-bored guns won the trial and Dr Walsh had to go into print to admit that the results were valueless.

The following year another cup was put up, this time by James Purdey, to the value of 50 guineas. The lessons of the previous trial being learned, concentrators were excluded. Moreover, the ranges at which the birds were to be released were increased to 30 and 40 yards and this time, as expected, the choke-bored guns were victorious. To the obvious satisfaction of Greener, one of his guns (the only Greener in the competition) was used by the winner.

As an aside, it is worthy of note that each pigeon trapped at the 1876 trial was costing the man who was attempting to shoot it two shillings and sixpence, and at this time a farm labourer, for a week's hard work, was paid thirteen shillings and sixpence.

It is perhaps surprising that the events we have described so far in this chapter should have had so little impact in the Patent Office. The probable reason for this is that the subtleties of the form of the inside of a gun-barrel do not lend themselves to a finite description required in a patent. That is not to say that there are no patents. Given the climate of the time, that would be too much to expect.

Most numerous among the choke patents are those concerned with forming longitudinal grooves in the bore. This is an ancient idea. Some authorities date its origin to the sixteenth century and claim that it was the root from which the idea of the rifle, with its spiral grooves, grew. Be this as it may, the idea of longitudinal grooves persisted and with it the claim that the shooting of such a barrel shot 'harder' or 'better' than a simple tube.

Within our span there are three patents solely or partly covering this idea. They are No. 4542 of 1875 and No. 2581 of 1876, both in the name of John Wallace Duncan, who quotes no trade or profession and who may have been an agent for he gives his address as Southampton Chambers, Chancery Lane, London; and No. 4425 of 1879 granted to the famous Belgian arms manufacturer, Henri Pieper of Liège.

To deal most succinctly with this notion we will quote from *The Gun and its Development*, where Greener reports on these longitudinally-grooved barrels:

> After repeated trials of such guns (Greener) is convinced that the shooting is in no way improved nor the value of the gun in any way increased by the process.

Another idea, perhaps even more ancient than the preceding one, which reappears as a patent in our period, is the scheme of an enlarged powder chamber in the rear of the barrel. The relevant specifications are No. 571 of 1873 granted to Thomas W. Miller and No. 3123 of 1878 taken out by Lionel Gye. The value, validity or virtue of such specifications eludes us.

To round off this chapter, we have purposely kept a variety of ideas that have persisted, in one form or another, to this day; indeed, some have been relaunched as 'novelties'. When the concept of the choke-bore became widely known, and its efficiency proven, there were many sportsmen who wished to avail themselves of this advance without incurring the expense of new guns. One answer was to fit new barrels. Alternatively, guns were re-bored, but proof of this in a specific gun is difficult to establish as the gun has to be accurately dated, and cylinder guns continued to be made after the introduction of the choke. In addition, there were ideas to achieve the desired close-shooting by modifications to the barrels other than, or perhaps in addition to, re-boring. Three of these became the subjects of patents.

The first of these, which never progressed beyond the provisional stage, was No. 312 of 1875, in the names of two giants of the era, John Rigby of Dublin and William Middleditch Scott of Birmingham. They proposed that either the muzzles of barrels be swaged in, or additional choke-tubes be fitted over existing muzzles.

A variant of this second idea was part of J. S. Heath's patent, No. 984 of 1880. Here we have a readily detachable pair of double tubes that fits, as a single unit, onto the muzzle of a double gun adapted to receive it. Rights to this patent were acquired by Thomas Turner who widely advertised the system which was favourably reported by Basil Tozer ('20 bore') in his book *Practical Hints on Shooting* (1887).

**T. T. has just patented an**

# ATTACHABLE MUZZLE.

Guns fitted with this invention can be converted from cylinder bore, or vice versa, in one minute, while in the field. The muzzle can be easily carried in the waistcoat pocket, a sportsman is then as well off as if he had two guns with him, one for close and the other for wild shooting.

THOS TURNER PATENT

Prices and all information on application.

*Part of Thomas Turner's advertisement of 1883*

Yet another idea from antiquity that reappeared, was the patent, No. 4294 of 1883, in the name of Paul Ambroise Bayle, a Parisian engineer. He proposed to bore a shotgun barrel as two cones, joined at their apexes with a cylindrical section. This idea called 'friction and relief' was usually applied to high-quality flintlock shotguns of the Regency period. With the coming of percussion ignition it was discarded for, when a barrel so bored is fired by the more efficient percussion system, the gun recoils excessively with a normal load.

Having dealt with the minor patents in this area, we return to a more important aspect.

By the last quarter of the nineteenth century, Britain had amassed a vast colonial empire. Naturally, the soldiers and administrators who controlled it made the most of the unparalleled sporting opportunities open to them in these distant lands. The fundamental difference that these overseas sportsmen found was the presence of large, and sometimes dangerous, beasts alongside game birds. From this mixed sport came a need for a sporting arm different to the classic 'game gun' of the home country. There were combination-guns made, in which one barrel was for a moderate-to-powerful rifle cartridge and the other barrel for shot. Such combinations were usually referred to in the British trade as 'Cape guns', after the main outlet for them.

A variant on this theme was the single-barrel actions that could be fitted with either a smooth-bored or rifled barrel. The best known of these, certainly the most widely advertised, was the 'Transvaal', promoted by S. W. Silver and Co. of London, which used a Martini-type action onto which could be screwed a variety of shot and rifle barrels.

The other answer to the challenge of mixed-game shooting was to fire solid ball from a shotgun. With the designs of bullet then available, the accuracy of such a combination was poor and for practical purposes the only use of it was shooting in very dense cover or jungle. Bearing in mind the various disadvantages of the gun/rifle combinations that were available, we can at once grasp the importance of an idea that would permit a double-barrel shotgun to fire a solid bullet accurately from either barrel.

Such was the achieved result of the British patent, No. 7568 of 1885, taken out by the patent agent H. H. Lake for George Vincent Fosbery, V.C., then living in Liège.

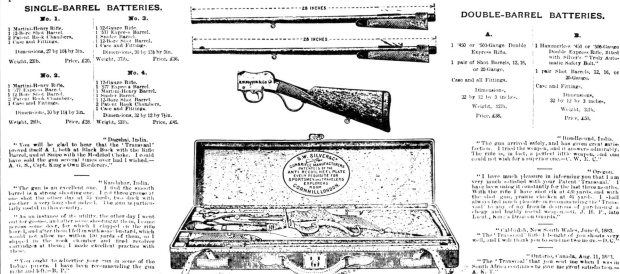

*S. W. Silver and Co. advertisement of 1883*

In large measure, this invention was made possible by the choke-bore with its constricted muzzle, for what Fosbery patented was the idea of rifling only this constricted portion. This was found to be sufficient to stabilise a bullet, but not enough to disrupt the shot pattern, as occurred when firing a charge of shot through a fully rifled barrel. Indeed, the published reports testify to the very high quality of the shot patterns obtained with all sizes of shot. This invention was commercially exploited by Holland & Holland as the 'Paradox' system. Before we consider this remarkable gun in greater detail, we would like to say a few words about the man who stands unique among the many inventors we have considered in holding Great Britain's highest award for gallantry in war. After leaving Eton, George Fosbery obtained a commission in the Bengal Army of the Honourable East India Company in 1851. He had the good fortune to be on sick leave in England when, along with many others, part of his native regiment mutinied in 1857. However, he was soon back in India and involved in the aftermath of this conflict. He won his Victoria Cross in what was known as the Umbeyla Campaign on the North-West Frontier in 1863. The troops he was leading on this occasion were firing from their Enfield rifles explosive bullets of his own design. While he obtained no patent on these

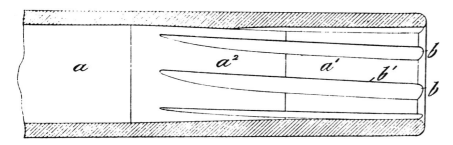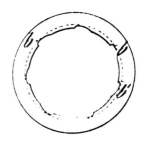

H. H. Lake (agent for G. V. Fosbery) patent
No. 7568 of 1885

bullets, from the beginning of his service career until old age, he took out a steady stream of patents to cover a variety of improvements to military weapons. In his development work, he made use of his skill as a machinist to produce in secrecy prototypes of his inventions. For instance, in *Land and Water*, on 24 November 1886, he records how he spent months testing all sorts of variations (rifling, bullet and powder charge, at ranges from 25 to 250 yards) of his rifled choke gun. The Holland & Holland Paradox was perhaps Fosbery's greatest invention and some 5000 were produced by Hollands in both hammer and hammerless forms. Because of the strains that the actions of these guns were called on to stand, they are most often seen with a back-action style of lockwork, which encroaches the least of any on the action bar. In calibre, these guns were made in all the usual bore sizes between 8 and 28. The large bores were more useful in Africa and Asia, as lightweight powerful rifles to take dangerous game; while the 16-bore and smaller sizes were especially useful in Europe and Australia, with their smaller and less dangerous big game.

The first guns of this type were proved and regulated for black powder, but later versions were designed for smokeless powder, the so-called 'Nitro Paradoxes'. Another version, intended to give even greater velocity, was the 'Magnum Nitro Paradox'. Guns of one or other of these types were very well reported by the big-game hunters/explorers of the era and so when the patent expired, in 1899, many other makers produced copies of the system.

While the protection was still in force Greener obtained a patent, No. 17,746 of 1889, in which the entire barrel was rifled except for a recess-choke. It was found, however, that this was not sufficient to control the shot after the disruption caused by the rifled bore and the idea languished.

Concerned as we are in this chapter with the way a shotgun throws its pattern, it is appropriate that we include a movement in the early-1880s toward the adoption of thin brass shotgun cartridges. Suffice it to say here that, in 1882, the Kynoch Ammunition Company was offering its 'Perfect' thin brass case, as both pin- and centre-fire, in all gauges between 8-bore and .360.

Surprisingly, the cost of such cartridge-cases was no greater than good-quality paper cases. In addition, it had been found that, with the folded crimp closure that was used, the quality of patterns noticeably improved. The snag was that because the case walls were so thin, a round with 12-bore external dimensions required 10-bore wads and so on up and down the scale of gun sizes. On this point the idea foundered because, despite the improved shooting, it emerged that not enough sportsmen were prepared to buy special guns, or have existing ones rebarrelled, to create a really significant market. However, for special applications, notably wildfowling in Britain and tropical use, the brass case remained in limited use until World War I caused the cessation of production.

Arising from this are two patents for chamber-sleeves to permit a gun bored for paper-case cartridges to use the brass case that took the wad appropriate to the bore size of the gun. These two are: No. 3137 of 1882, granted to C. D. Abel, patent agent for Wilhelm Lorenz

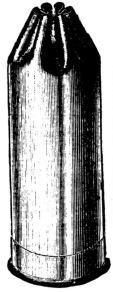
*Kynoch advertisement of 1882*

of Carlsruhe, Germany; and No. 4309, also of 1882, granted to George Lincoln Jeffries of Birmingham, another son of G. Jeffries of Norwich.

*W. Greener's advertisement of 1884*

Amid all these frenzied efforts to obtain a tighter shot pattern, we find an idea which has come to be applied to the opposite end. In the patent, No. 4217 of 1874, in the name of John Long Kerr of Alleghany, Pennsylvania, is a description of how a portion of the barrel towards the muzzle is enlarged between 0.03 inches to 0.12 inches, and 8 to 10 inches long to 'obviate bunching, welding and to secure the desired concentration'. As far as we know, no commercial use was made of this invention at the time, but within the last decade the idea has been revived in only slightly-modified form, the so-called 'Tula' choke for skeet clay-pigeon shooting.

It is not our role in this work to offer any advice on the boring that a sportsman should adopt, but we are bound to remark that the overwhelming experience of the last century, is that very few men are best served with the tighter choke-bores. To end this chapter we feel that we can do no better than to quote from a letter written in May 1887 by Frederick Beesley to *The Field*. It beautifully sums up the experience of the century:

> **Customers, somehow, will have heavy chokes and the slightest hint at their not being able to hold straight enough to hit with a small killing circle runs great risk of ruffling their dignity; yet 50 per cent of the guns I sell come back to have the choke relieved, with 'I wish I had taken your advice at first' . . .**

# CHAPTER THIRTEEN

# The Increase in the Popularity of Shooting

On 9 August 1870 it became law in Britain that an annual ten shilling gun licence had to be bought by everyone owning a gun, rifle or pistol, who did not have a licence to kill game. By 31 March the following year, 93,677 such licences had been sold and this figure was to rise to 172,643 for the year ending 31 March 1890. Game licences had meanwhile remained practically static. These are obviously crude statistics (and the increase noted resulted from many factors), but they do point to an upsurge of interest in shooting in the two decades up to the year 1890. The reason that lay behind this change in fashion, which incidentally provided rich material for Mr Punch, we must leave, not least for reasons of space, to the social historian. However, as a result of this influx of new sportsmen and, to a lesser degree, sports-women, a number of innovations and inventions appeared and this chapter provides us with a suitable 'catch-all' heading under which to consider them.

For instance, a fashion that achieved a degree of following in the late-1880s was that of drastically reducing the weight of a sporting shotgun (a normal 12-bore was nearer 7 pounds than 6 pounds) to the region of 5½ pounds. Like all fashions, this was not new, but the coverage that it generated in the readers' letters columns and the advertisements of the period necessitates our consideration.

UNNECESSARY QUESTIONS.

*Lady (with gun).* " Am I holding the thing right ? "

*How Mr Punch saw the lady with a gun*

---

**THOMAS TURNER,**
INVENTOR OF
**THE "FEATHERWEIGHT" GUN,**

A **12-Bore Gun**, with Barrels and Action of FULL STRENGTH, **Weighing 5¾lbs.** Barrels 28 inches long, firing the usual **charges of Black or Nitro Powder**, without any unpleasant **recoil**, and giving equally as good results as heavier guns.

**THE "LEVISSIMUS" GUN,**

**Weight, 4¾lbs.** 12-Bore, with 24-inch Barrels. With 27-inch **Barrels, 5lbs.** Barrels of full thickness.

**19, BROOK STREET, LONDON, W.**

*Thomas Turner advertisement of 1887*

The most vociferous advocate of the idea was Thomas Turner of 19, Brook Street, London who used the name of 'Levissimus'. Turner produced both hammer and hammerless light guns, but it is not clear whether he applied the name to both or only one of these types. It has been our good fortune to be able to study a 12-bore hammer gun in some detail. This gun weighs 5 pounds and 14 ounces and, to achieve this, the whole gun has been pared down with the exception of the barrels. For instance, the bar of the action is shorter than usual and is more the size of a 16-bore than that of a 12-bore; the forend is abbreviated to about half the length

*Thomas Turner lightweight hammer gun*

that is normal and, perhaps most striking of all, the stock is cut away on the lower sides to leave but a web of wood at this point. Not that the Levissimus was the only one of this type. We have examined Cashmore and Ford guns of this type, have seen references to Lang guns and do not doubt that other makers profited from the fad (as suggested by the fine Lincoln Jeffries advertisement) for ever lighter sporting shotguns.

*Cutaway stock of Thomas Turner lightweight hammer gun*

When all the dust had settled, the facts emerged that while it was perfectly possible for a good maker to build a sound 12-bore shotgun down to even 4¾ pounds to fire standard cartridges, such guns were not to be the next generation for the vast majority of sportsmen. While the idea did not gain general acceptance

*William Ford advertisement published in 1884*

(it was, in a sense, a step too far in the direction that was being followed), these featherlight guns hastened the reduction of weight of the ordinary game-gun. A point that such guns most naturally raised in the minds of all practical sportsmen was that of recoil.

Recoil, that is to say the rearward motion of a firearm when a projectile is fired from it, and the effect it has on different individuals is a fascinating aspect of the study of guns.

Some individuals are, it seems, far less affected than others. In this context a photograph that used to appear in the catalogue of the American Weatherby Rifle Company springs to mind. This showed a petite Italian Contessa, who was said to weigh less than 100 pounds, posed beside an elephant that she had shot using one of the firm's high velocity .460 magnum rifles. At the other extreme are those people who are very susceptible to recoil, either from individual discharges or from the cumulative effect of many shots. Attempts to mitigate these

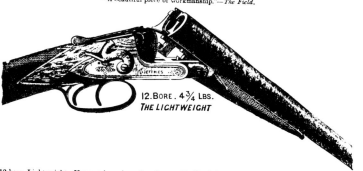

*Lincoln Jeffries advertisement of 1887*

227

effects by the use of a cushion-like pad fixed to the gun stock are of great antiquity, probably as old as firearms themselves, but within our present period we find several ideas protected by patents to this end. We feel that they can, with reasonable justification, be included in this chapter devoted to the increase in popularity of shooting because it is a feature of most novices that they fear the recoil of a gun.

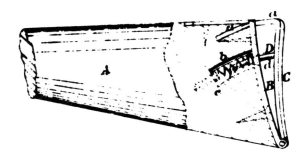

*A. Clark (agent for W. Miller) patent No. 4345 of 1875*

*Inside of S. W. Silver and Co. recoil pad*

The first of these patents, No. 1691 of 1871, was granted to Walter Scott of Birmingham. This covers the idea of an India-rubber pad. In addition, we have Hugh Adams Silver's specification, No. 2938 of 1874, for a soft and hard rubber combination to be used as a recoil pad. This idea is also covered, and presumably refined, in patent No. 17,054 of 1886, in which we learn that H. A. Silver was a colonel. However, he does not appear in Hart's Army List as a colonel or any other rank, and our researches have yet to discover in which army he served. The specification is also in the name of Walter Fletcher, who is quoted as being a gunsmith of 67, Cornhill, London, which was the address from which the firm of S. W. Silver & Co. traded. The idea of a rubber pad is also mentioned in E. C. Green's patent, No. 14,626 of 1885. But of all these it is the Silver's pad that is by far the best known and was once practically the generic name for a rubber recoil pad.

A novel pad was that proposed by John Percival Onderdonk of Philadelphia. This envisaged an air-filled pad with a vent at the bottom. In addition to this, he proposed a heel-plate supported on a pair of compression springs. Both of these proposals were included in his specification, No. 4372 of 1884.

The spring-loaded butt-plate had been thought of before. It is covered by the specification, No. 4345 of 1875, granted to A. M. Clark. He acted as agent for William Deeps Miller of Pittsburg. In this, the heelplate of the gun is hinged at its bottom and slots against a spring at the top, with the intention of resisting the upward flip of a normally-stocked gun as it is fired.

It is this upward motion that can bruise a user's cheek and so we find two cheek-pads also in the patents. Again the idea is ancient, but the novelty of Alfred Hall's patent was to have a slip-on rubber pad. He was an ironmonger from Cleckheaton in Yorkshire and he was granted patent No. 8922 of 1886. Another cheek-piece patent, No. 10,379 of 1889, this time on the idea of having the pad actually set

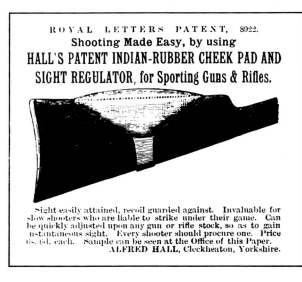

*Alfred Hall's advertisement of 1886*

into the stock, was granted to G. G. L. Bankart of Bolton Grange, Bradford.

However, for the vast majority of sportsmen, the answer to handling the recoil lies in a properly-fitted gun of appropriate weight, and the recoil-pad is an idea that has remained in only limited use.

There are few boons that can be conferred on a sportsman to compare with that of a well-fitting gun stock. A gun that fits seems to become part of the shooter's own body, in that, its manipulation is as easy and natural as that of a limb or digit. The value of a good-fitting stock has long been recognised. For example, in 1814, we find Col Hawker recording that 'the length, hand and casting off of a stock, must, of course, be fitted to the shooter, who should have his measure for them as carefully entered on a gunmaker's books, as that for a suit of clothes on those of his tailor'. But to achieve this desired end, there seems to have been little but intelligent trial and error.

The step from this state to the production of a gun with an adjustable stock would seem to be a very short one and we believe such guns were well-known. Curiously, the first description of one that we have discovered is in *The Field* of 22 May 1886, though of a similar date is the description included by Greener in *The Gun and its Development*. This described an adjustable gun to be used in conjunction with an aiming point, behind which the gun-fitter stood. It is not made absolutely clear in the description whether it was only the special aiming-point

that was the invention of Greener's London shop manager, Mr Oliver, or whether he had invented the measurement-gun as well.

There is a patent for a measurement-gun taken out by Henry William Holland, No. 2341 of 1889. The drawing with this specification shows a gun on which the length of the stock can be adjusted by a heel-piece sliding on two rods, and the comb of the stock raised and lowered on two guide rods. In addition, the angle that the barrels make with the head of the stock can be altered and locked by a bolt in the position of a Henry Jones double-grip. There is also provision to raise or lower the whole stock by means of a transverse hinge under the standing-breech. The final refinement is a species of rear sight mounted on the top of the breech-ends of the barrels.

A gun of very similar specification to the above is now in the collection of the author (IMC). Many years ago he was given it by a kind friend who rescued it for him from a London dustcart. Examination of this piece strongly suggests that it was made up from scrap parts found in a gunmaker's shop – the barrels, for instance, show every sign of once belonging to a pinfire gun.

Unfortunately, throwing up a gun in practice in a gunmaker's shop and actually shooting with it are very different exercises. So the next logical development was to make a measurement-gun that was capable of firing. In the terminology of the last century the inert gun was always called a measurement-gun and one

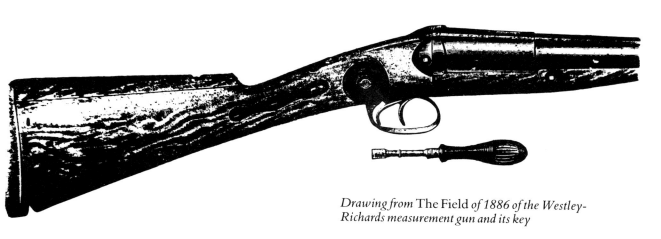

*Drawing from* The Field *of 1886 of the Westley-Richards measurement gun and its key*

229

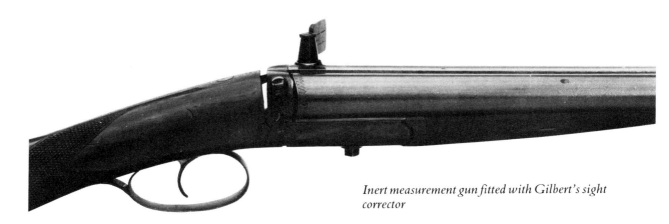

*Inert measurement gun fitted with Gilbert's sight corrector*

that could be fired and have its stock adjusted was a 'try-gun'. This useful distinction we shall preserve.

The production of a fully-adjustable gun that would fire proved to be a notion that was difficult to achieve in practice. To preserve the weight, balance and that subtle 'feel' of a good shotgun was a challenge that sorely taxed and, it is not unfair to say, defeated, in some cases, men who were among the most successful nineteenth-century shotgun inventors. Their efforts to produce a try-gun were naturally protected by patent.

The earliest try-gun that is recorded is the invention of Albert Hape and Alfred Shelton Oliver, both of Elberton, Georgia. They employed the patent agent, A.M. Clark, to protect their invention in Britain and it appears as specification No. 2407 of 1881. The drawing is a rather sketchy affair, but what it shows is a gun with a pistol-grip behind which is a species of hinge. This permits the rear portion of the stock to be raised or lowered and, at the same time, to be adjusted for length, by a slot and wing-nut type of arrangement. By the standards of the Westley Richards measurement-gun, these adjustments are limited and the lack of any adjustment for the cast of the stock, that is to say the deviation of the stock from the central vertical plane of the gun, is a grave defect. Nevertheless, all credit must be given to this pioneer idea and we cannot doubt that, if this patent had been kept in force and defended, it could have become a valuable master patent.

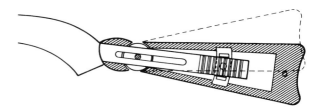

*A. Clark (agent for A. Hape and A. Oliver) patent No. 2407 of 1881*

This was evidently not the way things turned out, for, about eight years later we have the beginning of a small spate of try-gun patents. The first of these appears as a patent, No. 1157 of 1889, granted to the inventive William Palmer Jones of Birmingham. This is shown as a Henry Jones-type gun with bar-action external hammer locks. Just behind the trigger guard in the hand of the stock are a pair of hinges. The one at the front has a horizontal pivot and, just behind it, the other has a vertical pivot. These hinges are activated and locked by threaded bolts so that, with a turnscrew, a whole variety of stock configurations could be produced. In addition, the length of the stock could be adjusted, as the heel portion slid in and out on two rod-guides and could be locked in position by set-screws working on these rods. Yet more adjustments were provided in the shape of a moveable comb, and the heelplate could be pivoted about a horizontal central pivot.

If we can judge by the advertisements that appeared in the contemporary sporting press, this gun was a great success for its inventor.

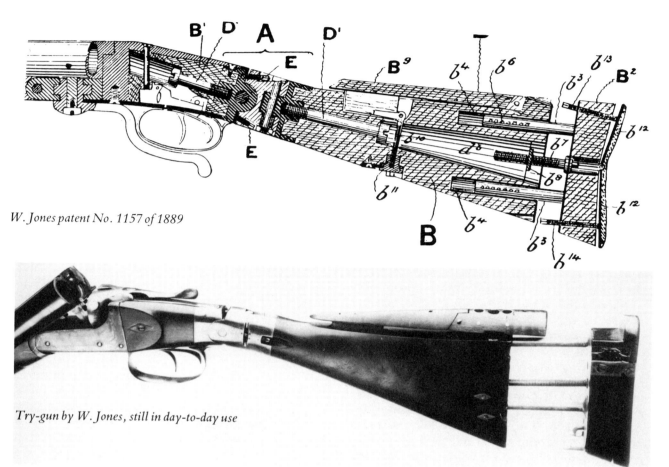

*W. Jones patent No. 1157 of 1889*

*Try-gun by W. Jones, still in day-to-day use*

While Palmer Jones kept for himself the right to use his invention in Birmingham, he licensed Holland & Holland to use the gun in London, and granted similar rights to Trulock and Harris in Ireland.

Evidently Palmer Jones felt that there was room for improvement in his gun, for later the same year he patented, as specification No. 5372, a new set of movements for the head of a try-gun stock. This specification most clearly demonstrates that it had proved to be a very difficult exercise to produce a fully-adjustable try-gun. Adjustability was evidently no problem, but incorporating the lockwork certainly was. So we have mention in the patent text of muzzle-loading guns and in the drawings, in some detail, of a Needham needle-fire type gun. This raises the intriguing question as to whether a needle-fire was actually made new in 1889 or

*Advertisement from* The Field *of 1891*

231

whether an existing gun was modified. Also drawn is what appears to be an external hammer centre-fire gun, but with no apparent provision for lock- or trigger-work. In fact, there are only two motions catered for in this particular gun. Just behind the head of the stock is a hinge with a horizontal pivot so that, about this, the whole of the stock can be swung up and down in relation to the line of the barrels. The second adjustment is a vertical pivot (some 3 inches forward of the first hinge), by which the alignment of barrels to stock could be altered. It is curious that there was no provision for any alteration of the shape of the stock.

Given the fiercely competitive nature of the London gun trade in 1890, it is interesting to see how the rivals of Holland & Holland reacted to the try-gun. Some resorted to the age-old ploy of playing down the usefulness of this tool, but Henry Thorn, 'Charles Lancaster', took up the challenge by inventing and patenting a try-gun of his own. Before we describe this gun, we feel it is relevant that we should briefly digress and record something of the events that had an influence, which we are now inclined to over-look, on the whole fabric of Victorian shooting.

One of Thorn's own claims to fame was that he was a successful gun-fitter and one of his greatest coups derived from this: he built guns for Annie Oakley. Miss Oakley first came to London in 1887, as the exhibition shooting star of The Buffalo Bill Wild West Show, which

entertainment was part of the American Exhibition (some say the only success of it). Within a few months of the opening at Earls Court, Annie Oakley had become a cult figure. Society, from Queen Victoria and the Prince of Wales downwards, idolised her. She was showered with flowers and gifts of every sort and she was invited to shoot, both at the live pigeon traps and at shooting parties. Her potential as an advertising medium was obvious to the gun trade and several makers presented her with guns, but it was Thorn who fitted her with a pair of 20-bores. He had realised that the 12-bore guns that she used were probably too heavy for her and with Lancaster's lighter guns and their well-fitting stocks Miss Oakley was evidently much pleased, for she wrote to him from New York in December 1888 to say: 'The pair of 20-bores (weight 5lb. 2oz.) I have been using now nearly two years . . . With many thanks for the pains you have taken in making me such perfect fitting and fine shooting guns. I am gratefully yours, Annie Oakley.'

Miss Oakley's importance to the evolution of shooting in this country has never been sufficiently stressed. Here was a woman who shot better than most men; in fact, her first encounter with her future husband was to beat him at live pigeon trap shooting. After the men of the gun clubs and the shoot owners had showered her with invitations, how could they refuse their wives and daughters who said, in effect: 'Why

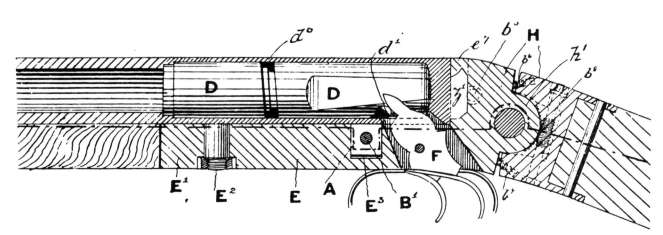

*W. Jones patent No. 5372 of 1889*

not us too?' In fact, Miss Oakley advertised private shooting lessons for ladies only at £1 per pupil per day, which lessons were given at Lancaster's shooting ground at Willesden.

Thorn's try-gun patent, No. 5688 of 1890, is remarkable in that there is no provision for any adjustment at the head of the stock. The reason for this is that such an adjustment, in Thorn's own words, 'has the disadvantage that when adjusting the said stock to touch the face, the handle and also the butt are moved disproportionately'. So, the only provision is for a full range of movement at comb and heel.

If we upset our chronological sequence by just one day we can consider next another try-gun that had a fixed-hand portion to its stock and depended for its movement on mechanism behind this point. This is the William Ford patent, No. 8621 of 4 June 1890, which used a universal, knuckle-type joint just behind the shooter's hand, with provision to alter the length and configuration of the comb of the stock. Also covered by this specification is an adjustable rib. This is supported by two slotted cross-members, one at the breech, the other at the muzzle, and the rib could be adjusted within the limits of the two slots.

Patented the previous day was Henry William Holland's design, No. 8549. Evidently this was an improvement of the first Jones patent of 1889. Jointing at the hand of the stock is retained, but what is new is a simpler adjust-

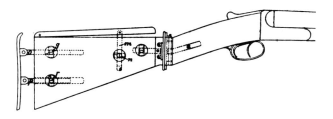

*W. Ford patent No. 8621 of 1890*

ment for length of stock. There are still two guide rods, but only a single adjusting bolt in the centre. The heelplate is only adjustable at its bottom and is pivoted about two-thirds of its way up. The major change, however, is in a much longer comb, which can be adjusted laterally by a screwed-rod set on the diagonal of the stock from right to left.

The try-gun has proved to be something of a mixed blessing to the gun fitter. It is not the magic way to certain success that some claim it to be. In the hands of a skilled man it can be of the greatest value in determining the stock necessary to fit a client, but for those less skilled, it is a subtle snare that leads to the production of curious forms of gunstock that are neither use nor ornament.

It is beyond our brief to concern ourselves with the technique of actually shooting a shotgun to hit a moving target. Therefore, we must ask that the reader accept the bald statement

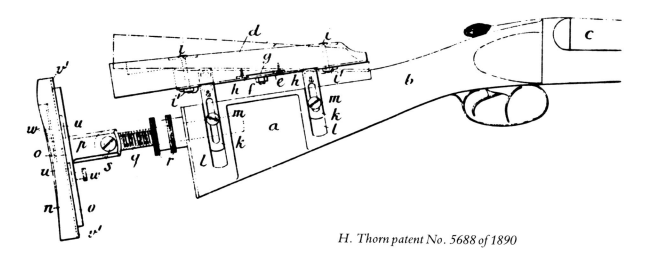

*H. Thorn patent No. 5688 of 1890*

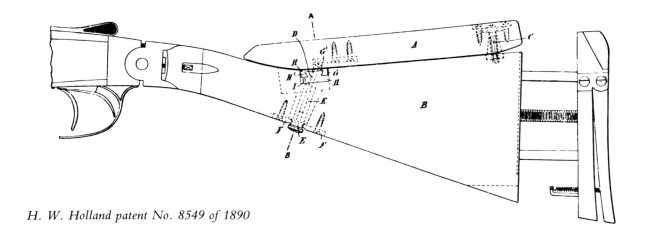

*H. W. Holland patent No. 8549 of 1890*

that, for a right-handed man, shooting from the right shoulder with a gun of conventional proportions, the right eye has to be the one that aligns the gun. If, for some reason, the left eye takes too great a share of this, some remedy is required. This can be a specially-shaped gun or a shooter can be taught to close, partially or completely, his left eye. To this same end we have two patented gadgets, both of which partially obscure the vision of the left eye. First there is what has become known as 'The Gilbert Shooting Corrector', the invention of Thomas Gilbert, 'gentleman' of 54, Great Marlborough Street, London. This was patented as No. 53 of 1884, and is designed as a metal plate, made to fit on the upper left-hand side of the gun barrel. The second is less well known, the patent of W. W. Watts, No. 4226 of 1885. Watts was, we believe, the proprietor, certainly the chief instructor and manager, of an establishment known as the London Sporting Park. This was an independent shooting school and occasional guns are encountered bearing its name, which would seem to indicate that the establishment also sold guns that it had had made 'in the trade'.

What Watts patented was the idea of a ring, presumably worn on the shooter's left thumb, with a disc mounted on it to obscure the vision of the user's left eye.

While we are concerned with sight, there is even a patent on the idea of a coloured foresight as part of Edwin Green's specification, No. 14,626 of 1885.

This chapter is concerned with all sorts of notions that could be said to originate from the upsurge in popularity of shooting. Of all these, the idea of a shooter photographing his quarry with the same motion that he uses to produce its demise will, we are sure, appear to be one of the most bizarre. But such was the subject of Victor Freiherr von Kalchberg's patent, No. 12,613 of 1890, in which he proposed to mount a camera underneath the barrel of a rifle or shotgun and

*Thomas Gilbert advertisement of 1884*

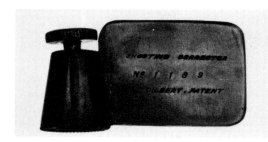

*T. Gilbert's 'Shooting corrector', patent No. 53 of 1884*

trip its shutter via a link to the trigger mechanism of the gun. It appears from the specification that the intention was solely to photograph the shooter's quarry, which is understandable to anyone with experience of trying to combine a photographic and shooting expedition. (Perhaps this idea could be developed, using today's instant and miniature photographic technology, into a camera gun which would demonstrate to a shooter where he had pointed his gun and hence be an aid to better marksmanship.)

There are times when, by the most oblique routes, insights into the way our sporting forebears thought are glimpsed. One such is offered by the subject of 'game scorers', devices by which a sportsman could keep his own tally of game brought to bag. These took two basic forms, one a gadget to be carried in the pocket, often shaped like a pocket watch, the hands of which could be advanced in some way; and the other, a mechanism to the same end, usually made of brass, that was set into the stock of the gun. Today the use of such an excrescence would be looked upon as being in the most doubtful taste, but in the 1890s a little group of them are to be found patented by well-known figures in the gunmaking and shooting world.

An example is provided in the two patents for game-counters in the name of Sir Ralph Payne-Gallwey of Cowling Hall, Bedale, Yorkshire. No. 12,014 of 1884 is the cruder, in that a separate device is required for the tens and units. Let into the side of the forend is a cover-plate through which projects a knurled knob. In front of this is a slot in which a pointer moves, and the edges of the slot are graduated so that one quarter turn of the knob moves the pointer one

division via a worm gear. Payne-Gallwey's second patent, No. 4083 of 1885, makes no mention of the first, but it is obviously designed to overcome the shortcomings of its predecessor. There is the same knurled knob, but this time it directly turns a disc that is set so that its edge shows through a slot in the cover-plate. Through this slot, numbers engraved on the edge of the disc are visible. In fact, there are a pair of discs with a stud-and-spring arrangement so that when '9' is passed on the unit disc, this advances the tens disc to '1'.

There was, apparently, some customer-demand for a gadget of this nature for we find patent No. 5962 of 1887 granted to the well-known gunmaker, Henry William Holland, to the same end. This rather larger device had to be set in a slot, cut into the top of the stock. This was covered by a rectangular metal plate with rounded ends. In it was cut a small opening, through which the recorded number could be viewed. The number was advanced one unit by pushing down on a small stud that projected through the metal cover. The internal mechanism consists of a vertical disc, or rim, with ratchet teeth projecting laterally from it. Bearing on these teeth was a horizontal lever, pivoted at the rear, upon which a downward projection from the stud bears so that pushing down the stud moves the ratchet-wheel one tooth onward, which corresponds to one unit on the scale. The size of the disc was such that there was no need for a tens and units system – the numbers could simply run on as a series.

What is, to all intents and purposes, the second Payne-Gallwey design is contained in the patent, No. 10,343 of 1887, in the name of William Mansfield. He traded as Joseph Brazier and Sons, The Ashes Works, Lord Street, Wolverhampton.

Another patent, No. 15,910 of 1887, dealing in a much more wide-ranging way with counters of all sorts, was obtained by James McHardy of Dollar, 'North Britain' (i.e. Scotland), who describes himself as a 'Scientific Expert' and James Livingstone of West Grange, Bogside, Alloa, who was a keeper. The version of their counter that is of particular interest is a simple ratchet-wheel for recording the number

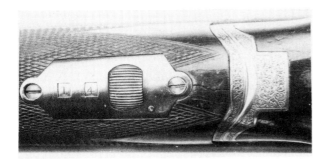

*Counter fitted into forend of a Horsley hammerless gun built circa 1887. The counter is probably a later addition*

of shots fired. To do this, it was linked, either to the trigger or to the heelplate of the gun, to advance the wheel one notch per shot. The number reached is viewed through a porthole in the cover and the only other practical detail is the mention of a knob fitted to the centre-spindle by which the counter could be rotated on to zero.

The continuing interest of the London trade is reflected in a patent obtained by Henry Thorn. This device is well known from the fact that it is described in the early editions of *The Art of Shooting*, written by the patentee under his famous pseudonym, 'Charles Lancaster'. The patent, No. 16,343 of 1887, describes two forms: one, a single-number series set on the face of a ratchet wheel that was advanced by a thumb slide mounted on the outer cover of the counter. Also covered by the same patent, is a more complex counter, capable of recording greater numbers, in which are two ratchet wheels, one for tens, the other for units. A pawl on the units wheel, with each rotation, moves the tens wheel on one notch.

The judgement of subsequent generations has been especially severe on such counters. The pocket type are now known almost exclusively as 'Norfolk Liars'. It is also far more common today to find a neatly let-in piece of walnut, to camouflage the site of one of the built-in counters, than to find the counter itself.

Thus, we come to the end of another two decades that witnessed an amazing level of effort applied to the improvement of the sporting shotgun.

The 'Norfolk Liar' has now been relegated to the antique shop; historical judgement has, at the same time, winnowed from the inventions crammed into the two decades encompassed by this book most of the essential features of guns. Many of these have not changed into this century.

It has been our intention to explain logically the contemporary rivals of those designs we now regard as truly successful. In this varied group we have, on the one hand, inventions which, given only a little more luck, might have survived and, at the other extreme, notions so impractical that we wonder they ever warranted serious consideration.

Hopefully, in this second volume of *The British Shotgun*, we have provided a broader view and a wider understanding of this remarkable period of competitive British invention. For it is all these strands, woven together, that combine to produce the complex tapestry of this golden age of British gunmaking. By fostering a greater understanding and appreciation of this period, we hope to contribute to the preservation of this part of the British national heritage.

The evolution of the sporting shotgun in Britain did not of course cease abruptly in 1890. The spate of invention continued with very little slackening until the outbreak of the First World War, after which it proceeded on a much reduced scale.

The immense volume of this material, with the fascinating problems of single triggers and under-and-over gun, to name but two topics belonging to this period, demands, for adequate coverage another book – *The British Shotgun: Volume Three!*

# The British Shotgun Patents 1871–1890

This list of specifications was compiled from the patent abridgements and contains all those concerned with shotgun mechanisms. We have not included those concerned with gunmaking or those that mention in passing possible shotgun use of a mechanism that is clearly intended as a rifle or a pistol. Those marked P only received provisional protection and are usually less detailed than a full specification. Those marked ★ cover additional features.

*1871*

| | | |
|---|---|---|
| 251 | E. C. Hodges | *Barrel Bolting Action* |
| 825P | W. Ansell | *Barrel Bolting Action* |
| 929 | F. J. Abbey & J. H. Foster (E. C. Green, Agent) | *Barrel Bolting Action* |
| 1003 | T. Murcott | *Hammerless Action* |
| 1098 | J. Rigby | *Barrel Bolting Action★* |
| 1174 | W. Ansell | *Barrel Bolting Action* |
| 1512 | J. S. Heath | *Retracting Strikers* |
| 1572 | W. Richards | *Barrel Bolting Action* |
| 1619P | W. Scott | *Recoil Pad* |
| 2396 | J. Hall | *Barrel Bolting Action* |
| 2522P | F. J. Abbey & J. H. Foster (E. C. Green, Agent) | *Barrel Bolting Action* |
| 2891P | J. Turon | *Cap inside breech on muzzle loader* |
| 3058 | G. Penton | *Release Trigger* |
| 3091 | J. Thomas | *Barrel Bolting Action* |
| 3318 | S. J. Wallis | *Hammerless Action* |

*1872*

| | | |
|---|---|---|
| 42P | W. M. Scott | *Lever Work* |
| 129 | G. H. Wilson | *Safety* |
| 180 | W. F. Parker (E. T. Hughes, Agent) | *Rebound Lock* |
| 267 | J. Woodward & J. Emme | *Barrel Bolting Action* |
| 445 | H. Walker | *Barrel Bolting Action* |
| 1324 | A. Francotte (J. Piddington, Agent) | *Barrel Bolting Action* |
| 1825 | W. S. Riley | *Barrel Bolting Action★* |
| 1917 | S. J. Wallis | *Single Trigger Mechanism* |
| 2121 | R. Jones | *Barrel Bolting Action★* |
| 2349 | W. Ansell | *Barrel Bolting Action★* |
| 2579 | S. Mathews | *Barrel Bolting Action* |
| 3257P | F. Braendlin | *Barrel Bolting Action* |
| 3791 | W. Anson | *Forend Fastener* |

*1873*

| | | |
|---|---|---|
| 284 | G. Gibbs & T. Pitt | *Hammerless Action* |
| 571P | T. W. Miller | *Powder Chamber* |
| 940 | C. H. Maleham & T. Mirfin | *Hammerless Action* |
| 953 | E. Hollis | *Forend Fastener* |
| 1268 | W. M. Scott | *Forend Fastener★* |
| 1422 | J. Deeley & J. S. Edge | *Forend Fastener★* |
| 1465 | S. Remington | *Breech Block★* |
| 1563 | R. Hill | *Barrel Bolting Action* |
| 1826 | E. Crowley | *Barrel Bolting Action* |
| 2119 | F. Grey & W. Harris | *Barrel Bolting Action* |
| 2193P | W. Powell | *Forend Fastener* |
| 2328P | J. H. Apted | *Hammerless Action* |

| | | |
|---|---|---|
| 3084 | W. W. Greener | *Barrel Bolting Action* |
| 3552 | J. Roberts | *Safety* |
| 3756P | W. M. Scott | *Forend Fastener★* |

*1874*

| | | |
|---|---|---|
| 712 | W. M. Scott | *Forend Fastener* |
| 1205 | J. Needham | *Ejector★* |
| 1645 | W. R. Pape | *Barrel Bolting Action* |
| 1817 | W. R. Trevelyan | *Barrel Bolting Action* |
| 2052 | W. M. Scott | *Barrel Bolting Action* |
| 2238 | A. Wyley | *Hammerless Action* |
| 2530 | T. Perks | *Barrel Bolting Action* |
| 2938 | H. A. Silver | *Recoil Pad* |
| 3090 | W. W. Greener | *Barrel Bolting Action* |
| 3424 | W. M. Scott | *Hammerless Action* |
| 3442 | G. Jeffries | *Barrel Bolting Action* |
| 3548 | T. T. Lawden & J. Thomas | *Half-Cocking Action* |
| 4217 | J. L. Kerr (W. R. Lake, Agent) | *Interior form of Barrel* |

*1875*

| | | |
|---|---|---|
| 186 | W. M. Scott | *Barrel Bolting Action* |
| 312 | J. Rigby & W. M. Scott | *Interior form of Barrel* |
| 510P | W. P. Jones | *Barrel Bolting Action* |
| 921 | J-B Laine (E. P. Alexander, Agent) | *Three Barrel Gun* |
| 1014 | C. E. Lomel | *Barrel Bolting Action* |
| 1247 | J. Williams | *Barrel Bolting Action* |
| 1290 | E. Hughes | *Cocking Mechanism* |
| 1756 | W. Anson & J. Deeley | *Hammerless Action* |
| 1902 | W. M. Scott | *Barrel Bolting Action* |
| 2128 | A. J. B. Hollis | *Barrel Bolting Action* |
| 2793 | J. Needham | *Ejector* |
| 3223 | W. M. Scott | *Cocking Indicator* |
| 3549 | R. Piel | *Hammerless Action* |
| 3709 | H. Walker | *Retracting Strikers* |
| 3780P | J. Bardell | *Forend Fastener* |
| 4345 | W. D. Miller (A. M. Clark, Agent) | *Sprung Heel Plate* |
| 4351P | G. Jeffries | *Barrel Bolting Action* |
| 4542 | J. W. Duncan | *Lockwork* |

*1876*

| | | |
|---|---|---|
| 117P | T. Southgate & J. Woodward | *Cocking Mechanism* |
| 129 | T. Perkes | *Cocking Mechanism★* |
| 493 | W. Powell | *Barrel Bolting Action* |
| 585P | J. Johnson & R. Wayne | *Forend Fastener* |
| 600 | T. Southgate & J. Woodward | *Cocking Mechanism* |

| | | |
|---|---|---|
| 615 | W. M. Scott & M. Scott | *Barrel Bolting Actions★* |
| 651 | T. Woodward | *Hammerless Action* |
| 700 | H. Walker | *Barrel Bolting Actions★* |
| 1234 | J. F. Gastinne-Renette | *Forend Fastener* |
| 1329P | C. Price & W. Harris | *Hammerless Action* |
| 2235P | T. T. Lawden & J. Thomas | *Cocking Mechanism* |
| 2581 | J. W. Duncan | *Interior form of Barrel★* |
| 3240 | T. Bailey | *Half-Cocking Mechanism* |
| 3291 | T. T. Lawden & J. Thomas | *Cocking Mechanisms* |
| 4513 | W. Anson | *Safety Mechanism* |
| 4825 | C. Dumonthier | *Walking-Stick Guns* |
| | (A. M. Clark, Agent) | |
| | | |
| *1877* | | |
| 292 | C. O. Ellis & | *Forend Fastener* |
| | E. W. Wilkinson | |
| 461 | H. Tolley | *Cocking Mechanism★* |
| 928 | J. Stanton | *Lockwork* |
| 971 | R. Walterskirchen | *Cocking Mechanism* |
| | (W. R. Lake, Agent) | |
| 1251 | E. G. Lefaucheux | *Hammerless Action* |
| | (J. H. Johnson, Agent) | |
| 1590P | J. D. Dougall | *Trigger work* |
| 1623 | W. W. Greener | *Hammerless Action★* |
| 1981 | J. Adsett | *Hammerless Action* |
| 3718 | C. G. Bonehill | *Barrel Bolting Action* |
| 4215P | W. S. Woodward | *Barrel Bolting Action* |
| | | |
| *1878* | | |
| 397 | J. Purdey | *Barrel Bolting Action* |
| 545 | J. Lang | *Hammerless Action* |
| 761 | W. M. Scott & T. Baker | *Hammerless Actions* |
| 950 | L. Gye | *Hammerless Action* |
| 964 | G. Hackett | *Forend Fastener★* |
| 1085 | W. Richards | *Barrel Bolting Mechanism* |
| 1089 | S. Mills | *Cocking Mechanism* |
| 1143 | P. A. A. Laffiteau & | *Forend Fastener* |
| | L. H. Rieger | |
| | (A. P. Price, Agent) | |
| 1145 | E. C. Hodges | *Hammerless Action★* |
| 1968 | T. Perkes | *Hammerless Action★* |
| 1970 | W. Poutney | *Forend Fastener★* |
| 1735P | F. T. Baker | *Forend Fastener* |
| 2163P | I. Bullock & R. Bullock | *Cocking Mechanism★* |
| 2293 | J. W. Wilson & | *Barrel Bolting* |
| | & I. T. Milliken | |
| 2323 | C. G. Bonehill | *Hammerless Action★* |
| 2886P | H. Hammond | *Safety Mechanism★* |
| | & E. Hammond | |
| 3123P | L. Gye | *Enlarged Powder Chamber in Cartridge* |
| 3447P | T. Woodward & | *Safety Mechanism* |
| | & D. Bentley | |
| 3573P | S. Mathews | *Hammerless Action★* |
| 3611 | J. P. Clapbrough | *Hammerless Action* |
| 3929 | J. Mathews | *Hammerless Action* |
| 4294 | H. Walker | *Hammerless Action★* |
| 4647P | W. Rogers | *Hammerless Action* |
| 4980 | S. Mills | *Barrel Bolting Action* |
| 5106 | J. H. Walsh | *Barrel Bolting Action★* |
| | | |
| *1879* | | |
| 126 | T. D. Cross, J. W. Cross & | *Hammerless Action* |
| | W. W. Cross | |

| | | |
|---|---|---|
| 133 | J. Lang | *Hammerless Action★* |
| 134 | H. W. Holland & T. Perkes | *Safety Mechanisms* |
| 574 | J. Adsett & T. Adsett | *Hammerless Action★* |
| 649P | H. Tolley | *Hammerless Action* |
| 706 | J. V. Needham & | *Safety Mechanism* |
| | & G. Hinton | |
| 769 | W. W. Greener | *Hammerless Action* |
| 907 | W. Anson & J. Deeley | *Safety Mechanism* |
| 1065 | M. W. Parsons | *Hammerless Action* |
| 1128 | W. Adams | *Hammerless Action* |
| 1411 | J. Rigby & T. Bissel | *Barrel Bolting Action★* |
| 1728 | R. Hill | *Hammerless Action★* |
| 1754 | A. Wyley | *Hammerless Action★* |
| 2147 | J. Reeves | *Hammerless Action★* |
| 2177 | W. H. Tisdall | *Hammerless Action★* |
| 2816 | R. Ellis & H. Scott | *Hammerless Action★* |
| 2848 | J. MacNaughton | *Hammerless Action★* |
| 2879P | J. Rogers | *Hammerless Action★* |
| 3297 | G. Gibbs & T. Pitt | *Hammerless Action★* |
| 3684 | F. Crutchley | *Hammerless Action★* |
| 3883P | W. M. Scott & J. Tonks | *Hammerless Action★* |
| 4228 | H. Walker | *Hammerless Action★* |
| 4317 | E. James | *Hammerless Action★* |
| 4425 | H. Pieper | *Interior form of Barrel* |
| 4809 | H. Phillips | *Hammerless Action* |
| 4902 | L. Gye | *Hammerless Action* |
| 5002P | J. Tolley & W. Tolley | *Hammerless Action★* |
| 5111 | D. Fraser | *Hammerless Action* |
| | | |
| *1880* | | |
| 31 | F. Beesley | *Hammerless Action* |
| 278P | T. Southgate & | *Hammerless Action* |
| | E. Harrison | |
| 294 | J. Dickson | *Hammerless Action* |
| 881P | D. Bentley | *Hammerless Action* |
| 930 | W. W. Greener | *Hammerless Action* |
| 984 | J. S. Heath | *Detachable Choke* |
| 1422P | J. Lang | *Hammerless Action* |
| 1860 | T. W. Webley | *Hammerless Action* |
| 1952 | C. G. Bonehill | *Hammerless Action★* |
| | & W. J. Matthews | |
| 2505P | T. Woodward | *Hammerless Action★* |
| | & T. Woodward | |
| 2711 | J. F. Swinburn | *Hammerless Action* |
| 4210 | H. A. Silver & W. Fletcher | *Safety Mechanism* |
| 4291 | J. F. Swinburn | *Barrel Bolting Action★* |
| 4665 | D. Kirkwood | *Hammerless Action★* |
| | (W. R. Lake, Agent) | |
| | | |
| *1881* | | |
| 397 | J. T. Rogers & J. Rogers | *Hammerless Action* |
| 499P | H. A. A. Thorn | *Hammerless Action* |
| 525 | J. F. Swinburn | *Hammerless Action* |
| 1242 | H. A. A. Thorn | *Four-Barrel Gun* |
| 1872 | H. Walker | *Barrel Bolting Action★* |
| 2003 | W. W. Greener | *Ejector* |
| 2378 | W. Nokes | *Safety Mechanism* |
| 2407 | A. Hope & A. S. Oliver | *Try-Gun* |
| | (A. M. Clark, Agent) | |
| 2531 | E. James | *Hammerless Action★* |
| 2871P | W. Tranter | *Hammerless Action★* |
| 2993 | S. B. Allport | *Hammerless Action★* |
| 3027 | T. Woodward | *Hammerless Action* |
| | & T. Woodward | |

| | | |
|---|---|---|
| 3313 | M. Kaufman (W. E. Gedge, Agent) | Barrel Bolting Action★ |
| 3466P | F. M. Robertson & J. Joyce | Barrel Bolting Action★ |
| 4585 | L. Gye | Hammerless Action |
| 4872 | H. A. Silver & W. Fletcher | Safety Mechanism★ |
| 4916 | J. Lang | Hammerless Action★ |
| 5143 | T. W. Webley & H. Webley | Ejector★ |
| 5395P | W. Tranter | Hammerless Action |
| 5420 | Y. C. M. Tassel (W. H. Beck, Agent) | Safety Mechanism |

*1882*

| | | |
|---|---|---|
| 213 | H. A. A. Thorn | Four-Barrel Gun |
| 327 | S. Trulock, R. Trulock & W. Trulock | Hammerless Action |
| 617 | W. M. Scott & T. Baker | Gas Vents on Action Face |
| 873 | J. Dickson & A. Murray | Three-Barrel Gun★ |
| 1209P | W. M. Scott | Hammerless Action |
| 1282 | L. Gye | Side Opening Gun |
| 1320 | W. M. Scott | Hammerless Action |
| 1511 | T. W. Webley | Safety Mechanism |
| 1636 | C. M. Spencer & S. H. Roper (W. R. Lake, Agent) | Repeating Shotgun |
| 1881 | W. Tranter | Hammerless Action★ |
| 2061 | J. Williams | Hammerless Action★ |
| 2344 | T. Woodward | Hammerless Action |
| 2746 | L. Gye | Side Opening Gun |
| 2833 | J. Robertson | Hammerless Action★ |
| 3053 | T. W. Webley & T. Brain | Hammerless Action★ |
| 3089 | H. A. A. Thorn | Four-Barrel Gun |
| 3137 | W. Lorenz (C. D. Abel, Agent) | Chamber Sleeve |
| 3877 | W. Rogers | Hammerless Action |
| 4019P | F. B. W. Roberts & B. T. Moore | Electric Ignition |
| 4089 | W. Anson | Safety Mechanism |
| 4187 | E. James | Hammerless Action★ |
| 4309P | G. L. Jeffries | Chamber Sleeve |
| 4516 | W. W. Greener | Hammerless Action★ |
| 4541 | H. Hammond & E. Hammond | Safety Mechanisms |
| 4766P | D. Bentley & W. Baker | Single Trigger Mechanism |
| 5273 | A. Henry | Hammerless Action |
| 5759 | T. Gilbert | Safety Mechanism |
| 5710P | J. Needham | Safety Mechanism |
| 6194 | J. H. Hannay | Barrel Bolting Action★ |
| 6238 | N. G. Green | Electric Ignition |

*1883*

| | | |
|---|---|---|
| 23 | H. W. Holland & J. Robertson | Hammerless Action |
| 125 | E. A. Monfort | Electric Ignition |
| 145 | J. F. Swinburn | Hammerless Action★ |
| 687P | T. Woodward | Hammerless Action★ |
| 727P | W. M. Scott | Hammerless Action |
| 823 | F. Beesley | Hammerless Action |
| 1137 | W. Nobbs | Ejector Mechanism |
| 1215 | M. V. K. Cooper & J. Kriz (G. M. Cruickshank, Agent) | Novel Gun |
| 1463 | T. W. Webley, G. Bouckley & E. C. Hodges | Hammerless Action★ |

| | | |
|---|---|---|
| 1515 | H. Tolley | Hammerless Action |
| 1571 | H. Pieper | Electric Ignition |
| 1833 | W. Anson & J. Deeley | Hammerless Action★ |
| 1903 | E. Harrison & F. Beesley | Hammerless Action |
| 2101 | S. A. Grant & W. Adams | Hammerless Action |
| 2224 | J. Darby | Safety Mechanism |
| 2813 | J. Woodward & F. Beesley | Hammerless Action |
| 3049 | T. Perkes | Ejector Mechanism |
| 3845P | T. Woodward | Hammerless Action |
| 3859 | W. M. Scott & C. Proctor | Hammerless Action★ |
| 3874 | T. Horsley & C. Pryse | Hammerless Action |
| 4294 | P. A. Bayle | Interior Form of Barrel |
| 4693 | G. H. Needham | Barrel Bolting Action★ |
| 4867P | D. Bentley | Hammerless Action |
| 4977P | E. Bled | Hammerless Action |
| 5292 | D. Bentley & W. Baker | Hammerless Actions |
| 5459 | J. P. Burhard & F. Novotuy (H. J. Hadden, Agent) | Barrel Bolting Action★ |
| 5848 | H. F. Phillips | Hammerless Action |

*1884*

| | | |
|---|---|---|
| 53 | T. Gilbert | Sight Corrector |
| 154 | J. S. Pinder | Hammerless Action |
| 425 | F. Beesley | Hammerless Action |
| 1064 | H. A. Silver & W. Fletcher | Safety Mechanism |
| 1657 | T. Keight | Hammerless Action |
| 3002 | C. Pryse & E. J. Cashmore | Hammerless Action |
| 3606 | J. H. Apted | Selective Trigger Bolting Mechanism |
| 4292 | W. Anson | Hammerless Action |
| 4372 | J. P. Onderdonk | Recoil Pad |
| 4458 | T. Southgate & J. Lang | Hammerless Action |
| 4786 | T. Wood | Electric Ignition |
| 5249 | J. Andrews | Electric Ignition |
| 5405 | J. W. Smallman | Safety Mechanism |
| 5564 | W. M. Scott | Hammerless Action |
| 6624 | J. F. Swinburn | Hammerless Action |
| 6673 | J. Tonks (W. R. Lake, Agent) | Hammerless Action★ |
| 6787 | W. Tranter | Safety Mechanism★ |
| 6883 | T. Keight | Hammerless Action |
| 7939 | N. O. Waymire (A. M. Clark, Agent) | Extractor |
| 8471 | C. G. Bonehill | Hammerless Action★ |
| 8591 | E. Bled & E. Richoux | Hammerless Action |
| 8620 | A. L. S. Leighs | Safety Mechanism |
| 9110 | J. Victor | Hammerless Action |
| 10101 | H. Tolley | Hammerless Action |
| 10903 | H. Allender (H. H. Lake, Agent) | Hammerless Action★ |
| 11382 | E. Harrison & F. Beesley | Safety Mechanism |
| 11625 | W. Bentley | Barrel Bolting Action |
| 11898 | S. P. Wilding | Safety Mechanism |
| 12014 | R. Payne-Gallwey | Game Counter |
| 12586 | C. G. Bonehill & A. J. Simpson | Hammerless Action |
| 13199 | Dresse, Laloux et Cie (W. R. Lake, Agent) | Hammerless Action |
| 13688 | J. Gibson | Hammerless Action |
| 14008 | S. Russell | Electric Ignition |
| 14488 | F. Beesley | Safety Mechanism |
| 14526 | J. Deeley | Ejector Mechanism |
| 14628 | J. B. Bull | Safety Mechanism |

| 15209 | J. Darby | *Safety Mechanism* |
| 15299 | W. Anson | *Ejector Mechanism* |
| 16307 | T. Southgate | *Ejector Mechanism* |
| 16930 | J. Bulloch & | *Safety Mechanism* |
| | G. P. Appleyard | |
| 17037 | D. Bentley | *Semi-Hammerless Lock* |
| 17088 | J. F. Swinburn | *Safety Mechanism* |

*1885*

| 984 | R. Redman & | *Forend Fastener* |
| | S. Whitehouse | |
| 1011 | J. H. Hannay | *Safety Mechanism* |
| 1467 | J. W. Smallman | *Hammerless Action* |
| 4083 | R. Payne–Gallwey | *Game Counter* |
| 4226 | W. W. Watts | *Sight Corrector* |
| 4258 | A. Hyde | *Hammerless Action* |
| | W. P. Thompson, Agent) | |
| 5049 | J. Deeley & F. J. Penn | *Hammerless Action* |
| 6943 | D. Moore & F. S. Moore | *Safety Mechanism* |
| | (T. Stead, Agent) | |
| 7568 | G. V. Fosbery | *Interior form of Barrel* |
| | (H. H. Lake, Agent) | |
| 7715 | R. James & W. Taylor | *Barrel Bolting Action* |
| 7895 | G. Jeffries | *Ejector Mechanism★* |
| 8314 | W. C. McEntee | *Hammerless Action* |
| | & J. Hughes | |
| 8851 | G. Hacket & E. Belcher | *Hammerless Action* |
| 9048 | T. Bailey | *Hammerless Action★* |
| 14626 | E. C. Green | *Barrel Bolting Action★* |

*1886*

| 659 | W. A. G. Birkin | *Hammerless Action★* |
| 1290 | G. Flaischen | *Loaded Indicator* |
| 2283 | Winchester | *Repeating Shotgun* |
| | Repeating Arms | |
| | (H. H. Lake, Agent) | |
| 2663 | H. Tolley | *Hammerless Action★* |
| 2725 | W. P. Jones & H. A. Smith | *Hammerless Action* |
| 3400 | G. Jeffries | *Ejector Mechanism* |
| 4251 | R. Chaplin | *Hammerless Action* |
| 4289 | J. Deeley | *Ejector Mechanism* |
| 4437 | J. W. Smallman | *Hammerless Action* |
| 4446 | G. D. Potter | *Ejector Mechanism* |
| | (B. J. B. Mills, Agent) | |
| 7205 | H. Parsons | *Ejector Mechanism* |
| 8657 | F. Beesley | *Hammerless Action* |
| 8922 | A. Hall | *Cheek Pad* |
| 9411 | Winchester | *Repeating Shotgun* |
| | Repeating Arms | |
| | (H. H. Lake, Agent) | |
| 9414 | Winchester | *Repeating Shotgun* |
| | Repeating Arms | |
| | (H. H. Lake, Agent) | |
| 10303 | H. Tolley | *Hammerless Action★* |
| 10679 | T. Perkes | *Ejector Mechanism* |
| 12329 | H. A. Silver & W. Fletcher | *Safety Mechanism* |
| 12402 | E. G Anson | *Ejector Mechanism★* |
| 12869 | J. T. Cooper | *Novel Gun* |
| 13400 | J. Rochatte | *Hammerless Action★* |
| | (W. H. Beck, Agent) | |
| 14348 | J. Thomas & J. G. Thomas | *Barrel Bolting Mechanism* |
| 14404 | W. Nobbs | *Ejector Mechanism* |
| 14874 | A. Bertrand | *Hammerless Action* |
| 14968 | A. Francotte | *Ejector Mechanism* |
| | (W. H. Beck, Agent) | |

| 15272 | E. Harrison | *Hammerless Action* |
| 15763 | H. Parsons & W. Brown | *Hammerless Action* |
| 16138 | W. Anson | *Ejector Mechanism* |
| 16214 | E. Harrison | *Hammerless Action★* |
| 17054 | H. A. Silver & W. Fletcher | *Recoil Pad* |

*1887*

| 805 | Winchester | *Repeating Shotgun* |
| | Repeating Arms | |
| | Arms (H. H. Lake, Agent) | |
| 1281 | J. W. Smallman | *Ejector Mechanism★* |
| 2116 | W. Monton, E Brettell | *Hammerless Action* |
| | & W. Bentley | |
| 4920 | T. Woodward | *Ejector Mechanism* |
| 5224 | J. Cox | *Forend Fastener* |
| 5834 | H. W. Holland | *Ejector Mechanism★* |
| | & J. Robertson | |
| 5962 | H. W. Holland | *Game Counter* |
| 7222 | C. O. Ellis & | *Ejector Mechanism* |
| | E. W. Wilkinson | |
| 7346 | H. Smith | *Hammerless Action★* |
| 7470 | I. Bullock & R. Bullock | *Ejector Mechanism* |
| 8841 | W. Ford | *Ejector Mechanism★* |
| 9399 | J. Dickson | *Ejector Mechanism* |
| 10343 | W. Mansfield | *Game Counter* |
| 10487 | T. Brain | *Ejector Mechanism★* |
| 10621 | J. Dickson | *Ejector Mechanism* |
| 10888 | W. H. Brighton | *Ejector Mechanism* |
| 11623 | H. W. Holland & | *Ejector Mechanism* |
| | & J. Robertson | |
| 12176 | T. Perkes | *Ejector Mechanism* |
| 14444 | E. Harrison & E. G. Anson | *Hammerless Action* |
| 15910 | J. McHardy & | *Counter for shots Fired* |
| | J. Livingstone | |
| 16343 | H. A. Thorn | *Game Counter* |
| 16356 | T. H. Morton & | *Ejector Mechanism* |
| | & E. Hughes | |
| 17792 | R. I. Hampton | *Hammerless Action* |
| | (A. J. Boult, Agent) | |

*1888*

| 1496 | J. Truscott | *Safety Mechanism* |
| 2294 | T. W. Webley | *Ejector Mechanism* |
| 2622 | W. Ford | *Ejector Mechanism* |
| 2677 | J. Lang & A. Jeffries | *Ejector Mechanism* |
| 3100 | W. Wem | *Ejector Mechanism* |
| 4360 | S. A. Grant | *Ejector Mechanism* |
| 5672 | R. Paulson | *Ejector Mechanism★* |
| 6913 | F. J. Penn & J. Deeley | *Ejector Mechanism* |
| 7274 | W. Anson | *Ejector Mechanism★* |
| 7813 | I. Bullock & R. Bullock | *Ejector Mechanism* |
| 7823 | C. G. Bonehill | *Safety Mechanism* |
| 9348 | W. Ford & J. Clifford | *Ejector Mechanism* |
| 9677 | C. H. Maleham | *Ejector Mechanism* |
| 9872 | L. E. Parfitt | *Ejector Mechanism* |
| 10084 | T. Perkes | *Ejector Mechanism* |
| 11550 | E. Harrison | *Ejector Mechanism* |
| 11560 | P. Brun-Latrige | *Hammerless Action* |
| 12033 | J. S. Heath | *Safety Mechanism* |
| 13857 | J. Dallaway & J. Cox | *Ejector Mechanism* |
| 16176 | L. Jeusette, D. Henrard | *Barrel Bolting* |
| | & H. Henrard | |
| 16278 | L. Neuman | *Hammerless Action★* |
| 16691 | H. W. Holland | *Ejector Mechanism* |
| | & J. Robertson | |

| | | |
|---|---|---|
| 17732 | W. P. Jones | Three- or Four-Barrel Guns |
| 18157 | E. Harrison | Ejector Mechanism |
| 18163 | R. B. Jentzsch | Safety Mechanism |
| 18164 | R. B. Jentzsch | Safety Mechanism |

**1889**

| | | |
|---|---|---|
| 357 | W. R. Miller | Hammer for Winchester Model 1887 |
| 1157 | W. P. Jones | Try-Gun |
| 1249 | W. H. Brighton | Ejector Mechanism |
| 1880 | J. Rogers & J. Rogers | Ejector Mechanism |
| 2341 | H. W. Holland | Measurement-Gun |
| 2450 | J. W. Smallman | Mounted snap Cap |
| 2563 | A. Nouvelle | Hammerless Action★ |
| 2784 | T. Perkes | Ejector Mechanism |
| 2790 | O. Horton | Hammerless Action |
| 3413 | R. Jones & W. Taylor | Ejector Mechanism |
| 4697 | J. W. Smallman | Ejector Mechanism |
| 5077 | W. H. Brighton | Ejector Mechanism |
| 5159 | T. Woodward | Ejector Mechanism |
| 5372 | W. P. Jones | Try-Gun |
| 5966 | T. Green & J. Green | Ejector Mechanism |
| 6148 | J. Cox | Barrel Bolting Action★ |
| 8323 | W. Phillipson & W. Baker | Ejector Mechanism |
| 8667 | P. Brun–Latrige | Hammerless Action |
| 8915 | J. Rogers | Ejector Mechanism |
| 9062 | J. W. Smallman | Ejector Mechanism |
| 9209 | L. E. Parfitt | Ejector Mechanism |
| 10379 | G. E. L. Bankart | Cheek Pad |
| 12003 | C. E. Batcock & H. W. Bateman | Safety Mechanism |
| 12008 | W. H. Brighton | Ejector Mechanism |

| | | |
|---|---|---|
| 12314 | T. Southgate | Ejector Mechanism |
| 13158 | C. H. Maleham | Ejector Mechanism |
| 13591 | E. Harrison | Ejector Mechanism |
| 15313 | C. Rosson | Ejector Mechanism |
| 17746 | W. W. Greener | Interior form of Barrel |
| 18275 | F. J. Candy | Safety Mechanism |
| 18781 | W. Phillipson & W. Baker | Ejector Mechanism |
| 20979 | F. Beesley | Ejector Mechanism |

**1890**

| | | |
|---|---|---|
| 662 | T. Southgate | Ejector Mechanism |
| 1955 | J. Ross | Ejector Mechanism |
| 2760 | S. B. Allport | Ejector Mechanism |
| 2830 | W. H. Brighton | Ejector Mechanism |
| 5688 | H. A. A. Thorn | Try-Gun |
| 6444 | R. Darne (W. E. Gedge, Agent) | Hammerless Action |
| 7759 | J. MacNaughton | Ejector Mechanism |
| 7969 | A. Agnel | Hammerless Action |
| 8549 | H. W. Holland | Try-Gun |
| 8621 | W. Ford | Try-Gun |
| 12178 | R. Trulock | Ejector Mechanism |
| 12613 | V. F. Von Kalchberg | Camera mounted on Gun |
| 14886 | J. Ross | Ejector Mechanism |
| 17292 | W. Baker | Ejector Mechanism |
| 19156 | Winchester Repeating Arms (H. H. Lake, Agent) | Repating Shotgun |
| 19395 | J. Ross | Ejector Mechanism★ |
| 20196 | L. Menestre & P. Pasquier | Safety Mechanism |
| 20234 | E. Harrison | Ejector Mechanism |
| 20880 | G. Lilleyman | Ejector Mechanism |

# Select Bibliography

Akehurst, R., *Game Guns and Rifles*, G. Bell & Sons Ltd, 1969

Baker, D. J., *The Royal Guns at Sandringham*, Phaidon, 1989

Beaumont, R., *Purdey's: The Guns and the Family*, David & Charles, 1984

Booth, J. N., *Booths in History*, Ridgeway Press, 1982

Browning, J. and Gentry, C., *John M. Browning – American Gunmaker*, Doubleday & Company Inc., 1964

Burrard, Major Sir G., *The Modern Shotgun*, Vols 1, 2 and 3, Herbert Jenkins, 1931 and 1932

Chamberlain, W. H. J. and Taylerson, A. W. F., *Adams Revolvers*, Barrie & Jenkins, 1976

Cooper, C. R., *Annie Oakley*, Hurst & Blackett Ltd.

Crudgington, I. M. and Baker D. J., *The British Shotgun: Volume I 1850–1870*, Barrie & Jenkins, 1979

Davenport, Neil, *The United Kingdom Patent System,* Kenneth Mason, 1979

Edgeworth, M., *Ormond*, Gresham Publishing Co.

Greener, W. W., *Choke Bore Guns and how to load for all kinds of game*, Cassell, Petter & Galpin

Greener, W. W., *The Gun and its Development* (5th and 9th editions), Cassell, 1892 and 1910

Harris, Clive (ed), *The History of the Birmingham Gun Barrel Proof House*, Guardians of the Birmingham Proof House, 1946

Hastings, M., *English Sporting Guns and Accessories*, Ward Lock, 1969

Hinman, B., *The Golden Age of Shotgunning*, Winchester Press, 1971

King, P., *The Shooting Field,* Quiller Press

Kirton, J., *The British Falling Block Breechloading Rifle from 1865,* Armory Publications, Tacoma, 1985

'Lancaster, Charles' (Henry Thorn), *Illustrated Treatise on the Art of Shooting* (1st edition), Charles Lancaster, 1889

Long, J. W., *American Wildfowl Shooting*, Orange Judd Company, 1879

Payne-Gallwey, Sir R., *Letters to Young Shooters*, Vols 1, 2 and 3, Longmans Green & Co., 1890, 1894 and 1896

*A Part of the Holland & Holland Collection with a Brief History of the Company & Notes on Related Subjects*, Holland & Holland, 1976

Rattenbury, R., *The Browning Connection*, Buffalo Bill Historical Center, 1982

Riling, R., *Guns and Shooting: a Bibliography*, Greenberg, 1950

Rose, R. N., *The Field 1853–1953*, Michael Joseph, 1953

Sharp, H., *Modern Sporting Gunnery*, Simpkin, Marshall Hamilton Kent and Co. 1906

Shelton, L. P., *California Gunsmiths 1846–1900*, Far West Publishers, 1977

Taylerson, A. W. F., *The Revolver 1889–1914*, Barrie & Jenkins, 1970

Taylor, L. B., *A Brief History of the Westley Richards Firm 1812–1913*, Shakespeare Head Press, 1913

Teasdale-Buckell, G. T., *Experts on Guns and Shooting*, Sampson, Low, Marston and Company, 1900

'20-Bore' (Basil Tozer), *Practical Hints on Shooting*, Kegan, Paul, Trench Co., 1887

Walsh, J. H., *The Modern Sportsman's Gun and Rifle*, Horace Cox, 1882

*Stonehenge's British Rural Sports*, (14th edition), Frederick Warne & Co., 1878

Various issues of the following periodicals have also been consulted: *Arms & Explosives, The Field, Land and Water, Shooting, The Sporting Goods' Review* and *Wildfowlers' Shooting Times and Kennel News* (otherwise known as *Shooting Times*).

# Index